"…. BUT HOW YOU PLAYED THE GAME!"

A HISTORY OF INTERCOLLEGIATE
ATHLETICS AT HOPE COLLEGE

PART I - 1862-1955

Gordon M. Brewer - Hope '48

Published by Hope College
Holland, Michigan

IDENTIFICATION OF COVER PICTURES

Top row, from left to right: **1933 Hope College golf team**--standing left to right: Russ Paalman, Coach Bud Hinga, Harvey Scholten; seated: Ben Timmer, Les Serier; **1910 Hope track team**, see p. 41; **Riverview Park, 1951**: John Hamilton circles left end against De Pauw; **Donald "Duke" Mulder - Hope '48**; **Jack Schouten and the Hope baseball team, circa 1907**; **The 1920-21 Hope basketball team**--top row left to right: Gordon Van Eenenaam, Coach Jack Schouten, William "Jake" Joldersma; seated: Garret De Jong, Gerritt Wassenaar, captain Dick Japinga, J. Dyke Van Putten, Meinte "Mike" Schuurmans.

Bottom row, from left to right: **The 1943 "Blitz Kids"**, see p. 120; **Jack Schouten - 1881-1978**, Hope's first full time coach; **Miner Stegenga, Hope '15**; **Hope women's basketball team, 1904-05**, see p. 27; **Hope coaches, 1952**--left to right: Nick Yonker, Ken Weller, Larry Green, Al Vanderbush; **Coach Milton L. "Bud" Hinga**.

Photos courtesy of the Joint Archives of Holland and the collections of Gordon Brewer, Russell DeVette and Randall VandeWater.

First Edition

Library of Congress Catalog Number: 92-73357
International Standard Book Number: 0-9634061-0-8

Cover design by Rich Nienhuis Advertising Design, Holland, Michigan
Design and typesetting by Hope College Public Relations Office
Printing by Thomson-Shore, Inc., Dexter, Michigan

For Lorraine - -

Whose quiet patience filled late nights and long weekends --

while I boarded bus and plane, to worship at the shrine of sport.

"…. BUT HOW YOU PLAYED THE GAME!"

A history of intercollegiate athletics at Hope College.
Part I - 1862-1955
Gordon M. Brewer - Hope '48

CONTENTS

THE AUTHOR

Gordon Brewer has been a participant in or observer of the Hope College sports scene since his enrollment as a freshman in the fall of 1941. The second son of Robert and Helen Brewer, Gordon was born in Kalamazoo, Michigan in 1923. At age six months, his family moved to the small town of Martin, some 18 miles north of Kalamazoo. Educated in the Martin Public Schools, he was influenced to attend Hope College by high school principal Herman Laug (Hope '29) and the Reverend Albert Mansen.

The Japanese attack on Pearl Harbor in December of Brewer's freshman year served notice that his education would be interrupted. He was called to active duty on March 29, 1943, in his sophomore year. After 31 months of service with the 8th Air Force in England he was discharged at Fort Sheridan, Illinois in November of 1945. He then served as interim basketball coach at Martin High School until his re-enrollment at Hope in February, 1946. His graduating classmates in June of 1948 included sisters Margery and Lorraine Virginia Bult who would become Mrs. Brewer later that summer.

The Brewers were first employed by the Byron Center Public Schools where Lorraine taught elementary grades and Gordon initiated a football program and also coached basketball and baseball. Moving to Kelloggsville High School in 1950, Brewer taught history and literature while his coaching responsibilities included football, basketball, and track.

Following eight years in the high school ranks, Brewer was invited to return to Hope in 1956 as head track coach and an assistant coach in football. He also coached jayvee basketball for four years. His tenure as track coach would span 32 seasons. On April 27, 1991 the newly refurbished Hope track was named in his honor. In 1960 Brewer was named Director of Athletics, succeeding Al Vanderbush who now devoted full time to his responsibilities in the Department of Political Science. During this period Brewer was active as Hope's delegate to the NCAA, serving on various committees, including the Division III Steering Committee and the Post-Graduate Scholarship Committee.

After 20 years in the athletic directorship, Brewer was appointed Chairman of the Department of Physical Education, Recreation, and Athletics. He served five years in this capacity before retiring in 1988. His previous writings include sport essays entitled, "In Pursuit of True Sport", and "When the Cheering Stops". He also authored a short history of Hope's years in the MIAA as part of the 1988 Michigan Intercollegiate Athletic Association publication, Celebrating a Century of the Student Athlete.

The Brewers' children are Robert James, Lawrence Gordon, Daniel Richard, and Susan Marie (Hayes).

FOREWORD

"......BUT HOW YOU PLAYED THE GAME! A HISTORY OF INTERCOLLEGIATE ATHLETICS AT HOPE COLLEGE" is "must" reading for anyone interested in Hope College and Hope College sports. For those who enjoy a good story, this book includes some of the best in Hope sport history. Those who know Gordon Brewer well know that no one tells a story better than Gord.

The author has exceptional oral and written communication skills. He can always be counted upon to express the sentiment of the occasion be it a dedication ceremony, athletic banquet, or a team or departmental meeting. He is a clear thinker and brings a wealth of reading background into his communications. Readers will get a glimpse of what life was like during the first 93 years of the college. His is a lively tale which makes reading interesting and entertaining. The reader will become familiar with the great names of the past, persons who not only contributed to the rich legacy of Hope but also contributed in significant ways to the greater society upon graduation.

There are also other reasons why it is fitting for Gordon Brewer to author this segment of sport history at Hope. Gordon had first hand experience as a student-athlete, staff member of the Department of Physical Education and Athletics, coach, Department Chair, and Athletic Director over a five decade period. Gordon is the right person to compile this work because he enjoyed his own Hope experiences over a long career. He loves the College and it shows in this very well written book.

Gordon knew the coaches he wrote about personally. Schouten, Hinga, and Vanderbush in particular were men of strong character and commitment. These are the coaches who Gordon brings back into focus. Brewer, DeVette, and Green joined others to further the program in the segment of sport history after 1955 and yet to be written.

Gordon Brewer during his career at Hope emulated the highest ideals of Hope College. His commitment was deep and genuine. He was warm and inviting; his door was always open to those students and staff who sought his counsel. He was also fair. He knew what tough love was before it became a known term. He was an outstanding motivator of teams and individuals.

Few perhaps know that Gordon is a strong student of history and to this day, has many reading interests in the historical field. This background and academic preparation has led to a well documented and meticulous manuscript. The interesting asides and personal detail discovered through careful research give the reader a true picture of "Life at Hope" during this time period. Gordon brings out how the experience of sport at Hope has always centered on the student athlete rather than the end result of winning. His is a story beyond the box score and statistics of the game. Athletes lives outside the lines of the contests come alive in the book and lend support to the idea that an athlete's total experience at the college is more important than just his/her sport experience.

Due to Gordon Brewer's life experiences at Hope, communication skills, and commitment to Hope College, the author makes this an exciting part of the Hope story. Gordon makes it clear in his text that from Hope's beginning, the struggle to maintain the proper balance between academic and athletic pursuits has continued. The sport program geared to making the experience a rich personal experience for the participant first and foremost, has been the norm at Hope from the beginning. The foundation for the innovative present day program was established during these early years of sport because there were coaches and teachers who cared about each student-athlete's total experience at the College. You will enjoy Gordon Brewer's account of Hope's humble sport beginnings.

Bill Vanderbilt
Teacher, Coach, & Colleague
of Gordon Brewer from 1967-1988

PREFACE

Bright young faces in a sea of caps and gowns, Commencement Day at Hope College. In Holland's Municipal Stadium I waited with other faculty for the procession to begin. This culmination of the college experience has a certain appropriate flavor; it properly underscores academe and the institution's **raison d'etre**. Terms like **cum laude**, diploma, degree, and Phi Beta Kappa are in the air when the program is underway. Accomplishments are recognized and parents are proud.

But the stadium itself is testament to another side of college life, the extra curricular. Important in this category are sports, especially intercollegiate athletics. Within the hour the main address will call attention to Hope's outstanding year in athletics. Some will call it the best in Hope history. In the larger universities the cultural phenomenon of sports has often obscured the school's declared purpose, but this day, in this place, one senses balance, and the fact that these two realms need not infringe upon each other.

The afternoon draws to a close and caps are symbolically thrown in the air. As the crowd thins out, some linger for a nostalgic look at goal posts, or to the north where the vacant track and baseball field now hide their story. What is that story, and all the stories of games played in yesteryear and yesterday? Who did what to bring about this seemingly happy blend of scholastic and athletic pursuits?

Some preliminary investigation revealed that there existed no organized history devoted exclusively to intercollegiate athletics at Hope College. It seemed to me that here indeed was a story waiting to be told. I was encouraged by Bill Vanderbilt, then chairperson of the department of physical education, to begin the project during a 1985 sabbatical leave. Elton Bruins, at the time dean for the arts and humanities, also felt strongly that such a record should be part of Hope's overall history.

A diploma attests to my graduation from Hope College in 1948, but the school's real gift to me was beyond measure. My tuition was paid, but hardly my debt. Happily, I was invited to return in 1956 for a second Hope experience, this time as teacher, coach, and administrator. Repayment time had begun. And now perhaps the final installment, a chance to share with old grads some of their finest hours. The prospect of this kind of research had great appeal.

I would soon discover that the story in many ways would tell itself, with maybe just a nudge from me. I also felt strongly that this history must be more than a chronicle of box scores, of wins and losses. Surely sport transcends statistics. Most would see the narrative as incomplete without some attention to emotions at critical junctures. This dimension would come in part from interviews with former athletes and others associated with the school.

In choosing a title I have turned to Grantland Rice, the acknowledged dean of American sportswriters. Until his death in 1954, his syndicated column, "The Sportlight," set the standard for those on the sports beat. He is perhaps best remembered for creating "The Four Horsemen" of Notre Dame, and for a short bit of verse that became his credo:

When the One Great Scorer comes
To mark against your name
He writes - not that you won or lost -
But how you played the game.

For years this quatrain graced the walls of gyms and locker rooms across the land, where amateurs and would-be champions played the game. And then it fell from favor, especially with the barons of big time sports who view such sentiment as naive, hopelessly out of step with reality - - "Nice guys finish last," and all that. But as I examined decades of Hope athletes I found their answer to Rice's final line an eloquent one, that "how they played the game" was a tribute to themselves and their institution.

It is my intent to present Hope's athletic history in two parts. The present work covers the period from the inception of the college in 1862 through the 1954-55 school year, when Al Vanderbush decided to close out his coaching career and designate Russ De Vette as his successor. Part II will proceed through the halcyon years of the late '50s, the turbulent '60s, the changing decade of the '70s, dominance in the '80s, and finally the promise of the '90s.

While reaping great enjoyment and satisfaction from sport, I must concede that its transient nature has always bothered me. Young men and women challenge themselves in sports competition in a relatively short period of time. Seldom, if ever again in life, will they know the emotional and physical highs that accompany such participation. On the college scene it becomes a four-year capsule. Afterward they walk among us incognito. This is not all bad, for surely life moves on to more important things. But perhaps, just perhaps, yesterday's hero and his or her supporting cast deserve a trifle more, a replay, for those who would read it, of that brief span when energy and anticipation knew no bounds. A part of my purpose then, is to say in these pages that effort expended in athletics should not be totally lost, even if results were not always spectacular.

The information gathered has been revealing in a manner I had not fully anticipated. Each era of athletes had its own character, defined its own goals, performed in the face of unique handicaps, had leaders of principle, and, in the end, made a significant mark. Each in some measure, prepared the way for the next. My initial fascination ultimately deepened to genuine inspiration, and such is my hope for each reader. The rank and file of Hope athletes have made the most of sport without making it more than it is - - which certainly is not as simple as it sounds.

GMB

ACKNOWLEDGEMENTS

Many people have accommodated me in the preparation of this book. I am especially indebted to the following for generously granting me interviews: Gladys Hinga Bosch, Ekdal Buys Sr., Ed Damson, George Damson, the late Clarence Heemstra, Lee Kleis, the late Irwin J. Lubbers, Bill Poppink, Elizabeth "Bess" Schouten, Henry Steffens, Alvin Vanderbush, Ken Bauman, Don Piersma, Dave Kempker, and the late James Ver Meulen. Warren Vander Hill, Bruce Geelhoed, Bill Vanderbilt Sr., James Bultman, George Kraft, and Russell De Vette read parts of the manuscript and offered valuable suggestions. Randall Vande Water provided valuable source materials and photos.

The project could not have been completed without the willing assistance of Hope Archivist Larry Wagenaar, his assistant Craig Wright, and student assistants Kori Levos, Krystal Van Wulfen, and Rebecca O'Shesky. Also, a vote of thanks to former Hope Archivist Andrew Vander Zee who helped in the location of materials for the early chapters. Staff members at Holland's Herrick Library were most helpful in supplying microfilm. Preston Stegenga, a long-time friend and classmate, provided photos of his father's teams at Hope in the teens. Tom Renner, director of public relations at Hope interrupted his busy schedule numerous times to provide invaluable assistance in many areas, including the final publication. His enthusiasm and constant encouragement are deeply appreciated. Bess Schouten provided very special information about her illustrious father that could have come from no other source, and I am grateful for her generous sharing of these insights. The proof reading of Greg Olgers and type-setting of Karen Bos are deeply appreciated.

CHAPTER 1

THE EARLY PERIOD - ATHLETICS IN TRAVAIL

Hope College came into being with fully a third of the 19th century still before it. While athletic activity was not extensive in those early years, a point of view was being developed and our roots are there. What was the picture, and how should it be viewed in the light of later developments? Perhaps an appraisal of Hope's early period in sports can be seen in sharper focus against the backdrop of a handful of happenings on the national and state scenes.

For instance, in 1859, only 12 years after the intrepid Albertus C. Van Raalte established the Holland settlement, the first intercollegiate baseball game was played at Pittsfield, Massachusetts, between Amherst and Williams. Amherst won, 66 to 32. In 1869, three years after Hope's first commencement exercise, the midwestern Cincinnati Red Stockings turned pro and toured the east, winning all games played. Also in 1869, Rutgers and Princeton met in New Brunswick, New Jersey, in the country's first intercollegiate football game with Rutgers the winner, six goals to four. In 1884, the first intercollegiate football game in the state of Michigan was played in Ann Arbor, with Albion losing to the University of Michigan, 18 to 0. In 1888, one year after Hope's **Anchor** began publication, the Michigan Intercollegiate Athletic Association was formed with Michigan Agricultural College (later Michigan State University), Albion, Hillsdale, and Olivet as charter members. In 1891, the year following Hope's Quarter Centennial Celebration, Dr. James A. Naismith invented the game of basketball at the YMCA Training School in Springfield, Massachusetts.

Hope's enrollment, until 1878, was strictly male with most preparing for the ministry or some phase of religious work. They were serious students, few in number, and located in the western extreme of the state. This combination gave rise to a label of provincialism that would be hard to live down. They were not, however, as isolated as one might presume and took due note of the events mentioned above and the new sports that were becoming a part of campus life.

Early evidence of a need for respite from the rigors of academic life was the building of a gymnasium in 1862. The frame building, constructed largely by the students and Principal Philip Phelps, was dedicated on July 17, 1862. The grandeur of the program on that day far exceeded that of the building being dedicated. There were 41 numbers in all. The graduating class of the Holland Academy sang 11 songs. There were 18 recitations, three dialogues, an essay on the new gym by William Shields, plus addresses by the Reverends Peter J. Oggel and Joseph H. Kershow. Merely surviving the ceremony speaks well of the physical stamina of those on hand.

The actual location of the building was on the high ground just east of Van Vleck Hall, where stately Carnegie Gymnasium would stand for most of the 20th century.

> The original building was a simple structure with the entire framework visible from the interior. In 1878, the building was completed with ceiling, hardwood floor, platform, and a walnut balustrade, and was papered and painted. At that time, the building was raised from the ground on a brick foundation. Chairs replaced the old wooden settees.[1]

With the addition of such finery it became the first college chapel and served as such until the erection of Winants Chapel in 1894.

While gymnastics and other exercises in the gym offered some diversion, they could not match the excitement provided by the outdoor game of baseball. Popularized in army

Hope's First Gymnasium

Erected in 1862 primarily by the students, it survived the Holland fire of October 9, 1871, was renovated in 1878 and served as a chapel until 1894 when it reverted to its original function as a gym. It was torn down in 1905 to make way for Carnegie Gymnasium.

The above photo showing the gymnasium at the right was most likely taken from the top floor of the newly constructed Van Raalte Hall. Van Vleck Hall (1857) is at the left. Circa 1904.

Looking southeastward past Van Vleck Hall toward the gym entrance.

camps of the Civil War, it was brought home to every town and hamlet of America. In the early 1870s, an organized club at Hope College was playing more than intramural contests. The **Holland City News** of June 8, 1872, dutifully reported that: "A match game of baseball, played June 1st at Grand Haven, between the Hope College Club of this city, and the Eagle Club of Grand Haven resulted in the following:

Score: Grand Haven - 30
Hope College - 12
Time of game: 2 hrs. 45 min."[2]

The **News**, busily campaigning for the reelection of Ulysses Grant, offered no comment on the game, but did list the following Hope players by name and position:

Herrick c
Hegemon 3b
Bedell p
Krijger cf
Post lf
Ledeboer ss
Steele 1st b
Pfanstiehl 2b
Walsh rf

I could not help but recall my grammar school baseball days, when the worst player always played right field and batted ninth. I wondered if Mr. Walsh was so classified in 1872. A second observation would be that pitching was not yet an art.

The first issue of the **Anchor** (June, 1887) mentioned Hope's first baseball game of the season as being played on May 20th at the Fair Grounds, again against a Grand Haven team. This time the college boys prevailed 25 to 24. In the same issue appears a patronizing account of the team's struggle against a not too powerful foe:

> On the 4th of this month [June] we witnessed a very interesting game of baseball between the Muskegon High School and the Hope College nines, and although our boys were beaten they had no reason to be ashamed of the defeat, as they played well. The outfield did good work capturing all the flies. As in the previous game, our boys did their best work toward the last. The game ended with a score of Muskegon 15, Hope College 5. Time of game, 2 hours and 15 minutes. Henry Scott, umpire...[3]

The decade of the "Gay Nineties" began with optimism and increased activity for those interested in athletics. Generally speaking, this did not include faculty members, though there were exceptions. The Hope College Athletic Association was organized on May 10, 1889 with Winter as manager; Kuiper, secretary; Sietsma, treasurer; and Betten and Veldman, Captains. An **Anchor** notice advised that all challenges should be sent to the manager. The club numbered about 20 members.

Baseball continued to be the primary sport, but Hope was branching out to satisfy other interests. In October, 1892, the **Anchor** reported that "Hope College is ambitious to keep abreast of the times. In addition to the existing so-called baseball and football clubs, a lawn tennis club was recently started."[4] Apparently all three games were played well into the fall season with football continuing somewhat longer. An **Anchor** article titled "Athletics" speaks of the three sports and contains a priceless example of nineteenth century sports journalism. The account is mainly devoted to a baseball game played in early October. While some of the expressions evoke a smile, one must concede that the youthful scribe was attentive, conscientious, and quite thorough in his coverage of the contest:

> During the last two years there has been somewhat of a revival in the line of athletics at Hope College...and every afternoon students can be seen on the campus enjoying themselves in a game of lawn tennis, football or baseball. Through the kindness of the faculty a tennis court has been laid out which in due time may be in fine condition.
>
> Football is practiced a good deal, but what the boys need is a competent leader and teacher which we hope to have next spring.
>
> Baseball is mostly played of all the games; two clubs have been formed, one from the College department, and the other from the Grammar department. Great interest is shown in this game and especially when a match game is announced, the number of games won by each of these clubs is equal. The interest was great when the notice was put up on the bulletin board that a match game was to be played between a picked club from Hope College and the Holland City Juniors; the game was scheduled for the 5th of October to be played at the Ottawa County Fair, the prize being a League ball and bat. Everyone was out for practice a few days before the time but still some fear was expressed of not winning the game. The Juniors had the choice of innings and took the "outs" and when all were ready 'game' was called at 1:30 P.M. A close game was looked for by all who knew the strength of both teams. Ver Schure twirled the sphere for the Juniors and Brock for the College boys. At the end of the first inning the score was 2-1 in favor of the College boys. The end of the second added a goose egg to the score of each club, but at the beginning of the 4th the score was even. It was in this inning that the Juniors seemed to have it all their own way and that they would go off as victors of the game. Some hard batting was done and they managed to get six runs added to their score making it 8-2 in their favor. The score then rose but slowly until

the 1st half of the ninth inning when it was 10-6 in favor of the Juniors. It was now the time, or never, for the College boys to catch up, and each took up the bat with a firm grip and wielded it with success until all but one, had a score credited to his name; eight runs were made, making the score 14-10 in favor of the College boys. A white-wash on the Juniors in the last half of the ninth inning ended the game in favor of the College boys. Score 14-10. The game was closely contested and the Juniors show good strength although it would have been more evenly played had the Juniors not objected to some of the College boys playing their regular positions. By an agreement between the two clubs Heeren would not catch for the College boys as the Juniors feared too many men would be caught at second, so that second base was assigned to him where he distinguished himself by making a one handed catch on a backward run. The features of the game were the hard hitting on both sides and Williams' long hit over center, and Ballard's fine catch on a forward run for a fly which saved the game for the College boys. Considerable disagreement was shown at times on some of the decisions of the umpire, Mr. Watermueller, although no one can say that he favored either side. A number of flies were missed in right field on account of the crowd sitting in the field, but mention ought to be made of the boys appointed as marshalls who kept the crowd back from the diamond. We express our hearty thanks to them for their work.

> The College boys also express their thanks to the Directors of the Fair for the prize which has been awarded to them. We hope that the kind feeling which has been established between the city boys and the students may be kept up and be strengthened by the match games between the two clubs which may yet be played in the future. Come again boys.[5]

Followers of modern day sports may sense that this was Hope's age of innocence, so to speak. A game was an entity in itself, played for sheer enjoyment, and without serious consequences. Championships were not at stake and jobs were not on the line. But this would change. Such pastoral scenes would soon defer to "progress" and sport, as we know it, would be on its way.

When news from other colleges and universities reached the Hope campus it was eagerly digested. The desire to conform to norms of the day can be seen in bits of trivia that appeared from time to time in the college newspaper. The matter of school colors, or lack of same, was a source of concern to Harmon Van Slyke Peeke, Hope class of '87. In June of 1888 he wrote the **Anchor** from his mission station in Nagasaki, Japan, deploring the fact that Hope could not match Harvard or Princeton in this regard. His proposal of orange and some contrasting, harmonious color was based on Hope's Dutch heritage and the House of Orange. In December of that year an editorial suggested that orange might represent the Netherlands connection and blue the United States. The suggestion was deemed worthy and in due time Hope uniforms would sport these colors. The matter of uniforms of course, was a process of evolution, but it was mentioned as early as 1893: "Old cast off trousers, somewhat abbreviated, are used by some of the boys in athletic sports. Anything to give freedom of motion to the limbs."[6]

In February of 1889, the **Anchor** somewhat innocently reported that, "Football costs Princeton $3,000 a season."[7] Such information was hardly a catalyst for Hope's infant program. However, in 1891 the Athletic Association received a challenge from Michigan Agricultural College to meet in football and the ramifications of intercollegiate competition had to be considered. A down-to-earth student editorial in December, 1893, was the forerunner of many a philosophic treatise on the subject in years to come:

> Every college ought to have a baseball nine and a football eleven and meet teams from sister institutions. Intercollegiate contests promote a spirit of friendly rivalry, and to keep the latter from degenerating into semi-professionalism is the duty of all concerned. Study is the student's business. Whatever is allowed to come between him and his work, is a stumbling block to progress. The man who cannot exclude his athletic sports from the study hour had better leave them alone, and yet, every student ought to hold himself responsible for taking a certain amount of exercise daily.[8]

On June 26, 1894, the structure known as Graves Library and Winants Chapel was dedicated. Designed by Mr. W.J. Johnston of Chicago, and built of native stone from nearby Waverly, it was the first really impressive building on the campus. Winants Chapel made it possible for the frame chapel east of Van Vleck Hall to revert to its original function as a gymnasium. Alterations were made and various items of gymnastic equipment were added. The hazards of using such devices when uninitiated was not fully comprehended, and it was trial and error all the way with impulsive curiosity getting the best of discretion. In any case, the remodeled facility was enthusiastically received by the students. The December, 1894, issue of the **Anchor** spoke proudly of "Our Gymnasium:"

> The old chapel building has at last undergone such changes as will make it look like a gymnasium. With the money so liberally subscribed last year the committee has done some profitable work; the old stage has been removed, the gallery has been extended so as to make a fine running track which requires thirty four laps for one mile(!!). Four travelling rings have been hung in line which afford amusement to the boys; a trapeze has been made which we are sorry to say has been the source of three injuries already, but we trust the boys will be more careful in its use hereafter; a kicking standard and horizontal bar are in course of construct-

ion and will soon be ready for use. [Parallel bars were added in 1895]. The committee which was appointed last year have the management in hand and are having the Gymnasium open from 4:00 to 5:45 P.M. every day. The fees have been fixed at 50 cents a term or three terms for $1.00. Among other things which will be enforced is the wearing of rubber-soled shoes; we have noticed the desirable effect of this rule already although the rules will not be in force until next term...[9]

The fascination of football for Hope students, especially in the early years, is not readily explained. The object of the game was not altogether clear to spectators and perhaps to some participants as well, but the very activity tended to generate excitement. The **Anchor** reported that football was in high favor and almost every afternoon an excited, struggling mass of humanity could be seen on the south campus "contending for possession of the ball." One speculates that the rough and tumble nature of the game struck a responsive note in America's identification with rugged individualism and the frontier spirit. Students described it variously as "the royal game," "the greatest college game," "the king of athletic sports," and "the game that makes for true manhood and the largest school spirit."

The so-called south campus was the area on the north side of 12th Street between College and Columbia Avenues. In the 1890s this sizeable plot of ground was entirely without buildings and provided more than ample room for both practice and contests. The ground, however, tended to be sandy and was liberally sprinkled with sandburrs.

A series of circumstances, beginning in 1893, combined to excite Hope students with the prospect of intercollegiate football at an early date. Professor Gerrit J. Kollen had become Hope's third president in 1893 and the college was on

Interior of Hope's first gymnasium. Built in 1862 largely by students, it was refurbished in 1878 to serve as a chapel. In 1894 it reverted to its original function as a gym. The gymnastics equipment indicates that the picture was taken sometime after the latter date.

the move. Also arriving in that year was a young professor of English and Modern Languages named Erastus A. Whitenack. Professor Whitenack had some knowledge of and great interest in the new sport of football. His offer to coach the team was a godsend to the young men seeking to elevate their program to the level of other colleges in the state. Also, such encouragement from a faculty person further identified the team with the school. An additional touch of sophistication was the formation in September of 1895 of a Football Association to promote and manage the program:

> At a meeting of the Football Association held Sept. 20, A.L. Warnshuis was elected Manager and H. Sluyter, Captain. Much enthusiasm is manifested and it will undoubtedly be a successful football season; the grounds will be improved as much as necessary, and if in any way possible two clubs will be organized, thus promising some good games. Alma College has made an offer of a challenge, and it is now under consideration.[10]

It is quite understandable that in this atmosphere of optimism and anticipation the team would give little credence to a somewhat dormant directive of the faculty and Council (known as the Board of Trustees beginning in 1927) which forbade any of Hope's athletic teams to leave the city during term time to enter into a contest with an outside team. The restriction, however, was of long standing and was now invoked by a faculty and administration concerned about adequate preparation time for classes as well as the expense involved. When all attempts at negotiation failed, the impact came as a bombshell. The affected students gave vent to their frustration in the pages of the **Anchor**:

> As already remarked in an editorial, the boys caught the right football spirit this term, but foot-ball has now received a deadly blow for Hope. A short time ago a petition was handed to the Faculty, kindly asking them to remove the restrictions now existing against intercollegiate athletic contests. The petition was answered by a long document containing the Faculty's reason for refusing all requests. This has taken away the interest entirely, and not a dozen boys have been on the foot-ball grounds since. Without some incentive, without that of mere exercise, there can be very little interest in foot-ball, or any other sport at Hope. Not one of the resolutions passed by the Faculty will endure criticism, if viewed from a reasonable standpoint; by that we mean as Hope students would view it, not as Yale or Harvard, etc. It would be sheer folly to play Albion or other distant college clubs. But would one or two games played with Grand Rapids High School or some similar institution harm Hope students? Pray, where does distance come in? Where is the sporting world? What are the expenses? How much time would be expended? As it is at present there is very little to boast of, there is no college spirit to speak of in this direction, nor do we find the usual signs of college life. These are not casting reflections on our college, for we love it sincerely, but a change must come, as the college advances, and why should it not come now?[11]

Of all the protests perhaps the most touching was that voiced by team member John J. Banninga. A sophomore at the time, Banninga was deeply disappointed but collected his thoughts in the waning weeks of the fall and, after some reflection, wrote an informative essay titled "Football at Hope College." The commentary begins with some appropriate lines from Whittier, traces the evolution of football at Hope, and concludes without rancor. I include it here in its entirety as a valuable link with Hope's football past:

"Of all sad words of tongue or pen
The saddest are these: 'It might have been!'"

FOOTBALL AT HOPE COLLEGE

The history of football at Hope College is like the history of some great historic movement, as that of the phalanx, for example. First, there is no phalanx at all, then Epaminondas came and made a beginning; later Alexander himself appeared, and the phalanx assumed a definite and practical form.

It is about five years ago that football came to life at Hope. Some of the students who entered College that year had played football before, or had seen it played, and, consequently thought that it would be a good thing to play it here also. An association football was purchased, and that fall, and the succeeding one, the boys could be seen limping around the campus, having found difficulty in kicking in the right place at the right time. No eleven was formed. Each afternoon when a sufficient number of boys had come out, sides were chosen, and then each side would try to kick the ball through the opponent's goal. Hither and thither they would surge, kicking each other as often as they kicked the ball, until all were too breathless and tired, or too lame to play anymore.

In the fall of '93 our Alexander came, in the person of Prof. Whitenack. The boys soon learned that he was a foot-ball man, the man for Hope, to teach her intercollegiate football. The Professor kindly consented to extend a helping-hand after obtaining the consent of the President of the College. Now football assumed a definite shape, the boys took hold of it in earnest. A Varsity was formed with Henry Sluyter as captain. One game was played with the Holland City boys in which our team was victorious. The playing, of course, was that of beginners, but a good beginning had been made, and there were bright prospects for the future.

Last year (1894) very little was done. The boys played quite frequently, but rather for the exercise and fun, than for practice, in order to become good players. However, the boys were kept in practice, and developed into good material for this year's team.

The history of this fall's football is a history of what might have been. That which occupied the minds of former players was football. More than ever before did there seem to be a desire to form a good team and do some thoroughly good work. At a meeting of those interested, A.L. Warnshuis was elected manager, and Henry Sluyter, captain. Later in the term upon the resignation of the manager, H. Wiersum was elected to that office.

Challenges were received from Alma, Kalamazoo, Grand Rapids High School, and from the Ionia High School. The business men of the town encouraged the players, and if a game had actually been arranged for, the expenses could easily have been raised among them. [Earliest downtown Quarterback Club??] This filled the boys with enthusiasm. A second team was organized, and every afternoon the two teams could be seen on the field, doing hard work. The varsity procured suits, and everything assumed a business like aspect, when the whole structure suddenly fell to the ground.

The readers of the **Anchor** are well acquainted with the reasons. Those that are in authority do not seem to believe in Intercollegiate Athletics, and so the anticipated victories of our team vanished in the air. A petition signed by all the students failed to remove the restrictions, and there is no more football at Hope College at present.

In this number of the **Anchor** appears the picture of our 'might have been' team. We believe we have material for a good team and were we given an opportunity to show our powers, we believe we could demonstrate that Hope need not take a back seat in foot-ball, or other athletics. This fall is almost past, and no more can be done now, but we sincerely hope that circumstances will be such next year, that we can have a team in the field.

Alumni, what is your opinion? If we are not

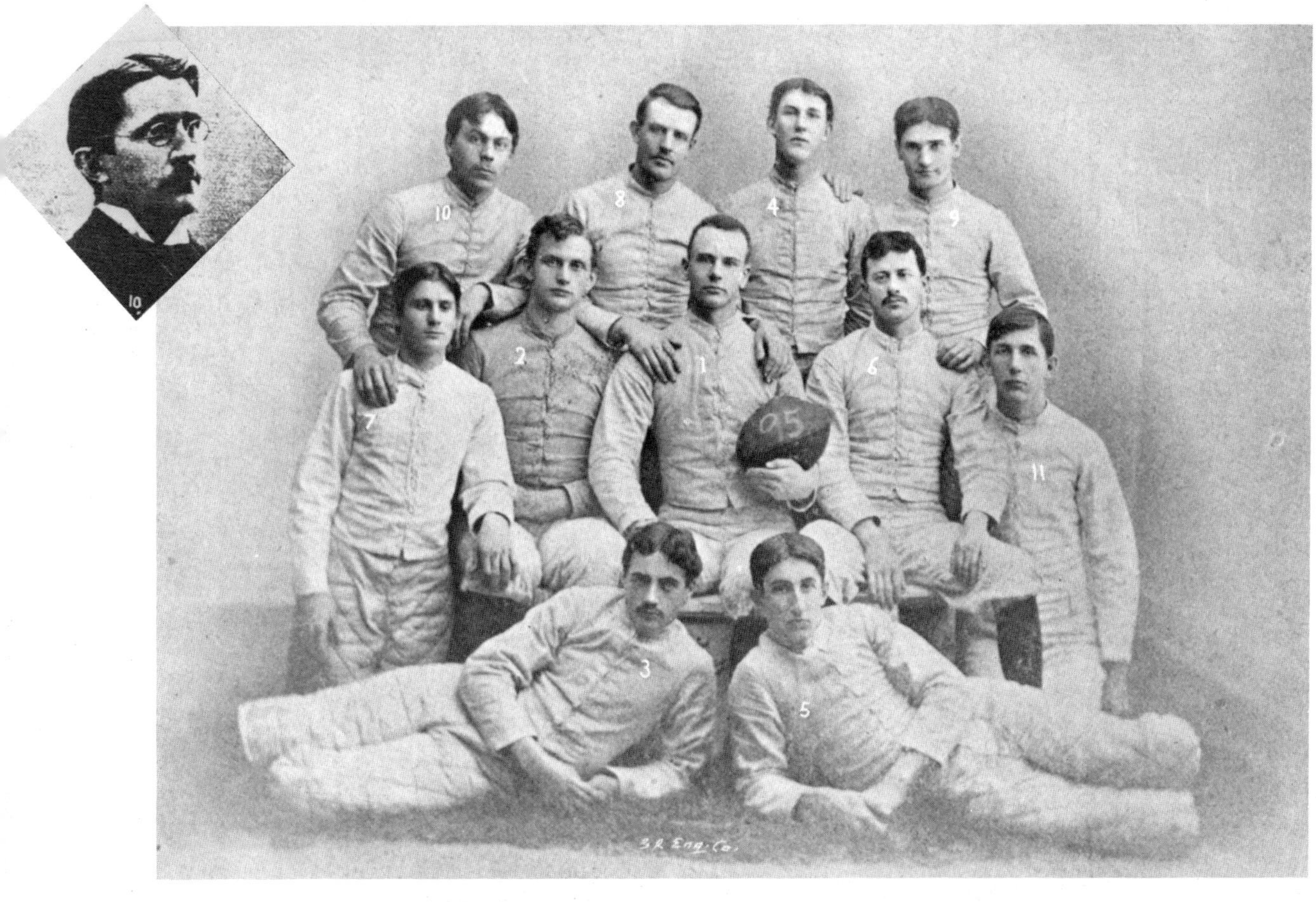

Hope's 1895 "Might Have Been" Football Team

Top Row L to R: E. Kelder, William Van Der Haart, Martin Hyink, John J. Banning. **Middle Row:** J. De Bey, Henry Schipper, Captain Henry Sluiter, J.J. Wiersum, A. Livingston Warnshuis. **Front Row** (Reclining): John E. Kuisenga, F.C. Warnshuis. **Inset:** First Coach, Professor Erastus A. Whiteneck.

mistaken, there was, once upon a time, a baseball team at Hope, that played outside games. What do you as former athletes of Hope think of having a football team at your Alma Mater that will sustain the reputation you then made? Possibly we are too enthusiastic, but certainly we cannot view the matter in the way the faculty does.

The football players have put their suits on the shelf for the remainder of this year, but they sincerely hope that, next year, they will be able to make good use of them.[12]

John J. Banninga 12

Despite Banninga's fondest hopes, he would graduate in 1898 without ever having worn his football "suit" in a regulation game. It would not be until 22 years after that fateful fall of '95 that the ban would finally be lifted and Hope would begin the catch-up process. There is evidence however, that John Banninga's value system was intact and that his sense of purpose was not shaken by this disappointment. In January of 1903 the **Anchor** reported the following: "Rev. J.J. Banninga of Timmangalam, South India, has already preached his first sermon in the Tamil language. We look for great blessings on his work."[13] A final glimpse of the man is seen as he appeared at the 1907 alumni banquet and addressed the gathering. His remarks included the following:

...Each one, passing through these halls, must consider himself a contribution of his people to mankind, and as such, be he minister, lawyer, or farmer, he must have a world-vision and a world-purpose. He can no longer draw a circle about himself as the center and say, "Herein will I live," for he belongs to the whole world and must serve all mankind. He becomes no magnet that draws all things to itself, but a dynamo, sending out power and light and heat in all directions.

We can best serve our college and the world by living ourselves absolutely to our God and our fellowmen. Not by writing our own names high on the walls of the temple of fame, but by writing Christ's name on the hearts and lives of men, can we best honor our Alma Mater. Let him who will, seek glory; let us seek service. Let him, who will, live to himself and live alone; let us live for the world and Him who made it, and thus we shall best serve our Lord and also our college.[14]

The decision of 1895 was a blow to physical activity in general and athletics in particular. The faculty had left little doubt as to who was making the decisions. One student account deplored the fact that the gymnasium could count only 25 members. As the students closed out the century a somewhat cynical assessment of the athletic situation was used as preface for another plea for reason and some sort of compromise:

This lack of interest...was also noticeable during the last few years in sports. It is true, we have often seen familiar figures arrayed in white pantaloons and red sweaters, running up and down our campus in chase of a ball, but the wearing of white pantaloons and red sweaters is not necessarily an indication of great enthusiasm. It is equally true that a few of our number claim to be members of the college eleven, or the baseball team; but pray, what honor is there in being a member of a college team that never plays and that, so far as the world at large is concerned, is a nonentity? Unearned honors may make a man vain but seldom enthusiastic. The fact is, we have at present no enthusiasm whatever for athletics of any kind.

...Let us arouse a greater enthusiasm for athletics and make it possible for every student of Hope College to be graduated a well developed man. Let the faculty take the initiative and allow the students to try intercollegiate baseball for one season, at least, and then watch the result.

Let us not be misunderstood. The students do not desire "to run the college" and are as capable of love for their alma mater as any students in the land; but a battle paean can never hope for immortality until it has stirred men's hearts to victory, and no banner can ever be as dear to a nation's heart as the flag that has waved in the smoke of the battle.

J.S.R. '00 [15]

The controversy surrounding football was not confined to Hope's campus. A love-hate relationship with the game had developed across the country and leading institutions reacted in a variety of ways. The sport was abolished at Harvard in 1885 following a report by the president stating that his investigating committee was "convinced that football as at present played by college teams is demoralizing to players and spectators and extremely dangerous." Within five years it had been revived as Harvard won its first victory over Yale before 20 thousand spectators! Columbia, a leading football power, also abolished the game. Northwestern and Union College prohibited football for one year. Stanford and California substituted rugby for football, a change that lasted ten years. A light-hearted poem appearing on the Penn State campus had more serious overtones: (see next page)

FOOTBALL DAYS

The football days have come again;
The gladdest of the year;
One side of Willie's nose is gone
And Tom has lost an ear.
Heaped on the field the players jab
And punch, and claw, and tear;
They knock the breath from those beneath
And gouge without a care;
They break each other's arms and legs
And pull joints out of place,
And here and there is one who gets
His teeth kicked from his face...

The objections to the game at Hope stemmed mostly from the threat it posed to study time and the added expense for an institution struggling financially. There was, of course, some concern about injuries, but this appears not to have been the major issue. Intramural play lacked the intensity of intercollegiate competition and it is likely that injuries were at a minimum. The consequence of rough play **was** the major issue on the national scene, as described by historian C.W. Hackensmith:

> Occupying the center of the intercollegiate athletic universe, football was at best a brutal affair. The great tactical plays...called for brute force and body contact at a dangerous speed, as judged by the 68 deaths and 804 incapacitating injuries recorded between 1901 and 1904. The situation reached a climax in 1905 when Harold Moore, a sophomore back at Union College, was killed in a game with New York University. The Sunday **New York Times** gave the incident front-page billing, and news services spread the grim story across the nation.[16]

While school authorities scrambled to bring the situation under control, Hope continued its low-key intramural games. The ban, distressing as it was, may be seen in some respects as a blessing in disguise. By the time Hope men were given the green light, rules had been altered limiting some of the early viciousness. Protective equipment, though far from ideal, was also improved during the intervening years.

Unfortunately, the faculty and administration's side of the ban is not well documented. Their restrictions, which seem overzealous by today's standards, were obviously instituted with the students' overall welfare in mind. It is doubtful if the seemingly adversarial relationship between faculty and students compromised overall student-faculty rapport. Mutual respect continued as the college found itself on the threshold of an exciting new century. The subject of the ban would erupt periodically, providing an emotional safety valve for young people in their identity-seeking years.

REFERENCES - CHAPTER I

1. Wynand Wichers, A **Century of Hope**. Grand Rapids: William B. Eerd-mans Company, 1968, p. 57.
2. **Holland City News**, June 8, 1872.
3. The **Anchor**, June, 1887.
4. _ ___, October, 1892.
5. _ ___, October, 1893.
6. _ ___, November, 1893.
7. _ ___, February, 1889.
8. _ ___, December, 1893.
9. _ ___, December, 1894.
10. _ ___, September, 1895.
11. _ ___, November, 1895.
12. _ ___, December, 1895.
13. _ ___, January, 1903.
14. _ ___, April, 1908.
15. _ ___, April, 1889.
16. C.W. Hackensmith, **History of Physical Education**. New York: Harper and Row, Publishers, 1966, p. 398.

CHAPTER 2

HOPE PREPARES FOR THE 20TH CENTURY

Professor Gerrit John Kollen was the first layman to serve as president of Hope College. For this and other reasons his election was opposed by some Council members and he failed to receive the necessary two-thirds majority vote until a second meeting of that body was called in June of 1893. His supporters stood by him, and when he finally prevailed, a new era began for the institution. If the college was to grow, its physical plant would have to be measurably improved. Dr. Kollen saw this need at once and possessed the driving force necessary to spearhead such a program. Within thirteen years four major structures rose on the campus and the denomination knew that its college in Michigan was here to stay. With the addition of Graves Hall and Winants Chapel, Van Raalte Hall, Carnegie Gymnasium, and Voorhees Hall, Hope became decidedly more attractive to students both in and out of Michigan.

Hope's athletic fortunes however, had reached a less than satisfying plateau and a boost was needed. It came from a somewhat unexpected quarter. In the late fall of 1891, Dr. James Naismith invented the game of basketball at Springfield College to ease student tedium during the grim Massachusetts winters. In the spring of 1892 a conference of YMCA directors met in Springfield, and Naismith used the occasion to demonstrate the game. According to Dr. George Meylan, who played in the game, the teams were captained by Naismith and Amos Alonzo Stagg, who would later become a legendary football coach. The use of peach baskets and a soccer ball is generally known, but Dr. Meylan also reports that the players shot underhanded, did a good deal of wrestling for the ball, and very little dribbling.

The game achieved almost immediate popularity and leap-frogged across the country. Climate and other conditions at Hope College were not markedly different from those at Springfield, and the new game was welcomed with great enthusiasm. It was in fact, destined to become Hope's brightest star in 20th century athletic competition.

A striking phenomenon of the period was the beginning evidence of an interest in sports participation by women. This was but one phase of their struggle for greater freedom in society and would culminate some 70 years later in federal legislation known as Title IX of the Education Amendments of 1972. Basketball was by no means confined to men and some of Hope's earliest records in the sport describe the women's activity:

Pictured above (circa 1900) are girls of Hope's Basquette Club about to engage in a drill with wooden dumbbells. The picture was taken in the original gymnasium. In the background can be seen a basket attached to the gallery with no backboard. The free throw circle and lane are also visible in the foreground.

A Basquette Club, composed of 18 girls was organized soon after the opening of the college year (1900) with Miss Floyd as President; Miss Riemens, Vice President; Miss Yates, Sec. Treas. The Basquette girls have possession of the gym two hours a week, at which times one half of the hour is occupied with physical exercise and dumb bell drill under the direction of Prof. Mast. The rest of the hour is given to basketball....Basketball is greatly enjoyed by the girls. They play the game beautifully, as was seen by the exhibition game played on Dec. 14 by two picked teams, before the faculty and about 50 invited guests. Everyone was surprised by the agility of the girls and pronounced basketball "all right." The rooters in the gallery almost raised the roof but were unable to rattle the players. The score was 4 to 4 with a line-up as follows:

Whites		Blacks
Alice Keppel (Capt.)	C	Carrie Herrell (Capt.)
May Veneklaasen	basket	Amy Dosker
Katherine Duffey	...	Minnie De Feyter
Minnie Vander Ploeg	guard	Avis Yates
Mamie Verwey	...	Anna Riemens

Anne Floyd, umpire; Grace Hoekje, referee[1]

Men's basketball was also on an intramural basis at this time, but by the 1901-02 school year a team had been organized to represent the school against outside independent teams. The earliest recorded score concerns a game played on February 1, 1902, between the Hope five and a team from Saugatuck. The final score was Hope 74, Saugatuck 4. Players for Hope included Cornelius Vandermel, Peter Pleune, James Van Der Meulen, Hessel S. Yntema, Evert Kruisenga, and Captain Frank Niessink. Niessink is not listed as a Hope grad and may have been a high school student (Hope Prep), as was Peter Pleune at the time. Eligibility rules had not yet been established and talented players from the prep ranks were considered "close enough." The lopsided score of this early contest is somewhat difficult to defend. It of course raises the question of "pouring it on" when an opponent is obviously outclassed. Since details are scarce, we will attribute it to a lack of substitutes rather than a lack of gallantry.

There can be little doubt that the game was fun to play and fun to watch. In March of 1902 the **Anchor** contained the following report:

> Basketball continues to be the favorite amusement. The college team is making a good record having won 4 out of 5 games with a score of 248 to 79, on points. The only real game our boys lost was that played with the strong Y.M.C.A. team of Grand Rapids, Feb. 24, which resulted in a score of 39 to 20, Grand Rapids getting the buttered half of the biscuit...[2]

The team played a return game at the Grand Rapids "Y" on the late date of April 25 and lost a second time 27 to 11. The fact that the game was played in Grand Rapids and that the following fall the football team made a trip to Muskegon indicates that there may have been periodic relaxations of the travel ban.

Intercollegiate athletics seemed to survive and even thrive during this period, despite the lack of any official sanction by the college. The college catalogue of 1902-03 included the following statement under the heading of "Gymnasium:"

> While physical culture is valued highly, it is not encouraged at the expense of education and morality. Believing that intercollegiate athletics have a strong tendency to interfere with the regular college work, and that they are generally not helpful to the development of moral Christian character, it is held that a denominational college like ours can not afford to support them.[3]

The statement does not appear in subsequent catalogues but it continued to be the college position. The Michigan Intercollegiate Athletic Association (MIAA) was alive and well after 15 years and seemed a natural for Hope College. However, since such affiliation would obviously encourage and support intercollegiate athletics, no move was made by college officials. Students, on the other hand, were determined to keep the issue alive and pled their case with some logic:

> The Athletic Association has an opportunity this year [1903] of entering into the Michigan Intercollegiate Athletic Association. As this offer is not made every year, we think it advisable that some action (pro or con) be taken at once. When we remember what a wonderful feeling of college brotherhood the entering into the Michigan Oratorical League has created for Hope; when we remember how much better we are known through this means, is it radical to stand for Intercollegiate Athletics, if there is much to gain and nothing to lose?...[4]

As basketball moved to center stage, other sports found the going a bit more difficult. The baseball team had its ups and downs. In 1903 they divided games with Mc Lachlan Business College of Grand Rapids. The 1904 team hoped to get along without help from city players but came up a little short. One of the city players who helped out in that spring was a catcher named Jack Schouten. Scores and opponents for the season were as follows:

Kalamazoo 13 - Hope 0
Hope 9 - Benton Harbor High School 1
Hope 8 - Allegan High School 5
Hope 5 - Grand Rapids High School 2

Hope Women's Basketball Team - 1901-02

Exact identification was not possible but the picture probably includes some of the following: Alice Keppel, May Veneklaasen, Katherine Duffey, Minnie Vander Ploeg, Anne Floyd, Mamie Verwey, Lilla Thurber, Carrie Herrell, Amy Dosker, Minie De Feyter, Avis Yates, Anna Riemens, Grace Hoekje, Estelle Kollen. (Photo courtesy of the Holland Historical Trust Collection of The Joint Archives of Holland)

Hope's First Basketball Team - 1901-02

Standing L to R: Evert Kruisenga, Hessel S. Yntema, James Van De Meulen. Seated: Peter Pleune, Captain Frank Niessink, Cornelius Vandermel.

In June of 1905 the **Anchor** reported that "for the first time in the history of Hope athletics has the baseball team been composed exclusively of college players." Sixteen tried out for the team and a successful season resulted. Scores were as follows:

Hope 9 - Holland High School 2
Hope 17 - Holland High School 7
Hope 19 - Holland High School 2
Hope 11 - Mc Lachlan Business College of Grand Rapids 6
Hope 10 - Allegan High School 1
Grand Rapids High School 7 - Hope 4

The schedule no doubt reflects both the limitations of the program and lack of involvement by the administration at that time.

Football continued to be played but enjoyed little spectator support from the student body or anyone else. A single game was played during the fall of 1903 with the "Preps" on November 21. There is no record of the score. Football, however, was only temporarily in the shadows.

Tennis was popular enough to warrant repair of the existing court and the laying of another. In May of 1901 the **Anchor** reported that there were now ample accommodations for all who were interested in tennis. The first campus tennis tournament was held in the spring of 1905 with a freshman, Arthur J. Misner, winning 6-4, 9-7 in a two-hour match over Bernard J. DeVries, who was a junior in the prep school at the time. This was considered a sports milestone and no attempts were made to initiate outside competition.

Track and Field is often termed the world's oldest sport, but it was slow in coming to Hope College. The dream of France's Baron Pierre De Coubertin to revive the Olympic Games became a reality in 1896, but the games failed to generate the interest and enthusiasm they deserved. The American aggregation of track and field athletes that journeyed to Athens put on a superb performance but the country yawned when they returned. Very little was made of their superior accomplishments. However, as St. Louis prepared to host the third Olympiad in 1904, track received some attention on the Hope campus:

> Along the south side of the campus a running track is being constructed and soon the fleet footed sons of Hope will pursue one another with mighty strides over its smooth surface, that they may gain strength of heart and swiftness of foot for coming contests with those of other schools. And then, on sunny afternoons, you may see students of every description engaged in forms of sport hitherto a little strange to Hope, jumping, shot putting, etc.[5]

Such anticipation was evidently a trifle premature, as the call for a team would not come for another four years. The track was somewhat short of the regulation quarter mile but was a welcome addition to Hope's athletic facility on 12th Street.

Basketball was clearly king of the campus, and its appeal was understandable. The action was fast-moving but easy to follow for those who watched, and as an indoor game it could be viewed and played in relative comfort by both men and women. The January, 1903, issue of the **Anchor** describes a women's game played on December 2, 1902, in the old gym between the "Whites" and the "Reds:"

> The teams were well matched. In the first half one point was scored. A basket was thrown after a foul by Miss Lilla Thurber of the Whites. In the second half enthusiasm ran so high that the sound of the official's shrill whistle was all but lost in the din occasioned by the alternate cheers and hoots of the two factions. In quick succession two baskets were thrown by the Reds, and the score stood four to one in their favor with only a few more minutes to play. The honor of having thrown the baskets belongs to Miss Estelle Kollen (daughter of President Kollen.)[6]

In February of 1904 the men's team made its debut in intercollegiate play. A student account of the first such contest took note of Hope's preparation and the payoff:

> The first match game of the season was between Hope College and Benton Harbor College. The faithful practice of the men evidenced itself in the team-work that was responsible for most of the scores. The Benton Harbor men played well individually, but were outclassed in team-work. The score was Hope College: 24; Benton Harbor College: 13.[7]

One of Hope's strongest opponents in the early years was the team from the Grand Rapids Y.M.C.A. The team was sponsored by a responsible organization and had ready access to practice facilities. When the Hope team defeated them on February 11, 1904, by a score of 24 to 11 it was something of an upset. Late in the season (March 25) the teams met again and this time the going was tougher. In a tightly played contest Hope again prevailed, this time by the narrow margin of 11 to 9. These victories, coupled with Hope's first win over another college, may have been a portent of things to come.

The season of 1904-05 was in many ways a landmark year in the annals of Hope basketball. The program achieved stability and distinction that one would scarcely expect from a group forced to rely almost entirely on student coaching. But leadership was good and a more attractive schedule was arranged. Team members were as follows:

1904-05

The first women's basketball team at Hope College to meet outside competition. The team was coached by George De Kruif of the men's team. Upper Row L to R: Ada Lahuis, Alyda De Pree, Edith Hodge, Maude Turnbull. Lower Row: Theodora Thurber, Mina Coggeshall, Lilla Thurber, Hannah Hoekje, and Jennie Veneklasen.

1904-05 Hope Basketball Team

Top Row L to R: Andrew Judson Kolyn, August Veenker. **Middle Row:** Henry Vruwink, Abraham J. Muste, Capt., Rudolph Nichols, Mgr., John C. Hoekje. **Bottom Row:** Peter Pleune, George De Kruif

R.F. - Judson Kolyn
R.G. - Henry Vruwink
L.F. - George De Kruif
L.G. - Abraham J. Muste, Captain*
C. - Peter Pleune
Sub. - John C. Hoekje
Mgr. - Rudolph H. Nichols
Sub. - August Veenker

The team's opening contest on December 2 was sort of a warm-up against the second team from the Grand Rapids "Y." Hope's 65-14 victory included a stellar performance by George De Kruif, who poured in 14 baskets. Most modern day coaches would be pleased with such point production by one of their forwards.

*A.J. Muste was a state oratorical champion in 1903. He later became a leading pacifist and advocate of non-violent action; upon his death in 1967, tribute was paid him throughout the world.

On December 9 Hope met a team known as the South Haven Rifles and again dominated the game with a 44-22 score. In addition to his other duties, George De Kruif had volunteered to coach the women's team. He arranged for them to play the prelim to the South Haven game. They were victorious over the girls' team from Holland High School, although there is no record of the score. As Christmas approached, the men's team played host on December 21 to a newly organized team from Grand Rapids Medical College. The Grand Rapids boys had played only one previous game. An embarrassing mismatch was the result as Hope won by a score of 101 to 8, probably the largest point spread in the school's history.

Following the holidays the team resumed play. On January 10 they hosted a traveling AAU team from Evanston, Illinois known as the "Crescent Five." When Hope prevailed 34 to 29 the team was jubilant. They had beaten a bona fide team with a regional reputation and the term "undefeated" could be heard about the campus. It had a nice ring. The very next day the team left for Kalamazoo to meet the Y.M.C.A. team of that city. How the travel ban was circumvented remains a mystery but it probably intensified the drama for this team now on a roll. In Kalamazoo the physical and emotional strain of the previous evening caught up to the seven-man squad and they were soundly beaten, 33 to 18. Through the years there would be many such quiet trips home while bruised egos recovered and the blues gradually dissipated in anticipation of the next encounter.

Eight days of practice were possible before the next game and the team put them to good use. On January 19 Hope's opponent was another Y.M.C.A. team, this time from Battle Creek. A determined Dutch team was back on track with a convincing 44 to 17 victory. A student observer commented on the fine display of sportsmanship by the Battle Creek squad despite the discouragement of defeat.

Saturday, January 28, was a memorable day for the Hope five and indeed for the entire college community. Somehow, the team from Michigan Agricultural College had been persuaded to make the trip from East Lansing and play in Hope's matchbox gym. When the final count was taken the score stood 44 for Hope, 30 for M.A.C. The margin was sufficient to make it an impressive victory, even with the obvious home court advantage. The general campus euphoria is reflected in an **Anchor** account:

> Our greatest triumph came in the game with Michigan Agricultural College. M.A.C. has held the championship of the state colleges for years. They had no intention of relinquishing it to Hope. But they did. We regret exceedingly that we cannot play M.A.C. in a return game on their own floor, just to confirm our title to the championship. Score: M.A.C. - 30; Hope - 44.[8]

One hesitates to presume that celebration of the M.A.C. victory lasted for an entire month, but for reasons unknown there were no games with outside teams during the month of February. It should be remembered that scheduling was the responsibility of the student manager, whose appointment may not have taken place until the beginning of the school year. Manager Rudolph Nichols did succeed in arranging a return game with the Kalamazoo Y.M.C.A. Hope's chance to avenge its only defeat came on March 1 when the Kalamazoo team came to Holland. Details are lacking in what must have been an exciting game. Hope's eventual one point victory (37-36) was a fitting climax to a most satisfying season. It is doubtful if Hope's claim to the state collegiate championship was recognized outside the city limits of Holland, but it didn't matter. The 7-1 record for the year and especially the M.A.C. victory clearly put Hope on the map in basketball circles.

The sudden prominence of basketball made the college aware of the old gym's shortcomings. When visiting teams and spectators arrived they found a building essentially without plumbing and no bathrooms or locker rooms. As early as June, 1901, the students had handed a petition to the Council requesting that these and other conditions be rectified. The petition was granted at the time, but the work was temporarily delayed. In 1902 President Kollen informed the students that the structure was not worth repair and that he had already raised $4,000 toward a new gymnasium.

President Kollen must be given credit for thinking big when it came to the gymnasium. He envisioned a structure that would be second to none in the state. Obviously such a project called for bold strokes in the area of funding, and Kollen was equal to the task. His target was Andrew Carnegie, the steel magnate who had given millions for libraries and academic research, but none for sports or gymnasiums. The intermediary was the Reverend Donald Sage MacKay, a former pastor at the Dutch Reformed

Collegiate Church of St. Nicholas in New York City. Carnegie was not a member of the church but attended services there whenever he was in New York. During a visit to Hope in the spring of 1905, Dr. MacKay had been impressed by the progress the college was making and the need for a combined auditorium and gymnasium. Through his good offices President Kollen was able to meet Carnegie and eventually persuade him to give $20,000 for a gymnasium to bear his name. Hope's good fortune, almost of fairy tale proportions, was received with great joy by the Council and students while the President returned to Holland a genuine hero.

In the course of his doctoral studies, Preston Stegenga (Hope '47) spoke with Mrs. J. Carleton Pelgrim nee Estelle Kollen, about her father's involvement with Carnegie. It is fortunate for Hope that a true friendship was established between the two. For instance, it was soon discovered that the grand design of the building, with some cost overruns, would result in a shortage, even with Carnegie's substantial gift. It was a sobering development but according to Dr. Stegenga, Kollen had one more card to play:

> Carnegie's initial grant of $20,000 was insufficient to complete the building. Therefore, Mrs. Pelgrim has reported, that her father made a second appeal to the industrialist, suggesting that he would not want his name on the gymnasium if others were sharing the cost. Carnegie then promptly contributed the necessary amount ($10,000) to complete the structure.[9]

Completed at a total cost of $30,688 including $1,718 for equipment, the building was dedicated on September 16, 1906. Speakers for the occasion included Dr. MacKay, Michigan Governor Fred M. Warner, Senator William Alden Smith, Gerrit J. Diekema, and President Kollen. The imposing new structure stood on the highest elevation of the 16 acre campus. It was quite possibly the state's finest gymnasium in 1906, and in any case it was one of the best. It came one year too late for Andrew Judson Kolyn, '06, who had been a regular on the 1904-05 basketball team, but he rejoiced with the others and even composed a song in connection with the dedication. According to Wynand Wichers, this rather blunt chronicle was sung to the tune of another song of the day called "Tammany" and remained a favorite for many years:

> A.C. Van Raalte in eighteen forty-seven came to town,
> And built old Hope College, of all his works the crown;
> But he chopped down trees to get his exercise, they say,
> Now a Scotchman, Carnegie, has shown a better way.
> Donald Sage MacKay is a preacher in New York, N.Y.
>
> He's a Scotchman; he met Andy - thought he'd take a try,
> Said he, I know a school where they can use your money.
> So Andy sent to Hope just 30,000 of his dough.
> Doctor Kollen is the man whom all the students love;
> He's the man we honor all the other three above.
> He can get the money; he's a friend of all the boys.
> He has got our gym for us, and that's why all this noise.
> Chorus
> Carnegie, Carnegie
> He's the man who built our gym.
> We will sing this song for him.
> Carnegie, Carnegie
> Prexy we love; he got the dough from
> Carnegie[10]

To backtrack a bit, when the students returned in the fall of 1905 they found the east end of the campus in the inevitable disarray of construction. The old gym had been torn down to make way for the new, and the playing fields were filled with equipment and building materials. The absence of a sports program during 1905-06 was borne patiently by the students who knew that in this instance it was for a good reason. In the spring of the year the men did manage a limited baseball schedule. The season got under way with three straight losses to Holland High School. The string was broken by a victory over the Zeeland Cigar Makers, 9-2, but Grand Rapids High School downed Hope 5-2. The team was able to end on a high note in a return game with the Zeeland Cigar Makers. The game went into extra innings and was won by Hope in the 11th by a score of 11 to 10. Earlier Henry Vruwink had tied the score with a dramatic grand slam home run in the ninth. He also contributed a great catch of a difficult fly ball in the 11th inning. As the school year ended, the students eagerly awaited the fall of 1906 and what they hoped would be a new era in sports with their splendid facility as a base of operations.

Sometime between the conclusion of the 1904-05 basketball season and the fall of 1906, Hope became a member of the Interurban Basketball League. The group included teams from Grand Haven, Muskegon, and Zeeland, as well as the Grand Rapids Y.M.C.A. The name derived from the rail passenger service which connected various towns in western Michigan. It was soon dubbed the "Trolley" league after the streetcar-like coaches employed by the line. While membership in the M.I.A.A. might have been preferred, the affiliation did give the team a new incentive, one they would appreciate by season's end. Early plans also included some impressive non-league opponents:

> The regular five have started practice in anticipation of a hard schedule. Among those whom we will play this winter are M.A.C., Ferris Institute, Olivet, Ann Arbor Y.M.C.A., Kalamazoo, and the Crescent Five from Evanston, Illinois. The last named team will make a trip to Buffalo, Chicago, Denver, San Francisco, and Honolulu(!).[11]

The games with Ann Arbor, Ferris Institute, Kalamazoo, and Olivet failed to materialize but 11 games remained when

Carnegie Gymnasium - 1906

Andrew Carnegie

Donald Sage Mackay

Gerrit J. Kollen

the schedule was finalized. Peter Pleune, Henry Vruwink, George De Kruif, and August Veenker returned from the highly successful team of 1904-05 and there was reason for optimism. The season opened on December 12 in spacious Carnegie Gym with the aforementioned Crescent Five from Evanston. Hope suffered a 38-29 setback in this first game in new quarters. It was a respectable score against a worthy opponent and the team moved on to its first league encounter with the Grand Rapids Y.M.C.A. Spectators were treated to a tension-packed game with John Roggen's basket finally providing the margin of victory. Score: Hope 33, Grand Rapids 32. The next night the Dutch swamped the Grand Haven team 45 to 11. A second league victory ushered in 1907, when Muskegon fell by a 28-17 count on January 4, Hope also played back to back games for the second time in the season, and on Saturday, January 5, nearly two years after Hope's "finest hour" in basketball, again met the squad from Michigan Agricultural College. Few had forgotten the earlier game and expectations were high. But the boys from Michigan's so-called "Cow College" had not forgotten either. They came prepared and thrashed the Hope quintet, 50 to 30.

Hope returned to league play with Zeeland on January 11. During a campus visit 54 years later, August Veenker recalled that Zeeland had offered the league's stiffest competition "with its team of laborers, college kids, and a general mixture of players."[12] Hope gained a seven-point victory on the January 11 in Carnegie, then a week later on Zeeland's floor, won again, this time 37-20. Grand Haven found it necessary to forfeit their second game to Hope. This, coupled with a 44-16 Hope victory over Muskegon, clinched the championship for Hope despite a remaining game with the Grand Rapids "Y." Hope's very first championship was celebrated on January 25 at an oyster supper provided by Professor John E. Kuisenga at his home.

Victory has its rewards, but two games remained. On February 7 Hope played its final league game against the Grand Rapids Y.M.C.A. and suffered a 32-30 overtime defeat. A return game with M.A.C. closed out the season. This time the Dutch narrowed the margin somewhat in losing 33-23, but the boys from East Lansing were definitely superior in 1907. Hope's 7-4 record was more than respectable, and with their title safely packed away, the team posed proudly in front of the championship banner.

For athletes the team experience becomes an intangible, but for most it is also indelible. In the summer of 1961, Peter Pleune and "Gus" Veenker returned for a bittersweet campus visit. They were the only survivors of "that championship season." The banner had long since disappeared. A remodeled Carnegie Gym, quiet in the summer sun, had lost its balcony and stage, but the echoes of 1907 were strong enough to prompt some reminiscing. The **Alumni Magazine** records the following:

> Dr. Pleune organized the first (basketball) team in 1901 when he was starting in the academy to get his high school diploma after he had been out of school for several years. "I was the equivalent of a high school freshman but was the age of a college senior when a group of us got together and decided to form a basketball team," he remembered.
>
> "Gus" Veenker came to Hope in 1902 and joined the newly formed team. The two recalled that "Dr. Gerrit Kollen, then president of Hope, was a stern, but kindly man who didn't go too strongly for athletics but after a couple of years allowed us to play off campus if we maintained an average of 85. Of course we didn't have any eligibility rules back in those days, so I ended up playing eight years with the Hope team," Dr. Pleune reported with delight. Mr. Veenker played basketball six years, baseball four years, and football three years before he was graduated.[13]

Jack Schouten, who had played from time to time on the Hope baseball team, served as its coach in the spring of 1907. Results of this season are somewhat sketchy, but it began with three successive victories over Holland High School. A 4-1 win over Grand Rapids High School preceded a loss to Mc Lachlin Business College of Grand Rapids. The Dutch were also victims of Grand Haven High School 7-2. Hope closed out the season with victories over Grand Rapids St. Alphonsus, 6 to 5, and the Holland Independents, 2 to 1. Hope's pitcher was one Pierre Adolph Rigard, a sophomore in the prep school, who hailed from Caracao, Dutch West Indies.

Hope's football team was back in action by the fall of 1907. On September 26 they were downed by Holland High 6-0 but bounced back with victories over the Holland Independents 8-6, and Grand Rapids High School 8-4. A second game with Holland High produced a scoreless tie, while a third game finally found Hope the victor 6 to 0. A 5 to 0 shutout of Grand Rapids High School ended the season. The Hope relationship with Holland High proved interesting to say the least. The fact that Hope played the high school three times in one season may be due to the fact that the Hope boys convinced the Holland coach, a Professor A. J. Helmer, to also coach their team. Where he stationed himself during the three contests is not known. Perhaps he was the referee. In any event, his remuneration consisted of two season tickets for Hope basketball games, which speaks to the ascendancy of the latter sport by 1907.

It would certainly have been premature as winter approached in 1907, to state that Hope had established a basketball "tradition." At the same time, there was present an eager anticipation of the season ahead. The players were not yet folk heros but some were becoming household words and the populace began to identify with them. The word was out that an evening in Carnegie Gym was time well spent. Gate receipts were not overwhelming, but the Athletic Association was able to show a net of $300 when the 1906-07 schedule had been played.

As the 1907-08 season began it was decided that practice would be conducted five nights a week at 9:00. Prospects again were bright as outlined in an **Anchor** article:

> ... The predominating sport is basketball. Pleune, Veenker, Oltmans, and the Vruwinks of the regulars are back determined to make even a more brilliant record than last year. (George) De Kruif, our star forward, will not play. This year he will be the official coach. His influence in this capacity will very probably counterbalance the loss.[14]

But a short year after Hope's exhilarating championship, the Interurban League was defunct. Only Zeeland, of the original group, remained as a Hope opponent. A variety of teams filled out the schedule, with Y.M.C.A. teams predominating. The strongest opponent by all odds was a team from Muscatine, Iowa, which was on an extended tour of the U.S. and Canada. On December 4 they humbled the Dutch, 70 to 26. There was some consolation in the fact that the Iowa five concluded their tour with 64 wins and 10 losses. Following this early setback, the Hope squad proceeded to another fine season, compiling an overall record of eight wins and three losses. Scores were as follows:

Hope 37 - Mc Lachlin Business College 11
Hope 81 - South Haven 18
Muscatine 70 - Hope 26
Hope 34 - Jackson Y.M.C.A. 32
Hope 70 - Kalamazoo Y.M.C.A 23
Hope 60 - Zeeland 33

Hope's First Championship Basketball Team
Interurban League - 1906-07

Top Row L to R: Abe Van Houten, Mgr., John A. Roggen, Harvey Oltmans, Henry Rottschaefer, John Vruwink. **Middle Row:** Henry Vruwink, Peter Pleune, Manley Stegeman. **Seated in front:** George De Kruif, August Veenker.

Zeeland 50 - Hope 40
Hope 45 - Zeeland 29
Detroit Y.M.C.A. 51 - Hope 22
Hope 50 - Palmer Park of Chicago 33
Hope 41 - Collins of Grand Rapids 18

By virtue of taking two out of three from Zeeland and downing the Kalamazoo "Y," Hope's players declared themselves "Western Michigan Champions," and the team picture bore this caption. August Veenker was captain-elect for the 1908-09 season, and on March 10 Professor and Mrs. Kuisenga again rewarded the team with an oyster supper. From its meager funds the Athletic Association presented coat-style sweaters with the coveted "H" to the team members. This award, practical and eye catching, was a genuine status symbol and remained popular through the 1940s.

The 1908 baseball season began with the arrival of new maroon uniforms and for a time all was upbeat. A 5 to 2 victory over Grand Rapids Union High School was followed by an 11-1 win over Grand Haven High School and a 12-1 decision over Holland High in a practice game. The record is unclear from that point on. Apparently some of the early enthusiasm waned, a condition that was blamed in part on lack of spectator interest. The team was disbanded on May 23 even though some time remained for additional games.

Henry Vruwink, a baseball player of considerable ability, volunteered to act as manager for Hope's first track squad in the spring of 1908. His call for candidates received a hearty response, according to the April **Anchor**. However, as with many new ventures, some of the response was mere curiosity. One month later the report conceded that the group was struggling:

> A few enthusiasts are working hard to make a creditable showing for our school. The most interest centers in the dashes, jumps, and long runs. The squad is small, but in spite of seemingly insurmountable difficulty, is determined and enthusiastic. The candidates have the proper spirit and are bound to win.[15]

But they could not win without opponents, and there is no record of any outside competition during this initial season. The MIAA Field Day Track Meet was held at Alma with Olivet getting the best of the host school, 55 to 39 1/3, but Hope as a non-member could only look longingly at this well-established meet.

Thanks to intervention by President Theodore Roosevelt in 1905, football began to incorporate rules designed to lessen brutality. Legalization of the forward pass in 1906 opened up the game considerably and brought about a change in field markings as well. Beginning in 1895 fields had been marked every five yards with lines parallel to the goal line. From 1906 to 1910 they were also marked with longitudinal lines every five yards parallel to the sidelines, a change designed to aid officials in the enforcement of the various forward pass rules. The resulting "gridiron" effect gave the field a name that remains despite elimination of the longitudinal lines after four years. In the fall of 1908 a touchdown counted 5 points. The point after was worth one as today, but a field goal counted 4 points and was usually dropkicked.

"Western Michigan Champions"
The 1907-08 Hope Varsity

Back Row L to R: Abe Van Houten, manager; Peter Pleune, captain George De Kruif, coach. **Middle Row:** Henry Heusinkveld, Henry Vruwink. **Front Row:** John Vruwink, August Veenker, Henry Rottschaefer.

Coach Helmer of Holland High was convinced to guide the Hope boys again in 1908 and he was greeted by 25 candidates. Veenker, Pleune, and the Vruwinks, Hope's perennial athletes, were key figures on the squad as were Henry Rottschaefer, and Frank Damson. On October 3 their lone touchdown was enough to beat Grand Haven High School 5-0. A week later the team began to roll with a 26-0 win over the Holland Independents.

The Hope players, most of whom also played basketball, had by now grown accustomed to the inspiration provided by the cheering crowds in Carnegie Gym. They were disappointed at the absence of support at football contests. As a gimmick to provide an additional draw, a high school-college double header was arranged for Saturday, October 17. The games were played on Hope's gridiron opposite Carnegie Gymnasium. The idea seemed to work, as a larger than usual crowd was on hand. There were, however, no accommodations for spectators. Those who watched stood along the sidelines or seated themselves on the bank that extended from the south side of the gymnasium.

The partisan crowd was pleased with Holland High's 11-0 victory over Allegan in the early game and hoped for a local sweep. Hope's opponent for the day was Benton Harbor College. The game was perhaps the most exciting played by Hope up to that time. The new rules gave it many of the ingredients of the modern day game. Benton Harbor drew first blood with 10 minutes gone when Maxon, their talented running back, scored on a run and kicked the point for a score of 6-0. Hope was held on downs and forced to punt. Benton Harbor reached the 20 yard line where Maxon drop-kicked a field goal making it 10-0. Following the kick off, an aroused Hope team moved to the Benton Harbor 20 on successive running plays. At this point Hope suddenly put the ball in the air and scored on a pass from Henry Vruwink to August Veenker. Veenker missed the point after and the score stood 10-5 at halftime.

Veenker got the second half under way by kicking off to the Benton Harbor goal line. Following an exchange of punts, Benton Harbor scored their second touchdown but the reliable Maxon somehow missed the point after. With the score 15-5 Hope used a variety of runs and passes to maintain control and move down the field. John Vruwink went the final distance and Veenker converted, making it 15-11. The visitors failed to move the ball and punted to Vruwink, who made a 10 yard return. A series of plunges by Pleune, Rottschaefer, and Damson put the ball on the Benton Harbor 20. An **Anchor** account picks up the action at this point:

> Captain Veenker was called back (from the scrimmage line) and sent a pretty drop-kick between the goalposts, tying the score. Pandemonium reigned, and it was with great difficulty that the students were refrained from carrying the team off the field.[16]

At this point Benton Harbor chose to kick off. Hope subsequently fumbled on their own 20 and lost possession. Inbound

1908 Hope College Football Team

Top Row L to R: Albertus C. (Chris) Van Raalte, Henry Rottschaefer, August Veenker, Henry Heusinkveld, Peter Pleune, Coach A.J. Helmer (bow tie), Henry Vruwink, Frank Garvelink. **Front Row:** Wietse Stegenga, Jacob Heemstra, Henry Roest - Manager, Earnest C. Brooks, Isaac Van Westenburg, John Vruwink.

Hope College Basketball Team - 1908-09

Top Row L to R: Edward De Pree, Henry Vruwink, August Veenker (Capt.). **Front Row:** Frank Kleinheksel, John Vruwink, John L. Laven, Alexander Van Bronkhorst.

Hope's First Distance Relay Team - 1909

Standing L to R: Earnest C. Brooks, Marinus Den Herder, Harry Anker, Martin Verburg. **Front Row:** M. Purlier Burkholder, Herm Stegeman, Nelson Dalenberg, Henry Pasma, Lloyd Kanters, Alex Van Bronkhorst.

hash marks were not part of the game in 1908 and Benton Harbor was obliged to work the ball to the middle of the field where Maxon matched Veenker's splendid kick with another of his own. Score: Benton Harbor 19, Hope 15. Again the **Anchor** account:

> Hope received the ball and worked it steadily down the field. Everything looked fine for a glorious victory, but time was called with the ball in Hope's possession. That Hope outplayed their opponents after the first 15 minutes is evident. It was a glorious defeat.[17]

The young scribe's final summation was perhaps not a consensus opinion, but it can be understood as a refreshing expression of true sport: two well matched teams, successful execution on both sides, uncertainty and excitement to the very end. The final score could hardly erase the overall experience. Hope concluded a rewarding season with a 4 to 0 shutout of Ferris Institute.

Hope's basketball record in 1908-09 showed eight wins against but a single defeat. This accomplishment suggests another superior unit, but it belies a schedule somewhat suspect. Opponents ranged from De Paul University to the Grand Rapids Boat and Canoe Club. Blame for this lack of consistency in scheduling cannot be laid at any particular doorstep. While several faculty members were kindly disposed to athletic activity, none stepped forward to lend stability and direction. As indicated earlier, this left the responsibility in the hands of an elected student manager, often with limited time and contacts. The problem was compounded by lack of any league affiliation, and the carryover of traditional rivalries was hard to come by. Scores for the season were as follows:

Hope 71 - Grand Rapids Boat and Canoe Club 16
Hope 50 - Muskegon High School 20
Hope 53 - Muskegon High School 20
Hope 57 - De Paul University 14
Hope 106 - Grand Rapids Y.M.C.A. 36
Jackson Y.M.C.A. 46 - Hope 32
Hope 37 - Detroit Y.M.C.A. 36
Hope 40 - Armour Institute 24
Hope 57 - Burroughs Adding Machines 22

Of interest is the fact that Muskegon High School was coached by Bob Zuppke, who would later guide the football destinies of the immortal Red Grange and the "Fighting Illini."

The spring of 1909 was not an outstanding one in the annals of Hope athletics. The excitement occasioned by basketball seemed difficult to recapture on the outdoor playing fields. The Athletic Association continued its policy of charging 15 cents for a "permit" to view the baseball games. Since the campus diamond was not enclosed in any way, and there was no policing, the measure amounted to a voluntary contribution. The season opened with two practice game victories over Holland High by scores of 7-5 and 13-2. The team then suffered losses at the hands of the Holland Independents, 8-2, Grand Haven High School, 3-1, and Grand Rapids High School, 6-5. The latter contest went 10 innings and was the high point of the season. It featured "sensational" double plays by Hope's combination of John Laven and Mack Yamamoto.

Track was growing in popularity, but the problem of scheduling persisted. In addition, An **Anchor** article contained a veiled reference that indicated a lack of faculty support:

> The outlook for a good track team is more encouraging each year. Last year we had some good material but lacked sufficient enthusiasm. This year we have both, but lack that shining road to success that is paved with the bricks of faculty sanction. The great apostle has said, "Know ye not that they which run in a race run all, but one receiveth the prize? So run, that ye may obtain." We would suggest the last sentence as the motto of our track team, so that in the coming race we may obtain not only the laurels but also the approval of both the public and faculty.[18]

Muskegon got the better of Hope in a cross country run and spirits were temporarily dampened, but Manager Henry Pasma did manage to arrange a very novel distance event with the Grand Rapids Y.M.C.A. It took the form of a relay race covering the 33 miles between Grand Rapids and Holland. Each team was composed of 10 men with the inaugural race going to the Hope team. The relay attracted considerable attention and became a regular feature of the track season for several years.

In the fall of 1909 Hope secured the services of a Mr. Mitchell to coach the football team. Little is known of Coach Mitchell other than the fact that he had played football at Carlisle in Pennsylvania at the institution whose favorite son was Jim Thorpe. The season would confirm his grasp of the game. The team was off to a winning start with a 13 to 0 victory over Wayland High School. A 5-0 win over Holland High was followed by a hard-fought, scoreless tie with Muskegon High School. Hope then dropped a 9 to 8 decision to Grand Haven High School for the team's only defeat of the season. In a second meeting the Dutch took the measure of Holland High, 11 to 6. Hope's game with Grand Rapids St. Alphonsus resulted in a 21-0 shutout for the Hollanders and set the stage for Hope's first meeting with Western State Normal School of Kalamazoo on November 6.

Hope won the toss and chose to take the wind. This led eventually to good field position, and Hope capitalized. The first touchdown was scored on a 35 yard sweep by Earnest Brooks behind good interference. Quarterback John Lavan converted for a 6-0 Hope lead. The heavier Western team was expected to retaliate but had trouble moving the ball. Hope scored again on a pass from Lavan to Brooks and Lavan's conversion made it 12-0 at halftime. Hope's line twice tackled Kalamazoo runners behind their own goal line for safeties but such did not figure in the scoring under 1909 rules.

In the second half Western came closest to scoring when Mc Ginnis, their captain, picked up a fumble and ran for his goal line. John Abbink shot after him, outran the tackle and brought him down. Hope's defensive line and Lavan's punting staved off other threats until speedy John Vruwink received a pass and streaked 60 yards for the score. A missed conversion left the score at 17-0. Hope's final tally came when Western, attempting to pass, fumbled the ball. A Hope lineman scooped it up and rambled into the end zone. Lavan's kick closed out the scoring. Hope's 23-0 win gave them a season's record of 5-1-1 and served notice that basketball would not be the school's only major sport. Five of the seven opponents had failed to cross the Hope goal line.

Hope students were quick to seize upon the propaganda value of the significant victory over Western, and via the **Anchor** badgered the faculty and council to lift the ban and support the program:

> Working against the greatest difficulties during this football season, kept down hard under the strict rules prohibiting intercollegiate sports, crippled miserably by an arbitrary permit edict that was well fit to throw the most optmistic football enthusiast into fits of melancholy, Hope College, on November 6, nevertheless put out an eleven that, equipped with Coach Mitchell's strategies, beat the husky Kalamazoo Normal College squad to a frazzle.
>
> The opportunity to somewhat find our rank among our sister colleges is not the only benefit to be derived from this intercollegiate foot-ball game. The victory over Kalmazoo Normals also brought out proof what good fighting spirit and efficient coaching may accomplish in athletics. It also brought out the fact that faculty members and members of Hope College council delight to see how the men of their college compare with those of other colleges. And we sincerely hope it will bring out one more fact, namely, that wholesome enthusiasm, gained on the athletic field carries over to other spheres of college life...[19]

The travel restrictions, objectionable as they may have been, were clearly understood by the various teams. To a researcher some 76 years later, they are less clear. Obviously some of the teams, mostly basketball, were allowed to travel at certain times, but the criteria which made such trips legitimate gives rise to speculation. The fact that basketball could be played in the evening and was of shorter duration may have been a factor. Vacation periods were free but Saturdays were not necessarily in the same category. The faculty and Council did not forbid football absolutely, but students sensed a subtle disapproval.

It is apparent as the basketball season of 1909-10 approached, that definite attempts had been made to beef up the schedule. Team members were confident in their ability and wanted to insure that their efforts were not wasted on questionable opposition. A proposed contest with Olivet College did not materialize, but when the schedule was confirmed it did include four games with colleges of established reputation. Manager James Verburg announced a holiday vacation tour of central and eastern Michigan, but practice had scarcely begun when the fates intervened. An epidemic of scarlet fever struck the community and the college was closed on December 6 by order of Dr. Boot, the city health officer. The women of Voorhees Hall were quarantined for four days before being released to their homes, and the men's basketball team lost two weeks of valuable practice. It was decided to go through with the tour in spite of this handicap. The team played and lost four games to various AAU teams in the space of a week. Scores were as follows:

Brinks of Grand Rapids 35 - Hope 22
Battle Creek Y.M.C.A. 34 - Hope 23
Jackson Y.M.C.A. 43 - Hope 40
Detroit Spauldings 42 - Hope 25

A second game with Battle Creek had to be canceled due to a severe snowstorm.

The team returned to Holland unshaken by the reverses and proceeded to down the Zeeland team, 48 to 20. Mount Pleasant Normal School was the next opponent and Hope's fine athletes came into their own with a 71-15 victory. A return game with Zeeland pushed the string to three with a 51-24 win. The touring Hull House team from Chicago was reportedly the AAU power in the state of Illinois, but the final score showed Hope 36; Hull House 27. An unprepared Hope team had dropped its opener to the Grand Rapids Brinks team and the Dutch were eager to prove that their excuse had been valid. In Carnegie Gym a resounding 88-11 victory proved the point.

A few days later Carnegie was again filled to capacity as Hope met, for the first time, the Irish of Notre Dame. The veteran August Veenker led Hope in scoring while the all round play of center John Vruwink and guard John Lavan sealed the historic 37-26 Hope victory. Maloney and Fish stood out for Notre Dame.

The background and environment of Hope's next opponent differed somewhat from that of Notre Dame. The Hope team journeyed to Jackson where they met and defeated the prison team 58-28. Needless to say, all of the prison's games were played at home and there were no arguments about a travel ban! Next on the schedule was a renewal of the earlier rivalry with Michigan Agricultural College. The Dutch traveled to East Lansing and were soundly beaten 40 to 21. A

Hope College Football Squad - 1909

Top Row L to R: James Houloose, Jay Den Herder - Manager, Coach Mitchell, Henry Dieters. **Middle Row:** John Lavan, John Abbink, John Warrenshuis, Charles Stoppels, Earnest C. Brooks, Henry Stegeman. **Front Row:** Gebhard Stegeman, John Vruwink, James Weurding, Cornelius Addison, Pierre Adolph Rigaud. **Seated in front:** J. Addison (mascot)

Hope College Basketball Team - 1909-10

Top Row L to R: Henry Vruwink, John Vruwink, James Verburg, Herm Stegeman, Earnest C. Brooks. **Front Row:** Alex Van Bronkhorst, Martin Verburg, John Lavan, August Veenker.

fiercely loyal student reporter described it this way: "Owing to the fact that the floor was wretched and that the crossbeams were so low that it was almost impossible to make a basket except directly in front of the basket, Hope's quintet was exceedingly handicapped.[20] Earnest Brooks was a bright spot for Hope as he sank a basket from the center of the floor.

On March 11 the "Aggies" (later Spartans) returned to Holland, determined to prove that their performance was no fluke. But the Dutch, with their Carnegie following and no crossbeams, were too much, and the final score was Hope 38 - M.A.C. 30. The student reporter was vindicated while the coaches agreed not to have a playoff as examinations were imminent at both schools. Hope's 8-5 record was not a true measure of one of the college's better teams.

The ebb and flow of baseball fortunes at Hope College is somewhat puzzling. It was the school's oldest sport but interest seemed to fluctuate from season to season. 1910 was one of the better years though the schedule was not extensive. The season's opener and finale present a study in contrast. The **Anchor** record of the former is as follows:

> Hope's baseball team has made a successful start for the season of '10, the first game with Grand Haven High School ending in a decisive victory for Hope. The game was called in the first half of the eighth inning on account of the inability of Grand Haven to retire the Hopeites, who, with only one out, were holding a dress parade around the bases. The score at that time was 38 to 4, with prospects for reaching 100. The Grand Haven team was helpless against the clever pitching of [Pierre Adolph] Rigaud, who, with fair support, allowed only three hits.[21]

On April 16, Hope met the Holland Independents with a different battery. John Lavan, quarterback on the football team and a regular on the basketball team, took the mound pitching to catcher Geb Stegeman. The result was a 4-0 shutout. This was followed with a 6-3 win over Holland High School, and another 4-0 shutout, this time over a team known as the Holland Cubs. Having established local supremacy, it was time for a new challenge. On May 20 the team from Western State Normal School came to town obviously hoping to avenge their football defeat of the previous fall. This first meeting between the two schools in baseball was a classic in every respect. Hope scored in the first inning when Lavan singled, stole second and third, and then came home on Jim Weurding's single to left. Lavan's temporary wildness in the third plus two Hope errors accounted for a Western run to tie the count. From that point on, spectators witnessed a spectacular pitcher's duel between John Lavan and Western's Tub Berger. Finally, in the bottom of the 12th inning, "Mack" Yamamoto of Hope beat out a bunt. He took third when Lavan sent a clean single to center. Geb Stegeman then drove the ball to deep short and the speedy Yamamoto beat the throw to the plate, sealing the 2 to 1 victory. The talented John Lavan was clearly the star of the game, as he pitched the entire 12 innings giving up but two hits. Also, his two singles and pair of stolen bases figured in the scoring of both Hope runs. Hope had six hits off Tub Berger including Shorty Vruwink's sixth inning double "beyond the oak in left field."

Track and Field in the spring of 1910 was actually a combination of that sport and cross country. Earnest Brooks served as manager and succeeded in providing a schedule with unusual variety. An invitational cross country meet opened the season on April 9. Five teams competed, with Michigan Agricultural College beating out Olivet College for top honors. The Grand Rapids Y.M.C.A. finished third, with Hope fourth and Muskegon High School fifth. Each team consisted of six runners and it was M.A.C.'s Tillitson edging Voelker of Olivet for first place in the four mile run. The individual champion received a gold watch provided by Hardie Jewelry Company, while the Holland Businessmen's Trophy went to the winning team.

Saturday, May 14, was the date of the second annual relay race between Hope and the Grand Rapids Y.M.C.A. The uniqueness of this event had captured the imagination of the entire Holland community and added to the amiable town and gown relationship. A student account of the finish is as follows:

> We do not hesitate to say that Hope crossed the tape in the second annual relay race between Grand Rapids and Holland before one of the largest and most enthusiastic crowds that has ever turned out for any athletic contest in Holland. Bulletins at H. Van Tongeren's [sporting goods store] kept the restless mass informed as to the runners. The 50 yard gain of the first runner increased to a half, three quarters, and even a mile seemed hardly plausible to those informed as to the relative strength of the teams. The blowing of the curfew whistle, however, warned everyone that Hope was still leading in the last lap. At the finish (Herm) Stegeman, the Hope captain, worked his way through the jam on Eighth Street, three and one half minutes ahead of M. Vander Visse, the Grand Rapids captain. By this victory Hope places the splendid Van Tongeren trophy beside the Jarvis cup, which was won last year.[22]

On Saturday, May 21, Manager Earnest Brooks engineered with great success, the first annual interclass track meet. The meet was won by the freshmen by virtue of a large number of entries and John Vruwink, who scored 34 of his team's 69 points. The juniors were second with 15 points. Again a large crowd of students and townspeople turned out for the competition. Captain Herm Stegeman did not take part, as he went instead to Ann Arbor where he represented Hope in an interscholastic meet, placing third in the two mile run in a field of 27.

Hope's next competition occurred on May 30, when the two-man team of Vruwink and Stegeman participated in an invitational meet in Grand Rapids. The two made a great showing, garnering 21 points and second place for Hope. John Vruwink won the medal for individual points for the entire meet (16) as he took first in the 220 and 440 yard dashes as well as seconds in the broad jump and shot put. Stegeman was an easy winner in the mile run.

Vruwink, anxious to test his abilities in stronger competition, closed out the season by entering the Y.M.C.A. interstate meet at Lake Geneva, Wisconsin. Included were track stars from Iowa, Wisconsin, Illinois, Indiana, North Dakota, Missouri, and Michigan. Vruwink entered the 100 yard dash, the 220, the broad jump, and the shot put. He came home with a gold medal in the broad jump (19' 5") and thirds in the 220 and shot put. Stegeman, meanwhile, entered an interscholastic meet in Chicago that was directed by Amos Alonzo Stagg. The Hope miler was second in his specialty in a field of 22.

The athletic accomplishments of the 1909-10 school year reflect the athletic talent that had come together at Hope quite by accident. Significant victories in football, basketball, and baseball, plus the coming of age of track and field, made it the outstanding year up to that time. The fact that the program was administered entirely by students adds a special dimension to the achievement. The seeds of an athletic tradition had been planted, and credit for this early harvest rests exclusively with these student-athletes. At this point in time, John Leonard Lavan, one of Hope's brightest stars, elected to transfer to the University of Michigan to pursue a career in medicine. The loss of his ability and leadership in three sports would be keenly felt.

The seeming resurgence of football at Hope was dealt a blow in 1910, when no coach could be found. Despite the absence of Lavan, several of those who had tasted success in 1909 returned and the group decided to proceed without a coach. Three games were played in October. Captain Herm Stegeman led his team to victories over St. Alphonsus of Grand Rapids, 20-0 and Wayland High School, 21-0. The third and final game marked the first meeting between Hope and Kalamazoo College in any sport. The final tally showed Kalamazoo an 11 to 6 victor in the first of a long series that would eventually center around a pair of wooden shoes. Hope's 2-1 record was something of a let-down after the fine showing in 1909, but it would go in the record books as a winning season. Seven long years would pass before Hope fans could again savor a football victory.

The picture in basketball was considerably brighter. The team was heartened by news that alumnus George De Kruif, who had guided the team in 1907-08, would return as coach. John Vruwink, Hope's all time star athlete, was elected captain of a team that could boast of experienced players in Herm and Geb Stegeman, Alex Van Bronkhorst, Frank Kleinheksel, and James Weurding. Peter Ver Hoek and Miner Stegenga rounded out the squad. Hope opened at home with a win over the Grombecker and Major team from Grand Rapids, then took time off for Christmas. The team resumed action with a four-game trip in early January. Scores were as follows:

Hope 39 - Grand Rapids Grombecker & Major 24
Hope 57 - Mount Pleasant Normal 24
Detroit Y.M.C.A. 38 - Hope 26
Hope 46 - Jackson Y.M.C.A. 43

Mount Pleasant Normal came to Holland for a return game on January 20 and the Dutch again prevailed, this time 55-29. The Lansing "Y" was no match for a Hope five that was gaining momentum; final score: Hope 64, Lansing 15. The return meeting with the Jackson Y.M.C.A. was a different story but Hope took the hard fought game 44-40. On February 10 Hope initiated athletic competition with Alma College, defeating the Scots 92-32. Each school would have its moments in the years to come, and 75 years later the relationship, built on mutual respect, would be prized by both institutions.

A week later the rivalry with Michigan Agricultural College was renewed at Carnegie Gymnasium. Hope's 41-21 victory was rough treatment for John Macklin, M.A.C.'s new coach, but the Hope team and fans were much impressed by Coach Macklin both as a person and in his role as coach. It was apparent that the state college had chosen wisely. On February 25 the Dutch were edged 23-21 by the Hull House team of Chicago. Stegeman suffered an ankle injury that would sideline him for several games. A badly crippled team journeyed to East Lansing on March 2 as John Vruwink was also out with an injury. Hope played surprisingly well but finally succumbed 35-32. Of interest is the fact that the opposing coaches served as officials for the game. There is no indication that lack of objectivity was a problem.

On March 6 the team, still without Vruwink and Stegeman, met the strong Detroit Athletic Club. John Roggen, who had graduated in 1907, (no eligibility rules) was pressed into service replacing the injured Stegeman, but all was for naught as the Detroiters triumphed, 51-31. One week later Vruwink was back in the lineup as Hope defeated Lewis Institute of Chicago, 31-17. In the season finale Hope's team was finally intact as they downed the Detroit Y.M.C.A., 40-32. It was somehow appropriate that Herm Stegeman should star in the victory and that the rebounding of John Vruwink, "the idol of the fans," was outstanding. With an 11-4 record the Hope team declared themselves collegiate champions of the state as well as AAU co-champions with the Detroit Athletic Club.

In spite of unexpected and often unwarranted success, the Hope athletic program lacked the stability afforded by administrative continuity. The exhilaration of Hope's 1910 baseball victory over Western Normal had scarcely subsided when it was decided to allow the sport to lapse for a season.

Hope College Track Team - 1910

Standing L to R: John Vruwink, Harry Anker, Gebhard Stegeman, James Verburg. **Seated L to R:** John Tillema, Harry Telman, Alex Van Bronkhorst, M. Purlier Burkholder, Earnest C. Brooks - Manager, Herm Stegeman, Peter Ver Hoek, Edward Tanis, Nelson Dahlenburg.

The Relay Race - May 14, 1910

A large crowd awaits the finish of the 30 mile relay race from Grand Rapids to Holland. Some spectators may be seen atop the building which holds the finish line banner. Hope won when Herm Stegeman crossed the line 3 1/2 minutes ahead of the Grand Rapids YMCA captain. The photo looks east on Eighth Street from Central Avenue towards College Avenue.

Attention was turned to track with great resolve and the usual pre-season optimism:

> With spring term and warm weather here, and baseball on the shelf, the question of track athletics looms up bigger than ever before. "Track" means no longer one cross country run, and one relay race, - it means a department with a regular schedule. One of the reasons for abolishing baseball schedules was the booming of track work. Here is your chance, athletes, to make track work a regular branch of college sport. No sport requires so little time, no branch involves so little expense. All that is needed is a pair of "gym" shoes and a lot of Dutch determination.[23]

The cross country invitational opened the 1911 season at Hope's four-mile Waverly course. Tillitson and Geib of Michigan Agricultural College finished 1-2 in the race, but the Grand Rapids Y.M.C.A. bunched its men very well and took the next four places, that being enough to win the meet. Peter Ver Hoek, in seventh place, was Hope's first finisher. The teams finished as follows:

Grand Rapids Y.M.C.A.
Michigan Agricultural College
Muskegon High School
Hope College

Olivet College did not return in 1911 for the meet. A lack of consistent and systematic practice was cited as the reason for Hope's last place finish.

The second annual interclass track meet was held on Saturday, May 6, under the direction of Manager George Steininger. John Vruwink again brought his class (sophomores) the championship by scoring 39 of his team's 62 points. He placed first in seven events (!), and second and third in two others. Clarence Holleman was the star for the freshmen, who finished second with 50 points.

The 1911 distance relay with the Grand Rapids Y.M.C.A. began well but soon fell victim to unusual if not bizarre circumstances. The runners left Van Tongeren's Cigar Store in Holland promptly at 2:45. Rain threatened. At the end of the second mile, John Vander Broek of Hope stepped on a loose stone, twisting his ankle so severely that another runner, Herman Stegeman, was substituted. The rules did not permit substitutions in the middle of a lap, but the race was continued anyway. The real difficulties began in the third lap, as reported by a student covering the event:

> Mazurkiewicz of Y and [Herbert] Van Vranken of Hope were the next runners, and it was then that the heavy rain and trouble started. Some of the machines carrying the runners found it impossible to climb the hills and were forced to turn back. [Cornelius] Muste of Hope and Hoogesteeger of Y ran the next lap, which proved to be the last, since Muste took the wrong road and was lost. The judges then forfeited the race to the Grand Rapids team.[24]

The season ended on a positive note in Grand Rapids on May 30. The meet, known as the Michigan State Track Meet, was held at Comstock Park. Four teams and several independent performers competed. John Vruwink's performance was again outstanding. After winning his preliminary heat in 10.8 in the 100, he captured the final in the excellent time of 1O.1. He also took the 220 in 23.6 seconds and placed second in the open 440 which was won in a time of 53.1. In the field events he was first in the broad jump. He closed out the day by running the anchor leg on the winning mile relay team. Other members of this relay team were Clarence Holleman, George Steininger, and Herm Stegeman. The time of 3.41 was not outstanding but would go down as Hope's first victory in that event, and the team was awarded a silver loving cup as proof of the accomplishment. Stegeman won the 880 yard run in 2:15 and placed second in the mile run, the latter being won in 4:43.4. Hope's overall performance gave them the team championship for the first time in a regulation track and field meet.

The weather had cooperated in the spring of 1911 and the clay tennis courts were reported in fine condition. An on campus tournament was organized and in the finals it was John J. "Jock" Riemersma defeating Cornelius Muste in straight sets, 6-4 and 8-6. Many a Holland High graduate will recall this same "Jock" Riemersma with affection (and fear) as their stern but fair principal.

Followers of college athletics are aware that in each school's history certain "eras" exist when a fortuitous combination of talent results in fine teams over a period of years. In the summer of 1911 at Hope College it appeared that perhaps the first such era was about to end. John Lavan had departed the previous fall and now two more stalwarts would leave. Herm Stegeman decided to transfer to the Conrad Teacher Training School in Montana and John Vruwink elected to go to the University of Chicago for studies in medicine. Lavan and Vruwink both hailed from Grand Rapids and were long-time friends. Lavan's earlier choice may have influenced Vruwink's decision. All would be missed, but the departure of Vruwink attracted the most attention. With perhaps a flare for the dramatic, John chose to leave by steamer from Holland harbor. His home town **Grand Rapids Press** covered the story:

> When the steamer **Puritan** left its docks last night it carried on board the star athlete of Hope College in the person of John Vruwink:. A large number of the fellows gathered at the dock to bid farewell to the man who will be missed in every line of athletics, and hearty cheers were given as a token of the esteem in which he was held.

> Vruwink left for Chicago where he will take up work at the University of Chicago. For several years he has been a strong man in football and track work. But in basketball will Hope suffer the greatest loss. Vruwink has played center on that team and was considered one of the best in this section of the country. If he had remained this year he would have filled the position of athletic director to which he was elected last spring.[25]

In its first two decades of organized sport Hope could name a score of fine athletes, but John Vruwink was by all odds the school's first superstar. His subsequent performance under Coach Stagg at Chicago would confirm this label.

REFERENCES - CHAPTER 2

1. The **Anchor**, January, 1901.
2. _ ___, March, 1902.
3. **Catalogue of Hope College**, 1902-03.
4. The **Anchor**, April, 1903.
5. _ ___, April, 1904.
6. _ ___, January, 1903.
7. _ ___, February, 1904.
8. _ ___, February, 1905.
9. Preston J. Stegenga, **Anchor of Hope**. Grand Rapids: William B. Eerdmans Company, 1954. p. 135.
10. Wynand Wichers, A **Century of Hope**. Grand Rapids: William B. Eerd-mans Company, 1968, p. 137.
11. The **Anchor**, November, 1906.

12-13. **Hope College Alumni Magazine**, January, 1962. pp. 8-9.

14. The **Anchor**, October, 1907.
15. May, 1908.

16-17. November, 1908

18. April, 1909
19. _ ___, November, 1909.
20. _ ___, March, 1910.
21. _ ___, April, 1910.
22. _ ___, July, 1910.
23. _ ___, May, 1911.
24. _ ___, July, 1911.
25. **The Grand Rapids Press**, September 22, 1911.

CHAPTER 3

IN THE "TEENS" - CONTINUED QUEST FOR STATUS

Hope's need for a faculty or staff person to take charge of the program of intercollegiate athletics was obvious to the students and they continued to petition for such an addition. It is ironic that the solid success of basketball and sporadic success in the other sports actually weakened the students' case. Faculty who were not at all opposed to athletics continued to feel that the boys were doing a good job and the status quo was just about right. The great majority of faculty, Council members, and personnel in the Particular Synod of Chicago were without any background in athletics. Fun and games were all right but in their opinion contributed very little to one's overall growth, and certainly such activity did not merit the hiring of a full-time person. In the early decades of the 20th century Hope students felt that the lack of a coach or director placed them at a disadvantage and denied them the opportunity to realize their potential as athletes, but there was little movement in "the corridors of power" and converts were hard to come by.

In 1911 the absence of a coach of any sort for football was especially unfortunate. The old guard of players had departed and the new faces were inexperienced. Hope opened with St. Alphonsus of Grand Rapids and put up a good fight. The Grand Rapids team scored on two well executed pass plays. The Dutch were without the services of quarterback George Steininger and halfback John Vander Broek. Despite outstanding play by Harris Meyer, Hope found its best effort stopped on the one foot line. Final score, St. Alphonsus 10, Hope 0. Muskegon High School proved even more troublesome as they downed the Dutch 15-0. An injury to Harris Meyer hindered the Hope cause. The team's best performance of the season came against Kalamazoo College. Hope's defense limited Kalamazoo to one touchdown and a field goal* but lack of any offensive punch resulted in an 8-0 defeat.

* Beginning in 1909 a field goal counted 3 points instead of 4.

On November 4 a game but outmanned Hope team hosted the squad from Western State Normal. The 23-0 Western victory ended Hope's most disappointing season to that time. The failure to score a single point throughout the season compounded the frustration.

In contrast to football, the basketball team of 1911-12 enjoyed some continuity. George De Kruif was again available to coach a squad that included returnees Miner Stegenga, Frank Kleinheksel, Peter Ver Hoek, Geb Stegeman and Alex Van Bronkhorst. Scores were as follows:

Hope 77 - Grand Rapids Battalions 13
Hope 63 - Mount Pleasant Normal 24
Grand Rapids Y.M.C.A. 32 - Hope 27
Jackson Y.M.C.A. 55 - Hope 35
Hope 45 - Saginaw All Stars 42
Hope 53 - Mount Pleasant Normal 27
Detroit Rayles 41 - Hope 40
Hope 41 - Michigan Agricultural College 40 (OT)
Jackson Y.M.C.A. 33 - Hope 24
Hope 34 - Evanston Reds 18
Michigan Agricultural College 55 - Hope 23
Zeeland Olympic Club 47 - Hope 25
Hope 34 - Detroit Athletic Club 29
Hope 34 - Grand Rapids Y.M.C.A. 20
Hope 36 - Zeeland Olympic Club 8

Hope's fine rivalry with Michigan Agricultural College continued in 1912. The first game, played in Carnegie Gym, saw the Dutch capture a thrilling 41-40 overtime victory. A one-point margin held up for Hope as Vatz of M.A.C. missed a free throw attempt that would have again tied the score. A month later in East Lansing it was a different story as the Aggies dominated play throughout and downed Hope 55-23.

One account spoke of the wearisome train ride followed by a three-mile ride from the station in an open sleigh as not conducive to good play, but most would concede that the M.A.C. win was the result of a solid performance.

In the game with the Detroit Athletic Club only three Detroit players made it through the heavy snow to Holland. Several boys from Holland High were rounded up and joined the Detroit trio in order that the game might be played. Frank Kleinheksel missed the first game with the Zeeland Olympic Club but was on hand for Hope's one-sided victory in the second meeting. Some regrettable incidents born of Zeeland frustration marred this final game and the season ended with a negative note. But overall, Hope's 9-6 record was evidence of yet another good year in a sport that Hope and Holland had taken to its heart.

Spring sports were not spectacular at Hope in the spring of 1912. Jacob Poppen and Otto Vander Velde were pitchers on the baseball team with Peter Ver Hoek their receiver. The opening game on April 13 saw the Dutch eke out a 5-4 victory over Holland High. A week later the team met Mc Laughlin Business College of Grand Rapids and again managed a one-run decision, this time 4 to 3. Hope's seven errors were offset by the strong pitching of Poppen. The May 11 game with Kalamazoo College was rained out, but Western State Normal, the other team from the celery city, came to town on June 1 and went home after shutting out the Dutch, 9 to 0.

The 1912 track team was organized with George Steininger as manager and Alex Van Bronkhorst as captain. The much anticipated cross country invitational was held on April 27 but lost some of its luster when M.A.C. and Olivet did not participate. Muskegon High School won the meet with 19 points. The Grand Rapids YMCA scored 47 for second and relegated Hope to third with 58. Clarence Holleman, in seventh place, was Hope's first man. The interclass meet on May 4 was a lot more fun. Otto Vander Velde abandoned baseball for the day and scored 17 1/2 points as his freshman team won the meet with 40 1/2 points. The 30 mile relay with the Grand Rapids Y.M.C.A was staged on May 18 with the Grand Rapids team claiming the fine silver cup donated by Mr. Boter of the downtown merchants. No individual stars emerged and the season ended on an anticlimactic note.

All football seasons begin on a positive note and 1912 was no exception at Hope. Lambert Eidson, Professor of Pedagogy, agreed to coach the team and Manager Geb Stegeman arranged a six-game schedule. The opening game, however, was disappointing and a portent of things to come as Hope lost to Holland High, 21-2. Allegan High School failed to show up for the second game and in a return game with Holland High the college boys suffered through a 30-0 shutout. Kalamazoo College and Western State Normal showed no mercy as they thumped the Dutchmen, 60-0 and 45-0 on successive weekends. The battered Hope players closed out the season with a respectable 12-9 loss to Grand Rapids Union High School.

Hope Basketball Team - 1911-12

Top Row L to R: Alex Van Bronkhorst, Lawrence Dalman, Gebhard Stegeman, Richard Vandenburg - Manager, Peter Ver Hoek, Lambertus Hekhuis. **Bottom Row:** William Lokker, Miner Stegenga, Frank Kleinheksel.

If preseason football hopes had been ill founded, there was certainly some justification for optimism as the basketball season approached. All of the 1911-12 team returned and Manager Richard Vandenberg provided an attractive schedule. Early season scores were as follows:

Hope 50 - Mount Pleasant Normal 20
Hope 90 - Manistee Azas 14
Grand Rapids Y.M.C.A. 27 - Hope 19

The Holland High varsity played the prelim for Hope's game with Manistee as the two schools continued to cooperate in sports. During the Christmas vacation of early January a northern swing resulted in the following:

Manistee Azas 35 - Hope 27
Hope 30 - Traverse City Needhams 27
Ludington Wolverines 25 - Hope 21.

Perhaps the season's highlight occurred on January 10, 1913, when Hope met Albion College for the first time in athletic competition. The game was played in Hope's Carnegie Gym and the Dutch were able to turn back their future MIAA opponent, 59 to 21. Also of note was the prelim game in which the Hope Bloomer Girls lost to the men's reserve team, 31 to 9. Sue Koeppe and Alice Tilly led the way in this contest which pre-dated Title IX by some 59 years.

Hope gained an even split in its final six games with scores as follows:

Grand Rapids Y.M.C.A. 35 - Hope 30
Hope 37 - Detroit Rayles 35
M.A.C. 33 - Hope 23
Hope 33 - Northwestern (Naperville, Ill.) 30
Hope 28 - Chicago Midway Five 21
M.A.C. 58 - Hope 25

Despite the double loss to arch rival M.A.C., the Hope five had compiled a .500 record including some notable victories. The basketball tradition was alive and well.

Hope's baseball squad for the spring of 1913 included familiar names:

Catchers - Peter Ver Hoek, Ed Hoeven
Pitchers - Jacob Poppen, Otto Vander Velde
lb - Henry Poppen
2b - Millard Vander Meer
3b - Jock Riemersma
ss - Lavinus De Ruiter
of - Miner Stegenga, Henry Potgetter, Clarence Hospers

The team was off and running as they downed Holland High 1-0 and 11-4, but on May 10 the Holland Independents took the measure of Hope, 7 to 4. The season ended with a 2-0 loss to Ferris Institute, a team which remained undefeated.

As usual, the big track news in the spring of 1913 was the Holland to Grand Rapids relay run against the Grand Rapids Y.M.C.A. The series stood at two victories each as the teams prepared for the 30 mile run. When the last runner reached the "Y" in Grand Rapids, it was Hope the victor once again. The 10-man team consisted of Clarence Holleman, Peter Ver Hoek, Edwin Koeppe, George Pelgrim, John Muyskens, Frank De Roos, Henry Bilkert, Charles Peet, George Heneveld, and John Van Strien.

The 1913-14 school year would prove a momentous one for Hope College athletics. It began with a call for football players in mid-September. Professor Eidson, if somewhat chagrined by the 1912 performance, was not about to abandon ship. His new assistant, Marinus Van Putten, was an inspiring addition and 28 men turned out, all determined to erase the negatives of the previous fall. John Van Strien had been elected captain but for unexplained reasons resigned the post at an early date. He was replaced by George Veenker. The season opened on October 4 with Grand Rapids Catholic Central High School. The Grand Rapids team, lacking in size and experience, had the additional misfortune of meeting a team with something to prove. Details of Hope's 81-0 victory are not available.

On October 11 the Dutchmen entertained the team from the Grand Rapids Veterinary school and recorded a second straight shutout, this time 27 to 0. But one week later Kalamazoo College put an end to Hope's resurgence with a 25-0 win. All of Kalamazoo's scoring occurred in the first half. Western State Normal completed the Kalamazoo jinx with a hard fought 14-0 victory on October 25. Again, all of the scoring took place in the first half. In its final game on November 2, Hope rediscovered its offense and scored an impressive 24 to 8 victory over Ferris Institute. In the season's afterglow none could foresee the events that would stymie Hope football at the very moment that it seemed to be reestablished.

When Ame Vennema became the fourth president of Hope College in 1911 he was no doubt aware of the Council's travel ban preventing athletic teams from making treks outside the city during school time. He could not, however, have anticipated the furor that would be unleashed when in the fall of 1913, the basketball team felt sufficiently established to defy the rule. All were confident, including Manager Henry Van Houte who arranged a one thousand mile tour, most likely to showcase the team's prowess. After an opening 74 to 11 victory over a team called the "Ramblers," the team departed Holland on December 19. In Grand Haven they were proudly hosted for dinner by the Reverend Jim Ver Berg, who had been manager of the memorable 1909-10 team. The next stop was Milwaukee where the team was entertained by Miner Stegenga's brother, who served as Secretary of the Milwaukee Y.M.C.A. In Sheboygan Hope met and defeated the team from Mission House (later Lakeland College) by a score of 46 to 21. After a week's intermission for Christmas, the tour was resumed with three more victories: Hope 33 - Traverse City 31, Hope 32 - Manistee 12, and Hope 35 - Grand Rapids Y.M.C.A 2.

The 5 and 0 Dutchmen, returning in triumph, were shocked when President Vennema, with faculty support, suspended the team. The nature of the suspension is not known, but it brought action from the Student Council, which requested permission to hold a mass meeting on the campus. The request was denied and the situation became tense when the mayor of the city invited the students to hold their meeting in the city hall. Suspicion lingers that this course was abetted by a few faculty mavericks. The result was a student strike, an action quite out of character for the Hope College of that era. The faculty was shocked by this precursor of the 1960s and responded in frustration with the following resolution:

> The president was entirely within his rights in suspending the basketball team for violating the out-of-town rule. It was only the lawless interference and flagrant violation of their own wise and law-abiding constitution that the Student Council headed the student strike. The revolt of the student body was without justification, and the strike for recognition, so called, is only to be condemned.[1]

1913-14 Hope College Basketball Team

Top Row L to R: Otto Vander Velde, Miner Stegenga, Dick Smallegan, George Veenker, Clarence Lokker. **Front Row:** Paul Stegeman, Henry Van Houte - manager, Lawrence Dalman, Prof. Lambert Eidson - coach, George Steininger.

The strike was quickly settled and the season continued as scheduled. There would, however, be repercussions.

Hopes for an undefeated season were dashed when the Detroit Y.M.C.A. did the Dutchmen in to the tune of 65-19 on January 8, but the Hope five was back in form a week later taking the measure of Mount Pleasant Normal, 49 to 23. Detroit continued its domination as the perennially strong Rayles took a 33-20 decision before the Hope team reeled off five consecutive victories to record the school's most impressive won-lost record to that time. Scores were as follows:

Hope 35 - Northwestern 33
Hope 35 - Western State Normal 22
Hope 43 - Grand Rapids Y.M.C.A. 28
Hope 35 - Kalamazoo College 30
Hope 33 - Olivet 20

The game with Western marked the first meeting of the two schools in the sport of basketball. For the first time in several years, Hope was unable to schedule Michigan Agricultural College and this detracted somewhat from an otherwise illustrious season. Undaunted, the Hope team sought additional status by engaging in the age old game of comparative scores. Hope and M.A.C. had a common opponent in Northwestern of Naperville. The Aggies were beaten by the Illinois five and the Dutch promptly proclaimed themselves State Collegiate Champions by virtue of their two point decision over Northwestern. There is no record that M.A.C. or anyone else challenged the claim.

In the spring of 1914, through the generosity of Mr. C. Dosker of Grand Rapids, two additional tennis courts were provided. This made a total of three on the northeast corner of 12th Street and College Avenue. They served the college well for 15 years, finally giving way to Dimnent Memorial Chapel in 1929. In baseball Hope opened the season by registering an 8 to 2 victory over Holland High. Otto Vander Velde went the route on the mound and stroked a home run to aid his own cause. Grand Rapids Central High School was next and edged Hope 5-4 in ten innings before Kalamazoo College beat the Dutch, 5-3. Reports claimed that the latter contest was witnessed by two thousand spectators. Also of interest was the fact that the game's umpire was Jack Schouten, who would not be on the college payroll for another six years. The season continued as the battery of Jacob Poppen and Lawrence Dalman proved too much for Ferris Institute, the team from Big Rapids falling 9-2 to the Dutch. Western State's 4 to 2 victory over the Hope men closed out the season

A high point for trackmen that spring was the sixth running of the Grand Rapids to Holland Relay. The Hope Runners' victory over the G.R. Y.M.C.A. gave them a 4-2 advantage in this unique sporting event. Team members included Charles Peet, John Muyskens, Edwin Koeppe, Marion Gosselink, Herm Stegeman, George A. Pelgrim, Bert Vande Brake, John L. Mulder, Clarence Holleman, and John Van Strien.

When the Council met in April, President Vennema sought to resolve the continuing tension caused by the travel ban and read the following statement:

> ... There is an unwritten rule of the college, of long standing, which prohibits any of our athletic teams from leaving the city, during term time, in order to enter into a contest with outside teams. This rule is supposed to be in accordance with the wish of the Council as reflecting the sentiment of the churches, particularly in the Particular Synod of Chicago, from which we draw most of our students. So strong is the desire on the part of the students that they are constantly tempted to violate the rule out and out, or to evade it by not going as regular organization teams, but by forming a different combination known as a Pickup Team, and then going. This is a somewhat involved matter and a many sided question, having a bearing upon the finances, the scholarship, the morals and college spirit of our student body. The rule is more difficult to enforce because some of our students come from other of our church academies, having enjoyed the freedom before they came to Hope. What especially the writer of this report is desirous, is whether the Council would have us maintain this position or whether, according to the wish of the students, we may feel at liberty to recede from it, and if so, to what extent? Personally we have no disposition to deny to any student any pleasure, if it is thought that they may engage in it without working harm to themselves or to the good name of the college.[2]

No definite action was taken, and at the end of the school year the students presented yet another petition. This irritated some faculty to the point that a motion was made to abolish athletics altogether. (!) Wynand Wichers, who would become Hope's sixth president, was at the time a young faculty member and very much involved. His first-hand account is as follows:

> ... Wiser counsels prevailed and the matter was referred to a committee, which recommended that the petition be allowed subject to the appointment of a Board of Control, consisting of Professors Milton J. Hoffman and Wynand Wichers, representing the faculty, L.(Lambertus) Hekhuis representing the alumni, and Messrs. M.(Miner) Stegenga and G.(George) Steininger the Athletic Association. There were the following restrictions: A three-year trial, parental consent, proper chaperones, and all games to be played after the close of recitations on Friday and in such time that the teams could be home by midnight of Saturday. There was to be no intercollegiate football.[3]

If there were regrets in the fall of 1914 at the absence of football, such sentiments were not expressed in the **Anchor** with its new weekly format. There was however, general anticipation that basketball might reach an all-time high. Miner Stegenga, Otto Vander Velde, Dick Smallegan, Teunis Prins, and Marinus Van Putten all returned from the 1913-14 team, and talk of an undefeated season was understandable. This was not to be. A stronger schedule and other circumstances conspired to saddle the Dutch with an unimpressive 7-9 record. Things began well as the team seemed to pick up where it had left off by downing Grand Rapids Bethany Church, 44 to 14. This was followed by a decisive 36-15 win over Mount Pleasant Normal, but a two-day trip into the Chicago area resulted in defeats at the hands of Northwestern (North Central), 36-10, and the Illinois Athletic Club, 31 to 29. The team, somewhat shaken, rallied to edge the Detroit Rayles 31-29 on the Detroiter's home court and hopes were revived, but the following night Hope fell to the Detroit Y.M.C.A., 36 to 16. The up and down nature of the team continued as they drubbed the Pontiac Y.M.C.A. 59 to 23 to end the eastern trip.

Hope ushered in 1915 with a January 1 victory over the Grand Rapids Y.M.C.A., 33 to 27, but M.A.C. was back on the schedule and the trip to East Lansing was made without two regulars. The resulting 56-20 shellacking was the first of four consecutive defeats. On January 21 the Detroit Rayles invaded Carnegie Gym and won in overtime, 30 to 28. Play and sportsmanship were superb in the contest, which some felt was the best all-round game played in Carnegie to that time. The Detroit "Y" downed the Dutch for the second time, 30-16, and Northwestern also gained a second win, 56-23.

It was a discouraged but determined Hope team that journeyed to Kalamazoo to meet Western State on February

12. The hard-fought game stood 22 all at the end of regulation play. The evenly matched teams then battled into a third overtime before a confused Western player passed the ball to a surprised George Steininger, who quickly dropped in the winning basket. The return train trip via Grand Rapids was upbeat, to say the least, but celebration time was short. Kalamazoo College, next on the schedule, trailed Hope 18-16 at half time but prevailed in the end, 34 to 27. Things did not improve when M.A.C. journeyed to Holland and returned to East Lansing with a solid 46-28 victory. The Dutch rallied for the season finale against the Grand Rapids Y.M.C.A. Fans were not disappointed as Miner Stegenga, Otto Vander Velde, and Dick Smallegan played their last game before the Hope crowd and won it, 44 to 30.

Stegenga and Vander Velde had been truly outstanding athletes for all of their four years and would join John Vruwink and John Lavan as perhaps the top athletes at Hope in the pre-World War I era. Vander Velde pursued medical studies at the University of Michigan and subsequently returned to serve Holland as a prominent physician. He also donated hours of service to Hope College for many years as team physician. Stegenga, affectionately known as "Stogie," graduated from Western Theological Seminary in 1918 after two years at New Brunswick. He held several pastorates in the east and then, during World War II, enlisted in the army, achieved the rank of major and served as the base Chaplain at Camp Gordon, Georgia. Each spring, at Hope's Honors Convocation, the top male athletes are recipients of the Otto Vander Velde All-Campus award and the Miner Stegenga award.

Baseball had its moments in the spring of 1915, despite a 4-5 record. Victories were recorded over Holland High (2), the Grand Rapids School of Business (4-3), and Ferris Institute (15-3). Western State and Alma scored one run victories, 3-2 and 4-3, while Mount Pleasant Normal handled the Dutch, 9-4. The Alma loss was blamed by some on a missed train connection in Grand Rapids, resulting in a late arrival and no warm-up time. After taking the measure of Ferris 15 to 3 and Holland High 14-13, Hope dropped a 2 to 1 heartbreaker to Olivet. Otto Vander Velde went the entire 10 innings giving up but 3 hits and striking out 17, but Dutch bats failed to respond. The Zeeland Independents came to Hope's 12th Street diamond for the season's final game and put on an offensive display that netted 10 runs. A bright spot in Hope's comeback try was Lawrence Dalman's grand slam home run, which landed alongside Van Vleck Hall, but seven runs was the best the Dutch could do. The team picture includes sophomore Irwin J. Lubbers, who would become better known by winning the State Oratorical Contest and later becoming the seventh president of Hope College.

A determined effort to promote track included an invitational two mile run. The event was won by Paul Stegeman, followed by Dowie De Boer and Glen Belknap, but disappointment was in store as the Hope team was beaten by the Grand Rapids Y.M.C.A. in the Grand Rapids to Holland relay. Muskegon High School added to Hope's frustration by winning the four mile cross country run.

Otto Vandervelde and Miner Stegenga - Hope '15

Vandervelde and Stegenga were star athletes in the teens and made significant contributions in later years. Stegenga returned to coach the '17-'18 basketball team and Vandervelde served as team physician for many years. Special athletic awards are given in their names at the annual honors convocation.

In the fall of 1915 football was kept alive by the organization of an interclass league which included a team from the prep school. After this team was mauled by the freshmen, it was decided that the small prep team should not continue. The juniors eventually won the championship as enthusiasts clung to the hope that the Council would ease its restriction.

Hope's basketball success in the early years is remarkable in that coaching continuity was nonexistent. The team was fortunate in 1915 when Carl Bowen agreed to serve as coach. A graduate of the University of Iowa, Bowen had played for that institution and now took over a team that had lost its superstars. His main job as Holland's city engineer allowed time for the daily practice sessions. Teunis Prins captained the team, which was not seen as equal to the previous two. It was therefore a pleasant surprise when the club won six of its first seven games. Scores were as follows:

Hope 61 - Grand Rapids Wolverines 12
Hope 24 - Mount Pleasant Normal 20 (OT)
Traverse City Olympics 30 - Hope 26
Hope 32 - Ludington Wolverines 17
Hope 12 - Grand Rapids Y.M.C.A. 11
Hope 20 - M.A.C. 14

The win over M.A.C. was a rare Hope victory on the Aggies' home floor. On January 19 the Illinois Athletic Club proved too strong for the Hope five, winning 35 to 14, and the going was more difficult from that point on:

Illinois Athletic Club 35 - Hope 14
Kalamazoo College 24 - Hope 21
M.A.C. 21 - Hope 19
Hope 35 - Alma 29
Mount Pleasant Normal 27 - Hope 21
Hope 27 - Western State Normal 24
Hope 18 - Grand Rapids Y.M.C.A. 15
Kalamazoo College 36 - Hope 19
Hillsdale 27 - Hope 21
Hope 56 - Detroit Timkin Roller 8

The overall 10-7 record was more than most had expected, and a genuine credit to Coach Bowen.

The high point in the Vennema administration was the celebration of the 50th anniversary of the incorporation of the college. Months of planning included publication of the first **Milestone**. A yearbook had been published in 1905 but the project was not resumed until the semicentennial year. A great deal of pride and enthusiasm went into the **Milestone**, a special pageant, and numerous other activities. It seemed to extend to the baseball nine as Hope captain Marinus Van Putten led his team to a fine 5 and 2 record. The opening 4-3 loss to Western State was followed by a five game winning streak before Ferris Institute edged the Dutch 8-7 in 10 innings in the season windup. The victories were as follows:

Hope 11 - Ferris Institute 6
Hope 7 - Holland High 4
Hope 3 - Mount Pleasant Normal 1
Hope 2 - Zeeland Independents 0
Hope 6 - Holland Y.M.C.A. 1

Other bseball news that spring centered around John L. Lavan ('11), Hope's gift to the major leagues, who was making it big with the St. Louis Browns. Lavan, a fine fielding shortstop, was part of an infield that included the famed George Sisler. Grand Rapids papers recounted a sensational play by Lavan in Comiskey Park that robbed "Shoeless" Joe Jackson of a sure base hit. Three years later Jackson would lose more than a hit as an accessory in the infamous Black Sox Scandal.

Track and field in 1916 came closer to the sport as presently conducted than in any prior year. Hope's first opportunity came in a meet hosted by M.A.C. Paul Stegeman placed second in the 880 yard run, freshman dashman Jacob Elting was second in the 100 yard dash. Next was a modified marathon sponsored by the **Grand Rapids Herald**. In this event Hope's Koppenaal brothers, William and Peter, placed fourth and seventh respectively. But the season's big event was Hope's first real dual track meet. The contest was staged at Mount Pleasant Normal just prior to a baseball game between the two schools. This allowed Hope to borrow Paul Stegeman and Marinus Van Putten from the baseball team. Both were fine athletes and contributed to Hope's 78 1/2 to 25 1/2 victory. Results were as follows:

100 yard dash: Jacob Elting (H), Lawrence Dalman (H), Farmer (MP) 10.4
880 yard run: Paul Stegeman (H), Andrews (MP), Lawther (MP), 2:12.01
high jump: Wilson Stegeman (H), Beddow (MP), Kyser (MP) 5' 1"
220 yard dash: Jacob Elting (H), Lawrence Dalman (H), Crane (MP) 24.0
1 mile run: Lawrence Johnson (H), Richard Zevalkink (H), Eidt (MP) 5:05
broad jump: Lawrence Dalman (H), Marinus Van Putten (H), Kyser (MP) 19' 1"
440 yard dash: Jacob Elting (H), Marinus Van Putten (H), Lippert (MP) 52.4
mile run: Lawrence Johnson (H), Eidt (MP), Richard Zevalkink (H) 10:55.0
shot put: Hindes (MP), Lawrence Dalman (H), Paul Stegeman (H) 36' 4"
pole vault: Lawrence Dalman (H), Beddow (MP), Baker (MP)-Clarence Heemstra(H) 9'3"
discus: Lawrence Dalman (H), Paul Stegeman (H), Hindes (MP) 101' 5"
mile relay: Hope College 3:37.3

Lawrence Dalman with three firsts and three seconds was clearly the star of the day, but Jacob Elting's victory in all three dashes was also an outstanding accomplishment, especially for a freshman. On the same day, with other personnel, Hope placed second in the annual cross country race with Muskegon High School and the Grand Rapids Y.M.C.A. Later in spring the all-round Dalman teamed with Gordon Oltmans in tennis to defeat the Grand Rapids Y.M.C.A. team of Rutledge and Bartz, 7-9, 6-2, 6-1. This avenged an earlier defeat and marked Hope's first engagement with outside competition in the sport of tennis.

On April 25 a student petition to the Council asked for a full-time coach. The Council approved this petition and promised to work diligently to find a qualified person. Four more years would pass before such a person was found.

Pressure for the return of intercollegiate football continued in the fall of 1916, but the best Hope could manage was a November 15 game with Holland High. A combination of two fine high school athletes spelled defeat for Hope. "Cappy" Cappon's pass to Dick Japinga resulted in a 7-0 win for Coach Drew's team. Cappon would later star for Michigan while Japinga would throw in his lot with Hope College.

A familiar figure emerged as Hope's basketball coach for the 1916-17 season. Jack Schouten had been a part of the Hope sports scene since the 1890s and now volunteered to take the non-paying position. Marinus Van Putten was named Captain and Bill Ten Haken Manager of a team that appeared to like the friendly confines of Carnegie Gym. Six of seven victories occurred on the home court while seven of eight losses were away games. A mixture of collegiate and independent teams made up the schedule:

Hope 49 - Ted and Ed's of Zeeland 18
Hope 47 - Muskegon Normal 9
Whiting Owls 56 - Hope 31
Illinois Athletic Club 41 - Hope 18
Flint Vehicle Workers 36 - Hope 32
Detroit Y.M.O. 27 - Hope 26 (OT)
Grand Rapids Y.M.C.A. 23 - Hope 20
Hope 23 - Western State Normal 12
M.A.C. 34 - Hope 20
Hope 46 - Alma 22
Hope 21 - Grand Rapids Y.M.C.A. 12
Kalamazoo College 33 - Hope 14
Hope 18 - Western State Normal 16
Hope 18 - M.A.C. 13
Kalamazoo College 49 - Hope 10

In March of 1917,with America's impending involvement in World War I, it was understandably difficult for students to give much attention to sports. On April 6 the United States declared war on Germany and a wave of patriotism swept the country. The Hope campus was no exception and on April 11 the following resolution was telegraphed to the White House:

President Woodrow Wilson
The White House
Washington, D.C.

The students and faculty of Hope College, in a large and enthusiastic mass meeting held this evening, unanimously voted loyal support and readiness to render service to our great and beloved country in this day of need.

A. Vennema
President
April 11, 1917[4]

As young men slipped away to join various branches of the service, a baseball team was assembled. After dropping games to Western State 2-1, and to De Pree Chemical 2-0, the team was disbanded. For the first time in nine years there was no Grand Rapids to Holland relay race. There were bigger issues.

Interest in athletics was not dead however, and when the Council met in June they received another petition with reference to intercollegiate football. This time the students bolstered their position by reminding that the other Reformed Church college, Central of Iowa, sponsored the sport and apparently with full support of its constituency. A reluctant Council finally granted the request by the narrow margin of nine votes to eight. Football would begin the long road back.

Jack Schouten was persuaded to coach the Hope men in their 1917 return to the gridiron, but it was necessary for him to be away for periods of time due to responsibilities with the Holland Fair Association. The team got a late start, but by October 10, 23 men were vying for positions. Willard Van Hazel, as team captain, assisted in preparing for a game with Grand Haven High School. The game took place on October 20 and Hope emerged the winner, 7 to 0. Fullback Clarence Heemstra scored the only touchdown and Bernard Hakken kicked the point after. The scheduling of additional games proved impossible and as the **Anchor** put it, "King football was forced to enter upon hibernation."

Harvey Ramaker and Clarence Heemstra were the only basketball returnees for 1917-18, but hopes ran high when it was learned that Miner Stegenga was back in town and would serve as coach. "Stogie" would take his senior year at Western Theological Seminary after spending two years at New Brunswick. Hope opened the season on Friday, December 7, hosting Calvin College. A small crowd of 350 watched as Hope dominated the inexperienced Calvin five. The halftime score of 28-4 ballooned to 55-8 at game's end. Fans and players of course, had no inkling that they were initiating a series that would become the top small college rivalry in the country.*

Wartime basketball had its ups and downs as Hope posted a 6-6 record. There were numerous occasions when the team could not practice due to the fuel shortage. An **Anchor** writer mentions rather casually that "An added feature (of the season) was a game played at Ann Arbor with the University of Michigan, who have broken into the caging game." While "breaking in" the Wolverines managed to double the score on the Dutch. The season record was as follows:

Hope 55 - Calvin 8
Hope 24 - Muskegon Y.M.C.A. 23
Western State 22 - Hope 15
Hope 35 - M.A.C. 21
Grand Rapids Y.M.C.A. 24 - Hope 23
Hope 26 - Holland Y.M.C.A. 14
Muskegon Y.M.C.A. 22 - Hope 19
Grand Rapids Y.M.C.A. 30 - Hope 23
University of Michigan 31 - Hope 15
Hope 28 - Western State 22
M.A.C. 34 - Hope 10
Hope 28 - Kalamazoo College 27

* Calvin officials maintain that this was not an official Calvin team but rather, a group of Calvin students who acted on their own in agreeing to the game.

The 1918 **Milestone**, appropriately bound in khaki, proudly displayed pictures of 36 Hope men in uniform, plus names of another 22 not pictured. Despite this loss of manpower, a game effort was made to do something with spring sports. Baseball was reduced to one intramural game, but the Hope-Grand Rapids relay was revived, and with great success. In an unusually close race Hope went one up on the Grand Rapids Y.M.C.A. The series now stood at 5-4 with the following men providing the edge:

Elmer Lubbers	John Flikkema
Francis Ihrman	Ed Stegeman
Henry Pyle	John Kempers
Edward Tanis	Peter Baker
Peter Vos (prep school)	John Dalenberg

A radical change took place on Hope's campus in the fall of 1918. Colleges and universities across the country were called upon to enlist their young men in the Student Army Training Corps. (S.A.T.C.) Hope's unit was activated on October 1 and continued in force for about a month beyond the November ll armistice. The men were housed in Carnegie Gym and had their mess hall on the third floor of Van Raalte Hall. In addition to tuition and fees, each man received $30 per month. Lieutenant J.D. Jacobson commanded the unit, which was disbanded on December 14.

The S.A.T.C. had the effect of keeping men on Hope's campus and provided men for the football squad, as well as Lieutenant Edward S. Dabney, who assisted "Cubby" Drew as coach. Hope's first game of the season was played at Kalamazoo College on Saturday, November 16. It was Hope's first intercollegiate game since 1913 and was eagerly anticipated by all. In the first half, tackle George Hoek blocked a Kalamazoo punt and recovered in the end zone for a touchdown. Perry Reiminga kicked the point and Hope led at halftime, 7-0. Kalamazoo scored twice in the third quarter and held a 13-7 lead with three minutes remaining in the game. At this point halfback Willard Elferdink plunged over for Hope and Reiminga again converted, giving Hope the hard-fought 14-13 victory. Hope had three substitutes but none got into the game. Hope fans were justifiably proud of their team's return to the gridiron.

One week later the 14-man squad again traveled to Kalamazoo to meet Western State. This time the Dutch were outclassed in every department, absorbing a 62 to 0 drubbing. As the Hope 11 limped back to Holland they found little consolation in the fact that Western had downed Hillsdale, 102 to 0, on the previous Saturday. Fortunately, no one was seriously injured and the team was able to close out its season on a positive note on Thanksgiving Day by taking the measure of Grand Rapids Junior College, 27-0. Dick Japinga and James Klomparens each scored two touchdowns and Perry Reiminga kicked three points. As a memento of this signivicant season, 12 men who had played in two or more of the games were presented with jerseys. The jerseys were done in brown and gold to also commemorate the days of the S.A.T.C.

The parade of basketball coaches continued at Hope in 1918-19. This time it was Clarence Lokker, Hope '14, who assumed the reigns. As the season got underway students were reminded of certain rules laid down by the Athletic Board of Control in regard to academic standards. An 80 percent average was required of all athletes. There was an additional restriction to the effect that no player could participate who had received a "C" during the previous semester! Today's moderate standards pale by comparison.

Due to the late departure of the S.A.T.C., Carnegie Gym was not available for practice and the season opener was not played until January 1, 1919. The team was, of necessity, ill prepared and lost to the Grand Rapids Y.M.C.A., 34 to 12. A number of fine athletes were still in the service as Hope dropped its second contest to the Camp Custer Officers, 22-15. But the tide began to turn as Hope edged the Muskegon Y.M.C.A. in overtime, 27-26. Dick Japinga had the winning field goal in this first of an eight game winning streak. The fact that several "name" schools were numbered among the victims added luster to the achievement. Scores were as follows:

Hope 27	-	Muskegon Y.M.C.A. 26
Hope 29	-	Western State 25
Hope 21	-	M.A.C. 18
Hope 29	-	Northwestern (Naperville) 18
Hope 62	-	Grand Rapids Y.M.C.A. 17
Hope 26	-	M.A.C. 20
Hope 34	-	Western State 26
Hope 31	-	Holland Y.M.C.A. 23

The inevitable letdown came as Hope lost to the Muskegon Y.M.C.A. by a score of 38 to 23. In the season finale the team rallied in a gallant effort, but fell before the strong Detroit Rayles, 26-17. The 8-4 record however, pleased Hope followers and confirmed Hope as a genuine power in state collegiate basketball. There were no trophies to display, but the team felt rewarded as they were honored at a chicken dinner prepared by Mrs. Prins, mother of Teunis and Peter Prins.

Hope's windup of the school year was less than spectacular. For some reason spring sports failed to match the performances of fall and winter. The baseball team, after taking a 6-3 practice game from Holland High, dropped games to Grand Rapids Junior College 6-3, to Western State 14-0, and to Kalamazoo College 4-2. In track meanwhile, it was the Grand Rapids Y.M.C.A.'s turn to win the relay and even the series at 5-5.

1918 Football Team

Hope's first team to play intercollegiate games after the 1914-16 ban. **Top Row L to R:** Lieutenant Edward S. Dabney (Coach), Henry Warnshuis, John Joldersma, George Hoek, Martin De Wolf (Manager). **Middle Row:** Mike Schuurmans, James Klomparens, Clarence Poppen, Willard Elferdink, Gerrit Wassenaar. **Front Row:** Perry Reininga, Earl Knutson (Captain), Nanko Bos, Henry Bolt. Missing from the picture: Dick Japinga - quarterback, Charles N. Drew - Coach.

Hope College Basketball Team - 1918-19

Top Row L to R: Garrett De Jong (Manager), Gerritt Wassenaar, Nanko Bos, James Klomparens, Clarence Lokker (Coach). **Front Row:** J. Dyke Van Putten, Peter Prins, Teunis Prins (Captain), Dick Japinga, Clarence Heemstra.

In retrospect, the decade of the teens must be viewed as a period of progress with sport in proper perspective. The continued prominence of basketball, student agitation for reforms, the establishment of governance and eligibility rules, the lifting of the travel ban, dealing with the trauma of World War I, and surviving the three-year football ban were all factors in bringing about greater cohesiveness. Few would dispute the fact that Hope's quest for status in intercollegiate athletics was on track.

REFERENCES - CHAPTER 3

1. **Preparatory School Minutes**, 1913.
2. **Minutes of the Council**, April, 1914.
3. Wynand Wichers, **A Century of Hope**. Grand Rapids: William Eerdmans Company, 1968, p. 150.
4. The **Anchor**, April 18, 1917.

CHAPTER 4

THE EARLY TWENTIES - INDEPENDENT COMPETITION

The Roaring Twenties were ushered in with expectancy as the 1919-20 school year began at Hope College. The decade would bring two major achievements, the hiring of a full time Athletic Director-Coach, and affiliation with the Michigan Intercollegiate Athletic Association. As mentioned earlier, both moves had been viewed by authorities as undue encouragement of activity that could only detract from the main purpose of the college. Gradually this perception was changing as the Reformed Church hierarchy took a more realistic look at the facts of American culture.

Neither Charles Drew nor Lieutenant Dabney were on hand in 1919, but Earnest Brooks, who had played on Hope's vaunted 1909 grid team, was available and willing to coach. The injury jinx, which stalks most teams, caught up with Hope in the first half of the season. The opening game with Kalamazoo College was scoreless until late in the third quarter when Willard Van Hazel, Peter Prins, and Earl Knutson were all forced out with injuries. Kalamazoo capitalized and took the contest 30-0. A week later at Alma things were even worse as Prins, Van Hazel, George Hoek, and Dyke Van Putten did not make the trip. The ranks were further depleted when quarterback Dick Japinga left the game in the third quarter with an injury. Final score: Alma 39 - Hope 0. The M.A.C. freshman team also downed Hope, this time 13 to 3 as Japinga's dropkick field goal produced the only Dutch score. It was a different story as the injured returned for the Ferris game. Hope scored 10 touchdowns as triple threat Dick Japinga ran, passed, and kicked Hope to a 71-7 victory. Japinga's dropkicking ability was especially evident as he was successful with a field goal and 7 of 10 extra points. Hope gained an even split on the season by taking successive victories from Grand Rapids Junior College by scores of 20 to 6 and 26 to 0. The latter contest was played on the field located on 19th Street between College and Columbia avenues.

The big news that fall came during a November chapel service when President Edward Dimnent announced that Jack Schouten had been hired as full-time athletic director and coach. Jack's daughter Bess relates that Dr. Dimnent sought out Jack in the latter's drug store on east Eighth street. The agreement was reached there and according to Bess, her father could hardly wait to get over to the gym and begin his duties. Students were gratified that their ongoing agitation had finally produced the desired result.

Jack was born Johannas Hendrikus Landskroon Schouten on June 12, 1881. Place of birth was the Beach House, 12th Street and Columbia Avenue in Holland. Later it would be known as the Emersonian House and Beach Cottage, and eventually it would make way for the present Kollen Hall. Jack was bitten by the baseball bug early and played on Holland and Hope teams even before the turn of the century. The son of a physician, he was also interested in medicine, but for a variety of reasons, most of them sport-related, he never quite zeroed in on that profession. His compromise was to learn all that he could about athletic training and the treatment of injuries incurred by athletes. Although the college had dabbled in fitness, Jack was, in a sense, Hope's first department of physical education. It is noteworthy that the program which he instituted included classes for women students. Despite a sometimes stern demeanor, Jack's genuine love for his students was soon apparent and for 32 years they would respond in kind. Mrs. Schouten, the former Marjorie Vyn, had married Jack on July 2, 1908. According to daughter Bess, Mrs. Schouten always called her husband John, but to most everyone else he was forever "Jack" - - with deepest affection and respect.

With Earnest Brooks in charge of the football squad, Jack's first official coaching responsibility was to take the five man cross country team to the M.A.C. Invitational. The Hope men, with their new coach, did themselves proud as only M.A.C. and the University of Michigan finished above them. Ten schools competed and the order of finish was as follows:

M.A.C.
University of Michigan
Hope College
Kalamazoo College
Detroit Junior College
Western State Normal
Albion College
Alma College
Hillsdale College
Ypsilanti Normal

Of the Hope runners, John Kempers finished first, followed by Francis Ihrman, Gerrit Muyskens, Charles Loomans, and Elmer Lubbers.

Jack Schouten was no stranger to Hope College basketball. When he took over, the 1919-20 squad he was actually returning to a post he had occupied during the 1916-17 season. The season's record this time of nine and seven would include splits with M.A.C., Western State, Mount Pleasant Normal, and Kalamazoo College, as well as a first ever meeting with Wabash College of Indiana. Scores were as follows:

Hope 43 - Grand Haven American Legion 14
Wabash 27 - Hope 10
Bluffton Phi Delta Kappa 43 - Hope 18
Whiting Red Crowns 45 - Hope 18
Hope 33 - Grand Rapids Y.M.C.A. 16
Hope 21 - M.A.C. 16
Mount Pleasant Normal 16 - Hope 15
Hope 24 - Kalamazoo College 15
Hope 15 - Mount Pleasant Normal 14
Hope 24 - Alma 18
Kalamazoo College 21 - Hope 19
Hope 39 - Grand Rapids Y.M.C.A. 12
Western State Normal 23 - Hope 21
Hope 27 - Western State Normal 26
M.A.C. 34 - Hope 23
Hope 28 - Holland Y.M.C.A. 20

As the baseball season approached Jack was in his element. His scheduled game with M.A.C. on April 11 had to be canceled due to a downpour, but Hope subsequently took on Holland High in two practice games, winning 6-5 and 7-3. The battery of Arthur Roggen and Dick Japinga was effective throughout most of the season but could not prevent Western State from recording a 6-2 victory. Roggen was back

John H.L. "Jack" Schouten

Hope's first Director of Athletics and full-time Coach Jack took over in the fall of 1919 at age 38.

in form as Hope took Grand Rapids Junior College 10 to 4. In an official game with Holland High the high schoolers put together a 3-1 win to the dismay of the Hope men who may have taken too much for granted after the practice games. The team rebounded to dominate Ferris 15 to 4 and edge Grand Rapids Junior College 5-4.

Jack also found time to coach the track team but the turnout was not large. The Grand Rapids Y.M.C.A. overpowered Hope 18 to 41 in a 4 1/2 mile cross country run. They were also successful in the llth running of the Grand Rapids to Holland relay, giving Grand Rapids a 6-5 advantage in the series. As the first year of the Schouten era drew to a close there was consensus that the college could now expect stability in the program of athletics.

Students and other followers of Hope sports had rejoiced at the restoration of football. Now, with the addition of a full-time coach, the prescription for success seemed to be in place. There would, however, be tough times in the 1920s. With the exception of two break-even years, each season would be a losing one. During this period the excitement of the game seemed to override the modern day obsession with winning and losing. Expressions of displeasure were minimal and at no time was there any suggestion that the sport be eliminated from the program.

Football was king again in the fall of 1920 but had to surrender some ground to politics. It was an election year and Holland received a campaign visit from Franklin Delano Roosevelt, the democratic candidate for Vice President. F.D.R. courageously invaded this republican stronghold and spoke before a polite crowd at the Knickerbocker Theater on Eighth Street. The Cox-Roosevelt campaign was an uphill struggle fraught with disappointment and the same might be said for Jack's initial season as football coach. The opener was Hope's first occasion for athletic competition with Hillsdale College. At game's end the Dutch found themselves on the short end of a 19 to 0 score. The Dales would provide some of Hope's toughest competition for the next 40 years. The game with Alma began well for the Dutch, as Bill Elferdink intercepted a pass and ran it back for a touchdown. Dyke Van Putten's kick was wide and the score stood 6-0 until late in the fourth quarter, when the Scots punched over a score and kicked the all important point for a 7-6 victory. Hope continued to improve against Ferris. Garrett De Jong's touchdown was the game's only score but it was enough for the Dutch to notch a 6-0 victory, their only one of the season. The schools from Kalamazoo again shut down the Hope attack, Western by a 47-0 count and Kalamazoo 18 to 0. The shutouts continued when Mount Pleasant Normal downed the Dutch 17-0 at the 19th Street field.

Meanwhile the cross country team journeyed to East Lansing and finished a creditable third for the second year in a row. Team scores were as follows:

M.A.C. 26
University of Michigan 31
Hope 48
Albion 61
Kalamazoo College 65
University of Detroit 67

Hope's runners finished the 4 1/2 mile course with Stanley Schipper leading the way. Captain Francis Ihrman was second, Tony Meengs third, and Marinus Hoffs fourth.

Dick Japinga was captain of the 1920-21 basketball team, which posted a splendid 15-7 record. The season opened with a 35-15 victory over the Lowell American Legion team. In its second game Hope hosted the first official team from Calvin College. The home team held a considerable edge in experience and took the contest 31 to 13. The series would even out over the years and become one of Western Michigan's leading sports attractions. After splitting games with two independent teams from Indiana, Jack engineered a swing through Iowa that produced six victories against a single loss. The Dutch dropped home and away contests to M.A.C. and to Western State, but took Mount Pleasant Normal 19-15 and overwhelmed Alma in the season finale, 51 to 10. In the prelim to the latter game Calvin tasted victory over Hope for the first time as their freshman team downed the Dutch frosh, 22-19. Scores for the season were as follows:

Hope 35 - Lowell American Legion 15
Hope 31 - Calvin 13
South Bend Y.M.C.A. 40 - Hope 15
Hope 30 - Whiting Owls 10
Hope 32 - Western Union College of Le Mars, Iowa 12
Hope 23 - Sheldon Company "E". 22
Hope 30 - Sheldon Company "E" 14
Hope 47 - Hull Independents 15
Iowa Sioux Club 40 - Hope 17
Hope 28 - Iowa Sioux Club 22
Hope 35 - Orange City American Legion 10
Hope 22 - Grand Rapids Y.M.C.A. 18
Hope 44 - Company "F" of Grand Haven 11
M.A.C. 31 - Hope 17
Hope 36 - Grand Rapids Y.M.C.A. 17
Hope 32 - Flint Buicks 20
Bay City Industrials 30 - Hope 26
Western State Normal 28 - Hope 24
Western State Normal 21 - Hope 14
M.A.C. 27 - Hope 23
Hope 19 - Mount Pleasant Normal 14
Hope 51 - Alma 10

The team's 15 victories were the most by any Hope team since the sport's inception at the turn of the century. Team members were understandably the toast of town and campus. The **Anchor** also had kind words for the coach:

> The coach, John Schouten also deserves high commendation. His hearty ways, his pleasing personality, and his encouraging talks helped to bring out the best that was in the fellows. Taking charge of a number of basketball teams and all the other physical directing besides, is no snap, yet Jack made a great success of it![1]

Track in the spring of '21 was limited to a cross country run with the Grand Rapids "Y." Hope emerged the winner 23 to 32 as Francis Ihrman and John Kempers finished second and third. April showers limited Hope's baseball schedule, and games with M.A.C., Ferris, and Albion were canceled. The season finally got under way at Orchard Lake, where the Dutch succumbed to St. Mary's, 13 to 3. Pitchers George Laug and Dyke Van Putten were unable to contain the St. Mary's sluggers. The Schouten men did score two one-run victories over Grand Rapids Junior College, 11-10 and 7-6, but lost to Ferris 14-8, and twice to Mount Pleasant Normal,

11-4 and 4-3.

Also in the spring of 1921, Hope accepted an invitation to participate in a tennis tournament at Kalamazoo College. Both men and women were included in the competition. Lester Brusse, Raymond Zwemer, and Dirk Stegeman brought home a fourth place finish behind Kalamazoo, Alma, and Western, but ahead of Albion and Mount Pleasant Normal. The Hope doubles team of Maxine Mc Bride and Rachel Gebhard lost to Albion 6-2, 6-1 as Albion subsequently won the women's tournament.

The rough and tumble nature of football calls for numbers and Coach Schouten was understandably concerned when only 18 men turned out for the team in the fall of 1921. Dick Japinga was back at quarterback after passing up the 1920 season and all hoped the great ability of this fine athlete could somehow offset the lack of bodies. It was not to be. J. Dyke Van Putten was captain of the team that opened the season on October 8 at Hillsdale. Only 15 men made the trip and the Dales were simply too much as they downed the Dutch 34 to 0. A week later the Alma Scots added to the gloom as they notched a 32-0 victory. On October 22 Hope hosted Grand Rapids Junior College at the Sixth Street field known at the time as "Waterworks Park." The afternoon's competition was actually a double-header with Holland High taking a 6-0 decision from Grand Rapids Union in the early game while Hope dropped a hard-fought game to J.C. by the score of 7 to 3. Dick Japinga's drop kick field goal would prove to be Hope's only score of the season. The double-header idea was attempted again on October 29 but rain delayed the start of Holland High's game and the Hope-Ferris contest which was to follow, had to be cancelled.

It was a game but outmatched Hope 11 that traveled to Kalamazoo on November 5 to meet Western State. A 34-0 Western lead at halftime ballooned to 65-0 at game's end despite liberal substituting by Coach Spaulding. Records list it as Hope's worst defeat ever. Battered but unbowed, the Dutchmen welcomed the end of a dismal season.

Cross country in the fall of 1921 was limited to a lone meet in East Lansing, where Hope's five-man team gave a good account of itself in finishing fourth behind M.A.C., the University of Michigan, and Ypsilanti Normal. Team members were Delbert Kinney, Gerrit Wissink, Irvin Borgman, Bert Kempers, and Captain Stanley Schippers.

If football results were disappointing, the anticipation of basketball was at the other end of the spectrum. Thirty men turned out for the initial practice session. The contingent was led by Captain Dick Japinga and the entire team from the previous season, a team which had posted an impressive 15 and 7 record. The season opener with the Grand Rapids Franklin Independents resulted in a resounding 44-12 victory, with Japinga scoring 21. On Friday, December 6, Hope hosted Calvin College before a capacity crowd in Carnegie Gymnasium. The heated rivalry of later years had not yet developed and the full house must be attributed early season curiosity based on the success of the 1920-21 team. Hope's second team downed their counterpart, the Calvin Rivals, 35-24 in the prelim game. In the varsity contest Hope's experience was evident as the Dutch emerged on the long end of a 54-20 score. The team's next challenge was a swing through Indiana and Wisconsin. Jack's charges dropped three of five games on this trip but gained valuable experience while learning to deal with the overconfidence factor. Scores were as follows:

Whiting Red Crowns 29 - Hope 24
Hope 39 - Cedar Grove 9
Hope 34 - Oostburg Quicksteps 11
Scheboygan Mathewsons 24 - Hope 19
Cedarburg 42 - Hope 36

Returning to Holland, the starting five of Japinga, Van Putten, Ben Riemersma, George Irving, and Mike Schuurmans put together a five-game win streak. A strong alumni team pushed Jack's unit before losing by a score of 35-26. Two Grand Rapids teams were the next victims. The Grand Rapids YMCA fell 36-12 while Grand Rapids Junior College was overpowered 32 to 5.

Hope's victory at Kalamazoo College was by all odds the most dramatic of the season. Ralph Young, later the outstanding Director of Athletics at Michigan State, was the Kalamazoo coach. His Hornets held a slim 30-29 lead as the final seconds ticked away. George Irving's shot from center court was of the desperation variety but it parted the net and Hope's fine team had a one point win to savor as they traveled the 50 miles back to Holland.

The Dutch were riding high as they prepared for the school's second encounter with De Paul University of Chicago. The Blue Demons would one day be a national power under legendary coach Ray Meyer, but in 1922 they did not enjoy such status and were quite unprepared to meet the charged-up Dutchmen. Hope's 57-17 victory included an outstanding performance by Captain Dick Japinga, who scored 33 points. His 16 field goals would be welcomed by any present day coach and when one recalls that until 1937 a center jump occurred after every basket, the achievement becomes quite remarkable.

Western State put an end to Hope's win streak with strong defense and an early instance of "slow down" tactics. The final score of 18 to 9 left Jack's squad in a state of mild frustration that lingered for two more games. A traveling team from the east known as the New York Nationals made a stop in Holland and pinned a 31-23 defeat on the Dutchmen before Kalamazoo College came to Carnegie Gym intent on avenging their earlier loss. Hope built an early 12 point lead, then saw it dwindle to one in the closing minutes. In a rebound scramble Milton "Bud" Hinga of Kazoo scored what proved to be the winning basket. Hope had one last chance. As time ran out Dick Japinga was fouled but failed to convert the free throw necessary to send the game into overtime. All in all, it was an evening of considerable excitement and not a little irony. Kalamazoo's Bud Hinga would become a coaching legend at Hope while Dick Japinga's son Bill would become a tennis star at Kalamazoo College before joining the Hope faculty and coaching men's tennis in the 1980s and '90s.

Hope returned to its winning ways by downing the Grand Rapids YMCA 21-12, but lost a 29-28 heartbreaker to M.A.C. Western State was next and Jack's now seasoned team was ready. Hope's 21-16 win avenged the earlier slow down loss. The momentum carried over and produced a 19-17 victory over Mount Pleasant Normal as well as a second victory over Calvin, this time by a score of 36 to 14. An impressive 40 to 12 win over Tri State of Angola, Indiana made it four in a row. To close out the season Jack's crew made a three game swing through the eastern part of the state. Dick Japinga and Dyke Van Putten were unable to make the trip, but Hope won two of the three despite the handicap. Scores were as follows:

Hope 46 - Detroit College of Law 14
Mc Graw's Independents of Jackson 22 - Hope 17
Hope 24 - Orchard Lake St. Mary's 10

The season's record of 16 and 8 against some tough competition was indeed impressive. Many would feel that this was Jack's finest team.

Spring sports in 1922 were limited to four baseball games and one track meet. In track a meet was arranged with the men from Western Theological Seminary. Seven events were closely contested on the 12th Street track with Hope emerging the winner by a score of 33 to 30. Hope's baseball opener with Western State featured a battery of J. Dyke Van Putten and Ben Riemersma. Several errors contributed to Hope's downfall as the Western team took the contest by a 10-4 score. Close scores were definitely not to be the order of this season as the Dutch trounced Grand Rapids Junior College 18 to 4, then lost to the Holland Independents, 21 to 2. In the season finale, Grand Rapids Junior College was again Hope's victim, this time 11-3. In addition to his baseball and track chores, Jack organized Hope's first spring football practice. Supervision was delegated to some of the players and though limited in scope, the program is evidence of Jack's genuine desire to upgrade the sport.

By September of 1922 the discouragement of the previous fall was forgotten. Twenty two men responded to Coach Schouten's call and Charles "Chuck" Van Zanten was elected captain. Hopes were high as the team traveled to Ramona Park to meet Grand Rapids Junior College on October 7. A steady rain hampered both squads but JC, with a 20 pound weight advantage, was able to punch over a score in the second quarter which held up for an eventual 6-0 triumph. A week later the team took a train to Big Rapids where rain was again the order of the day. This time neither team was able to score. Hope was thankful for small favors as the 0-0 tie enabled the Dutch to avoid defeat for the first time in two seasons.

Two weeks later Ferris came to Holland for a return game that was similar in many respects. There was no rain on this Saturday but the game was preceded by a contest between Holland High and South High of Grand Rapids. The final quarter of the college game was played in semi-darkness. Once again it was a defensive standoff. In the third quarter Hope's aggressiveness paid off as Ferris was forced behind its own goal for a safety. The game ended 2-0 in the darkness, but the Dutch rejoiced in their first gridiron victory in two years. The season finale was played against Western State's Reserve team with the Kalamazoo men winning, 6-0. As the season came to a close the mood was definitely upbeat for Jack's men.

To aid in the '22 cross country program Jack secured the services of Francis Ihrman who had graduated from Hope in 1921. Ihrman's squad included Irwin Borgman, Martin Hoeksema, Henry Louwsma, George Schutt, Elmer Van Lare, Ray Van Zoeren, and Gerrit Wissink. The team gave a good account of itself in the November 11 intercollegiate meet at East Lansing, finishing in third place behind Western State Normal and Kalamazoo College.

Also in the fall of '22, word came from Japan via Harvey Oltmans that Johnny Lavan, Hope's gift to major league baseball, was playing exhibition baseball in that country along with pitching great Herb Pennock. Of interest at home was the formation on campus of a girl's auxiliary known as the **Athletic Debt Diggers**. It was composed of four girls each from the sophomore, Junior, and senior classes. Members served as a mobile concession stand at various athletic events and were identifiable by their cardigan sweaters and "A.D.D." wooden shoe emblem. The organization flourished for a number of years, making a significant contribution to the economic well-being of the athletic program. Its eventual demise was due to a variety of reasons, including the advent of feminism, which viewed the activity as somewhat demeaning to women.

George "Pork" Irving and Captain Ben "Beans" Riemersma led the basketball returnees in 1922. Hope opened the season with victories over the Grand Rapids Franklins (13-7), and the Muskegon Independents (38-8), and then embarked on their now customary Wisconsin junket. The trip proved a sobering experience as the Dutch dropped all five contests. Scores were as follows:

Neenah Boosters 22 - Hope 5
Sheboygan 30 - Hope 22 (OT)
Plymouth 28 - Hope 13
Two Rivers 23 - Hope 17
Manitowoc 23 - Hope 22

The team returned to familiar haunts for an up and down season. The Grand Rapids YMCA fell before the Dutchmen

22 to 10 but Kalamazoo College, with another fine team, took the Hope team, 33 to 17. Victoria College, a traveling Canadian team, suffered a 28-18 defeat at the hands of Hope but two Indiana teams edged Jack's men in well-played games. Scores were: Indianapolis "Y" 27 - Hope 20, and Michigan City "Y" 34 - Hope 28. Hope got revenge of a sort by downing the Whiting Owls, 27-23, but in a return game the K College Hornets were again too much. The final this time was Kalamazoo 25, Hope 21. The team bounced back to defeat Anthony Wayne Institute of Detroit 20 to 11 but lost a close one to Western State Normal 22-20. Three straight wins boosted morale as Hope took Mount Pleasant Normal 17-13, Calvin 32-15, and Michigan City "Y" 24-22. Hope's 11th defeat came at the hands of Western State Normal, 40 to 14. Loyal fans were given a special treat in the season finale when the alumni team of 1918 came back for a go at the '23 unit. Despite the presence of Clarence Heemstra and Harvey Ramaker, the alumni were unable to match Jack's latest contingent. The final score showed Hope 33, Alumni 18. The season record stood at 10-11 in a transition year.

In the spring of 1923 Hope could manage only three victories in a 10 game baseball schedule. Home games were played at Waterworks (later Riverview) Park located at Columbia Avenue and Fifth Street. Freshman pitcher Jim Poppen made his presence known but the strong schedule resulted in seven defeats. Scores were as follows:

Western State Normal 6 - Hope 0
Hope 7 - Holland Furnace Warm Friends 1
Hope 3 - Ferris 1
Holland Independents 4 - Hope 3
Hope 16 - Ferris 7
Mount Pleasant Normal 7 - Hope 4
Orchard Lake St. Mary's 11 - Hope 2
M.A.C. 3 - Hope 1
Western State Normal 11 - Hope 1
Hillsdale 4 - Hope 1

1921-22 Hope College Basketball Team (16-8)

Top Row L to R: Coach Jack Schouten, Mike Schuurmans, Ken Van Lente. **Front Row:** George Irving, J. Dyke Van Putten, Captain Dick Japinga, Ben Riemersma, Garrett De Jong.

There was no track team in 1923 but two Hope men participated in a tennis tournament at Michigan Agricultural College. George Irving sustained an ankle sprain in the early going and was forced to withdraw, while Ray "Arab" Zwemer drew the number one seed and, after a strong effort, succumbed, 6-4, 6-1.

Ken Van Lente captained the '23 grid team from his center position. Adrian "Cappy" Buys was sidelined by early injuries but remained with the team as Jack's assistant. James Ottipoby and George Damson were mainstays on a team that earned an even split of an abbreviated schedule. Grand Rapids J.C. bested the Dutch 7-0 in the season opener on October 6, but two weeks later it was a different story as Julius Van Eenenaam's touchdown was enough to stop Ferris, 6-0. On October 27 Hope met Detroit City College. Some of Hope's regulars were unable to play due to severe reactions to smallpox vaccinations and the 20-0 loss was hard to take under such circumstances. The team was intact for a return game with Ferris on November 3 and the Dutch closed out the season with a 7-0 victory as Floyd "Flip" Vander Meer scored the only touchdown and Ted Vandenbrink kicked the point after.

In Hope's other fall sport the '23 cross country team achieved its customary third place finish at East Lansing with Egbert Schutt finishing first of the Dutch runners. Elmer Van Lare captained the team that also included Delbert Kinney, Barnerd Luben, Albert Berkompas, Fred Meyer, Richard Mallery, Walter Roughgarden, and Gerrit Wissink.

Jack's 1923-24 basketball aggregation, under the able leadership of Captain George Irving, was off to a good start with four straight victories. Coach Schouten had reason to be optimistic despite a tough schedule. Scores were as follows:

Hope 41 - Ottawa Athletic Club of Grand Haven 14
Hope 27 - Zion Athletic Club 12
Hope 38 - Calvin College 13
Hope 18 - Grand Rapids YMCA 15

The Michigan State Aggies halted the victory string by embarrassing Jack's crew, 20 to 7 in the season's only meeting between the teams. Next it was the University of Detroit who edged Hope by two baskets, 18-14, but the Dutch bounced back to take Huntington College of Indiana, 21 to 10. The victory set the stage for the battle with traditional rival Kalamazoo College. Hope managed a 31-27 win in overtime, then squeaked by the Indianapolis "Y," 29-28. Next it was Kalamazoo College again, this time in friendly Carnegie Gym. Hope's 37-19 victory marked one of the few times that the Dutch were able to take both games.

With Kalamazoo's other college however, it was a different story. Western State's 20-14 win preceded a two game split with the Michigan City "Y." The first game belonged to Hope in overtime, 31-30, while the Indiana boys had the best of it by a 31-21 score on the second night. Hope fell victim by the same score (31-21) as they met Valparaiso University for the first time. Another hard-fought six-point loss to Western State was discouraging. This time the score was 26-20. The pattern of close scores continued through the remainder of the season and included three more games against Hoosier opponents. Hope edged Manchester, 24-23, then suffered a similar fate at the hands of Huntington College, 17-16. In the second contest with Valparaiso, Jack's men narrowed the gap before losing out by a single basket, 22-20.

Hope fans were reluctant to see such a fine season conclude and Jack was persuaded to meet the city's strong Holland Furnace team in a best of three series. The Furnace team included former college stars from Kalamazoo and Michigan State and was coached by Charles "Cubby" Drew. An exciting first night saw the Furnace men win a close one, 26 to 24. Jack's team hoped to even the count on the second night but the Furnace team, led by former Kalamazoo College star Bud Hinga, was too much. Hinga scored 21 of his team's 33 points, 15 in the second half, and Hope took the loss 33 to 26. It had been great competition and Coach Drew's men were duly crowned City Champs.

Track was again dormant in the spring of 1924 but the baseball team did itself proud with a fine 5-3 record. Pitcher Jim Poppen found the going tough in the season opener at East Lansing as ragged fielding resulted in an 8-2 victory for the Aggies. Heine Albers took the mound against Western State but his effort was wasted as Hope bats were silent in a 4-0 shutout. Charles Maher, later an outstanding coach at his alma mater, caught for Western. Meeting strong opponents seemed to pay off as the Dutch downed Ferris 16-3, then took the measure of Kalamazoo, 4 to 1. Hope got above .500 by shellacking the Holland Independents, 12 to 1. Kalamazoo College had its revenge in a well played 5-4 victory before Hope shut out Ferris 3-0 in a second meeting. The game at Albion was rained out, but Hope was able to play the following day at Orchard Lake, edging St. Mary's, 3-2. Jack's talented crew closed out the season on a positive note with a convincing 11-7 victory over Central State Normal of Mount Pleasant.

Throughout the spring Jack also managed to set up twice-a-week football drills for those players not on the baseball squad. It was evidence of Coach Schouten's continuing efforts to upgrade performances in that sport.

Jack Schouten's fine record as a basketball coach in some ways obscured his gallant attempts to improve the football program. The recruiting of promising athletes was practically unknown in the 1920s and an overworked Jack would have been hard pressed to find time for it even if the practice were widespread. In addition to his duties as Director of Athletics it should be remembered that he coached all sports (four, sometimes five) and still felt a responsibility to conduct physical education classes for the women students. In addition, all students took a natural science at some level.

This meant a laboratory running into the late afternoon and leaving a short period of daylight for practice sessions. Football was especially vulnerable as there was no switch to daylight saving time. Since the labs were sacred, Jack endeavored to offset the handicap in the fall of 1924 by installing floodlights along the bank on the south side of Carnegie Gym. But all gimmicks including spring practice and even white footballs at one point, were of little effect when numbers were lacking. The small squads made it difficult to scrimmage, especially when injuries took their toll.

By the fall of 1924 Hope's enrollment had climbed to 458 and President Edward Dimnent had reason to be optimistic about the school's future. The grid campaign was off to a good start under Captain Floyd "Flip" Vander Meer. Ferris came to town for the opener and attendance was good. Ken Van Lente blocked a kick and Lee Kleis subsequently scored from the 4 yard line for the game's only score. But Hope's 6-0 win would be its only taste of victory during another frustrating season. The season's second encounter resulted in a 42-0 thrashing at the hands of the University of Detroit Reserves. But the Detroiters, in charge all the way, had high praise for the competitiveness of Jack's men to the very end. Hopes were still high as the Dutchmen journeyed to Houseman Field in Grand Rapids to meet the Junior College team coached by John Bos. Sparkling plays by halfback Lee Kleis were erased by officials' decisions. Early in the game Lee returned a kickoff to the J.C. 11 yard line. On a subsequent fourth down play Kleis appeared to be over the goal line but the officials ruled that J.C. had held and the ball went over. Later in the contest Kleis evaded all tacklers in a brilliant 72-yard punt return only to have the score called back by the all familiar holding penalty. There were no instant replays to review and the Dutch went back to Holland with a 0-0 tie. In the Kalamazoo game George Damson intercepted a pass and raced 50 yards to score. Ted Vanden Brink kicked the point. A subsequent score gave Hope a surprising 13-0 lead before Kalamazoo's strong passing attack gave them a 19-13 half-time lead. It was all Kalamazoo in the second half resulting in a final of 38 to 13. Hopes for a second victory over Ferris were dashed when injuries removed George Damson, Norm Vander Hart, Ken Van Lente, and Jim Ver Meulen. Jack's thin line of reserves simply could not fill the gap and the Ferris men prevailed 8-0. Hope traveled to Ohio for the season finale against a strong Defiance 11. In the opening quarter Ted Vanden Brink intercepted a pass on his own 20 and dashed 80 yards for the score. The quarter score showed Hope leading 7-6 but by halftime the Ohioans had built a 26-7 margin. The Dutch stiffened on defense in the second half but still were forced to give up two more touchdowns. Failing to mount an offense, Hope suffered a 40 to 6 defeat in a contest mercifully shortened by darkness. The trip home was a long one.

In cross country Jack was able to enlist the aid of Stanley Schipper (Hope '22) who helped prepare the team for the annual run at M.A.C. In 1924 the meet was held on October 25. Western State Normal took top honors followed by Ypsilanti Normal, and Hope in its usual third position. Six schools finished behind the Hope team. Jack Kik crossed the line first for Hope, and other team members were Del Kinney, Elmer Van Lare, Barnerd Luben, Ray Van Zoeren, Arnold Van Wyk, and Nelson Doak.

A section of the 1924 **Milestone** presented Isla Pruim and Fred Yonkman as having been elected the most popular Hope students for that school year. The popularity of "Fritz," coupled with his athletic ability, made him an odds on choice for basketball captain as the 1924-25 season opened. It would be a good season despite the somewhat limited schedule of 13 games. The fine record of 10 victories versus only three defeats is not surprising when one considers the unusual experience and depth available to Jack. In addition to Yonkman, the squad included George Irving, Ben Riemersma, Ken Van Lente, Ted Vanden Brink, James Ottipoby, Jim Poppen, John Henry Albers, Mel Lubbers, and the up and coming star, Lee Kleis.

The team was off to a running start with three consecutive victories. Three teams from Grand Rapids were the victims: The Royal Ravens, 49-10, Trinity Lutheran, 22-12, and Calvin College, 26-11. A traveling team known as the Denver Tigers broke the bubble by a score of 28-21, but the Dutch were not outclassed by any means. It was a confident team that took the measure of Manchester College, 41-28, and Concordia of Fort Wayne, 38-30. In the latter contest freshman Lee Kleis scored 13 points. Next it was traditional rival Kalamazoo College and the Dutch again prevailed (22-16) despite the early departure of James Ottipoby with a sprained ankle. A trip to Western State's campus in Kalamazoo resulted in a disappointing 31-20 loss but Hope fans still believed their team to be the best and jammed Carnegie Gym a week later for a rematch. They were rewarded with an impressive 32-16 Hope victory. As the season wound down the Hope faithful were aware that they were indeed watching one of Hope's better teams in the 25 years since the game began in Holland. In succession Jack's squad downed Michigan State College, 20-19, Kalamazoo College, 43-18, and the University of Detroit Titans, 29-15. A unique feature of the latter game was the fact that Detroit was held scoreless in the first half, the intermission score reading Hope 12, U. of D. 0. In a state of understandable euphoria, the team traveled to Detroit for the return game that would wrap up the season. Meanwhile, the Titans, still smarting from their embarrassment at the hands of the small town five, were more than ready. Their strong play forced the Dutch into a rare sub-par performance. One observer counted 27 missed shots under the basket by the Hope players. Detroit had revenge to the tune of 40 to 15. But one game does not a season make and the team quickly shook off the anti-climatic ending. Once again, by comparing season records and common opponents,

Hope declared themselves state intercollegiate champions. MIAA Champion Alma, 10-0 in the league and a splendid 18-3 overall, would seem to have had a legitimate claim but little was made of the matter and Hope fans were happy with their favorite sons. On May 14 the team bowed out appropriately with a special dinner at the home of Jack Schouten.

The baseball team of 1925 and Coach Jack experienced mixed emotions when it was learned that pitcher Jim Poppen had been signed by the Baltimore Orioles of the International League. Jim left early for spring training and was eventually assigned to Waynesboro of the Blue Ridge League. He was recalled by Baltimore after the Pittsburgh Pirates offered to buy Poppen in their trek to the National League pennant.

First baseman Ken Van Lente was elected captain of the '25 team while outfielder Jim De Pree served as manager. The season opened on April 11 against Western State and the slants of Jim Poppen were sorely missed as Western crossed the plate 10 times enroute to a 10-2 victory. A week later Hope posted a 6-2 win over Calvin. Big blows in this contest were a triple by Ben Riemersma and Ted Vanden Brink's home run. The team came into its own against Kalamazoo College behind the brilliant pitching performance of Heinie Albers. His 17-0 shutout included 17 strikeouts. On May 8 the Dutch downed Calvin in a second game 8 to 2 but Michigan State College pounded the Dutchmen 13 to 1 in East Lansing. Al De Groot's home run was Hope's only tally. Hope bounced back to take Central State of Mount Pleasant 9-6 but lost to Kalamazoo College 4-2 as pitcher Clint Cole was wild in the early innings. Jack's men outlasted Orchard Lake St. Mary's 3-2 in a 10 inning classic as Gerald Elenbaas singled in the tenth, stole second, and came home on Ben Riemersma's game winning single. The return game with Central State Normal resulted in Hope's second shutout victory of the season, this time 4-0. Ferris Institute came from behind in the ninth inning to beat Hope 11-9 in what had appeared to be an easy win. The season ended on a positive note in a fun game with an alumni team. Jack's crew shut out the "old timers" 16 to 0.

There was no track in 1925 but Western State Normal hosted an intercollegiate tennis tournament for the state of Michigan and three Hope men decided to enter. Eugene Damstra, Fred Yonkman, and Lee Kleis journeyed to Kalamazoo and managed to score 2 points in the tourney. Damstra lost, 6-0, 6-2, to Western's Lee Hart, the eventual state champion. Yonkman defeated the Ypsilanti entry but lost to a Kalamazoo man. In doubles, Damstra and Kleis defeated the Alma duo but succumbed, 6-1, 6-3, to the strong Western team of Hart and Zuidema.

A number of factors in the fall of 1925 seemed to indicate that Hope's football fortunes would be decidedly better. For starters, Jack had two assistants in Ray Nelson and Bruce Raymond, the latter a new history professor at Hope. They would ease the load of coaching the unusually large turnout of 47 candidates. The team had excellent leadership from Captain George Damson and Manager Jim Ver Meulen. Also, for the first time, Hope had a band. Herbert Johnson of Grand Rapids was engaged as director and the group performed at all home games. In a 1985 interview Jim Ver Meulen related to this writer how he had played in the pregame band program and then participated in the game. Brothers Matt and Bill Peelen were team members whose sons Matt and George would one day contribute to Hope's fine teams of the late 1950s. Almost unnoticed was a freshman from Baldwin, Wisconsin, named Alvin Vanderbush who would leave his mark on Hope College as Professor, Coach, and Director of Athletics in the 1940s and '50s.

For reasons unknown, Hope's first football game in '25 was not played until October 16, when the team traveled to Ferris. In a 1985 conversation George Damson recalled packing his football equipment at home on the night before the game, then racing down 8th Street with said gear at 6:00 a.m., fearful of missing the train to Big Rapids. Happily for Hope, George caught the train and later the passing combination of Damson to Lee Kleis accounted for both touchdowns as the Dutchmen shut out Ferris 12-0 on a muddy field. The game with Detroit City College (later Wayne State) was also played in the mud. Neither team was able to score until, with five minutes remaining in the game, Russ Japinga's punt was blocked. Two plays later Detroit scored to claim the 7-0 victory. Hope's third game was played in wet snow against Grand Rapids Junior College. Tackle Norm Vander Hart and halfback Lee Kleis turned in stellar performances, but Hope's 3-0 win resulted from Tom Van Zanden's dropkick field goal from the 20-yard line in the final quarter. The next train ride took the team to Findley, Ohio, where fumbles and a blocked kick led to a 13-0 Findley lead at halftime. Hope's second-half comeback featured Russ Japinga's TD plunge and an end run score by Kleis. Lee then place kicked the all-important point and Hope went home with a 13-13 tie. A great deal of publicity preceded Hope's Armistice Day game with Kalamazoo College and fans could sense a winning season as they made their way to Riverview Park. But Coach Chester Barnard brought a well oiled machine to Holland that included superstar Bob Black. Three of Kalamazoo's four first half touchdowns were the result of Black's passes. Hope closed the door in the third quarter, but in the final stanza Black scooped up a fumble and ran 26 yards for the score. The final was Kalamazoo 34 - Hope 0. Hope's 2-2-1 record would be its best in the decade of the '20s.

The cross country team also knew hard times. In the annual Michigan Intercollegiate meet at East Lansing, Hope had to settle for sixth place as their ace, Captain Jacob Kik, suffered a foot injury midway in the race. He was forced to drop out temporarily, then gamely finished the course in 24th place. Del Kinney, in 15th place, was first to finish for the Dutchmen. Other participants were Ray Fieldhouse, Barnerd Luben, Paul Van Ess, and George Clicquenoi. Lester Bossard served as alternate. Ypsilanti Normal finished first of the eight teams entered.

Five veterans were gone from the 1925-26 basketball squad, but the team, in new uniforms, was off to a good start. Heine Albers was captain of a group that included Lee Kleis, Jim Poppen, Ted Vandenbrink, Mel Lubbers, Russ Japinga, Clarence Diephouse, and Eugene Damstra. Despite early victories the team lost three, one-point games and ended with a 7-12 record, one of the few losing seasons in Jack's tenure as coach. Scores were as follows:

Hope 58 - Firlich Hardware of G.R. 15
Hope 35 - American Seating of G.R. 10
Hope 35 - Muskegon YMCA 10
Alumni 35 - Hope 34
Hope 26 Bethany Church of G.R. 22
Manchester 36 - Hope 28
Hope 28 - Central State Normal 19
Western State Normal 31 - Hope 15
Hope 38 - Basch Jewelers of G.R. 30
Kalamazoo College 36 - Hope 30
Albion 32 - Hope 31
Indianapolis "Y" 34 - Hope 27
Hope 30 - Central State Normal 20
St. Mary's 33 - Hope 31
Manchester 50 - Hope 17
Concordia of Indiana 25 - Hope 19
Kalamazoo College 34 - Hope 26
Holland Furnace 41 - Hope 32
Holland Furnace 48 - Hope 31

In the Alumni game, former stars Dick Japinga and "Chief" Ottipoby scored in the closing minutes to assure the one-point victory. Hope's first game with Manchester was officiated by Judson Hyames, Western State's fabled baseball coach, in whose honor Western's baseball stadium was later named. The "city series" at season's end was played in the Holland Armory, and the Holland Furnace team prevailed in both contests, with Dick Japinga and Bud Hinga doing most of the scoring for the winners.

Hope's 4-5 baseball record in the spring of 1926 belies the fact that some exciting baseball was played. Jim Poppen was captain of a team that "plunged right in," opening against Notre Dame. The Irish were too much for the Dutch on April 17 in a 16-1 victory that saw Lee Kleis collect the only hit and drive in the only run for Hope. A week later Jack's crew took out their frustration on a hapless Grand Rapids Junior College team to the tune of 14 to 3 behind the battery of Clint Cole and Russ Japinga. Heine Albers took the mound against Western State but the improved Hope nine still could not match the strong team from Kalamazoo and lost, 7 to 2. In Hope's first game with Kalamazoo College, Albers pitched against Bob Black, Kalamazoo's all-round star athlete. With Kalamazoo leading 3-1 in the fourth inning, the game was halted by rain and the contest went into the books as a Kalamazoo victory. But a week later, on May 7, the same teams met in Kalamazoo and it was a different story. Big Jim Poppen was on the hill for Hope and gave up but four hits while striking out seven. Poppen's two doubles aided his own cause while Albers contributed a three-run triple in the eighth; final score, Hope 9 to Kalamazoo 4. Hope continued to produce runs as they downed Ferris, 10-3, at Riverview Park. Poppen was again impressive with 16 strikeouts. On May 13 Hope met Michigan State College as part of the latter's Founders Day celebration. Heinie Albers went all the way for the Dutch, but the home team prevailed, 6-2, in a well-played game. The crowd was estimated to number three thousand, probably the all-time record for Hope College baseball.

After a second game with Ferris was rained out, Jack's men were back on track with a 14-4 pounding of Grand Rapids Junior College. This time it was Clint Cole registering 16 strikeouts on the mound for Hope. The game's big blow was Heinie Albers' home run over the center field fence. The season ended on May 29 with a 6-2 loss at Orchard Lake St. Mary's.

Hope's era as an independent in athletics was drawing to a close. On June 3, 1926, representatives of the Michigan Intercollegiate Athletic Association met in Albion. One of their actions was to approve Hope's application for membership. The inclusion of Hope in the various schedules would not take place until early December, but there was great rejoicing as the news was relayed to Holland.

REFERENCES - CHAPTER 4

1. The **Anchor**, March, 1921.

CHAPTER 5

LEAGUE AFFILIATION - FIRST CONTESTS IN THE MIAA

The acceptance of Hope College into the Michigan Intercollegiate Athletic Association would be finalized in December. This of course meant that for one more fall season Hope would compete as an independent. Jack Schouten was able to enlist the aid of Red Cornwall as an assistant football coach for the season, and Egbert Fell was elected captain. The 1926 starting line up included Al Vanderbush at left guard and Henry Steffens at center. Steffens would later assist Hope's next coach, Milton "Bud" Hinga, while Vanderbush would become head coach following World War II. Hope's contest with Flint Junior College on October 8 was all that a coach could ask for in a season opener. The defense was superb in shutting out the Flint team while Lee Kleis scored two touchdowns to lead the offense. Russ Japinga and freshman Paul Nettinga also crossed the goal line to make the final count 24-0. Albion of the MIAA was Hope's next opponent and the game was seen as a preview of things to come. After a scoreless first quarter, Albion pushed across a touchdown to take a 7-0 halftime lead. A hard-fought third quarter was scoreless but Dutchmen misplays in the final period allowed the Britons to score two more times. Hope's offense failed to materialize and Jack's men were beaten 21-0. A lack of offense continued to plague the Dutch as they dropped games to Detroit City College and Western State Frosh by scores of 3-0 and 10-0. The game with Grand Rapids Junior College ended in bizarre fashion. J.C. took an early 6-0 lead but Paul Nettinga's score tied it up 6-6. Late in the contest J. C. moved into field goal range and Russell "Rud" Formsma dropped back to attempt the important three pointer. The kick was low, but a Hope lineman's upraised hand deflected the ball upwards and over the goal post giving JC the 9-6 victory. The Hope attack had been weakened earlier when fullback Russ Japinga suffered a dislocated elbow. Hope closed out the season by dropping a close one to Findlay College, 13 to 6. In early December the Holland Exchange Club honored the teams from Hope and Holland High with a football banquet. Speaker for the occasion was George Veenker, Hope class of 1916. Veenker's time at Hope had included the infamous three-year football ban - - a worse fate, he insisted, than Hope's 1-5 record.

The main activity for Hope's 1926 cross country team was participation in the llth annual State Intercollegiate Meet at East Lansing. George Clicquenoi captained the team that finished in fifth place behind Michigan Normal (Ypsilanti); Kalamazoo College, Western State, and the Michigan State Reserves. Sixty-nine men participated in all. Jacob Kik finished 13th and Fred Dunnewold 18th, and both men received silver medals for placing in the second 10. Other Hope participants were Rob Ritchie (29th), Alfred Popma (30th), Clarence Berkompas (36th), and Clicquenoi (39th). Ken Brown of Western was the individual winner with a time of 26:28.

Hope's time for official league membership was now at hand and was proudly announced in the **Anchor**:

> The "consummation devoutly to be wished" has finally taken place". Hope College has been received into full membership in the Michigan Intercollegiate Athletic Association.
>
> On Friday, December 3, Coach Jack Schouten, Professor (Egbert) Winter, and Neil Van Oostenberg (student) journeyed to Albion where they met with representatives of the other colleges in the Association and received official announcement that Hope's application for membership had been considered and favorably voted on...[1]

Schedules were drawn for basketball, track, cross country, and tennis. Member schools at the time included Albion, Alma, Hillsdale, Hope, Kalamazoo, and Olivet. Michigan Normal of Ypsilanti, a member since 1892, had withdrawn in the spring of 1926. Adrian had withdrawn in 1922 but would rejoin in 1937. Hope's enrollment of 545 in the fall of '26 made the MIAA's newest member the second largest in the conference. Only Albion, with about 750 students, was larger.

Hope's prowess as a state basketball power was about to be tested. It was unfortunate that the school's first season in MIAA basketball would feature a team severely depleted by graduation. Russ Japinga and Captain Lee Kleis were the only returnees but Jack had high hopes for freshman Alvin "Boo" Cook. The opener saw Hope drop a four-point decision to the Muskegon Triangles, 31-27, but the next three games were victories. In turn, Hope downed Grand Rapids Boters, 18-17, Grand Rapids Bethany Majors 32-18, and the Wealthy Florals, also of Grand Rapids, 38-21. The stage was set for Hope's first ever MIAA contest. The game was played in Hope's Carnegie Gym on January 14, 1927, with Olivet College providing the opposition. The fates were kind to the home team and Hopeites reveled in their 40 to 31 landmark victory. With a four-game win streak, the Dutchmen now prepared to meet old rival, Kalamazoo College, the 1925-26 MIAA champion. Hope played well but bowed to the champions, 31-20. This was followed by an overtime loss to Alma, 28-22, and the Dutch were suddenly aware that competition in the MIAA would demand an all-out effort. A non-conference game with Flint Junior College proved a welcome respite at this point. In the course of the opening tip-off, the ball was batted to the sidelines where it struck scorekeeper Albert Lampen in the face, dislodging his glasses. The good natured professor was undaunted and continued to

1926-27 Hope College Basketball Team
Hope's First MIAA Team

Top Row L to R: Coach Jack Schouten, Nicholas Prakken, Alvin "Boo" Cook, J. Dean Martin, Paul Nettinga, Russ Japinga. **Front Row:** Clarence Diephouse, Bernard De Pree, Captain Lee Kleis, Harold "Brute" Japinga, Carl "Cox" Van Lente, Laverne Vander Hill.

document Hope's impressive 52 to 11 victory.

Hope's second encounter with Kalamazoo was like the first, but Jack's men narrowed the margin by five. The final this time was Kalamazoo 31, Hope 25. Boo Cook was sidelined by injuries and missed the Michigan State game, which Hope lost 46 to 31. Cook returned for the second meeting with Olivet and the Dutch were even more impressive than in the first game, the final count being Hope 33, Olivet 13. Lee Kleis scored 13 to lead Hope in their first MIAA contest with Albion. The teams battled to a 25-25 tie at the end of regulation play but Albion owned the overtime, winning 32 to 25. Despite strong play by Lee Kleis and Boo Cook, Western State got the better of Hope to the tune of 31-19, but Hope bounced back to thrash the hapless Flint J.C. team, 58 to 11. In another non-league game the Hope crew came up three points short, losing to St. Mary's, 37-34. MIAA teams continued to be tough and Hope dropped a second contest to Alma, this time 29-20. At this point the Dutchmen found the going difficult, to say the least, as they lost again to Western State, 46-25, to Holland Furnace, 36-28, and to Albion, 41-26. As the curtain came down on Hope's first season in MIAA play the standings showed the team tied with Hillsdale for fourth place. The order of finish was as follows:

Albion	10-0
Kalamazoo	8-2
Alma	6-4
Hillsdale	2-6
Hope	2-6
Olivet	0-10

Lee Kleis was named to the All-MIAA second team while Boo Cook received honorable mention.

Track and field had known some bright moments in the teens but the college had failed to field a team after the 1922 season. Membership in the MIAA now provided the needed catalyst to reawaken interest in the sport. In Hope's first meet on May 6 the small aggregation met Kalamazoo College and was soundly beaten. There is no record of the score but Hope's only first came in the broad jump, when John Nauta tied a Kalamazoo man for the top spot in that event. One week later Hope's team had jelled and downed Olivet 65 to 39. Twelve events were contested with Hope winning eight of the 12. Firsts were recorded as follows:

100 yard dash - John Nauta
220 yard dash - Frank Mosher
880 yard run - Walter De Velder
Mile run - Alfred Popma
2 mile run - Fred Dunnewold
discus - George De Roos
high jump - Marvin Meengs
mile relay - Hope team

Olivet took first in the 440 yard dash, the shot put, the broad jump, and the javelin. The MIAA track championship was determined by the order of finish in the MIAA Field Day Meet which, in 1927, was held at Albion College. Hope had at least one entrant in each of the 15 events but the Dutchmen's new found confidence was severely shaken when Fred Dunnewold's fourth place in the two mile run proved to be their only scoring performance. If Hope's return to track and field was less than spectacular, it was a beginning and the sport would not be abandoned again.

Jack Schouten's 1927 baseball aggregation under Captain Gerald Elenbaas posted a 4-9 record. The team was awarded third place in the MIAA standings as a result of the Field Day Tournament held at Albion. The season opened with a 13-1 loss to Western State which was followed by a 3 to 1 loss to Kalamazoo College. In the latter contest Clint Cole's pitching effort was wasted as eight men were left on base. Hope's lone run came on Clarence Howard's home run. A trip north saw the Dutch drop successive games to Central State, 11-8, and to Alma, 9-8, but on May 4 Clint Cole was brilliant in shutting out Kalamazoo, 1-0. He gave up four hits and struck out 12. The season was marked by close games as Michigan State got the better of Hope, 7-5, and St. Mary's edged the Dutch, 7-6, in 11 innings. Cole was back to stymie Olivet, 11-2, as he struck out 11 and Howard again homered. Three days later it was Olivet's turn as they set the Dutch down, 5-0. The Holland Independents took Jack's men, 3-1, and Albion beat Clint Cole, 3-2, before the Dutchmen broke loose against Alma, 14 to 5. Cole had his revenge against Albion on May 28 when Hope gained a 5-4 decision in Holland. Kalamazoo won another close one from Hope at the 38th MIAA Field Day, dropping the Dutch, 2 to 1.

In the spring of 1927 Hope's three tennis courts on the northeast corner of 12th Street and College Avenue gave way to construction of the Memorial Chapel. Despite this severe handicap a team was organized. Members included Bill Heydorn, Oscar Maddaus, Neil Mc Carroll, William Klerk, and Eugene Damstra. A strong Olivet team shut out Hope in the season's only dual competition. The State Intercollegiate Meet was held at Western State Teachers College and Hope was represented by Heydorn and Damstra. The latter posted a singles victory over a Ypsilanti Normal entry but in doubles the Ypsi contingent prevailed over Heydorn-Damstra.

As Hope students returned to the campus in the fall of 1927 there was understandable excitement. For the first time Hope would compete for a football championship, the MIAA Championship. As the season progressed there would be numerous obstacles and not all could be overcome. The MIAA Freshman Rule, then in force, was a particular hardship as the small Dutch squad was made even smaller. Russ Japinga captained the team that was able to fit in only six practice sessions before taking on Albion in the opener at Albion. The weather, unusually hot for October 1, wore down the Dutchmen early in the second half and the final score was

Albion 31, Hope 0. Two weeks later Coach Dwight Harwood brought his Hillsdale team to Riverview Park. The extra week of preparation and recuperation served the Hope team well, and a huge crowd turned out to support them. The faithful were not disappointed as Russ Japinga scooped up a fumble and raced 40 yards for the score. Later in the game John Winter caught a touchdown pass to provide the winning margin of 13 to 6. Hope's first home game in the MIAA was a victory.

Hope's game at Flint Junior College proved a turning point in the season. Things began well as the speedy Lee Kleis broke loose for a 56 yard touchdown run, giving the Dutch a 7-0 halftime lead. But sometime in the second half misfortune struck. Backfield men Kleis and Paul Nettinga both sustained serious knee injuries putting them out for the season. Olivet took advantage of the crippled Hope to the tune of 13 to 6 as Russ Japinga scored the only Dutch touchdown. Near blizzard conditions prevailed on November 5 at Alma but nothing could stop the aerial attack of the 1926 champions, and Jack's men went down to defeat, 39 to 0. Armistice Day saw the Dutch in Kalamazoo before a crowd of two thousand. Hope battled to a 6-0 halftime lead as Japinga passed to Winter for the score. Japinga's effort, including an 80-yard punt, could not offset the determined Kalamazoo comeback, which gave the Hornets a 26 to 6 victory. The final MIAA standings showed Hope tied with Olivet for fifth place, each with a 1-4 record. Russ Japinga and Al Vanderbush were selected to the All MIAA second team.

Hope's 1927 cross country team journeyed to Kalamazoo for the MIAA meet, which was won by Kalamazoo. Captain Fred Dunnewold finished sixth as the Dutchmen tied Alma for second place. Hope did not participate in the State Intercollegiate Meet at East Lansing due to injuries to Ted Boot and Edward Swarthout.

Dean Martin was captain of the 1927-28 Hope basketball team which posted an overall record of eight and 10 while ending the MIAA season in a three way tie for third place. All of this was accomplished without the services of Lee Kleis, Paul Nettinga, Boo Cook, and Russ Japinga. Hope won its opener from the Muskegon Krauses, 51 to 17. In this contest Lee Kleis made a game effort to participate but reinjured his football knee and was forced to retire for the season. Wealthy Florals of Grand Rapids fell before the Schouten men, 55-18, but the Grand Rapids Boters team gained a three point decision from the Dutch, 24-21. Hope rebounded to take the Basch Jewelers 43-29. A final warm-up game produced a 36-28 victory over the Grand Rapids Bethany Church team.

The MIAA season opened in Carnegie Gym against Hillsdale. The usual Holland basketball hype was enhanced

Hope College Tennis Courts

The view above looks east along 12th Street past Van Raalte Hall. The three courts in the foreground gave way in 1927 to construction of the Memorial Chapel, later known as Dimnent Memorial Chapel.

by the appearance of a Hope band under the direction of Herm Laug. The Hope five responded by borrowing a page from the football team, defeating the Dales, 35 to 24. Olivet was downed, 39-30, by Hope's intense play and there was talk of a title, but at this point the team seemed to lose its touch and proceeded to drop the next eight games. Scores were as follows:

Alma 33 - Hope 23
Albion 45 - Hope 19
Michigan State 36 - Hope 21
Kalamazoo 27 - Hope 22
Western State 47 - Hope 20
Alma 32 - Hope 25
Hillsdale 34 - Hope 28
Western State 29 - Hope 27

Hope finally turned the tide on a two-day trip to the east. Olivet was beaten decisively, 27-15, and the next night the Dutch took a non league thriller from St. Mary's, 42-41. Carl Van Lente ended the game in dramatic fashion by sinking a long shot in the last seconds of play. Captain Dean Martin led the team with 21 points. Next it was a superior Kalamazoo team taking the Dutchmen by 20 points, 47 to 27. A sub-par performance in the season finale against Albion might well have been expected. In an earlier game the Britons had outscored Jack's men by 26 points and prospects appeared dim indeed. But Jack's appeal to Dutch pride had its effect and his crew kept the score close from the opening whistle. However, despite LaVerne Vander Hill's 16 points Hope trailed, 37-36, as the last 30 seconds ticked away. At this point "Cox" Van Lente again produced his specialty, a center court shot that parted the net, giving Hope the 38-37 victory and a very positive finish to their season. The final MIAA standings were as follows:

Kalamazoo	9-1
Alma	8-2
Hillsdale	4-6
Hope	4-6
Albion	4-6
Olivet	0-9

Captain Ray De Young led a small but determined group of trackmen in the spring of 1928. The group included Fred Dunnewold, John Klay, Al Vanderbush, George De Roos, John Nauta, Frank Mosher, Marvin Meengs, Ed Swarthout, Floyd Kleinjan, Dean Martin, Herm Laug, Charles Rosema, and Stanley Van Lare. Hope opened the season with a creditable performance as they bowed to Kalamazoo College 78-53. First place finishes were recorded for Hope by Frank Mosher in the 100 yard dash (10.4), Marvin Meengs in the 220 yard low hurdles (27.7), Fred Dunnewold in the 2 mile run (10:52), Stanley Van Lare in the pole vault (9' 9"), and Herm Laug in the high jump (5' 4"). On Saturday, May 12, Hope hosted Olivet at the Fair Grounds on 16th Street. Frank Mosher was the star of Hope's 104-27 victory as he won first place in the 100, 220, and broad jump. The MIAA Field Day meet was won by host Albion with 66 1/2 points while Hope had to settle for fifth place with but six points. Marvin Meengs was third in the high hurdles, Walter De Velder took third in the javelin and fourth in the 440, and the Dutch mile relay team was fourth.

Hope's tennis team did not enter the MIAA Field Day meet in 1928 but did compete in three dual meets. Kalamazoo defeated Hope, 4-3, in a close one that saw Lester Vande Poel, Clarence Klaasen, and Eugene Damstra win in singles. Details are lacking of a second meet, which was also won by Kalamazoo. Olivet's margin of victory over Hope was 5-2. Other members of Hope's "no courts" team were Oscar Maddaus, Neil Mc Carroll, Gerrit Bovenkerk, and Bill Heydorn who also served as manager.

In baseball Jack's men posted a 4-7 overall record on their way to a fourth place finish in the MIAA. The season opened in Kalamazoo against Western State Teachers College with the home team winning 8 to 1. It was in this contest that senior Lee Kleis gave it a final try. To the disappointment of all, his football knee was re-injured, forcing his retirement from Hope sports. Thus ended a brilliant athletic career that was often obscured by bad breaks or losing seasons. Lee captained the 1926-27 basketball team and was outstanding in football and baseball as well. After graduation he would become a successful high school coach, taking the Zeeland basketball team to the Michigan State Finals in 1934.

Leon "Lee" Kleis - Hope '28

As captain of the 1926-27 basketball team Lee led Hope College into MIAA competition. An outstanding athlete in football, basketball and baseball, he continued the performance standards set by Dick Japinga in the early twenties.

Without Kleis, the Hope nine was beaten by Kalamazoo, 10 to 1, before getting into the win column twice against Hillsdale, 5-3 and 12-0. Clint Cole and Carl Van Lente provided the pitching power in these two contests. Hope's second game with Kalamazoo was close but the Dutch were edged 2-1 while Albion won handily, 7 to 1. Hope's third and fourth wins were at the expense of Olivet, 7-5 and 8-1. Two more games were played with Albion and the Briton's dominance continued, 10-5 and 17-6. The Hope nine closed out the season in East Lansing as Michigan State shut out Jack's crew 11-0 in the annual Founders Day game.

In the fall of 1928 Jack conducted two weeks of pre-season practice beginning on September 12. The sessions took place at a beach camp on the north Lake Michigan shore. Al Vanderbush was captain of a team that was tough on defense but had trouble scoring. The MIAA season was an unusual one in that three of the six teams failed to win a league game. The record also shows eight tie games. Hope gave up a total of four touchdowns in five league games, enviable defense in any era, but could not push across a single score. Olivet had similar troubles and the September 28 opener at Riverview Park ended in a scoreless tie. Hope threatened in the second quarter but John Klay's field goal attempt was wide. It was much the same story at Hillsdale on October 6, when defense was again the order of the day and neither team scored a single point. Alma finally was the first to cross the Hope goal line scoring a touchdown in each half to register a 12-0 victory. Hope lost a Homecoming heartbreaker to Kalamazoo College on November 10, when the Hornets scored a lone touchdown to register the 7-0 win. John Kobs, Michigan State's longtime baseball coach, was the referee in this hard-fought contest. A week later Jack's squad found themselves at Albion in the rain. Albion scored in the first two minutes of play and the game then settled into another defensive stalemate with Hope perhaps having the best of it. Vanderbush broke through on several occasions to throw Albion runners for losses and sophomore Clarence Becker intercepted both Albion passes, but the final score remained Albion 7, Hope 0. A frustrated Hope 11 entered its last game at Flint Junior College without a win or even a score, but determined even at this late date to turn things around. Flint scored first on a 35 yard run but from that point on, failed to register a first down as the Dutch defense again showed its metal. In the second quarter Clarence Becker scored for Hope to break the long drought and a second score gave Jack's squad that long awaited victory, 12 to 7. The only negative note was the dislocated shoulder suffered by Harold (Brute) Japinga.

There was no cross country team at Hope in the fall of 1928 and the Dutchmen eagerly moved on to basketball under Captain La Verne Vanderhill. The season began with a junket through Iowa in a Buick and a Packard furnished by Jack. Hope won two of seven games on the tour and then returned to meet the Grand Rapids Boters team and again meet defeat. No scores are available for these contests. The MIAA opener found Hope still on the short end as Hillsdale prevailed in Carnegie, 29-26. A trip to Alma produced the first league victory for the Dutch, 30 to 25. A series of close games followed. Hope was edged at Hillsdale, 27-25, and at St. Mary's, 28-26, then bounced back to take General Motors Tech, 35-31, and Kalamazoo College, 24-22, before Michigan State humbled Jack's crew, 51 to 18.

At this point the campus was saddened by news from the Near East that the Reverend Henry Bilkert, Hope '14, had been killed by Wahabi tribesmen as he journeyed from Basrah to Kuwait. The much revered missionary had been a member of Hope's winning 30 mile relay team in 1913.

The basketball season continued with Hope registering its second MIAA victory, this time at the expense of Kalamazoo, 28 to 20. For reasons unexplained, the Hope-Calvin series had been discontinued after the 1924-25 season. It was now resumed with great interest despite its non-league status. The first game of the new series was to be played in Holland, and Calvin insisted on certain conditions. Calvin's gym on the Franklin Street campus in Grand Rapids was too small to accomodate spectators. School officials felt that this deprived them of the so-called home court advantage as they were obliged to play their home games in the comparatively spacious Burton Junior High School Gym. The Hope College **Anchor** described the situation as follows: "After many years of separation the Calvin College team ventured down to Hope, to play on a neutral floor by their request, and drew a crowd which filled every corner of the gym."[2] The "neutral floor" was the Holland Armory and Calvin rewarded loyal followers with their first victory over Hope by the margin of one point, 31-30. About this time the term "arch rival" began to appear as each school referred to the other in the context of sports. La Verne Vander Hill was unable to play against Albion and Hope dropped the contest, 35-26 in spite of three "long Toms" from center court by Cox Van Lente in the last quarter. Neither Vander Hill or Van Lente were available for the Olivet game but Hope came from behind in the closing minutes to notch a 32-25 victory. On March 6 the Alma Scots took a five point decision from the Dutchmen, 37-32. John Klay made a valiant effort to fill the void left by Vander Hill and Van Lente as he scored a career-high 11 points. With its two aces still sidelined, Hope journeyed to Olivet. The home team was too much this time and the final showed Olivet 33, Hope 20. Referee for the contest was Harry Kipke, football coach at the University of Michigan. Next on the schedule was the second Hope-Calvin game, this time at the Burton Gym. One account claimed that two thousand people, the largest crowd ever to witness a game in Grand Rapids, saw Calvin win again, this time 25-20. Players who recall the Burton Gym express doubt that two thousand could have crowded in, even with standing room included. Vander Hill played for the first time in several weeks but Boo Cook was out with an injury suffered in the Olivet game. Roozeboom led Calvin with 10. An exciting Freshman game went to Hope, 21-20, as Watson Spoelstra scored 12. The Dutchmen closed out the season by taking the measure of Kalamazoo, 28-20. Hope's 4-5 record placed them fourth in the final MIAA standings.

Baseball in 1929 was dismal for the Dutchmen. Bernie Van Oss captained the team that posted a 1-9 record overall. Albion won the MIAA Championship and had a long time to celebrate as MIAA baseball went on a 29-year hiatus. Hope opened with Western State, committed seven errors, and lost the game, 11 to 0. The squad then settled down to some serious practice and actually played quite well in the next game at Kalamazoo College. Catcher Henry Steffens went three for five and helped force the game into extra innings, but Kalamazoo collected two home runs in the bottom of the llth, producing the eventual 11-10 victory. Hillsdale took two from the Dutch, 12-0 and 7-5, before Kalamazoo did it again, 14 to 9. Olivet was two better than Hope with a 6-4 decision and Albion won, 13 to 8, at Riverview Park. In a second game with Olivet, played on the field adjacent to Carnegie Gym, Hope finally tasted victory scoring 6 runs to 2 for Olivet. Albion downed Hope 10-4 in the last league game until after World War II. Hope's senior squad members were not available for the season windup against St. Mary's, which was won by St. Mary's, 12 to 3. Thus ended a dreary season for Coach Schouten, whose first love in sports was baseball.

Track and field came of age in 1929 under the capable leadership of Captain Walter De Velder. The season began with an exciting meet at Kalamazoo College. Fifteen events were contested, as the men from K took 8 first places to 7 for Hope. For the Dutchmen, Don Martin won the high hurdles in 17.7 and the Lows in 29.1. Anthony Popma took the mile run in 5:01.7 while Len Willett's 53.9 brought first place in the 440 yard dash. Captain De Velder's javelin heave of 159' 4" outdistanced all others, and Lew Scudder's broad jump of 20' 10" also took the top spot. Going into the final event, the mile relay, Jack's men held a slim lead of 62-60. Hope's team of Don Martin, Lew Scudder, Walter De Velder, and Len Willetts was equal to the task with a time of 3:47.8 and delivered the final victory, 67-60.

On Saturday, May 18, four members of the Hope team traveled to East Lansing for the State Intercollegiate Meet. A total of 171 men participated in the meet and the added incentive propelled Lew Scudder to second place in the broad jump with a remarkable leap of 22' 4 3/4". This was but 1/4" under the MIAA record set in 1914. Hope's mile relay team of Martin, Scudder, De Velder, and Willets placed fifth with the much- improved time of 3:27.0. A week later the team traveled to Olivet and registered a second team victory, this time by a score of 67 to 50. The pole vault and mile relay were not contested, but of the remaining 13 events Hope registered 7 firsts to 6 for Olivet. A one-two finish by Hope in both hurdle races was a significant factor in the victory. Marvin Meengs took first in the highs with Don Martin second, and in the lows the order was reversed. Len Willets won both the 100 and the 440 while Scudder took the discus and the broad jump. De Velder was first in the shot put with Scudder second. There is little doubt that the illness of Don Martin cost Hope their meet at Mount Pleasant, as Central State won by the narrowest of margins, 57-56. Meengs, Willets, and Scudder each won two firsts, but Martin's potential points were sorely missed.

Only seven men from the Hope team entered the MIAA Field Day Meet at Albion on Saturday, June l. By contrast, Albion's entrees numbered 23. As expected, Albion won with 52 5/6 points, but the Hope seven put on a surprising display with 41 points for second place. Kalamazoo was third with 31 5/6, Hillsdale fourth with 20 1/3, Olivet fifth with 11, and Alma sixth with 5. Hope's first-ever gold medal winners were Marvin Meengs in the highs (17.2), Don Martin in the 220 lows (27.5), Lew Scudder in the discus (111' 8 1/2"), and the Dutch mile relay team of Don Martin, Ray De Young, Walter De Velder, and anchor man Len Willets (3:39.5). In addition to medals the relay team received a special banner emblematic of their accomplishment. The Hope contingent might have scored even more had not Lew Scudder injured his heel on his first attempt in the broad jump.

Hope's new tennis courts, under construction in the "sunken gardens" facing 10th Street, suffered additional delays and would not be completed until the fall of 1929. The '29 team was determined to compete anyway, and some pretty good tennis was played as the season progressed. Kalamazoo defeated Hope on May 8 by a 5-2 count. Hope's wins were in number two singles when Les Vande Poel defeated Huizenga of Kalamazoo, 6-1, 6-2, and in number one doubles as Vande Poel and Clarence Klaasen defeated Huizenga and Hill, 8-6, 6-3. Olivet, the eventual MIAA champion, downed Hope, 6-1. Again it was Vande Poel and Klaasen registering the doubles win for Hope. In a close meet Central State Teachers of Mount Pleasant got by Hope, 4 to 3. Posting victories for Hope were Clarence Klaasen over West of Central, 6-3, 6-2, Cornelius Van Leeuwen over Spittler, 6-2, 6-0, and the doubles team of Bernard Arendshorst and Herm Kruizenga over Kearn and Wicksham, 6-4, 6-2. Vande Poel and Klaasen were handed their first defeat of the season by the team of Kelly and Converse 6-0, 7-5. The improving Hope team finally got its victory at the expense of Hillsdale which had taken the crown in both 1927 and '28. Vande Poel defeated Moore, 6-0, 6-3, Klaasen defeated Rose, 6-1, 6-2, Arendshorst was extended but defeated Mc Donald, 3-6, 6-3, 6-0. Herm Kruizenga defeated Buehl, 6-3, 6-4, and Sangor of Hillsdale defeated Cornelius Van Leeuwen, 6-4, just before the rains came ending the meet. On June 7 the imposing and inspiring Memorial Chapel was dedicated at the corner of 12th Street and College Avenue. The lost tennis courts were soon forgotten, even by the players.

There is no brand of optimism to match that of pre-season football and the fall of 1929 was certainly no exception. Jack was fortunate to secure the services of former great Dick Japinga, as his assistant. Boo Cook, a proven performer, had been elected captain and most of the veterans began pre-school workouts at Jack's beach camp. It was an upbeat group of Hope gridders who made their way to Hillsdale for the season opener, but the fates of football can be unkind, especially in first games. In the opening minutes Hope suffered two blocked punts. One resulted in a safety and the other was converted into a touchdown. From that point on it was all downhill and the Dutch finally limped home on the short end of a 42-0 score. Hope hosted Detroit City College in the second game and showed great improvement but in the end a Hope fumble led to the games's only score and Detroit gained the 6-0 victory.

Hard luck continued to plague the Dutchmen as they met Alma. Boo Cook, Clarence Becker, Ron Fox, and Tom Beaver sustained injuries and could not play. Loss of these key players was too great a handicap and the Scots got the win on their home field, 19 to 0. The pattern continued as Hope journeyed to Olivet. Boo Cook was back and early in the game threw a touchdown pass to Howard Dalman, but the play was called back due to a holding penalty. A dropped punt in the end zone resulted in an Olivet safety and the halftime score stood at 2-0. In the second half Brute Japinga went over on a quarterback sneak and Dalman ran the point to give Hope a 7-2 lead but Olivet came back with a late game touchdown to make the final count 8-7.

Hope's 0-4 record was deceiving. The squad included a number of talented players and they succeeding in getting it all together at Kalamazoo College. A Boo Cook pass to Japinga opened the scoring. Later a Cook to Cox Van Lente pass placed the ball on the three yard line and Lew Scudder plunged over for the score. In the course of the game John Winter blocked two Kalamazoo punts, which contributed to Hope's eventual 19-13 victory. An injury sidelined Scudder for the Albion game and the Britons spoiled Hope's Homecoming by winning 19 to 0. The post-season Exchange Club Banquet featured Michigan State Coach Jim Crowley as speaker. Crowley, best known as one of the famous Notre Dame Four Horsemen, was introduced by Holland High Principal "Jock" Riemersma.

Carl "Cox" Van Lente, noted for his center court accuracy, was the popular choice for captain of the 1929-30 Hope basketball team. As usual, the season began with some of the Grand Rapids City League teams. Hope was surprised by the Hub Clothiers team, 27-22, before rebounding to take the team from the Seventh Reformed Church, 39-19. The Raybestos Brakes aggregation gave the Dutchmen a good battle before succumbing 31 to 23 and then it was time for the league opener. Hopes for a fast start were dashed at Olivet when the home team won a close one, 33 to 29. The team journeyed on to Orchard Lake and pinned a 30-20 defeat on St. Mary's before returning to conference play against Hillsdale. In the most exciting contest to date, the Dales prevailed by one point in overtime, 27-26. Albion at Hope was next on the schedule but the game had to be postponed. Rather than have his team idle for a week, Jack scoured the Grand Rapids area for a substitute opponent. He finally came up with a group known as the Grand Rapids Whozits and a game of questionable merit ensued. Hope won by a score of 76 to 10. The Dutchmen were jolted back to reality against Michigan State, as the Spartans won, 55-16. The drubbing may have been good therapy as the team closed ranks to take Albion, 24-21, and Hillsdale, 37-24. In a second game, Hope lost to Albion, 22-21 and then fell to Kalamazoo, 22-19.

The first Calvin game was played in Grand Rapids and saw the Dutchmen back on track with a 10 point victory, 31-21. The second game with Olivet went to the Dutchmen, 26-24, before Alma trounced the Schouten forces, 44 to 27. The team played well against Kalamazoo but finally lost out in overtime, 23 to 21. Hope took out its frustration against Calvin in the Armory, winning 34 to 17, but St. Mary's got revenge for the early season loss by downing the Dutch, 33-26. Hope made a valiant effort to win its last game against Alma. Watson Spoelstra scored 19 of Hope's 29 points but fouled out in the closing minutes and the Scots were victorious 36-29. Hope ended in a fourth place tie with Albion. Watson Spoelstra was named to the All-MIAA first team, the first Hope basketball player to be accorded this recognition. Cox Van Lente received honorable mention.

With baseball no longer an MIAA sport, Hope played a reduced schedule in 1930. The opening game as usual was played against Western State Teachers College. Hope's one week of practice failed to prevent numerous errors and Western won easily, 12 to 1. Hillsdale shut out the Dutchmen, 9-0, before Jack's crew took on the Galewood Merchants of Grand Rapids and posted a 5-1 victory. On May 13 the Hope nine made the trip to East Lansing for the Founders Day game and lost to Michigan State, 13 to 3. Hillsdale beat Hope for the second time on May 24 scoring 11 runs to Hope's 3. The Dutch notched their second victory in the last game of the season when they prevailed over St. Mary's in 10 innings, 5 to 1. St. Mary's season record to that point showed but one loss.

The tennis season opened with a 5-2 loss to Kalamazoo College. Olivet, the eventual 1930 champion, downed Hope twice, 6-1 and 5-2. In the first encounter Hope's lone win was scored by the doubles team of Gordon Alexander and Jim Wiegerink, 6-4, 6-2. In the second meeting Hope's winners were Stan Ver Hey in singles and the doubles team of John Flikkema and Herm Kruizenga. Hope's first-ever competition with Calvin resulted in a 4-3 win for Hope, but details are lacking.

Marvin Meengs, Hope's MIAA champion hurdler, was elected captain of the 1930 track team. The 20-man squad included only four men with any track experience at all and it proved difficult to maintain the enthusiasm produced by the 1929 high water mark. In a triangular meet it was Kalamazoo

1929 Hope College Track Team 2nd Place - MIAA

Top Row L to R: John Mulder, Mgr., Edward Swarthout, Anthony Popma, Marvin Meengs. **Front Row:** Len Willets, Don Martin, Lew Scudder, Capt. Walter De Velder, Ray De Young, Herm Laug. Missing: George De Roos, Charles Rozema.

Hope College Mile Relay Team - 1929 MIAA Champions

L to R: Don Martin, Ray De Young, Len Willets, Walter De Velder.

first with 58 points, Olivet second with 48, and Hope third with 29. Hope's veterans did well, as Meengs won both hurdle races (16.7 and 27.0) and finished second in the high jump. Lew Scudder took first in the discus (110' 1") and second in the shot put while Fred Wyngarden won the shot with a put of 37' 1 1/2". Stanley Van Lare tied for second in the pole vault but overall depth was lacking. The MIAA Field Day Meet on June 7th was again held at Albion. Hope scored but 13 points and the sixth place finish was disappointing after the team's strong second in 1929. Captain Meengs did his part by winning the 120 high hurdles and finishing third in the lows. Lew Schudder took second in the discus and third in the broad jump while Fred Wyngarden collected a fourth in the shot put.

At the 1930 spring meeting of the Board of Trustees, Edward Dimnent, Hope's fifth president, announced his resignation. His successor, Wynand Wichers, was not immediately available and Dimnent was persuaded to serve until July of 1931. The 1930-31 school year began with Hope now feeling the effects of the stock market crash of the previous October. With some limitations the school attempted to conduct athletics in a business-as-usual manner. The cross country team included Bert Bossenbroek, Nick Cupery, Irving Decker, Lester Ellerbroek, Daniel Gryzen, and Harri Zegerius. The only recorded competition took place on November 1 at Kalamazoo College. In the triangular meet Kalamazoo took first with a perfect score of 15 to 50 for Hope and 55 for Albion. Nick Cupery, in seventh place, finished first for Hope. He negotiated the five mile course in a time of 32:27.

Allen Brunson was captain of the 1930 football team and Boo Cook, who had graduated the previous June, served as assistant coach. Jack was able to secure a new opponent for the opener and on September 27 the team traveled to Ohio to meet Bowling Green University. The Ohioans scored three times in the first half, but Hope closed the door in the second half and the 19-0 defeat was considered a moral victory against a team of such stature. Hope's game at Albion on October 11 was historic in that it was the first night contest ever played between MIAA teams. The game was well played, but Albion had the better of things and won 15 to 6. Hope's score came on a pass from Howard Dalman to Jim Tysse. A week later Alma came to Riverview Park and downed the Dutchmen, 21 to 6. Again Hope's only score resulted from a Dalman to Tysse pass. Hope's third Homecoming game was played on October 25th against Olivet. The defensive battle went scoreless until the third quarter when the visitors registered the game's only score and took the game 6-0. The physically and emotionally drained Dutchmen were no match for Hillsdale on November 1. The Dales held the upper hand from the start and gave Jack's men a 32-0 beating. The team regrouped and made a gallant effort in the season ending game with Kalamazoo but could not prevent the K men from scoring twice. The 14-0 final gave Hope its first winless season since 1921. Unknown to all was the fact that it would be Jack's last appearance as football coach at Hope. The overworked but indomitable Jack had labored through 11 seasons at great odds, giving of himself to do the best possible for the school and his players. A number of his innovations have been mentioned in these pages. He attended clinics throughout the Midwest and numbered among his friends were Amos Stagg, Bob Zuppke, and the great Knute Rockne. His request for additional staff would finally be honored at the end of the school year.

As the 1930-31 basketball season approached it was announced that for the first time all major games would be played in the Holland Armory. Clarence Becker was captain of the team, which opened with a 38-24 win over seventh Reformed Church of Grand Rapids. A second warm-up game produced a 29 to 27 victory over the Burton Heights M.E. Majors, as Becker led the team with 10 points. Coach Schouten took his team to Kalamazoo on December 11 hoping to upset the Hilltoppers of Western State, but Buck Read's quintet was again strong and won handily 39 to 21. A game at Ferris on December 11 saw the Dutch win a close one, 28-26, as Waddy Spoelstra scored 12.

For the second time in the space of two years, students returning from the holidays were greeted with grim news from the Middle East. This time it was the loss of Ray De Young, Hope '29, who had succumbed to blood poisoning and pneumonia. The popular De Young, a short term missionary, had captained the '28 track team and was also a member of the MIAA champion mile relay team in 1929. He was buried near Henry Bilkert in a Basrah cemetery.

On the first day of the new year, Hope traveled to Grand Rapids to meet a strong Bethany Majors team at the Y.M.C.A gym. Jack's team won in a squeaker, 26-25, but then dropped the MIAA opener to Olivet, 23-18, in the Armory. Hope won another close one in Albion's Kresge Gym, 17-16, but bowed to Hillsdale, 39-24, on the Dales home court. In one of the season's most exciting games Alma squeezed by Hope, 44-43, before wildly cheering fans in the Armory. Hillsdale took the measure of Hope for the second time, 36-29, before the Dutch got back to winning ways by taking rival Calvin, 31-26, as Clarence Becker led his team with nine points. Referee for the contest was Holland High Coach Bud Hinga. Hope's next victory came in Kalamazoo's Treadway Gym as they beat Coach Barnard's team, 31-28. Waddy Spoelstra with 17 and Chet Slighter with 12 were too much for Albion in the Armory as the Dutch posted a 36-31 win. Hope's trip to Olivet was disappointing as the home team dominated play throughout and sent the Schouten men home with a 46-28 loss. Kalamazoo got revenge by a 30-24 score when they played a return game in Holland and Alma got the best of the Dutch for the second time, due largely to the fine play of Carl Gussin, who scored 15 for the Scots. Spoelstra led Hope with 14. Jack Schouten's last game as Hope's basketball coach was a 31-25 victory over rival Calvin College. In this game Captains

Clarence Becker of Hope and John Van Appledorn of Calvin ended their court careers. Spoelstra again led Hope with 13 points. Hope finished fifth in the MIAA but had a commendable overall record of nine wins and eight defeats.

With baseball no longer an MIAA sport, Hope played but three games in 1931. Coach Juddy Hyames' crack Western State team shut out the Hope nine 7-0 as the Dutchmen were limited to a single hit. Michigan State stopped the Dutchmen 10-2 on April 23 and after a May 9 rainout, Hillsdale came to Riverview Park to hand Hope a 23 to 7 shellacking. Lost in this stinging defeat was an extraordinary performance by Carroll Norlin, Hope's center fielder. In perhaps the game of his life, Norlin cracked out two doubles, a triple, and an inside the park home run. He also made three outstanding catches in the outfield. It was the one bright spot in an abbreviated season.

Lew Scudder, the only remaining veteran of the famed '29 track team, was captain of the '31 squad. Hope's only dual meet was held at Alma's Davis Field, with the home team dominating the action. Alma's 98-22 victory featured Harry Wehrly, who won five events and placed second in a sixth. Nick Cupery was the only Hope man to capture a first place as he won the mile run in 5:10. Harri Zegerius was third in the same race. Hope failed to score a point in the MIAA Field Day Meet at Albion and finished in last place.

Credit for Hope's first golf team must go to Clarence Becker, who organized the group and served as coach. The first match was held at the Ridgemoor Country Club in Grand Rapids against Calvin College. Calvin won 3-2, but in a return meeting at the Holland Country Club lost to the Dutchmen, 5-0. Kalamazoo College was better than Hope, 21 1/2 to 4 1/2, as Chet Meengs recorded Hope's only win. Squad members, besides Becker and Meengs, included Russ Paalman, Les Serier, Harry Friesma, and Harvey Scholten. Golf would not become an MIAA sport until 1934, but thanks to the efforts of senior Clarence Becker, Hope would have a head start in the quest for the first title three years later.

The tennis season also opened with two successive meets with Calvin. The first action took place in Grand Rapids at Garfield Park with Calvin the winner, 3-2. Hope winners were Captain Cornelius Van Leeuwen, Jim Wiegerink, and the doubles team of Gerrit Wiegerink and Tom Zandstra. Hope won the second meet 4-3, and also beat Davenport-Mc Laughlin Institute, 5-2. On May 27 Hope had its best day of the season defeating Olivet 6-1. Olivet had taken the MIAA crown in both 1929 and 1930. Winners in singles for Hope included Jim Wiegerink, John Muilenberg, Gerrit Wiegerink, and Tom Zandstra. In doubles the Hope teams of Muilenberg and Gerrit Wiegerink, and Zandstra and Cobb Klaasen were also victorious. The high flying Dutchmen were stopped 6-1 by Kalamazoo College, the eventual league champion. Hope's doubles team of Gordon Alexander and Jim Wiegerink posted the only Dutch win. Hope played without the services of Van Leeuwen but Kalamazoo was beginning its long and amazing domination of MIAA tennis.

REFERENCES - CHAPTER 5

1. The **Anchor**, December 8, 1926.
2. The **Anchor**, February 27, 1929.

CHAPTER 6

THE THIRTIES - SPORTS IN THE DEPRESSION YEARS

As the decade of the thirties got underway Jack Schouten's repeated request for coaching assistance was finally heeded. A joint announcement was made by President Wichers and Holland High Superintendent E. E. Fell on May 21, 1931, that Milton L. Hinga had been engaged by the college to coach football and basketball. He would also teach in the History Department. Schouten meanwhile, would continue to coach baseball and track, supervise physical education, and serve as athletic trainer. The move was hailed by all as one that would certainly strengthen the Hope program. The popular Hinga had attended Kalamazoo Central High School and graduated from Kalamazoo College in 1923. He was immediately hired as football and basketball coach at Holland High where he served with distinction for eight years. Twice in the period his football teams suffered but one loss. He had been selected by a special committee of Hope's Board of Trustees, and President Wichers summarized their feelings: "Mr. Hinga is a fine Christian gentleman and has a record for wonderful sportsmanship. He has won the hearts of all who know him. As a classroom teacher he has been more than successful, and the committee feels that in every way he will be a strong and valuable addition to the college faculty."[1] Hinga's position at Holland High was filled by Gerald Breen, one of his former players, who had just graduated from Michigan State and had played under Harry Kipke and Jim Crowley. All parties seemed pleased and thus Milton "Bud" Hinga began a career that would span the next 29 years and touch the lives of countless Hope men and women.

The business at hand was to field a football team that would challenge the other MIAA teams in the fall of 1931. The 1930 team had struggled, but a bright spot had been the outstanding performance of the 1929 Freshman Team which won all three of its scheduled games. Paul Nettinga had coached the promising group of first-year men that included yet another of the talented Japinga brothers (Louis), also a fine receiver in Ed Damson, and Clark Poling, son of famed evangelist Daniel Poling.

Hope opened the season against Heidelberg College of Tiffin, Ohio. The task was not for the faint-hearted. The "Student Princes" of Heidelberg had been undefeated for three years and had outscored their opponents in 1930 by a margin of 290 to 20. It was therefore with some apprehension that Captain Ron Fox led his team onto the field. Heidelberg scored in the first and fourth quarters to win 14-0, but the game ended with Hope on the home team's 14 hard line and, all things considered, it was a positive opening game.

Bud Hinga's first home game was a rousing success. The Ferris Bulldogs came to Riverview Park and were surprised by the Dutch speed and alertness. Hope led at halftime, 6-0, on the strength of Louis Japinga's touchdown pass to Ed Damson. Howard Dalman returned the second half kickoff 27 yards, then reeled off a 45-yard run to the Ferris 15. Japinga again passed to Damson for the touchdown and this time successfully kicked the extra point. In the closing minutes Howard Dalman closed out the scoring by intercepting a Ferris pass and going all the way. Hope savored the 19-0 shutout and continued in the same vein against Albion on October 9. The Britons threatened in the first quarter but the stubborn Hinga men held on for a 0-0 halftime deadlock. The second half featured a 40 yard punt return by Louis Japinga to the Albion 15. The Dutch attack stalled at this point, but on fourth down Jim Nettinga threw a flat pass to Chet Slighter who got free and crossed the goal line. Japinga kicked the point and Hope had its second shutout in the space of a week, this time 7 to 0. The trip to Alma on October 17 resulted in a 20-6 loss, but the Dutch were far from embarrassed. Alma's initial score came as Jim Tysse's punt was blocked, but Hope stiffened and it remained 6-0 at half time. Alma's strong ground game pushed across another score with Borton going the final yards. Hope responded with a 58-yard drive deep into Alma territory only to have Brown intercept a Hope pass and streak 85 yards for the score. On October 24 the team met an old foe, St. Mary's of Orchard Lake. Although the teams had met for several years in basketball and baseball, it was their first meeting on the gridiron. St. Mary's was in but its third year of football and not quite ready for the offensive power of Hinga's single wing formation. Japinga opened the scoring with a touchdown pass to Dalman. The second score came soon after when the fleet footed Japinga ran a punt back 50 yards for the touchdown. Jim Nettinga scored two touchdowns as did Jim Tysse. During the course of the game Ron Fox blocked a punt and interceptions were registered by Milt Slagh, Howard Dalman, and Titus Van Haitsma. The 30-0 win was a confidence builder, even if the opposition did not match that of the MIAA.

The 1931 homecoming opponent was Dwight Harwood's unbeaten Hillsdale 11, and excitement ran high on the Hope campus. It was obvious by now that Hinga's combination of offense was a real crowd pleaser and the Homecoming game would be no exception. A jittery Hope back fumbled the opening kickoff and the Dale's Dwight Dunlap scored immediately. The kick was good and Hope found themselves down 7-0 almost before the game was under way. However, when the butterflies were gone the Japinga to Damson combination worked again and Louis' kick was true making it a new ballgame. Harwood's men scored again to make it 13-7 at halftime and it continued to be an uphill battle for the underdog Dutchmen. In the third quarter the relentless Hillsdale attack took them 90 yards for a touchdown, making the score 19-7, but once again the Dutch were able to respond. This time Howard Dalman brought the crowd to its feet as he broke away for a 50-yard touchdown scamper. In the fourth quarter Japinga hit Dalman with another touchdown pass and even though the point was missed, Hope's 19-19 tie was a decided moral victory with excitement to spare. The fans were aglow and a sizable number made their way to Kalamazoo for the next game. They were rewarded on the opening kickoff when Louis Japinga electrified the crowd by gathering in the ball on the 10 yard line and racing the remaining 90 yards for the touchdown. Japinga could be excused for missing the point-after kick but it would prove costly. Before the half ended, Deehr scored for Kalamazoo and Nefert ran the point successfully to give the Hornets a 7-6 halftime edge. The momentum had shifted to Kalamazoo as Warner scored making it 14 to 6. Hope fumbled the ensuing kickoff on the 20 and the K men scored again. This time Nefert's run for the point failed. The Dutch were not deterred by the 20 to 6, deficit and their comeback began with a 35-yard scoring pass from Japinga to Dalman. A pass attempt for the crucial extra point failed and the score stood 20-12. After an exchange Hope gained possession at midfield and Japinga gained 25 more yards on running plays. With the ball on the 25, Louis again found Dalman in the end zone. Dalman's run for the point was good and the Kalamazoo lead was reduced to one point, 20-19. In the closing minutes Hope mounted a 70-yard drive, but the threat ended with an incomplete pass in Kalamazoo's end zone. Hope's only bad game was a season-ending letdown at Olivet as the home team shut out the Dutch, 23 to 0. Throughout the season the team had played better than its overall 3-4-1 record would seem to indicate. With

Milton L. "Bud Hinga

Bud Hinga joined the Hope College faculty in the fall of 1931 along with his wife, the former Gladys Kendrick, and their two children, Connie and Billy. By general consensus he became one of Hope's all-time favorite people. In addition to coaching football and basketball, he later served as director of athletics, dean of men, and finally as Hope's first dean of students.

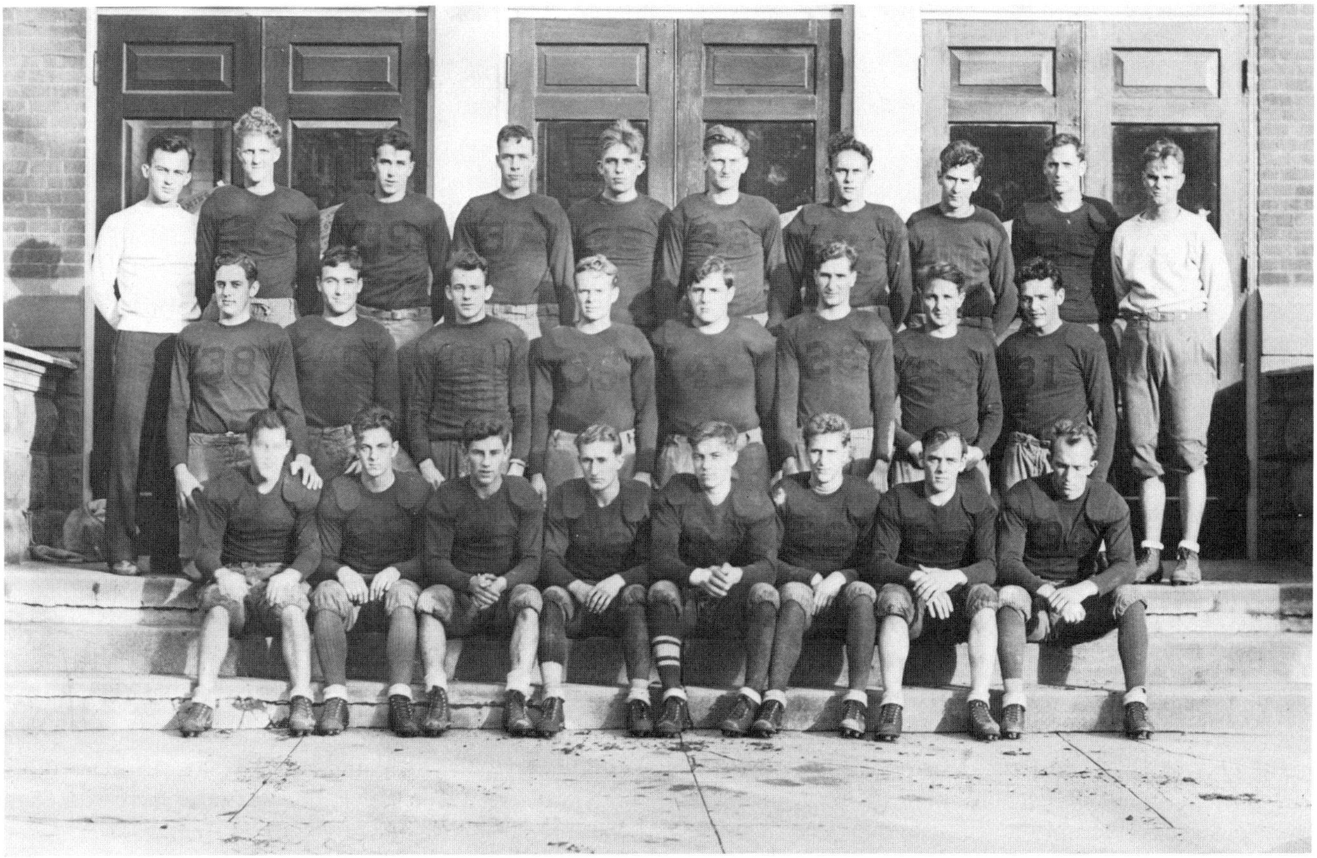

Bud Hinga's First Hope College Team
Varsity Football - 1931

Top Row L to R: Bob Notier, Manager, Gerrit "Curley" Wiegerink, Robert Freeman, Tom Beaver, Jim Nettinga, Jim Wiegerink, Gerald Nykerk, Andy Dalman, Jim Tysse, Coach Milton "Bud Hinga. **Middle Row:** Earl Moerdyke, Captain Ron Rox, Jack Plewes, Harold Seekamp, George Painter, Howard Dalman, Louis Damstra, George Van Peursem. **Front Row:** Chet Slighter, Lorenzo Meengs, Louis Japinga, Ed Damson, Milt Slagh, Titus Van Haitsma, Carroll Norlin, Jim Zwemer.

some justification the team considered itself better than its fifth place finish in the MIAA. Louis Japinga, a unanimous choice, was Hope's first football player to make the All-MIAA first team. Guard Jim Zwemer made the second team, and Howard Dalman, Ed Damson, and Ron Fox received honorable mention.

Hope's six-man cross country team was a respectable second in the October 31 MIAA meet at Kalamazoo College. Team members were Nick Cupery, Irving Decker, Harri Zegerius, Harvey Scholten, Lester Ellerbroek, and George Veldman. Kalamazoo took first place, as it had done since 1926, and its run of championships would continue until discontinuation of the sport in 1932.

Due to the late conclusion of the football season Coach Hinga had to make a hurried transition to basketball and found himself with but two weeks of practice before the opening game. He was fortunate to have seniors Watson Spoelstra and Howard Dalman as co-captains but Ferris Institute prevailed, 25-15, at the Armory on December 11. The first of many Hope basketball victories for Hinga occurred on December 17 as his team took the measure of the visiting Calvin Knights. The score was again 25-15 but this time Hope had the 25. The Dutch made it two out of three by downing Grand Rapids Junior College, 27-14, on December 30. Momentum seemed to be with the Hope team as it headed into 1932, but Hinga suffered an early lesson in humility in his home town of Kalamazoo. Buck Read's Western State quintet crushed the Dutchmen, 56-12, just four days before the opening game of the MIAA season. At Olivet Hope met Walt Sprandel's well-coached team and came away a 36-27 loser despite a 12-point effort by Howard Dalman. The team, however, was becoming accustomed to Hinga's fast break style of play. In the Albion game on January 15 the score stood at 12-0 before Albion could get started and Hope coasted to a 30-21 victory. Hope's 30-27 win at Alma was the Scots' first home court loss in two years as Dalman (11) and Spoelstra (9) led the way.

The team returned to the Armory to meet Hillsdale on January 28. Waddy Spoelstra had 13 in Hope's 41-22 victory, while the Dalman brothers scored 10 each, with Andy dropping in his first four attempts. A trip to Albion saw the Dutch squeeze out a 20-17 win before stopping Kalamazoo in the Armory 29-26. At Hillsdale, Howard Dalman scored 13 and Hope won, 35-28. Bad luck in Hinga's home town continued as Kalamazoo College got revenge in Treadway Gym, 32 to 27, in spite of a fine game by Gerald Nykerk, who scored 10. Hope was scheduled to meet Calvin in Grand Rapids on February 26, but due to the illness of several Calvin players school officials requested that the game be postponed until the regular season was completed. A second game with Western State was much like the first one. The state school was simply too strong and defeated Hope in the Armory, 52 to 23. Olivet's 35-28 victory over Hope gave them the MIAA championship with a perfect 8-0 mark. For reasons unknown Olivet canceled both its games with Albion. Gerald Nykerk, with 13 points, led Hope to a 38-33 victory over Alma in the MIAA finale for both teams. A week later, on March 14, the postponed game with Calvin was played in the Burton Gym. Andy and Howard Dalman with 12 and 11 points were the top scorers in Hope's 34-26 win. "Feike" Feikema, Calvin's giant center, scored 10.

In a break-even year Hope stood 8-8 overall and 5-5 in the MIAA, which placed them third in the conference. Waddy Spoelstra was again named to the All-MIAA first team. As the season ended a Hope alumnus was in the news. It was announced in Madison, Wisconsin, that George Veenker, Hope '16, had been appointed head football coach at the University of Wisconsin. Watson Spoelstra, who would pursue a career in sports journalism, reviewed Veenker's impressive coaching record in a well written **Anchor** article. "Vink" had coached high school basketball in Hammond, and later Gary, Indiana. His Emerson High team in Gary was undefeated in four seasons and won four state championships. This was no mean accomplishment, especially in the Hoosier state, and caught the attention of Athletics Director Fielding H. Yost at the University of Michigan. Yost hired Veenker to coach the Michigan basketball team and assist in football. Veenker's 1928-29 basketball team tied with Wisconsin for the Big Ten championship while his 1929-30 team finished in third place. In the fall of 1930 Veenker moved to Iowa State as head football coach. Iowa State had not won a football game in three years, but under Veenker the team won all but one contest (Nebraska) and finished second in the Missouri Valley Conference. Wisconsin was duly impressed and rightly so. "Vink" was Hope's gift to big time coaching.

Spring sports at Hope in 1932 were not impressive. The baseball team played one game, losing to Western State, 17 to 2. Bob Freeman pitched the entire game. The only other baseball action that spring was a game between the Freshman teams of Hope and Western with the latter winning 9 to 3.

Professor Albert Timmer coached the golf team in 1932.

Watson "Waddy" Spoelstra

Spoelstra was Hope's first All-MIAA basketball player. He was named to the honor squad in 1930, '31, and '32. Later he covered the 1932 Olympic games for the **Holland Sentinel**, enjoyed a successful career in sports journalism with Detroit newspapers, and founded Baseball Chapel for major league players.

Calvin scored an 8 1/2 to 3 1/3 victory over Hope in the opener as Harry Friesma was the only Dutch winner. Hope improved in a later match with Kalamazoo but came out on the short end, 7 to 5. Golf was not yet an MIAA sport, but Kalamazoo hosted a four-team MIAA meet at the end of the season. Scores were as follows: Kalamazoo 362, Albion 363, Olivet 383, and Hope 384.

Shortly after the basketball season concluded, Bud Hinga took over as coach of Hope's tennis team. Hope opened against Grand Rapids Junior College and was defeated, 6-1. The Dutch doubles combination of Frank Visscher and John Muilenberg defeated Shader and Kortlander of J.C., 3-6, 6-4, 6-2. The MIAA meet was held at Albion and Hope was represented for the first time. Don Vanden Belt and Jim Wiegerink participated with the latter, placing fourth in singles.

Hope's track team failed to score in the MIAA Field Day meet at Albion but in the Freshman competition Joe Esther led Hope to a second place finish behind Hillsdale. Kalamazoo made it a clean sweep of spring sports by claiming titles in tennis, golf, and track.

As the school year came to a close it was announced that for the first time award blankets would go to senior athletes who met the specified criteria. The proud recipients were: Watson Spoelstra, Howard Dalman, Nick Cupery, Ron Fox, Titus Van Haitsma, George Painter, Tom Beaver, Louis Damstra, Football Manager Bob Notier, and Basketball Manager Jack De Witt.

As the 1932 football season approached word came that Olivet had cancelled all its games. Coach Hinga began his second year with former Hope center Henry Steffens serving as his assistant. Hinga's policy was to name a captain for each game and then have the team elect an honorary captain or captains at the end of the season. Carroll Norlin and Jim Zwemer would be chosen in 1932. An added boost for the team that fall was the complete refurbishing of Riverview Park. Earlier the City of Holland had purchased the 16th Street Fair Grounds for additional cemetery space. The property included a covered grandstand adjacent to the race track. This was enough to start wheels turning in the minds of certain city fathers. The **Holland Sentinel** carried the story:

> Before the beginning of the 1930 season high school officials got together with the luncheon clubs and similar organizations to sod the field at Riverview park. This plan cared for the needs of the player but the spectator was yet afforded meager stands.
>
> Finally the City Council, backed by Hope College and Holland High, decided that the large grandstand at the Holland Fair (Grounds) was going to waste and that it would make an ideal football stand. Work was started under the direction of the unemployment committee of the Council and a number of jobless have been afforded labor for the past year.
>
> The stand has been set on concrete columns and has steel sub construction. All seats have been repaired and the place appears to be in tip top shape.[2]

In addition to the roof overhead, each seat had a back and a foot rest. Supporting pillars made a few seats undesirable and punts with a high trajectory were temporarily lost from view, but protection from the elements seemed to outweigh these nuisance factors. The playing field was changed from the original north-south layout to east-west in order to accommodate the grandstand, which faced south from the banks of the Black River. Official dedication of the facility took place on October 8, when Holland High met Kalamazoo Central.

For its opener Hope took on a Western State team which outweighed the Dutchmen 20 pounds to the man. The disadvantage was felt most keenly in the plunging of Bilski, Western's 210 pound fullback, who scored four touchdowns. Hope finally got on the board in the third quarter when Louis Japinga connected on a touchdown pass to Gerald Bonnette. At the final gun it was Western 31, Hope 6. Appropriately, Hope played its first game in the new Riverview against Hinga's alma mater, Kalamazoo College. In the defensive struggle, the game ended with the K men on Hope's 11 yard line and the Dutch were glad to escape with a 0-0 tie. The game at Albion also ended in a tie. In the second quarter Ted Watts broke loose for a 40 yard touchdown run and Albion led until the third period, when Gerald Bonnette hit Gordon Korstange for a touchdown pass. The play covered 40 yards but the all important point was blocked, leaving the final at 6-6. Hope's first victory came at the expense of Grand Rapids JC, 14 to 7. This was followed by a 46-0 romp over St. Mary's at Riverview. In the latter contest fans were treated to a fine display of the passing game. Louis Japinga threw three scoring passes, two to Ed Damson and one to Gordon Korstange. Gerald Bonnette passed to Korstange for a touchdown, and both Japinga and Bonnette scored on running plays. Hope entered its fifth Homecoming game against Alma with confidence despite the fact that they had never beaten the Scots in football. On a chilly, windy day, Hope drew first blood when Japinga passed to Korstange, who made a great catch on the three yard line. Japinga then ran the ball for two and Bonnette took it over from the one. Japinga's kick was good. Later in the game Hope stopped Alma on their own eight yard line. Norman Borton, attempting to punt out of danger, saw a strong wind catch the ball and blow it back into the end zone resulting in a safety. Hope's 9-0 victory was made to order for the Homecoming crowd.

On a snowswept field Hope made it four in a row by downing Detroit City College, 32 to 0. Once again Japinga made his presence known. After scoring himself on an end run, Louis passed to Damson and to Korstange for touchdowns. In the second quarter Ed Damson intercepted a pass and raced 80 yards for the score. Chet Slighter's fourth quarter touchdown closed out the scoring. In the season's last game, Hope traveled to Hillsdale to meet the league's strongest team. It was a 0-0 standoff until well into the third period when Hillsdale's Van Voorhees sneaked over to give the Dales a lead they never relinquished. The Dutchmen pushed to the 15 yard line as time ran out. The 7-0 defeat was again something of a moral victory and placed Hope third in the final MIAA standings. Louis Japinga and Jim Zwemer were named to the All-MIAA first team while Ed Damson and Carroll Norlin made the second team. Milt Slagh and Lorenzo Meengs received honorable mention.

Kalamazoo College again won the MIAA cross country championship in 1932 but the big news for Hope was Joe Esther's first place finish in the MIAA meet. Kalamazoo defeated Hope in a dual meet but Esther was the individual winner in this meet also. Other Hope team members were Gerald Heersma, Albert Holland, and Harri Zegerius. The Hope runners participated in the State Collegiate meet on November 12, and the Central States Championship meet on November 19. Both meets were held at East Lansing. MIAA cross country would not resume until the fall of 1946.

Hope's opening basketball game in 1932 was again with Buck Read's team from Western State Teacher's College. The outlook was ominous as Western had opened the season by defeating Olivet, 56 to 5. Olivet had been held to a single field goal. Hope managed to score 18 but Western's fast break rang up 63. Old rival Calvin was Hope's second opponent and the game in the Armory was close all the way. Calvin's Feike Feikema scored nine and eventually led the Knights past Hope, 24 to 22. The improving Hope five broke into the win

The Grandstand at Riverview Park - October, 1932

A press box and radio booth were added later.

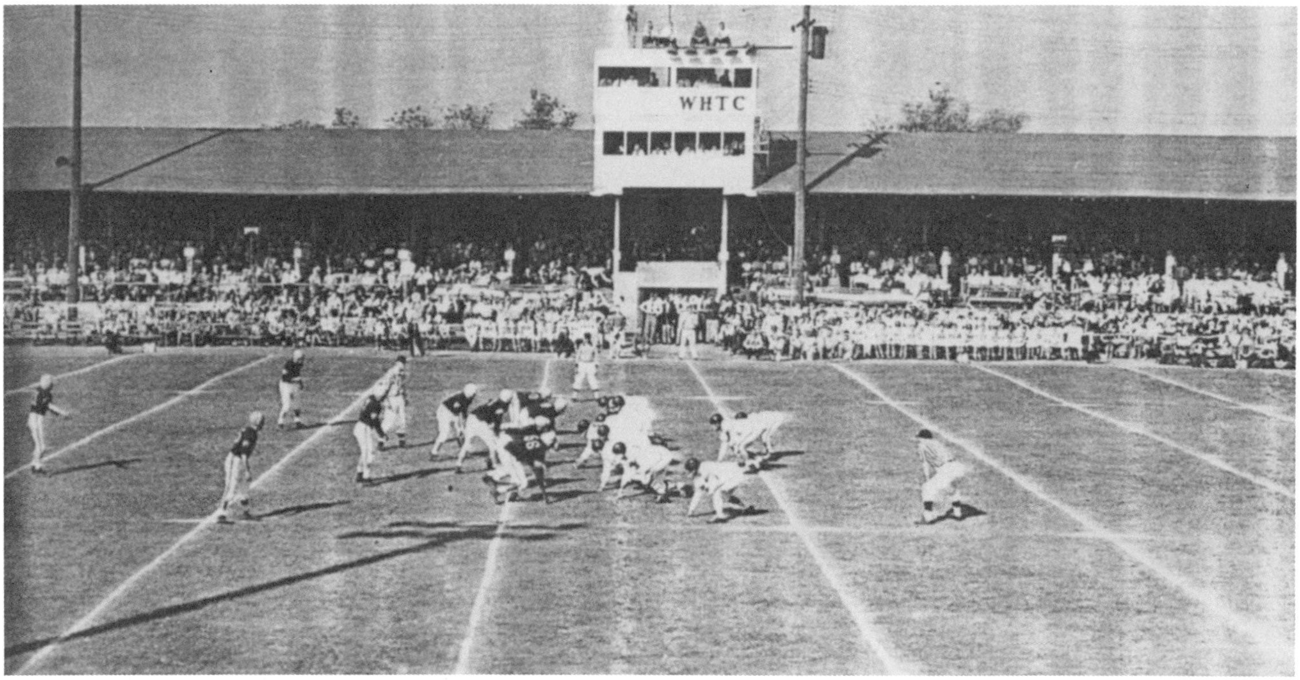

The Stadium in 1956

column by taking Central State, 36-33, but dropped the MIAA opener at Olivet, 56-36. In the latter contest Len Steffens scored 17 for the Dutchmen. Hope bounced back to take Albion, 31-26, then lost to Alma, 48 to 31, as Gordon Korstange scored nine. Hillsdale was also too much for the Hinga men winning 40 to 28. In a second game with Central State Hope played without Van Zanden, Nykerk, and Steffens and lost, 32-28. Kalamazoo's trip to the Armory resulted in an impressive 42-30 victory for Hope, but this was followed by three straight defeats. Hillsdale won handily on their home court, 34-20, Western State came to Holland and won, 56-31, and Calvin repeated their earlier 24-22 victory. Hope halted the skid by squeaking past Albion in Kresge Gym, 28-26, then surprised Olivet, 39 to 25. A trip to Kalamazoo produced Hope's fifth MIAA victory in tough Treadway Gym, this time 41 to 34. The fifth MIAA loss came at the hands of Alma in the last game of the season. The Scots, 40-30, gave them a 9-1 record and the league championship. Hope dropped to 5-5 and had to settle for fourth place. The Dutch were 6-10 overall.

Spring football practice was not new at Hope College, but Coach Hinga made it a serious matter in 1933. A full scale Orange-Blue game was scheduled for Riverview Park to climax the six weeks of workouts. Athletes who were not involved in football took part in golf, tennis, and track. There were no funds available for golf or tennis and the players were obliged to finance themselves. In tennis the Dutch were beaten 6-1 by Grand Rapids Junior College and were shut out 7-0 by Albion. In the MIAA meet the Hope entrees were eliminated in first round matches. A three-man Hope track team went to Albion for the conference meet. Hope's 10 point fifth place finish included Joe Esther's first place in the two mile run and a second in the mile run. Harold Seekamp scored the other two points with a third in the 440 yard dash. In the freshman competition, George Douma won the 100 yard dash. A bright spot in spring sports was provided by the golf team. Bud Hinga somehow found time to coach the team to a 7-1 record. Harvey Scholten was captain of the team, which dropped its opening match to Grand Rapids Junior College, then won the next 7. Opponents included Albion, Kalamazoo, Olivet, and Muskegon Jr. College. Besides Scholten, team members were Ben Timmer, Russ Paalman, and Les Serier. All but Serier would return for the '34 season when golf would become an MIAA sport. Senior award blankets for the 1932-33 year went to Jim Wiegerink (also valedictorian), Jim Zwemer, Carroll Norlin, Gerrit Wiegerink, Lorenzo Meengs, and football manager Harold Fairbanks.

Hope's upward climb in football would continue in the fall of 1933. Henry Steffens was again on hand to assist Coach Hinga while Jack Schouten coached the freshman team. 32

Louis Japinga - Hope '34

Japinga was Hope's first All-MIAA football player. The speedy halfback was also an effective passer and place kicker. He was named to the honor team in all three years that he played; 1931, '32 and '33.

men reported for practice, including 11 veterans. The team entertained Ferris Institute in the opener and was off to a good start with a decisive 26-0 win. Louis Japinga passed to Gerald Bonnette for Hope's first score, then followed it with another, this time to Ed Damson who took the ball away from two defenders covering him. Japinga's kick was good. Don TeRoller scored the third touchdown on a one-yard buck and Japinga again converted. In the fourth quarter Arnie Van Zanten blocked a Ferris punt, giving Hope possession on the 12. Japinga scored on the first play but his conversion attempt was wide. Hope scored a second non-league shutout by taking Grand Rapids Junior College, 19-0, at Riverview. Fans who had come in anticipation of an offensive show by Japinga were not disappointed. In the first quarter the speedy halfback broke loose on a 51-yard touchdown scamper and the Dutch were never headed. The second Dutch score came when Arnie Van Zanten again blocked a punt. This time Gordon Korstange recovered in the end zone for the score. Japinga's kick was good making it 13-0. Louis Japinga scored the final touchdown on a four-yard run. Milt Slagh's attempt for the point was not good.

October 14 was Homecoming and Hope played host to Alma. Al Glance scored first for the Scots but Milt Slagh was able to break through and block the point try. Japinga, with considerable help from team mates, then took charge of the game. His 40-yard touchdown run tied the score. This was followed by successive scoring passes to Ed Damson and to Gordon Korstange. Louis split the uprights for Hope's final point. In the game's waning minutes Alma scored on a clever reverse by Leroy Block making the final tally Hope 19, Alma 12. The joyous alumni crowd left the stadium convinced that their team was now a contender. October 21 was a cold and rainy day at Albion and this was reflected in the final score of 0-0. A week later at Kalamazoo it was more of the same. Hope' offensive potential failed to materialize and once again it was 0-0. On November 4 the Dutch traveled to the Motor City to meet Detroit City College. This game replaced Olivet on the schedule, the latter having discontinued football for a period of three years. Hinga's team was severely handicapped as Japinga nursed a bruised shoulder and did not play until the fourth quarter. In the third quarter the Detroiters got within field goal range and made good on the kick. The 3-0 score stood up in spite of the presence of Japinga in the final period. The last game was played at Hillsdale on Armistice Day. Hope's offense was again held in check while the Dale's Ray Pempin scored twice in the second quarter and kicked one point. Hillsdale's 13-0 victory game them the MIAA championship with a perfect 4-0 record. Hope recorded its highest finish to date in the MIAA as they tied for second place. The improbable 1-1-2 record was matched by Kalamazoo College. The Dutch were 3-2-2 overall and certainly in every ball game. Hope seniors Louis Japinga and Ed Damson received a double honor when they were elected honorary co-captains of the team and were also selected to the All-MIAA first team. Milt Slagh, Jim Nettinga, and Vern Klomparens made the second team while Clarence Tysse, Jim Nettinga, and Robert Freeman received honorable mention. On December 4 the Hope College Athletic Board of Control sponsored a banquet at the Warm Friend Tavern for the 17 football letter winners and for the 16 coeds who comprised the Athletic Debt Diggers organization.

Despite the non-league status of cross country, Hope made a determined effort to keep the sport alive. Kalamazoo College had won the last seven championships in the sport and was also anxious to see it survive. Two dual meets were scheduled between the schools, with Kalamazoo winning by scores of 25-30 and 23-32. Joe Esther of Hope was the individual winner on both occasions. At one time or another during the season the Hope squad consisted of Esther, Al Holland, Harold Mc Gilvra, Woody Maris, Maurice Snyder, Harold Ver Steeg, D. Ivan Dykstra, Adelphos Dykstra, Wynton Hotaling, Gerrit Rientzes, and George Douma.

Upon joining the MIAA in 1926 Hope had found the competition to be keen, perhaps more so than anticipated. The top spot in any sport continued to elude the Dutch. However, the runner-up position in football was seen as a good omen, a sign that Hope's hour might be at hand. As Coach Hinga and his football squad journeyed home from Hillsdale, his mind was already on basketball. Two days later practice began in earnest as the team prepared for its 17-game schedule. The home opener was a 29-21 victory over Ferris Institute as Gerald Nykerk led the team with 11 points, but in a return game. at Big Rapids Ferris evened things by edging the Dutch, 27-25. The third game was played in the Armory against the Hurons of Michigan Normal and it turned out to be an early season thriller. The final seconds found the game tied at 30-all, but as time ran out Gerald Nykerk was fouled in the act of shooting. All eyes were on the free throw line as Nykerk missed his first attempt, then gave the crowd a thrill by dropping in the second shot to give his team the 31-30 win. Central State was the next victim in the Armory as Hope won handily, 42 to 16. On January 5 Hope hosted Olivet in the season's first MIAA contest. Nykerk's 17 points helped the Hinga five squeeze out a 31-29 win. The good team performance continued at Albion's Kresge Gym. Hope's scrappy defense held the Britons to just three field goals in the 24-13 victory. Hope's four-game streak was halted by Calvin, 29-20, in the Burton Gym. Nykerk and Feikema neutralized each other but De Groot scored 10 to lead the Knights. At Alma Hope built a 21-12 halftime lead, then fell apart and was outscored, 28 to 11, in the second stanza to lose, 40-32. The team regrouped at Hillsdale winning, 36-25, but was stung by the Hornets at Kalamazoo, 31-21. Andy Dalman's eight points at Olivet helped produce a much needed 30-23 victory and Gordon Korstange scored an under the basket shot to beat Hillsdale, 28-26, in Holland. Alma's fine team outscored Hope by eight in the return game to win, 42-30, but Len Steffens with 14 led the Dutchmen past Albion, 37-30.

Western State's 47-21 drubbing of the Hinga men was more or less expected but Hope's home game with Kalamazoo College on February 27 was deadly serious. The last week of the season found Kalamazoo, Hope, and Alma all in the running for the MIAA championship. The Hope-Kalamazoo contest, like so many before and after, was pressure packed from beginning to end. After a halftime score of 13-13 Kalamazoo gained a 26-25 lead with but a minute left in the game. At this point guard Louis Japinga, who had so often brought his team from behind on the gridiron, maneuvered to the free throw area and sank the go-ahead basket. With 15 seconds remaining Gerald Nykerk was fouled and made good on the free throw, giving Hope the 28-26 victory and the long awaited championship. The following night Alma edged Olivet, 29-28, to share the crown with Hope. The jubilant Hope crowd streamed out of the Armory and announced the news by ringing church bells throughout the city. With a church "on nearly every corner" the din was considerable. On the following day all classes were cancelled and Hope's first athletic "Glory Day" was declared. A parade was organized at the chapel and proceeded to Eighth Street, to City Hall, and to both high schools before ending in a rally at Carnegie Gymnasium.

One game remained. If the meeting with Calvin was anticlimactic for Hope, it certainly was not for Coach William Corneliese and the Knights who pinned a final 29-25 loss on the Dutch. Calvin's boast of two wins over an MIAA champion was not an empty one, but did not noticeably detract from Hope's signal accomplishment. The team was 10-7 overall and 7-3 in the MIAA. Gerald Nykerk was named to the All-MIAA team while Teed Van Zanden made the second team. Len Steffens and Andy Dalman received honorable mention. Nykerk and Steffens were elected honorary co-captains. In addition, a group known as "Friends and Supporters in Holland" presented gold basketballs to each of the newly crowned co-champions. The tokens were prized by

First MIAA Championship
The 1933-34 Hope Basketball Team
MIAA Co-Champions with Alma

Standing: Coach Bud Hinga, Ben Timmer, Gerald Nykerk, Ken Vander Velde, Gordon Korstange, Harvey Scholten, Manager. **Seated:** Leonard Steffens, Andy Dalman, Gerald Bonnette, Ted "Teed" Van Zanden, Louis Japinga.

the recipients, who realized that they came from a business community mired in the depths of a crippling depression.

The troubled economy had already forced the MIAA to cancel all freshman team schedules. Now in the spring of '34 attempts at economic recovery included various government work projects under the Public Works Administration (PWA). One such project was undertaken on the Hope campus. It was designed to rebuild Hope's athletic field adjacent to Carnegie Gym. Plans included grading and construction of a running track with cement curbing. Progress was slow and the field was rendered unplayable. The delays finally resulted in cancellation of spring football practice and the baseball program.

Hope was left to concentrate on tennis, track, and golf. Professor Harvey Kleinheksel of the Chemistry Department coached the tennis team with assistance from Captain Don Vanden Belt. A full schedule was arranged and results were as follows:

Grand Rapids Junior College 4 - Hope 2
Albion 4 - Hope 3
Hope 7 - Hillsdale 0
Western Frosh 5 - Hope 2
Western Frosh 4 - Hope 3
Hope 7 - Hillsdale 0
Hope 5 - Kalamazoo College 2
Albion 6 - Hope 1
G.R. Jr. College defeated Hope a second time, score not available.

Special note should be taken of the victory over Kalamazoo, as it would be 28 years before it would happen again. The match was played at the Holland Country Club and K was off on the right foot as Ver West defeated Vanden Belt, 6-0, 6-3. Frank Visscher of Hope then took Mantele, 6-3, 4-6, 6-4. Leland of Hope defeated Dibble, 6-2, 6-3. Linden Lindsey of Hope beat Bullock, 7-5, 6-4, and Earl Vande Poel of Hope edged Chapman, 6-4, 6-4. In doubles Visscher and Lindsey of Hope defeated Ver West and Mantele, 6-4, 6-4, and the Kalamazoo team of Martin and Smith took Vande Poel and Don Te Roller, 6-3, 6-4. In the MIAA meet at Kalamazoo on May 25-26 it was Albion first, Kalamazoo second, and Hope third.

The 1934 track team participated in two meets. Albion hosted and won a triangular meet in which Hillsdale finished second and Hope third. Coach Schouten's squad made a good showing despite the third place finish. Harold Seekanp won the 440 in 54.5 while Joe Esther won the two mile run and placed second in the mile. The mile relay team of George Douma, James Quist, Clarence Tysse, and Harold Seekamp took first place in a time of 3:41. Tysse also took second in the 440 and third in the broad jump. Art Mc Gilvra placed third in the pole vault to complete the Hope scoring. In the MIAA meet at Kalamazoo Hope placed fourth with 19 points. Harold Seekamp was the favorite to win the 440 yard dash, but at the time the race was not run in lanes all the way as it is today. As a result Seekamp found himself boxed in while team mate Clarence Tysse won the race in 53.3. Seekamp did manage to finish third. George Douma got third in the 220 and fourth in the 100. Joe Esther, slightly off form, finished third in both the mile and two mile runs. Bob Freeman finished third in the Javelin and Hope's mile relay team of Tysse, Douma, Ed Damson, and Seekamp claimed second place. At season's end Joe Esther was elected captain for the 1935 campaign.

For the first time in 1934, golf became an official MIAA sport and Hope was ready. Bud Hinga again coached the team made up of Ben Timmer, Russ Paalman, Harvey Scholten, and Marv Kruisenga. Hope won six of nine matches and edged Kalamazoo in the MIAA meet to claim the championship. Scores were as follows:

Grand Rapids Jr. College 8 1/2 - Hope 3 1/2
Hope 8 - Albion 4
Hope 11 1/2 - Hillsdale 1/2
Kalamazoo 6 1/2 - Hope 5 1/2
Hope 11 - Olivet 1
Hope 7 1/2 - Kalamazoo 4 1/2
Hope 10 - Muskegon J.C. 2
Grand Rapids Jr. College 7 1/2 - Hope 4 1/2
Hope 12 - Albion 0
MIAA Meet: Hope 344, Kalamazoo 347, Albion 351, Olivet 365, Hillsdale 394.

With MIAA championships in basketball and golf safely tucked away, Coach Hinga looked forward to the 1934-35 school year. Henry Steffens was again on hand to assist Hinga and the team leaders were Co-Captains Vern Klomparens and Gerald Bonnette. Bonnette had made the sometimes difficult transition from running back to center and gave stability to a good line that included Klomparens, Gordon Korstange, Ekdal Buys, Stan Boven, George Heeringa, and Russ Van Tatenhove. Hinga's first three teams at Hope had been noted for speed and quickness, but suffered somewhat from lack of size. The '34 team by comparison, was heavier and would be remembered for a strong line. The team was tagged "The Beef Trust" and would give a good account of itself. In the opener at Riverview with Ferris, Hope snatched victory from the Big Rapids team in the last 32 seconds of the game when Fred Japinga passed to Bill Poppink in the end zone. Poppink leaped high in the air to make the catch and give Hope a 6-0 victory. At Alma's Bahlke Field, in an unusual game, Hope failed to register a first down. Fred Jappinga intercepted a Leroy Block pass and ran it back 65 yards for a touchdown. The kick was wide and the score stood at 6-0. Leroy Block then scored on a 22-yard run to tie the score but Wilson Block's kick hit the goalpost and bounced back. Later Alma got into the end zone but fumbled the ball, which Hope recovered. It was first ruled a touchdown but the officials reversed themselves and called it a touchback. Considerable controversy ensued as the game ended in a 6-6 deadlock. Alma lodged an official protest with the league's Judge Advocate, De Gay Ernst but after considerable review, the protest was disallowed. It was another tie when Coach John Bos brought his Grand Rapids Jr. College team to Riverview. Hope stopped J.C. on the one foot line in the first quarter but neither team could score and the final was 0-0. A notable feature of the game was Fred Jappinga's 70-yard punt. The Homecoming game featured a strong Albion team, which scored a safety against Hope in the first quarter. Jappinga completed a pass to Roger Leetsma. As Leetsma was tackled the ball was jarred loose but Korstange recovered and on fourth down Jim De Weerd went in for the score. The kick was wide. In the fourth quarter Don Te Roller went eight yards around left end to score and kick the point giving Hope its 13-2 Homecoming victory. October 27 brought the Hornets of Kalamazoo to Riverview. The game's big play was a 60-yard breakaway by Kazoo's Harold Kriekard. A subsequent touchdown from the seven yard line was the game's only score. The 6-0 loss to Hinga's alma mater was hard to take but, as always, regrets were soon lost in preparing for the next game. It was Homecoming at Hillsdale's Martin Field and the favored Dales shocked the Dutch by scoring in the first three minutes of play, but also in the first quarter, Korstange intercepted a pass at midfield and returned it to the Hillsdale 29. On the next play Jappinga passed to Te Roller for the touchdown and the latter's kick was good giving Hope a slim 7-6 lead. In the second quarter Jappinga intercepted Cole's pass on the Hope 25 and raced 75 yards to score. Te Roller's kick was again good. The second half was scoreless, but at one point Hillsdale fumbled on Hope's one yard line with the ball rolling into the end zone, where Jappinga

Hope's First MIAA Championship In Football
The 1934 Hope "Beef Trust" Team
Co-Champions with Kalamazoo

Back Row L to R: Donald Kooiman, Custis Fletcher, John Robbert, Don Te Roller Leo Mahan, Renier Papegaay, Hubert Heyboer, Stuart Gross. **Middle Row:** Assistant Coach Henry Steffens, Ken Tysse, Jim De Weerd, Ekdal Buys, Gordon Korstange, Co-Captain Vern Klomparens, George Heeringa, Alvin Klomparens, Coach Milton Hinga. **Front Row:** Stan Boven, Russ Van Tatenhove, Don Albers, Co-Captain Gerald Bonnette, John Buteyn, William Gaston, Roger Leetsma, Fred Jappinga.

recovered, clinching the 14 to 6 victory. Through the years, victory rides home from Hillsdale would be memorable but few and far between. In the season finale Hope hosted Wayne University. The Detroiters scored just before the half but missed the point. In the third quarter Don Te Roller got loose for a 10-yard touchdown run and kicked the point to give Hope a brief 7-6 lead, but in the fourth quarter a Demaree to Dobbins pass gave Wayne a touchdown and the eventual 12-7 victory. Hope's overall record was 3-2-2, but its MIAA mark of 2-1-1 gave the Dutch their first football title, a co-championship with Kalamazoo. Gordon Korstange, Gerald Bonnette, and Vern Klomparens were named to the All-MIAA first team while Fred Jappinga and Don Te Roller made the second team. Stan Boven received honorable mention. A casualty of the season was end Bill Poppink, whose arm was severely fractured in the Alma game. It was necessary for the arm to be placed in traction for an extended period of time and the injury ended Poppink's football career. It also caused him to miss the first eight games of the 1934-35 basketball season.

The early weeks of December saw Hope take its opening basketball game from Ferris, 26-17, and then fall before Western State, 44 to 13. In a second game with Ferris, Captain Gordon Korstange scored 16 in an impressive 46-14 victory. Two days later the Dutch beat Michigan Normal at Ypsilanti, 35-30, and this time it was Korstange and Harold Nienhuis leading the way with 10 points apiece. On January 5 Hope opened the MIAA campaign at Olivet. The confident Dutchmen received a mild shock when the Comets, led by George Wilson's 10 points, easily defeated the Hinga men, 30 to 17. The team bounced back to take Hillsdale in the Armory, 30-23, behind George Heeringa's 10 points, but lost at Alma, 36-30, in spite of a fine 18 point performance by Korstange. Hope won a close one at Albion, 33 to 32, as Harold Nienhuis put in the winning field goal. Bill Poppink made his debut against Kalamazoo and the Dutch prevailed, 31-20. As January came to an end Calvin downed Hope, 26 to 23. The Hope five got revenge on Olivet to the tune of 44-26 and did the same to Alma by a score of 37 to 33, but the MIAA schedule ended with three straight losses. Hillsdale beat Hope, 44-33, Albion won a close one, 27-26, and in an overtime game at Kalamazoo Hope lost, 18 to 16. Despite these setbacks, the Dutch closed out the season in style by downing old rival Calvin, 23-19. Hope was 9-7 overall and 5-5 in the MIAA. The latter was good enough for a third place tie with Kalamazoo. Albion and Hillsdale ended the regular season with 7-3 records, then played off the tie on a neutral floor in Jackson. Hillsdale was the eventual winner, 31 to 25. Gordon Korstange and Chink Robbert were named to the All-MIAA second team and George Heeringa was given honorable mention. Basketball rules for the next season would include the three second rule for the lane area in an attempt to neutralize to some extent the tall, stationary pivot man. The center jump rule would be modified somewhat with the ball to be taken out of bounds following a successful free throw rather than being returned to center court.

Hope College served notice in the spring of 1935 that it intended to upgrade its track program. With assistance from the Federal Emergency Relief Administration (FERA) a new layer of cinders was spread on the track adjacent to Carnegie Gym and the track was packed down with a heavy roller. Though the track was somewhat short of the regulation 440 yards, it was greatly improved and made practice sessions more effective. The season opened with a triangular meet at Kalamazoo and the defending MIAA champion won the meet with 58 points to 48 1/2 for Alma and 32 1/2 for Hope. Captain Joe Esther led Hope with eight points. A highlight of the meet occurred when Esther edged Joe Newell of Kalamazoo in the two mile run. Joe also took second in the mile run. Ek Buys won the shot put and George Douma took the 220 with the outstanding time of 22.5. Hugh De Pree scored six points by placing second in both the 440 and 880. On May 7 Hope met Muskegon Junior College at Hackley Field and came away with a 72-59 victory. The Dutch had no hurdlers but swept the shot and discus. Joe Esther also placed first in the mile and 880 yard run. At Albion on May 14, Coach Schouten's men placed third in a quadrangular billed as a warm-up for the MIAA meet. Host Albion won with 51 1/2 points to Hillsdale's 47, Hope's 45, and Olivet's 20 1/2. The conference meet was held at Upjohn Field in Kalamazoo and the Hornets successfully defended their title with 57 points, but Hope surprised the league by finishing second with 32 points to 30 for Alma. Jack juggled his lineup somewhat and it paid off. George Douma won the 440 with the fine time of 51.4 and took second in the 220. John Robbert won the 100 in 10.3 and placed third in the 220. Joe Esther took second in the 880 and fourth in the mile. Ek Buys put the shot 42' 2 3/4" for second, and Hugh De Pree was third in both the 440 and 880. Don Albers was third in the javelin. It was the first time Hope had finished as high as second since 1929.

The '35 tennis team under Coach Harvey Kleinheksel got off to a shaky start as a strong Grand Rapids Junior College team beat them, 7-0. Four days later Kalamazoo downed Hope, 6-1, as the doubles team of George Heeringa and Earl Vande Poel produced the Dutchmen's only win. Hard times continued as Western State took Hope, 5-2, and Albion did the same. In the latter meet Pete Vanden Berg and Les Van Tatenhove were winners for Hope in singles. Improvement was evident as the Dutch met Kalamazoo a second time. Kalamazoo got by this time by the narrow margin of 4-3. Earl Vande Poel defeated Mantele, 4-6, 6-4, 6-4, Don Te Roller proved better than Kazoo's Dibble, 7-5, 6-2, and Pete Vanden Berg won over Witshunki, 5-7, 6-3, 6-4. Kalamazoo hosted the MIAA meet but Albion dominated play by claiming the championship and runner-up spots in both singles and doubles. Hope again surprised the league by finishing in a tie for second with Kalamazoo. George Heeringa went to the semi-finals before being eliminated by Albion's Leigh Prettyman, the eventual singles champion. The doubles teams of Heering-Vande Poel, and Te Roller-Vanden Berg also made it to the semis.

The spring of '35 found Bud Hinga deeply involved in spring football practice. As a result it was agreed that Bruce Raymond of the History Department would take over as coach of the golf team. After a period of tryouts, the team was made up of Bill Poppink, Jack Claus, Jay Bush, and Ralph De Roo. The opening match against Olivet at Charlotte ended in a 6-6 tie. In the second match against Grand Rapids Junior College Jack Claus was the only Hope man to score as the superior Grand Rapids team posted a convincing 11 1/2-1/2 win. Another defeat came at the hands of Kalamazoo, 7 1/2-4 1/2, before Hope finally got into the win column with an 8 1/2-3 1/2 victory over Albion. Western State had trouble with the improving Dutchmen as they won by the narrow margin of 6 1/2-5 1/2, but the final dual match found Kalamazoo's Henry Brown in form with medalist honors at 72, and Hope lost 10 1/2-1 1/2. In the MIAA meet Brown was again medalist with 70, and his team mates were strong enough to give Kalamazoo the championship with 338 points. Olivet had 348 for second and Hope was third with 369.

In 1934-35 the MIAA decided to initiate an All Sports Award. The school with the best combined record in the five league sports would receive, at the end of the school year, a trophy emblematic of the accomplishment. Kalamazoo was the first recipient with 41 points. Hope was second with 35 and Albion third with 27. It was hoped that the award would provide incentive for schools to build balanced athletic programs. It has continued for more than half a century and in 1981-82 was expanded to include women's sports. Also during the 1934-35 school year Hope College took steps to standardize its own system of awards.

> At a recent meeting of the Hope Board of Athletics, new regulations were formulated and passed regarding the awarding of letters and sweaters to those who have earned them ....
>
> A suitable sweater will be awarded to each player the first year he wins a varsity letter. For football the type of sweater will be a shaker-knit pull-over, navy blue in color. For basketball, a shaker-knit coat sweater, burnt orange in color. For tennis, track, and golf, a jersey knit coat sweater.[3]

Athletes on the various freshman teams were awarded numerals denoting their year of graduation. Sweaters continued to be the award until the late forties when wool melton jackets became popular.

1935 was a break-even year for Hope College football, and, after the championship year of '34 perhaps something of a letdown. Nonetheless, some exciting football was played, including an opening day 7-6 win over Ferris. In the second quarter Russ Van Tatenhove blocked a Ferris punt and the ball ended up on the one yard line. Three plays later Leo Mahan scored for Hope and Al Klomparens kicked the point. In the third quarter Cisco scored for Ferris on an 18-yard run, but George Heeringa and Ken Vander Velde broke through to block the point. A determined Alma team, recalling the controversy of 1934, scored two touchdowns in the first four minutes to beat the Dutchmen, 13-0. Leroy and Wilson Block again were the stars for Alma. On October 11 Hope met Grand Rapids Junior College at Houseman Field and all of the scoring was done in the second quarter. The good news was that Hope did the scoring. The first score came as Fred Jappinga passed to Russ Van Tatenhove who lateraled to Al Klomparens, who went the remaining distance. Klomparens' kick was good making it 7-0. Klomparens also scored the second touchdown, this time on a direct pass from Jappinga. Klomp was not quite perfect as he missed the second try for point, but Hope's defense played tough to preserve the 13-0 win. On October 19 Hope traveled to Albion and won the war of statistics, but had to settle for a 0-0 tie. Hope had 214 yards of offense to 82 for Albion and in first downs it was Hope 16, Albion 4. In the first half the Dutchmen moved to the 5 yard line but failed to score. A Hope field goal attempt from the 14 failed and the final frustration came when Hope fumbled and lost the ball on Albion's three-yard line. A week later the Hinga men were in Kalamazoo for the Hornet's homecoming. The day belonged to Kalamazoo. Barnes passed twice to Wally Survilla for touchdowns, then scored himself on a deceptive reverse play from the four-yard line giving the Hornets a 20 to 0 victory. The only bright spot for the Hope was a record punt by Fred Jappinga on the windswept field. The exact scrimmage line is not known, but standing on his own goal line Fred is reported to have kicked the ball 70 yards in the air. It then rolled the remaining distance into the Kalamazoo end zone.

November 2 saw the Dutchmen win their own Homecoming game 6-0 over Hillsdale. Hope's score was set up by a 16 yard pass play from Klomparens to John Robbert placing the ball on the four-yard line. After a series of line plunges, Jappinga went over from the one. Klomparens' kick was blocked by Beckett. Hope's victory was costly as Jappinga was injured and could not play in the November 9 game in Detroit against Wayne University. Wayne scored touchdowns in the first and third periods and added a field goal in the second quarter to post a 16-0 victory. Michigan Normal came to Holland on November 16 for the season's final game. For a time it appeared that Hope might score the upset of the year. Don Kooiman recovered a Ypsi fumble on the 25 and four plays later Jim De Weerd went over and Klomparens' try for point was good. The 7-0 lead held up until late in the fourth quarter when the Normal team marched 53 yards to score. Hanneman's kick was good and the Dutch were forced to settle for the 7-7 tie. Hope finished 3-3-2 overall and 1-2-1 in the MIAA. The latter mark gave them a third place tie with Hillsdale. Fred Jappinga made the All-MIAA first team while

George Heeringa and Ken Vander Velde were named on the second team. The nine Hope seniors were presented bronze medals of honor by the Holland American Legion. George Heeringa was elected honorary captain and received a gold football, as did Don Kooiman, who was named the player displaying the best spirit.

Morale in the MIAA received a boost in 1935 when it was announced that the three- year ban on freshman sports would be lifted. Coach Hinga received additional good news when Teed Van Zanden returned to school after a year's absence. The Dutch squad faced a tough 18-game schedule which began with a close one against Muskegon Junior College. Sophomore Don Thomas scored the first basket of the season, then served notice that he was a force to be reckoned with by putting in a one-handed side-court shot in the closing seconds to win it for Hope, 29-28. Bill Poppink led the team with 11, but Thomas was close behind with 10. Western State dropped Hope, 38-24, but Bill Poppink limited Western's star center, Dave Arnold, to eight points while scoring seven himself. Poppink and Thomas continued strong against Michigan Normal with 10 and nine points, and the Dutch were impressive in the 30-22 win. On January 6 it took a last minute rally for Hope to slip past Ferris, 34-33. The MIAA season opened for Hope at Hillsdale, and Don Thomas' 14 points were instrumental in the 36-33 victory. It was Olivet in the Armory on January 13 and the Comets led all the way. Hope's 17-9 halftime deficit became a 33-23 defeat at game's end, but the procedure was reversed four days later as the Hinga five built a 23-eight halftime lead against Alma, then coasted to a 46-17 victory. Again it was the one-two punch of Poppink and Thomas leading the attack with 16 and 15 points respectively. On January 21 Don Thomas scored 13 against Albion but Hope blew a 10 point lead as Poppink and Ken Vander Velde departed via the foul route. The one point defeat, 38 to 37, would prove costly. At Kalamazoo the up and down Hope five built a 14 point lead, then saw it slip away to a tie at the end of regulation play. Finally, in the third overtime period the Dutchmen got it together for an 11 point flurry and the eventual 52-43 win. Poppink had 18 and Thomas 12. Hope dropped another one point decision in the return game at Ypsilanti when Michigan Normal came out on top, 26-25. Hinga's ability to bring his squad back was evident once again as the Dutchmen traveled to Olivet and upset the Comets, 40 to 32. In a low scoring game in Grand Rapids Hope prevailed

Members of the 1937 "H" CLUB proudly display their award sweaters in navy blue and burnt orange. **Front Row L to R:** Gleon Bonnette, Russ Van Tatenhove, Harold Nienhuis, Bill Wishmeier, Les Hopkins. **2nd Row:** Ray Boot, Mayo Hadden, Ed Heneveld, Bob Vandenberg, Bill De Groot. **3rd Row:** Bill Arendshorst, Lou Northouse, Bill Van Dussen, Paul Boyink, Joe Borgman, Fred Jappinga, Art Mc Gilvra. **4th Row:** Hugh De Pree, Al Klomparens, Peter Vandenberge, Bob Marcus. **Back Row:** Ek Buys, John Wyngarden, Ralph De Roo, Bill Poppink, Howard Schaubel.

over Coach Al Muysken's Calvin five, 21-20. Eleven of Hope's 21 points were free throws. In the Armory on February 14 Thomas scored 17 and George Heeringa 10 as Hillsdale was subdued 35 to 13, but things weren't as easy at Alma. The Scots utilized their narrow floor to the maximum by using a zone defense to great effect and the Dutch were once again forced into overtime. John Robbert and Bob Barber proved effective in this period and a grateful Dutch squad journeyed home with a hard-earned 29-27 victory.

The game at Albion on February 21 was crucial in Hope's bid for the title but the fates were not kind and the Dutch had an off night. Hope made two of nine free throws and adding to the misery was a brilliant 20-point performance by the Briton's Russell Kroeze. The final was Albion 43, Hope 31. Three days later Hope downed Kalamazoo in the Armory, 44-20, as Poppink scored 10 and Heeringa nine, but the damage was done and Hope's 7-3 record gave them third place in the MIAA as Albion and Olivet ended in a tie for the top spot. A playoff took place on a neutral floor in Battle Creek, and Albion emerged the winner by a score of 42 to 39. George Heeringa made the All-MIAA first team while junior Bill Poppink and sophomore Don Thomas were on the second team. Ken Vander Velde and Teed Van Zanden were elected honorary co-captains.

Jack Schouten's 1936 track team would make Hope's strongest bid to date for the MIAA championship. Captain George Douma provided superb leadership and despite a dearth of distance runners, there were several men with genuine first place potential. Don Martin, who had been a member of Hope's champion mile relay team in 1929 had dropped out of school to do a stint in the U.S. Army. While in the service he had become an outstanding dash man. His belated return to Hope was welcomed by all and provided tremendous point potential as he joined John Robbert, the 1935 gold medal winner. On April 25 Albion hosted a quadrangular meet which included Alma, Kalamazoo, and Hope. Eyebrows were raised when Hope won the meet with 49 1/2 points to 46 for Kalamazoo, 36 1/2 for Alma, and 28 for Albion. Martin lived up to his reputation by winning the 100 in 10.2 and the 220 in 23.1. John Robbert was close behind to make it 1-2 for the Dutch in both races. Clay Tellman's 53.5 took the 440 and Douma placed second. Hope's fourth 1-2 finish came as Ek Buys put the shot 42' 8" and Lou Northouse was second. Clay Tellman jumped 21' to take the broad jump, Hugh De Pree was second in the 880, and the mile relay team of Douma, De Pree, Martin, and Tellman breezed to victory.

Alma surprised Hope, 75-55, in a dual meet but Hope managed six firsts with Martin, Tellman, and Buys repeating. Hugh De Pree switched to the 440 and won with a splendid 53.0. Hope's relay team won by forfeit. On May 2 the Dutch finished second in a triangular at Kalamazoo. The host school won with 75 3/4, Hope had 55 1/4, and Olivet 31. Hope's firsts were Tellman in the 440 with the fine time of 52.1, Martin in the 100 with 10.2 and the 220 with 22.5, Buys in the shot with 40', and Art Mc Gilvra in a four-way tie for first in the pole vault. The State Intercollegiate Meet was held at the University of Michigan on May 15 and 16. Don Martin placed fourth in both the 100 and 220. His 220 prelim time of 21.7 gave him a first place tie in the heat. It would prove to be the fastest time of Martin's career. Clay Tellman also took part in the meet and had a career best broad jump of 21' 6." The mark failed to place, attesting to the caliber of the meet. The MIAA meet was held at Kalamazoo College on May 30. The stakes were high for Hope College and the team made a gallant effort to bring home the school's first championship. A first in track would give Hope the MIAA All-Sports Trophy by a margin of one point. With but two events remaining the Dutch held a 40 to 36 1/3 lead over favored Kalamazoo. John Lambooy of Kalamazoo won the 220 low hurdles as expected, but Hopeites watched helplessly as an Albion hurdler sauntered across the finish line allowing Mellens of Kalamazoo to nose him out for fourth place. This put first place out of reach for the seven men who had performed so well. Now even a victory in the mile relay would leave the Dutchmen short by 1/3 point. Along the way Hope had done about everything right. Don Martin tied the league record in winning the 100 (10.0) and took the 220 in 22.4. Robbert was second in the latter race. George Douma repeated as 440 champion in 52.2 while Clay Tellman finished third. Tellman won the broad jump with an impressive 21' 5 3/4" and Hugh De Pree surprised the field by winning the 880 in 2:03.9. Ek Buys won the shot put with a throw of 42' 11 3/4" and Lou Northouse took third. Hope's mile relay team finished second. In the final tally it was again Kalamazoo the champion with 47 1/3 to 43 for Hope, 21 1/3 for Alma, 20 1/3 for Albion, 16 1/2 for Olivet, and 14 1/2 for Hillsdale. It was clearly Hope's finest performance in MIAA track up to that time.

The '36 golf team, with Bud Hinga back at the helm, made a strong showing with a second place just two strokes behind champion Olivet and one stroke ahead of Kalamazoo. Hinga experimented with a variety of players in the various matches throughout the season. Included were Bob Blanchard, Jay Bush, Ralph De Roo, Mayo Hadden, Les Hopkins, Renier Papegay, Bill Poppink, and Bill Van Dussen. The season opened with a 6 1/2-5 1/2 loss to Grand Rapids Junior College. Next at the Ridgemore Country Club in Grand Rapids it was Hope 7 1/2, Calvin 7 1/2. On April 30 Olivet defeated Hope, 9 1/2 to 2 1/2, and Kalamazoo did the same on May 7. In the latter match Kalamazoo's Henry Brown continued his fine play with a 70. Poppink led Hope with a 73. On May 19 Hope surprised Olivet, 8 1/2 to 3 1/2, then dropped a practice match two days later to Western's Frosh, 8-4. A team of Poppink, Bob Blanchard, Renier Papegay, and Les Hopkins conquered the tough Grand Rapids Junior College team, 9 1/2 - 2 1/2, on May 26 in a final tune up before the conference meet. The team selected by Coach Hinga for the MIAA match at Kalamazoo included Bill Poppink, Les Hopkins, Bill Van

Dussen, and Ralph De Roo. Henry Brown was again the class of the league as medalist but Olivet captured the title with a score of 331, just two better than Hope's 333. Hope's second place was especially gratifying as the team inched past Kalamazoo by one stroke.

Coach Harvey Kleinheksel directed the '36 Hope tennis team to a third place finish after a slow start. Grand Rapids J.C. defeated Hope 6-1 as Bill Arendshorst at number 3 singles was Hope's only winner. It was Kalamazoo 5, Hope 2 with Arendshorst again a winner and also the doubles team of John Leland and George Heeringa. Hope got its first win by shutting out Hillsdale, 7-0, then dropped a close one to Albion, 4-3. In the latter meet Hope's winners were Arendshorst and Russ Van Tatenhove in singles, and the doubles team of Arendshorst and Van Tatenhove. Another shutout of Hillsdale, this time 5-0, preceded a 6-1 loss to Kalamazoo, as George Heeringa was Hope's only winner. Albion again defeated Hope, 4-3, before the Dutchmen took Olivet twice, 6-1 and 4-3. John Leland missed the second meeting with Grand Rapids Junior College due to injuries but it made little difference as Junior College shut out the Dutchmen, 7-0. Hope's team for the MIAA meet at Kalamazoo was made up of Leland, Heeringa, Arendshorst, and Van Tatenhove. All advanced to the quarter finals, but all were defeated there. Hope's doubles teams suffered the same fate. Harold Simpson of Kalamazoo defeated Leigh Prettyman of Albion, 6-2, 6-1, for the singles championship but Prettyman and James Rouman took the doubles title. Final results showed Kalamazoo with 18 points, Albion 12, Hope 10, Olivet 2, and Hillsdale 0. Alma did not enter a team.

For the football season of 1936 MIAA officials adopted a round-robin schedule with each team playing three of the schools twice and the other two once. Hope's one time opponents were Hillsdale and Kalamazoo. The arrangement was supposed to continue over a five-year period but was dropped after one year due to strong opposition from coaches and others who objected to giving up games with traditional non-league opponents. Olivet fielded a team in 1936 for the first time in three years, and Albion had a new coach in the person of Dale Sprankle who moved over from Adrian. Coach Hinga's co-captains were two proven veterans, Ekdal Buys and Fred Jappinga. Hope lost its opener on September 26 at Alma, with the 6-0 defeat coming as a result of two long passes by the Scots in the third quarter. A week later the Dutchmen got started by downing Olivet at Riverview 26 to 0, then on October 9 took the measure of the visiting Albion team, 6-0. Don Thomas passed to end Howard Schaubel for Hope's only score in a game played in a steady drizzle. After a 0-0 tie at Hillsdale the stage was set for Hope's Homecoming game with Kalamazoo on October 24. Pre-game dopesters made note of the fact that in five years as Hope's coach, Hinga had been unable to defeat his alma mater, though two games had ended in ties. Defense prevailed in the first half and neither team scored, but in the second half Kalamazoo's George Finley scored and kicked the point for a 7-0 lead. Hope responded with a Jappinga to Ed Heneveld touchdown pass and the score was knotted at seven and it looked like another standoff. Hope took to the air and Hope fans agonized as Kalamazoo's Clifford Hunt intercepted and ran 55 yards down the south sideline for the winning score. The 13-7 loss was a bitter pill for the entire team but especially for Ek Buys, Lou Northouse, and Howard Schaubel, who made an outstanding effort. The gloom deepened on Sunday morning when Hope's beloved Professor John B. Nykerk was found dead in his Voorhees Hall room. It was apparent that his last act had been to attend Hope's Homecoming game.

A week later the Hope faithful were grateful for their covered grandstand as the second Alma game was played in a downpour. Despite the adverse conditions, Bob Marcus passed to Don Thomas for a second quarter touchdown. The point attempt was not good. Alma took the ensuing kickoff and marched to a score with Clyde Dawe going over from the one. Jake Miller's dropkick was good and the Scots led, 7-6. The Dutch, however, were not to be denied this day. Early in the fourth quarter Fred Jappinga went over for a touchdown and Hope had its third victory, 12 to 7.

The game at Olivet on November 7 belonged to Co-Captain Ekdal Buys. From his defensive tackle position he knew a lineman's dream. Observing that the Olivet quarterback was taking only a one-step drop back before passing, Ek advised end Howard Schaubel that he was going for the ball. On the next play Buys charged the surprised passer, took the ball off his hand and raced 45 yards for the score. The maneuver worked not once, but twice. The second time Buys again scored, running away from the field on a 52 yard jaunt! Jappinga kicked the point after the first touchdown and Hope's high scoring tackle went home with a sweet 13-0 victory, not to mention a scrapbook item that might well serve as a challenge to all future Hope linemen.

At Albion on November 19 Hope repeated their performance of October 9 again beating the Britons, 6-0. In the second quarter Homer Lokker recovered a fumble on the Albion 14. On the second play Jappinga threw a touchdown pass to Lokker for the game's only score. It was somehow appropriate that Ek Buys should close out his career with added heroics. In the waning minutes of the contest Albion's Harry Kircher intercepted a Hope pass and broke free. Buys, now thankful for Jack Schouten's forced wind sprints, pursued and caught Kircher on the seven-yard line. The defense held and Hope had its fifth victory. The 5-2-1 record gave Hinga's team a second place tie with Alma. Ek Buys, Fred Jappinga, and Howard Schaubel were named to the All-MIAA first team.

Through the years the 1936-37 Hope basketball team has been characterized in a variety of ways, but there is consensus that prospects were bright from the start. Four veterans returned in the persons of Bill Poppink, Don Thomas, John Robbert, and Harold Nienhuis. All had been regulars on a team that, save for a couple of lapses, seemed to be of championship caliber. The four were backed up by substitute Art Mc Gilvra and an impressive group of sophomores that included Paul Boyink, Bob Marcus, Bill De Groot, Bob VandenBerg, and Ed Heneveld. Hope would play a 17 game schedule but there would be something missing. For the first time since 1928 there would be no games with Calvin College. The series had been interrupted for three years in the mid-twenties but in general, Hope's season was seen to include the regular MIAA campaign and a so-called "second season" made up the two games with Calvin. Now the popular but intense rivalry would go on a six-year hiatus for reasons not fully explained. Players on both sides enjoyed the sometimes frenzied competition, but it was known that the relationship between Coaches Hinga and Muyskens was strained at times. Fan behavior before, during, and after the games was often less than exemplary, and there was a tendency to use game results to bolster denominational positions on Sunday morning. In any event no games were scheduled in 1936-37 and Hope picked up one game with Michigan State instead. The Dutch had not played Michigan State since 1930.

Coach Hinga had reason to be optimistic as the season opened, but his team was not ready for the well-oiled machine of Buck Read at Western State on December 4. After a 55-19 shellacking the Dutch went back to basics and it showed a week later when they downed Muskegon Junior College, 40 to 14. Scoring was evenly divided with Paul Boyink getting 10. In the game at Ferris on December 15, Hope was off to a slow start and led by only one point at halftime. A second half surge however, brought a 43-33 win, again with even scoring. Don Thomas had 13, Boyink 12, and Poppink eight. In succession Hope took Michigan Normal 27-23, Ferris a second time 33-19, and opened the MIAA season by doubling the score against Hillsdale 40 to 20. In "the pit" at Olivet on January 11 Hope was able to cash in on only three of 15 free throws and saw the game go into overtime. Olivet emerged the winner, 31-29. This early season jolt got the Dutchmen back on track and four days later they downed Alma, 36-25, as Poppink scored 13 and Thomas 11. A convincing 51-36 victory at Albion was followed by a 39-28 win over Kalamazoo in the Armory. Again Poppink and Thomas led the scoring, with 12 and 11 points respectively.

On January 29 the Hope squad traveled to East Lansing to take on a Michigan State five that had already taken the measure of the University of Kentucky and Syracuse University. The Spartans were off to an 8-0 lead before the Dutchmen came back to trail 10-8 at the half. State led 21-18 with eight minutes remaining but Poppink and John Robbert each scored six as Hope battled to a 23-21 lead in the closing minutes. State missed the shot that would have tied the game. Poppink's rebound and long pass to Bob Vandenberg closed out the scoring and gave the Hinga men a 25-21 victory. Momentum was now with the Dutch as they prepared to host Olivet. In the meantime, labor unrest in the Flint area had resulted in activation of the National Guard, and Bob Marcus had been called to active duty. He was able to secure leaves to play in the season's final games but could not be present for any practice sessions. On February 5, 1380 fans squeezed into the Armory for the all important contest, and some 1,200 were turned away. Bob Marcus exchanged his army uniform for basketball gear, scored 14 points, and led his team to a 43-31 victory. Poppink and Boyink each added 10. The inevitable letdown took place as the team made the long trip to Ypsilanti the next day. The team simply went flat and Michigan Normal was the winner, 30-22. A trip to Hillsdale on February 12 saw the Dutchmen back in form, and Hope was a 56-23 winner as Bob Marcus was again high with 16. Thomas contributed 12 and Poppink 10. In two home games Hope enjoyed consistent play as they defeated Alma, 38-22, and Albion, 39-22.

The victory over Albion, coupled with Albion's earlier upset of Olivet, assured Hope of at least a championship tie but Hinga, Hope, and Holland were after that first-ever undisputed championship which seemed so elusive. All roads led to Kalamazoo for the showdown on February 23. Three Greyhound busses and a fleet of automobiles transported 800 Hopeites to Kalamazoo, where they outnumbered the Hornet following by a considerable number. The much feared Treadway jinx seemed to be in force as Kalamazoo built a lead and held it until the final 37 seconds of.the game. At that point Harold Nienhuis tied the score with a free throw and Bob Marcus scored the game's final three points to make it Hope 28, Kalamazoo 25. Captain Bill Poppink with 12 points, led his team to its long-sought and undisputed championship. Before leaving town the team was invited to the home of Western State Registrar John C. Hoekje for a post-game meal. Hoekje had played on Hope's 1904-05 team with pioneers,Peter Pleune, August Veenker, and Captain A.J. Muste.

Holland church bells could be heard as late as 2:30 a.m. and "Glory Day" preparations continued through the night. The idea, however, was not received with great enthusiasm by some faculty members and a crisis of mild proportions arose in the morning when the chapel doors were found to be secured with chains. Coach Hinga intervened, admonishing the offenders, who may possibly have included some football players. In any event, the chains were removed and the day-long celebration continued without further incident. Bill Poppink and Bob Marcus were named to the All-MIAA first team and Don Thomas and John Robbert made the second team.

As the spring sports seasons approached the main topic of conversation was the MIAA All-Sports Trophy. It was agreed that Hope's main competition would again come from Kalamazoo, and that finishes in track, tennis, and golf would determine the outcome. Despite the presence of Don Martin, Ek Buys, Hugh De Pree, and John Robbert, the turnout for track was discouraging. The **Anchor** sponsored an

The 1936-37 Basketball Team
Hope's First Undisputed MIAA Champion

Seated L to R: Art Mc Gilvra, Don Thomas, Bob Marcus, Captain Bill Poppink, Paul Boyink, John Robbert, Harold Nienhuis. **Standing:** Manager Jack Burkett, Bob Vandenberg, Joe Borgman, Coach Bud Hinga, Ed Heneveld, Bill De Groot, Professor Edwin Paul McLean.

Historic Moment

Hope's Don Martin wins the 100 yard dash with an MIAA record 9.9 at Kalamazoo's Upjohn Field - Saturday, May 29, 1937. The mark would stand for 30 years, finally being broken by Alma's Chris Mc Kee in 1967. Martin also set marks this day in the 220 yard dash (21.7), in the 120 yard high hurdles (15.5), and finished second in the 220 yard low hurdles. He scored a meet high 18 points for his team.

Shown here with Coaches Bud Hinga and Jack Schouten, Bill Poppink was a campus leader and top performer in basketball and golf.

In 1937 Ek Buys was the MIAA's number one tackle and shot putter. An enthusiastic supporter of his alma mater, he became chairman of Hope's Board of Trustees in 1961. Buys and Poppink were roommates in their senior year.

interfraternity track meet on April 23 in an attempt to drum up interest. The Cosmopolitans won the meet and a few more bodies joined the Hope squad, but it became obvious that most of the point scoring would come from the four veterans. In a triangular meet at Kalamazoo on May 23, the Hornets won easily with 78 points while Hope squeezed past Hillsdale by one point, 43 to 42. Captain Don Martin was impressive with 16 individual points. He was a busy man with firsts in both dashes and seconds in the two hurdle races. Ek Buys came through with a first in the shot put and Hugh De Pree was second in the 880. Ed Buteyn and Charles Waldo were second and third in the mile run. The MIAA meet was held on May 28 and 29 at Kalamazoo's Upjohn Field and Hope's five qualifiers managed to retain second place by the narrowest of margins as they beat out Albion 29 to 28. Hope may have finished in second place but Don Martin closed out his brilliant career in championship fashion. His first place finishes in the 100 (9.9), 220 (21.7), and 120 yard high hurdles (15.5), were all league records. In addition, his 2nd in the 220 yard low hurdles pushed John Lambooy of Kalamazoo to a new record in that event. Ek Buys repeated as shot put champion with a fine put of 43' 1 1/4."

Coach Bruce Raymond's golf team won five of eight dual matches in the MIAA and posted a strong second place finish in the Field Day meet. Once again it was Olivet edging Hope, 331 to 335. Hope's team in the conference meet consisted of Bill Poppink, Bob Marcus, Bill Van Dussen, and Ralph De Roo. At the end of regulation play Poppink and Olivet's Ed Novak were tied at 76. In the playoff Novak was brilliant with a 69 as Poppink repeated with a 76.

Under Coach Harvey Kleinheksel Hope's tennis team defeated Olivet and Albion in MIAA dual meets but lost twice to Kalamazoo College. Hope's Field Day team consisted of Bill Arendshorst, Paul Boyink, Bill De Groot, Gordon Pleune, and Pete Vanden Berg. In singles play Arendshorst drew Harold Simpson, Kalamazoo's defending champion, and after a well played match, was eliminated, 6-1, 6-1. Boyink and Pleune managed just two points and at the end of singles play, Hope trailed Albion, 3-2. As the day wore on Boyink and Pleune did the job for Hope by winning the doubles championship as they defeated Carr and Misner of Albion, 6-2, 6-1. This gave the Dutchmen second place in tennis and the school's first MIAA All-Sports Award, by a 41-37 margin over Kalamazoo. After 10 years of membership the school was proud to display this symbol of a well-balanced athletic program.

As the Class of '37 left the halls of Hope, at least two of its athletes did so with an understandable sense of achievement. Roommates Ekdal Buys and Bill Poppink had major roles in Hope's championships in football and basketball, and in securing the coveted All-Sports Trophy. Buys was a product of Grand Rapids Central High School while Poppink hailed from East High in Rochester, New York. In addition to athletics both had been involved in many areas of college life, but most-missed would be their standard of leadership. Hope's loss would be society's gain. Buys, a successful broker, outstanding churchman and humanitarian, would become the 24th president of Hope's Board of Trustees in 1961. Poppink, who began as a high school coach at Rockford, Michigan, became one of the State's most respected school administrators. Both had the satisfaction of seeing all their children attend Hope College.

Big news in the fall of 1937 was the advent of night football at Riverview Park. A Lion's Club committee headed by Russ Vande Poel initiated the $5,400 project. Local businessmen contributed $2,000 and the City of Holland supplied the remainder. For the first time Hope's football team would be equipped with two sets of jerseys, the whites being used for night games. The 1937 season would be different in a number of ways. After a one-year trial the league abandoned the double round robin schedule concept. In order to field a team Olivet found it necessary to play freshmen. As a result, their games were considered non-conference and did not count toward the MIAA championship or the All-Sports Trophy. Adrian rejoined the MIAA after a 15-year absence, but did not field a football team until 1938. The campaign for Hope would take a strange turn at mid-season. For the first four games no opponent was able to cross the Hope goal line and it appeared that the Dutch possessed a defensive powerhouse. Then the worm turned, and in the final four games the team gave up a total of 54 points and was not able to score a single point in its own cause.

The Olivet game was played in a downpour at Riverview Park on the night of September 24. The game's highlight was a 42-yard touchdown scamper by sophomore Lee Brannock. It was Hope's only score but enough to give Hinga's men the all-important opening game win. Tackles Mayo Hadden and Lou Northouse were injured in the rough contest, but the only other casualties seemed to be $75.00 worth of light bulbs which burst when pelted with the rain. Grand Rapids Junior College was back on the schedule and suffered a 12-0 shutout at the hands of the Dutch in another night game. Hope hosted Hillsdale on the afternoon of October 9. The teams were evenly matched but Hope fans were rewarded when Bob Marcus passed to Howard Schaubel for a touchdown. The Dales had their chance late in the fourth quarter but fumbled on the three-yard line and Hope notched its third victory, 7-0. A Homecoming night game at Kalamazoo proved to be Hope's undoing. The Dutchmen were never really in the contest and the Hornets walked away with a 26-0 victory. A week later, at Ypsilanti, Michigan Normal's Valleau and Walsh combined for 19 points and the Dutch were shut out again. Hope's Homecoming was held on November 6 and the team made a valiant effort to reverse the pattern. Lack of offense was again a problem and a fourth quarter Alma field goal proved the difference.

The 3-0 setback spoke well for Hope's defense but the inability to score continued to be a problem in the final game at Albion on November 13. In this encounter Hope lost possession on a fumble, and the Britons capitalized by completing a long pass. A subsequent penalty on the Dutchmen put the ball on the Hope three-yard line. On the next play Albion pushed over to claim the 6-0 victory. Hope ended play at 3-4-1 overall and their 1-3 mark in the MIAA left them in a fourth place tie with Albion. Kalamazoo repeated as champions with a perfect 4-0 record. Mayo Hadden made the All-MIAA first team at tackle and Howard Schaubel was accorded the same honor at one of the end positions. Named at the other end was Alma's Bob Devaney who would later become a coaching legend at the University of Nebraska. Ed Heneveld made the second team and Bob Powers was given honorable mention. Schaubel and Hadden were elected honorary co-captains of the '37 team.

A major rules change in basketball was effective with the 1937-38 season. Except for the opening of each half, the long standing center jump was eliminated. This speed-up of the game added considerable excitement but increased fatigue. Coaches were pressed to revamp their conditioning programs. The new MIAA season welcomed Adrian back into the league and Hope looked forward to defense of.its title. Despite the loss of stalwarts Poppink, Robbert, and Nienhuis, Hope was in good shape. Don Thomas captained the team that returned Paul Boyink, Bob Vanden Berg, Bill De Groot, and Ed Heneveld. Bob Marcus would be out of action until the first of the year due to a shoulder injury suffered in the Kalamazoo football game, but much was expected from sophomores Lee Brannock and Ken Honholt.

Brannock served notice that he would be a factor by leading his team with 15 points in the opening 39-17 victory over Ferris. Six days, later on December 8, the team traveled to East Lansing where they found a Michigan State team smarting from the previous year's upset. Don Thomas scored the first four points, but the Spartans took over for a 30-17 halftime lead and were never headed in their 51-27 victory. A good Michigan Normal team came to the Armory on December 16 and went home with a 35-26 triumph over the Dutchmen to close out 1937. The new year began with a January 3 trip to Kalamazoo to meet Western State, where it was more of the same. Western was in charge all the way and as time ran out the scoreboard showed Western 50, Hope 35. Bob Vanden Berg led Hope with 10. Sophomore Ade Slikkers started at guard and Bob Marcus also saw action for the first time. Hope's final warm-up was a 38-27 victory at Ferris on January 5. The MIAA season opened with Olivet at the Armory and Hinga's team, seasoned by some tough competition, was ready. Hope's team effort left the Comets on the short end of a 62-20 score. Don Thomas was high with 12 but he had help from sophomores Lee Brannock and Ken Honholt who chipped in with 11 each. The high scoring continued as Hope took Alma 61 to 30, but Albion put up a real battle before falling to the Dutchmen, 47-41. The January 21 game at Kalamazoo was typical with excitement all the way plus overtime at the end. The Hornet's 39-37 win would loom large at the season's end. Bob Marcus was back in form as he led his team with 11. The team pleased Coach Hinga with road victories at Alma, 38-26, and at Olivet, 40 to 19. In a close one at Ypsilanti the Dutch lost, 33-30, but were encouraged by the fine performance of Ade Slikkers, who led the scoring with 12. Adrian was not quite prepared for its first-ever game against Hope on February 8. Hope's balanced team, strong bench, and the enthusiastic Armory crowd left the Bulldogs on the short end of a 74-23 score. Ed Heneveld was high with 16 and Thomas had 13. Three days later it was again Thomas with 13, this time leading his team to a 49-28 win over Hillsdale, also in the Armory. The Dales had a second chance on their own floor on February 15 but this time Hope won 50 to 27 as Lee Brannock scored 17. In a crucial game at Albion the Britons were six points better and claimed a 44-38 victory. After a 50-23 win at Adrian Hope prepared for the big one against Kalamazoo in the Armory. A Hope victory would tie the teams for first place in the MIAA. 1,500 fans crowded into the Holland Armory on the night of February 25 to see if Hope would be able to reverse the overtime loss of January 21. Harrison Jones, Kalamazoo's fine center, was the game's high scorer with 15 and forward Don Spalsbury added 11, but Lee Brannock with 13 led Hope's balanced scoring and eventual victory, 48-41. The stage was now set for a playoff and the Grand Rapids Civic Auditorium was chosen as a neutral site. The March 7 game was witnessed by nearly four thousand people from Kalamazoo, Holland, and Grand Rapids. After an opening basket by Hope, the forces of Coach Chester Barnard took charge and led at halftime, 22 to 12. The lead was never relinquished as Don Spalsbury scored a game high 17 in the 44-31 win which sealed the championship. Lee Brannock had 15 for Hope. The March 8 issue of the **Anchor** was termed the "Mourning Edition" and was edged in black. By all accounts Kalamazoo's victory was well deserved and the game provided considerable publicity for the nation's oldest conference. Figures released later showed a gross take of $1,323, with $600 going to the league. Captain Don Thomas was Hope's only graduating senior and Hopes remained high for the 1938-39 season. Bob Marcus was named to the All-MIAA first team while Thomas and Brannock made the second team. Ed Heneveld and Ade Slikkers were given honorable mention.

Prospects for retaining the All-Sports Trophy were not good in the spring of 1938. The outlook was especially dim in track and field as Hope finished last in the March 16 meet held at Hillsdale. Lou Northouse's third in the shot put accounted for all two of Hope's points. Conditions brightened somewhat in an outdoor triangular held at Kalamazoo on April 30. The meet departed somewhat from the standard format and included five relay events: 440, 880, mile, 2 mile, and sprint medley. As expected, Kalamazoo won the meet with 59 points. Olivet was second with 36 and Hope third with 33. Lou Northouse won the shot put with a throw of 37' 7" and the discus with 111' 5." Bob Powers was third in the shot and Harvey Hop took second in the discus. In spite of obvious limitations Hope managed to finish third in the MIAA Field Day meet held at Kalamazoo. Kalamazoo again won the meet with 66 points to 59 for Albion, and 36 for Hope. Joe Howard of Kalamazoo had a new record of 23' 0" in the broad jump but a Saturday downpour in generally prevented the outstanding performances of the year before.

Coach Kleinheksel's tennis team also came up with a third place finish after a successful dual meet season of 6 wins and 4 losses. Hope lost twice to Kalamazoo and Albion, but posted wins over Alma and Olivet as well as two victories over Hillsdale. In the MIAA meet Paul Boyink and Gordon Pleune advanced to the semi-finals in doubles before losing to Marion "Buck" Shane and Edward Born of Kalamazoo, 6-4, 6-0. Shane also won the singles championship. He would go on to be one of the MIAA's all-time great tennis players.

Hope's 1938 golf squad included Bob Marcus, Ade Slikkers, Bill Van Dussen, Les Hopkins, Bob Haack, and Ed Heneveld. Coach Bruce Raymond guided the team to a 9-1 record in MIAA play and came close to a championship. In the MIAA meet it was Slikkers, Van Dussen, Hopkins, and Marcus being edged by Kalamazoo 345 to 348. The second place finish allowed Hope to tie Albion for the runner-up spot in the All-Sports Trophy race with 41 points. Kalamazoo was a runaway winner with a perfect 60 points, having notched championships in all five of the MIAA sports.

Thanks to Jack Schouten, baseball remained alive in '38 as an interfraternity team was again organized. The team split with Western State Frosh, winning, 6-5, and losing, 6-4. Victories were recorded over Bill Poppink's Rockford High School team and Grandville High, but Holland High beat Hope as they had done in the early days of the sport. Other spring activity included a genuine attempt to bring back women's athletics. A Women's Athletic Association (W.A.A.) was formed and produced a tennis team which took second place in a tournament held at Western State Teachers College. Jean Hoekje was Hope's top performer, reaching the semi-finals. As the 1938 school year came to close the **Milestone** was distributed. The college community was pleased to find it dedicated to a deserving Jack Schouten.

Prospects for a successful football campaign in 1938 were considered dim. Captain Bill De Groot was one of but seven returning lettermen. The backfield, however, offered real promise. Transfer quarterback Bob Vander Laan had been a standout at Grand Rapids Junior College and fullback Bob Marcus was a proven performer. Halfbacks Lee Brannock and Paul Boyink were talented athletes and completed the foursome. The season opened with a home night game against Ferris on September 23. Brannock opened the scoring with a 28-yard touchdown run, then broke loose again later in the half on a 45-yard scamper to the Ferris 16. Marcus then passed to Brannock for the score and Hope led, 12-0. Hope's third score came in the third quarter as a result of a recovered fumble on the Ferris 10. Two plays later Vander Laan went in for the score. None of the extra point attempts were successful but Hope added a safety when Ken Honholt tackled Le Seney before he could get off a punt. The 20-0 final was perhaps more than expected but Hope would soon know the sting of being shut out.

Albion came to Holland for a night game on September 30 and scored early when 200 pound tackle Duane Callahan dropkicked a field goal from the 18 yard line. Hope threatened twice. In the third quarter Bob Marcus' would-be touchdown pass was intercepted in the end zone by center Ray Gies. Late in the game Hope got within field goal range but Paul Houtman's place kick was blocked. Despite the 3-0 setback Hope had played well and bounced back against Grand Rapids Junior College on October 7. In the see-saw battle J.C took an early 7-0 lead. Brannock scored for Hope on a 25-yard run and Marcus later went 35 yards around right end to score. Junior College clung to a 14-12 halftime lead but saw it disappear in the second half as Marcus passed twice to Brannock for touchdowns. The 24-14 victory was welcomed, but Hope continued to search for a place kicker.

On October 15 Hope traveled to Adrian and experienced Indian summer with a vengeance. Game time temperatures reached an uncharacteristic 87 degrees and the teams, now accustomed to fall weather, were plagued by early fatigue. Marvin Den Herder scored from the two-yard line and Bob Marcus kicked the point to give the Dutchmen a 7-0 halftime lead. In the second half Hope scored on a Marcus to Ken Honholt pass and Cornie Pape kicked the point but Clemment scored for Adrian to make it 14-6. A turning point occurred in the fourth quarter when Hope's Denton Norlin tackled Rourke in the Adrian end zone before he could get off a punt. With the score at 16-6, Bob Vander Laan broke free at midfield and raced 50 yards for Hope's final tally and a 22-6 victory. Coach Gordon Mac Donald's Alma Scots, led by Captain Bob Devaney, proved too much for the Dutch in the Homecoming game on October 22. Lee Brannock scored for Hope but later a blocked punt in Hope's end zone spelled the difference and Alma emerged the winner, 13 to 7.

A week later the Hinga men made the trip to Kalamazoo for the Hornet's homecoming. After a scoreless first half Hope got a third quarter score when Brannock passed to Paul Boyink for the touchdown. Pape's kick was good and it appeared that Hope's 7-0 lead might hold up. Kalamazoo, however, sustained a late game drive with Dalla going over from the two and kicking the point to salvage a 7-7 tie. Hope was back home on November 4 for a night game with Olivet. Despite a steady rain, Hope showed plenty of offense. The Dutchmen scored first on a pass from Boyink to Vander Laan, then it was Vander Laan to Pape. Touchdown runs by Brannock, Boyink, and Jim Flannagan followed with Marcus kicking two extra points. The 32-12 victory was Hope's fourth and final win. A season-ending trip to Hillsdale was tough on the Dutchmen. Hillsdale, the state's only undefeated, untied team, was in charge all the way, winning finally by a score of 33 to 0. It was Hope's worst defeat in eight years. The overall record of 4-3-1 was respectable but 0-3-1 in the MIAA resulted in a fifth place finish. Guard Bob Powers and fullback Bob Marcus were named to the All-MIAA first team and Bill De Groot, Lee Brannock, and Cornie Pape made the second team. The campaign was officially closed on December 7 at the annual Exchange Club Banquet. Speaker for the occasion was Clarence "Biggie" Munn, who at the time was serving as line coach at the University of Michigan under head coach Fritz Crisler.

Nine veterans returned to Bud Hinga's 1938-39 basketball squad, and coach and players alike were still smarting from their 1938 playoff loss to Kalamazoo. In the opener against Muskegon Junior College Hinga used two separate units in defeating J.C., 45 to 27. In the second encounter Hope scored a convincing 55-18 win over Ferris as Lee Brannock led the attack with 18. On January 3 the team made its annual trek to Kalamazoo to meet Western State. Buck Read's crew led by eight at halftime, thanks to a superior performance by Ken Maddocks, a Grand Haven product. Hope's great second half effort paid off as Lee Brannock tied the score at 41 with less than a minute remaining in regulation play. Western prevailed in the overtime, 46-43, but it was Hope's best showing against Western in many years.

On January 6 it was Michigan Normal in the Armory and Hope was again in command. Brannock with 13 and Ken Honholt with 10 helped produce the 49-24 victory. Hope's overall scoring depth was in evidence as Hope overwhelmed Adrian in the MIAA opener. Howard Becksfort was high with 15, followed by Honholt with 14, Lokers with 14, Brannock with 12, and Marcus with 12. The final showed Hope with 91, Adrian 20. Things were decidedly different at Kalamazoo on January 13. Hope struggled throughout against this long time rival. Lee Brannock scored only one field goal in the contest, but it tied the game in the final two minutes. Bob Vanden Berg then tipped in the winning basket and the Dutchmen took home a hard earned victory, 29 to 27. Marcus was high with 11. Brannock and Slikkers took charge with 15 and 13 at Hillsdale in yet another MIAA win, 55-32. Only the names changed on January 21 as Hope built a 22-2 lead against visiting Olivet. This time it was Paul Boyink with 13 and Slikkers with 11 in the eventual 57-34 win.

January 23 saw the Dutchmen at Kresge Gym in Albion to meet Coach Ed Voltmer's Britons. In a fine defensive effort, Hope's big guns were held in check and the Dutch suffered their first loss in league play. Bob Marcus' eight points were the most scored by any Hope player in the 43-34 loss. The jolt seemed to arouse Hinga's men as Alma invaded the Armory on the 27th. Ray Lokers was a starter for the first time and the two Bobs, Marcus and Vanden Berg, scored 13 each in the 61-29 rout. Following the semester break, Hope downed Michigan Normal, 48-32, at Ypsilanti as Brannock returned to form with 12. In another non-league tussle, Hope traveled to Ferris to better the Bulldogs 52-28. Becksfort and Lokers led the Dutch with eight as all squad members got into the game. Hope made the long trip to Adrian in a resumption of MIAA play. Balanced scoring once again resulted in a lopsided win, this time 66 to 34. Brannock had 13, Vanden Berg 11, Honholt and Boyink 10 each.

Kalamazoo came to the Armory with their fine forward Don Spalsbury on February 13. Spalsbury was high for the night with 14 and the Hornets avenged their earlier loss, 42 to 34. Lee Brannock had an excellent game on the 17th, scoring 25 as Hope hosted Hillsdale and beat them, 56-34. Lokers chipped in with 10. It was Paul Boyink's turn at Olivet on the 21st as he dropped in 16 and Lokers again followed with 10. The 59-22 win kept Hope in the running and set the stage for the big one with Albion at the Armory three days later. Once again Hope fans were treated to a great game. After an 18-18 halftime score, Albion built a 36-28 lead with six minutes to go. Hope battled back to a 39-39 tie at the end of regulation play. The Britons took an early lead in the overtime but a Brannock bucket gave Hope a 44-43 lead. Bob Vanden Berg got the final field goal to give the Dutchmen a big victory, 46 to 43. Hope's 40-23 win at Alma in the season's last game gave the Dutch an MIAA record of 10-2 and placed them in a three-way tie with Kalamazoo and Albion for first place.

For the second year in a row Hope found itself involved in a playoff. At a special meeting MIAA officials came up with an interesting format. The playoff would take place on Wednesday, March 8, at the Men's Gymnasium on the campus of Western State Teachers College in Kalamazoo. Six 15-minute halves would be played with a 10-minute rest period between the periods of play. Thus, the total playing time (barring overtime) for each team would be 60 minutes instead of the customary 40. Hope would begin by playing Albion for 15 minutes, then play Kalamazoo for a like period. Kalamazoo would follow with a half against Albion and then the schedule would be repeated. Balance in the MIAA was in evidence as this was the fourth playoff in five years. A 120-piece mass band was assembled from the three schools to play during the intermissions.

Hope suffered several injuries in the spirited game with Albion and ended up on the short end of a 36-26 score. Bob Vanden Berg scored 10. The encounter with Kalamazoo was close all the way with Hope clinging to a 29-28 lead as seconds waned. At this point Don Spalsbury intercepted a Hope pass and scored the winning basket, making the final Kalamazoo 30, Hope 29. The Hornets proved their metal by repeating the 30-29 squeaker against Albion on Dick Walker's long shot in the final minute. Kalamazoo was again the champion and Hope, despite an outstanding year, had nothing to show but a third place finish. Bob Marcus and Paul Boyink were elected honorary co-captains, while Marcus and Lee Brannock made the All-MIAA team along with Don Spalsbury and Bob Warren of Kalamazoo, and Bill Feduniak of Albion.

In the spring of '39, Hope's second place in tennis was the best that could be mustered. The Dutchmen were fifth in golf and fell to sixth in the conference track meet held at Houseman Field in Grand Rapids. Albion won the meet and thereby gave Kalamazoo a run for the All-Sports Trophy, but in the final tally it was Kalamazoo again with 53 points to 48 for the Britons. It was left for women athletes to save the day for Hope in '39. A women's tennis tournament for MIAA schools was held at Albion on May 19 and 20. Hope's Jean Hoekje won the singles championship by defeating Margaret Mc Kee of Albion, 1-6, 6-3, 6-2. The doubles championship was taken by the Hope team of Thelma Kooiker and Alethe Brower as they defeated Nancy Todd and Mildred Rosenbaum of Kalamazoo, 6-2, 6-4. Hope won the tournament with nine points while Olivet, Kalamazoo, and Albion each scored four.

When students returned to the campus in September of 1939 headlines spoke of **Stukas**, **Panzers**, and **Blitzkrieg** as Adolph Hitler methodically dismembered Poland and war returned to Europe. The sobering spectre of world conflict however, did not noticeably alter campus life. Neutrality was a popular stance, and somehow the Maginot and Siegfried Lines seemed less important than Albion's line.

Twelve football lettermen returned and 25 freshmen reported to Jack Schouten. One of Coach Hinga's first moves was to shift Captain Bob Powers from guard to center. The season opened on a positive note in a night game against Ferris at Riverview Park. Fullback Marv Den Herder scored first for Hope, but Honholt's kick was wide. Hope's second tally came as a result of a 55-yard punt by Lee Brannock which was fumbled by Ferris on their five-yard line. Art Kronemeyer then plunged over for the touchdown. Brannock's try for the point failed but in the third quarter Ken Honholt recovered a fumbled Ferris punt reception in their end zone. In the final minutes Ted Bidwell of Ferris got away for a 75-yard touchdown run to take the sting out of the 18-6 defeat. September 29 brought Grand Rapids Junior College to Riverview for a game that featured defense. The Dutch were fortunate to come away with a 0-0 tie as J.C. missed a field goal attempt from the 12 yard line. Hope's offense reappeared on October 6 as Adrian made its first appearance on Dutch soil in another night contest. After six minutes of play fullback Art Kronemeyer went over left tackle for the game's first score and Bob Powers kicked the point. In the second quarter, tackle Marty Bekken blocked an Adrian punt and recovered it in the end zone for a touchdown. Adrian chose to kick off and Kronemeyer returned the kick to the Adrian 49. On the next play Lee Brannock covered the remaining 49 yards for the touchdown adding to the general Adrian frustration. In the fourth quarter Ed Luidens recovered an Adrian fumble on their 10 yard line, and Ray Meyers subsequently scored from the three for the last score. The final count showed Hope with 35, Adrian 0.

In a night game at Alma on October 13, Hope was without the services of quarterback Bob Vander Laan, who had been injured in the Adrian contest. Alma's Fred Hill opened the scoring early in the second quarter on a one-yard run, and Bob Kirby added the point after. The drive covered 65 yards. Late in the half the Scots mounted another drive, this time for 75 yards, which was climaxed by Francis Cappaert's touchdown plunge. Bob Kirby again added the point and Alma led at halftime, 14 to 0. The third quarter featured a punting duel between Don Smith and Lee Brannock and there was no scoring well into the fourth period. Hope appeared to be running out of time, but with 4 1/2 minutes remaining with the Dutch on their own 35, Bob Idema passed to Phil Waalkes who rambled to the Alma 12, where he lateraled to Brannock who was finally downed on the eight. Three running plays failed before Don Poppen went in for the score. Bob Montgomery's kick was blocked but he picked up the free ball and ran it in for the point, making it 14 to 7. In the final minute of play Idema threw a desperation pass to Ken Honholt in the end zone. Honholt made the reception to bring Hope within one. All eyes were on Montgomery as he split the uprights with a near perfect kick. The Hinga men savored their fantastic comeback to tie at 14.

In another night contest, on October 20, Hope hosted Kalamazoo College. Hope's 7-0 victory was the first in seven years against the Hornets. Ray Meyers scored for the Dutch in the second quarter and Montgomery added the point. The remainder of the game featured threats and fumbles by Kalamazoo, and goal line stands by Hope. One Kalamazoo drive ended with a fumble on the one foot line. If lady luck was with the Dutchmen, she was a welcome guest. Hope was the guest of Olivet at their Homecoming before 1,200 fans on October 28. It would prove a disappointing day for the Comets, as Hope registered its second consecutive shutout. Bob Montgomery scored from the three-yard line early in the game, but the try-for point was blocked. Bob Idema set up Hope's second score with a breakaway run from Olivet's 25 to the three. Brannock went over for the score and this time Montgomery's kick was true. In the third quarter Bob Powers intercepted an Olivet pass on their 40. The ball was advanced to the 25 by Den Herder. On the next play Brannock broke loose on a broken field run and went all the way. Montgomery's kick was good. As the fourth quarter opened, Hope was in possession on the Olivet 15. Ted Cimock carried to the one yard line and Ray Meyers went in for the score. Montgomery's extra point made it 27-0 and wound up a successful trip for the Dutchmen.

Hope had a taste of its own medicine at Homecoming on November 4. Dwight Harwood's strong Hillsdale squad dominated play from the start and posted a convincing 30 to 6 victory. It was Hope's first defeat of the season and put a damper on championship hopes. The Dutchmen closed out the season at Albion on November 11. The Britons' Elwood Lindow scored first on a brilliant 56 yard run. The point attempt was not good and the score stood at 6-0 until the second quarter when Steve Beban plunged over from the one and Long added the point giving Albion a 13-0 halftime margin. In the second half a series of passes clicked for Hope. George Heneveld was the victim of pass interference on the two-yard line but the Albion defense was stubborn. Finally, after three tries, Lee Brannock scored on a left end run and Montgomery kicked the point. The teams were evenly matched but Hope's effort fell one touchdown short and Albion wrapped up the championship. Hillsdale finished second and Hope, with a 3-2-1 record, 5-2-1 overall, was third. Bob Powers was named the All-MIAA center and along with Kalamazoo's Danny Wood, was selected the MIAA's most valuable player. The recognition was the first received by a Hope player in any sport. Lee Brannock, Ken Honholt, and Bob Hudson made the second team and Bill Tappan received honorable mention. In a season post-script, Chancellor Robert Hutchins of the University of Chicago announced that his school would abolish football and withdraw from the Big Ten Conference.

As the days dwindled down in the decade of the thirties, attention was focused once again on basketball. The fine teams of the two previous seasons had not fared well in post-season playoffs, and the goal now was to prevent this situation in 1940 by winning the title outright. Consistent play would be necessary but the outlook was again bright for the team captained by Lee Brannock and Ken Honholt. Seventeen candidates turned out to tackle the 18 game schedule. The season opened with three home games in December. Holland continued to be a great basketball town and fans crowded into the Armory to watch Hinga's latest combination build a 22-10 halftime lead over Ferris on December 5 before coasting to a 47-19 victory. Lee Brannock led the parade with 12 points, while sophomores Gil Van Wieren, Ken Vanden Berg, and John Visser made their first appearance. They would be heard from. The December 14 game with Michigan Normal was definitely tougher but Brannock came through with 18 counters and Hope had its second win, 36 to 23. Three days after Christmas the local fans enjoyed a holiday treat as the Dutchmen hosted Central College of Pella, Iowa, in the first ever meeting between the sister institutions. With balanced scoring Hope posted a 54-37 victory. Brannock and Bob Montgomery each scored 13 and Ray Lokers had 12. Central moved on to Grand Rapids for a game with Calvin the following night.

Thoughts of an undefeated season were dashed in Kalamazoo on January 3 when the team met its old nemesis, Western State. The Dutchmen trailed by 12 at halftime but actually outscored the Hilltoppers in the second half. It proved too little, too late, and the Dutch were downed, 47-37. Ade Slikkers was high with 11 and Brannock added 10. Two days later the team was back in form at Adrian as Ray Lokers led his team to victory with 17 points. Slikkers was again effective from outcourt with 10. Kalamazoo visited the Armory on January 9 and suffered a 46-29 setback. Dick Lemmer scored 13 for the Hornets but Hope countered with 15 from Brannock and 8 from sophomore Ken Vanden Berg. Hillsdale gave the Dutchmen a scare on January 12 as they led 17-16 at halftime, but the locals pulled away to win by 10, 43-33. Ray Lokers had 13. A trip to Olivet on the 16th netted the Dutchmen yet another MIAA win, 64 to 20. This time Ken Honholt was high with 18 while Lokers added 12. Hope's scoring potential was increasingly evident as a number of team members took turns as high scorers.

One of sport's axioms is that success breeds success. Few would dispute this truism, but a deadly byproduct is overconfidence, and Hope was stricken as Albion visited the Armory on the 19th. Hope built a 19 to 8 halftime lead and the script seemed to be repeating itself, but Albion went on an 18 to 0 run and quite uncharacteristically, the Hope team lost its poise. The Dutchmen were five for 25 from the free throw line including zero for five in the closing minutes. Albion took the contest by five points, 32-27, and the missed charities loomed larger than ever.

A non-league tussle at Ferris saw the team return to form. Honholt with 13 led Hope to a 54-32 victory. Brannock, Slikkers, and sophomore John Visser each scored eight. The combination of Alma's narrow floor and outstanding sophomores was a source of concern for Coach Hinga on the 27th. The Scots enjoyed a 23-22 lead at halftime but the pattern followed the Hillsdale game and Hope pulled away to win 45 to 32. The ever reliable Brannock came through with 18 points and Lokers, coming off an injury, added eight. As the season moved into February the team was on target at Ypsilanti and took the measure of Michigan Normal by the comfortable margin of 65 to 34. It was Bob Montgomery's night as he dropped in 17 while sophomore Gil Van Wieren chipped in with 11. It was Honholt's turn on the 6th at Adrian as his 13 points helped produce the 20 point margin of victory, the final being 47-27. Three days later at Kalamazoo's Treadway Gym the spread was even greater as the Dutchmen beat their long-time rival, 42-19. Hope's depth of talent was again evident. Co-Captain Lee Brannock was unable to play due to a back injury, but sophomore Gil Van Wieren picked up the slack and led the team with 13. Hillsdale had proven troublesome in January but the February 13 game on the Dales' home court was never in doubt. Defending the Dutch was a problem for Coach Harwood as each starter was now a bona fide scoring threat. Brannock was back and scored 12, as did Honholt. Montgomery had 11 and Lokers 10. The final was 58-26.

Olivet traveled to Holland on February 17. There was some concern that Hope might look past this Saturday game, knowing that on Monday they must play at Albion in the most important game thus far. Coach Hinga, however, was able to convince his team to attend the business at hand and they won going away, 58 to 25. There were no standouts but every squad member played and the scoring once again was evenly divided. With but one day of rest the Dutchmen made their way to Albion, where a victory would avenge their only MIAA loss and assure at least a championship tie. Both teams "came to play" and the contest at Kresge Gym may have been the hardest-fought of the season. In the end it was the defensive play and rebounding of Ade Slikkers that spelled the difference. Hope won by six, 30-24 as Brannock, Hope's leading scorer for the night, was held to eight points.

The night of February 24 still generates a glow in the hearts of those who were on hand in the winter of 1940. Coach Gordon Mac Donald was in town with a strong Alma team that had steadily improved, thanks to the play of Keith Carey, Bob Kirby, and the Howe brothers. Alma was determined to force another three-way tie by defeating Hope, and the Dutchmen were just as determined to prevent the spectre of another play-off. 1,178 fans crowded into the Armory and numerous others were turned away. Excitement reigned from the opening tip as Hope fought its way to a narrow 17-14 halftime lead.

The tension was relieved somewhat during the intermission as Captain Bob Powers of the football team was presented the league's Most Valuable Player award by Hope President Wynand Wichers. As play resumed Alma forged ahead 20-18. The Scots clung tenaciously to their lead and with seconds remaining were on top, 34-33. At this point Ade Slikkers realized the dream of every player who ever donned a uniform. He closed his collegiate career with a long set shot which parted the net and won the championship for his team. Keith Carey with 10 led his team in its great effort,while Brannock was high for Hope with 14. It was Hope's second outright title in four years. Hope's first-ever bid for post-season play came with an invitation to represent Michigan in the AAU Tournament in St. Louis, Missouri. The offer was declined by school officials due to the expense involved and projected time away from classes. Lee Brannock, Ken Honholt, and Ade Slikkers made the All-MIAA first team along with Keith Carey and Bob Kirby of Alma, William Feduniak of Albion, and Marion Diehl of Olivet.

With the conclusion of winter sports Albion led Hope in the All-Sports Trophy race, 22 points to 21. As usual, the outcome would depend on spring sports performances. There was general dismay in the Hope camp due to the lack of track candidates. Prospects in tennis and golf were above average but all realized that a low finish in track would give the trophy to someone else. There were no Hope entries in the MIAA indoor meet held at Hillsdale on March 13 and a May 10 interfraternity meet failed to generate the needed interest. Due to the limited squad size, no dual meets were scheduled. Hope's token force did enter the MIAA Meet held at Marshall on May 23 and 24. The loyal few promised a sixth place finish and were able to deliver. Lee Brannock took third in the broad jump and Bob Powers did likewise in the shot put. Larry Bruggers garnered Hope's other point with a fifth in the 880.

Coach Kleinheksel's tennis team included Al Joldersma, Don Poppen, Bob Vegter, Howard Hoekje, Bill Tappan, Ed De Pree, and Frank Zweering. The hoped-for second place did not materialize, but the team did manage to hold on to third place.

The golf team was made up of seniors Ken Honholt and Ade Slikkers, junior Bob Dykstra, and sophomore Ted Cimock. Under Coach Hinga the team did well in dual meets posting wins over Hillsdale, Alma, Kalamazoo, and Olivet. Golf seemed to offer Hope's best chance for a title but in the Field

Bob Powers - MIAA Co-Most Valuable Player - 1939

Powers, who captained the '39 team, was the first Hope athlete in any sport to be named the league's most valuable. He shared the honor with Kalamazoo's Danny Wood.

Day meet at Marshall the team had an off day and slipped to fourth place. Kalamazoo took first place in both tennis and golf but Albion won the track championship and thereby the All-Sports Trophy.

Jack Schouten coached a non-league baseball team that included some well known athletes. Jack Jalving and Dave Morrison pitched, with Bob Montgomery behind the plate. It was Ray Lokers at first, Kenny Vanden Berg at second, Chuck Zoet at third, and Bob Vander Laan at short. Outfielders were Art Timmer, Ernie Ensing, Howard Becksfort, and Dick Van Strien. Hope lost to Hillsdale, 9-3, and to Muskegon Junior College, 10-4, but defeated Grand Rapids University, 13 to 5. As yet there seemed little interest in returning the game to MIAA status.

As the decade of the thirties came to a close Hope had made its mark in the MIAA. Much of the credit must go to Milton Lage Hinga, whose efforts netted league championships in basketball (three), football, and golf. More important, perhaps, was his overall influence, which tended to boost morale. His concern for the welfare of all students was felt and became contagious. Athletics at Hope had survived the Great Depression's limitations but faced an uncertain future as war clouds darkened.

REFERENCES - CHAPTER 6

1. The **Anchor**, May 27, 1931.
2. The **Holland Sentinel**, Saturday, September 27, 1932.
3. The **Anchor**, December 11, 1934.

The 1939-40 MIAA Champions

With an 11-1 MIAA record and 16-2 overall, the team was invited to represent Michigan in the AAU Tournament in St. Louis. The invitation was declined due to projected expense and time away from classes. **Top Row L to R:** Harold Colenbrander, Elmer "Bud" Morgan. **Middle Row:** Coach Jack Schouten, Gil Van Wieren, Kenny VandenBerg, John Visser, Don Formsma, Bill Tappan, Coach Bud Hinga. **Front Row:** Bob Montgomery, Ray Lokers, Co-Captain Lee Brannock, Co-Captain Ken Honholt, Ade Slikkers, Howard Becksfort.

First MIAA Most Valuable For Hope

In '39 Bob Powers was selected Co-Most Valuable in football with Dan Wood of Kalamazoo. The award was presented to Powers by President Wynard Wichers at halftime of Hope's championship basketball game with Alma.

CHAPTER 7

THE EARLY FORTIES - COPING WITH WORLD WAR II

In the fall of 1940 Hope's convocation speaker was the Honorable Everett M. Dirksen of Illinois. A congressman at the time, Dirksen had not yet achieved the luster he would later enjoy as the Senate's golden-voiced orator, but he was a member of the Reformed Church and this was the likely connection. He was also a Republican.

As the school year got under way there were other happenings to report. Ade Slikkers took a coaching job at Coopersville High School and Lee Brannock did likewise at Lake Odessa. During the summer months Bernard Arendshorst, Hope accounting instructor, had mounted a campaign aimed at electing Bob Powers to the College All-Star football squad for the **Chicago Tribune**'s annual charity game at Soldiers Field. The effort fell short but 28 thousand votes spoke well for the former Hope captain and drew some attention to the Hope grid program. Powers, meanwhile, enrolled in the Wayne State Medical School.

Bud Hinga, now in his 11th year as Hope mentor, faced a limited seven game schedule due to the late cancellation by Olivet of its football program. In the home opener on September 20 Hope met hapless Ferris Institute under the lights at Riverview Park. The Dutch backfield of quarterback Bob Montgomery, halfbacks Ray Meyers and Bob Idema, and fullback Marv Den Herder dominated play, along with Captain George Heneveld at left end. At one point Coach Hinga inserted an all-sophomore team and the group held its own. The 35-0 rout included touchdown runs by Idema, Den Herder, Art Timmer, and Wallace "Whitey" Riemersma. Extra points were added via Montgomery's placements and Don De Fouw dropkicks. Tackle Harvey Koop contributed a blocked punt and Art Timmer an interception. Hope was almost as impressive at Adrian a week later. George Heneveld's defensive play stopped three early Adrian drives before Art Timmer reeled off a 70-yard touchdown run. The sophomore's admirers had already dubbed him the "Grandville Gazelle" and such performance seemed to validate the moniker. Hope's second touchdown came on a short Montgomery pass to Heneveld who lateraled to De Fouw who rambled the remaining 40 yards for the score. Montgomery's second kick made it 14-0. The game's final tally was registered in the fourth quarter, when Bill Tappan intercepted a pass on the Adrian 30 and ran it in for the touchdown. The 20 to 0 score left Hope's goal line uncrossed but the Alma Scots had other ideas when they invaded Riverview on the night of October 4. Bob Kirby broke the spell with a 12-yard scamper around left end to give his team an early 6-0 lead but in the second quarter Grandville was heard from again. Timmer broke loose on his own 48 and ran 52 yards for the score. Montgomery's kick made it 7-6 Dutchmen until the third quarter, when Alma's Jack Tait exceeded Timmer's feat by going 63 yards unmolested. Tait then wrapped up the ball game by intercepting a fourth quarter Montgomery pass and crossing the goal. The 19-7 setback was hard to take, but the talented Alma athletes would haunt the Dutchmen for the next two years. Hope's trip to Kalamazoo on October 12 produced a rewarding comeback. The game's only score came when Whitey Riemersma went in from the Hornet 15 on a fake reverse. The remainder of the contest featured a punting duel between Steve Dallas and Bob Montgomery. George Vander Hill's excellent coverage of Montgomery's kicks aided the Hinga men in registering their third shutout and taking home a sweet 7-0 victory.

Hope played well at Hillsdale's homecoming but had to settle for a tie. Early in the game the Dales moved to the Dutch two inch line but came away empty. However, in the closing minutes of the half Bert Eklund scored for Hillsdale. The conversion attempt failed. In a second half drive Marv Den Herder suffered a dislocated elbow and was sidelined for the season. Hope finally scored on a run by Whitey Riemersma but the all important point was blocked and the game ended, 6 to 6.

Hope's own homecoming contest was played on November 2 with Albion furnishing the opposition. A full-page ad in the Hope football program proclaimed in large letters that "WE WILL ALL WIN WITH WILKIE," but FDR and Albion would prove too much for Wilkie and Hope. The teams were evenly matched and for a time Hope held the upper hand. A Timmer to Heneveld pass placed the ball on the Albion six-yard line, but the Britons held and Hope's best scoring opportunity was gone. Also in the first half Albion blocked a Montgomery punt and Ed Alsip subsequently scored the game's only touchdown. The kick was wide and Albion led 6-0 at the half. The margin held up throughout a hard-fought second half and Coach Dale Sprankle had his second consecutive MIAA championship.

Hope's season, which had begun with such promise, ended on an anticlimactic note in a non-league game with Grand Rapids Junior College. J.C. drew first blood when John Crell dropkicked a field goal. The 3-0 lead was erased early in the fourth quarter by an Art Timmer touchdown. Don De Fouw's kick was blocked leaving Hope with a slim 6-3 lead. As the game and the season wound down Hope's defense weakened enough for Louis Charon to score the winning touchdown with Crell adding the point. The 10-6 loss gave Hope an overall record of 3-3-1, while their 2-2-1 MIAA mark was good enough for a third-place tie with Hillsdale. Bob Montgomery was named to the All-MIAA first team while George Heneveld and Bill Tappan made the second team. Bob Hudson and Marty Bekken were accorded honorable mention. Ray Meyers and Bill Tappan were elected co-captains for 1941, but Meyers would not return.

As winter and basketball returned to Holland pleasant memories lingered of Hope's dramatic championship of the previous season. Things would be different in 1940-41. Alma's young team, which had gone to the brink of a championship in 1939-40, was the overwhelming favorite. Hope, meanwhile, returned only Gil Van Wieren and Captain Bob Montgomery as starters. This was somewhat misleading, as Kenny Vanden Berg and tall John Visser had also played effectively. Transfers Jackie Baas from Grand Rapids J.C. and Ken Newendorp from Northwestern J.C. of Orange City were expected to help.

The 1939-40 champions had closed the season with a nine-game winning streak, and Hinga's new contingent made it 10 in the season opener on December 7 in the Armory. The Dutchmen displayed considerable confidence in their 59-39 victory over Muskegon Junior College as forward Kenny Vanden Berg led with 14. Montgomery and Visser followed with 12 and 11. For the first time Hope began league play before Christmas as they hosted Adrian on December 12. The victory margin was cut in half, but the Dutch prevailed, 45-35. John Visser was high with 11 and Montgomery had 10. As the squad made its way to Kalamazoo on the 17th they knew that the easy ones were over. The Hornets, always tough in Treadway, moved to a 24-21 halftime advantage and led by Dick Lemmer's 15 points, almost pulled it off. But at the gun it was Hope 43, Kalamazoo 37. Center John Visser played a strong game and was high for his team with 11.

Following the Christmas break Hope met Grand Rapids University on January 3. In another close one Hinga's quintet again came away the victor, this time 47 to 42. It was Visser again with 12 and guard Everett "Ets" Kleinjans with 10. On January 7 Hope made its annual trek to Western State's campus to meet Buck Read's Hilltoppers (not yet Broncos). The win streak, now at 13, was in jeopardy, to say the least. During the previous week the ever-strong Western five had scored an impressive 56-43 victory over UCLA. They had also taken the measure of a good team from the University of Chicago. Determined to take advantage of the strong competition, the Dutchmen were surprised to find themselves in the lead at halftime, 28-26. In an evenly-played second half Hope maintained the intensity and came away with the upset of the year, 48 to 45. Captain Montgomery with strong overall play and 11 points, led the team. Elsner was high for Western, also with 11.

In a return to league play two days later, Hope beat Hillsdale by 30 as a red-hot Gil Van Wieren scored a season-high 20 points. The final was Hope 62, Hillsdale 32. Olivet gave the Dutchmen a scare on January 14 when the Comets stayed with Hope for a 19-19 halftime score. The Dutch were ice cold from the free throw line making only three of 13, but a second half surge netted 32 points and the Hinga crew went on to win, 51-28. It was Van Wieren again with 14 and Kenny Vanden Berg with 10. A sobering development three days later put the Albion game in doubt. Bob Montgomery was put out of action with a back injury and John Visser went home to Grand Rapids to seek treatment for a worsening stomach ulcer condition. Ets Kleinjans was pressed into service at center and Hope trailed much of the way. Late in the game Vanden Berg tied the score at 31 and Van Wieren added two field goals to seal the 35-31 victory.

The long anticipated meeting with Alma took place in the Armory on January 23. Hope fans remembered the dramatic game of the preceding season and hoped for more of the same, but Alma's "super sophomores" of the year before were now seasoned veterans and pulled away with three minutes remaining in the half. Keith Carey with 20 and Bud Howe with 10 made the victory a decisive one, 44 to 23. Montgomery had nine to lead Hope while Art Timmer did his best to fill in for the missing John Visser. The Dutchmen bounced back from disappointment to take Michigan Normal, 53-45. Ken Vanden Berg led with 13 and Jackie Baas contributed 10 from his guard spot. A February 4 trip to Adrian produced a 55-30 victory that saw Baas again score 10 and Van Wieren return to form with 19. Two days later Hope met Kalamazoo in the Armory and a controversy of some significance marred the contest. The argument concerned a tap-in by Kazoo's Gerald Gedman as the half ended. A heated discussion was carried on for several minutes before the officials finally allowed the basket to stand. The decision loomed large at game's end when Kalamazoo won by a score of 36 to 35. Dick Lemmer led his team with 15 while Vanden Berg and Kleinjans each had 10 for Hope. A bright spot was the return of John Visser. It had been feared that he would be lost for the season but he played half of the game and would gradually work back into shape. Hope won handily at Hillsdale, 68-31, behind balanced scoring. Vanden Berg was high with 16, Montgomery had 13, and Kleinjans 12.

Olivet College withdrew from the MIAA in 1940, but continued to play MIAA schools on a non-league basis. Hope's contest there on February 14 was one such game. The 57-36 Dutch victory featured Ken Vanden Berg's 15 points, Ets Kleinjans with 14, and Gil Van Wieren with 10. Back home in the Armory, Michigan Normal reversed an earlier decision and took the Dutchmen, 43-32. Captain Burman Misenar was the outstanding man on the court with 17 points. Kleinjans had nine for Hope and substitute Don De Fouw followed with eight. The team's title hopes were fading but Albion was defeated, 32-25, after a struggle on the Armory floor. Montgomery was high with 10 and John Visser was on the road back with eight points.

Despite some mid-season disappointments, Hope found itself traveling to Alma with a solid ball club. With the return of Visser, Coach Hinga had high hopes for a return to the level of play that had netted a 17 game win streak. But Alma's team was one of the best in its history and its subsequent 52-32 victory proved beyond all doubt that the Scots were the best in the league. Bob Kirby led the scoring with 15 and Bud Howe was next with 13. Gil Van Wieren had eight for Hope and Bob Montgomery scored seven in his final game. Alma was invited to participate in the NAIA Tournament in Kansas City, where they defeated Panhandle State of Oklahoma before falling to Murray State of Kentucky. Bob Montgomery was named to the All-MIAA team along with Kirby, Carey, and Bud Howe of Alma, and Dick Lemmer of Kalamazoo. No second team was selected but Gil Van Wieren was given honorable mention.

In the spring of '41 Hope's first ever spring trip took

Hope's First Southern Trip

The 1941 tennis team leaves for the south. **Left to Right:** Frank Zweering, Bob Hoek, Howard Hoekje, Bob Vegter, Bill Tappan, Coach Bernard Arendshorst.

place. The venture was organized by Bernard Arendshorst, Hope's new tennis coach. Five players accompanied Arendshorst on the southern jaunt. The group included Frank Zweering, Bob Vegter, Bill Tappan, Bob Hoek, and Howard Hoekje. The team defeated Catawba College of Salisbury, North Carolina, 4-3, and Tennessee State of Nashville, 6-1, but lost to powerful Presbyterian of Clinton, South Carolina, 7-0. At each college, Coach Arendshorst presented a pair of wooden shoes as a remembrance. Without exception they were invited back for the next year. A match with the University of South Carolina, Columbia was rained out. In dual meets the Dutchmen were shut out, 7-0, by Kalamazoo, but recorded 6-1 wins over Alma and Hillsdale. In the final MIAA standings, Hope finished second to Kalamazoo.

Coach Hinga's 1941 golf team included Bob Dykstra, Jim Baar, Bill Pelon, Bill Alderink, Art Timmer, and Frank Lokker. The team dropped dual matches to Kalamazoo (12-0), Hillsdale (7 1/2-4 1/2), and Albion (9-3) but showed up well in the conference meet and managed an overall fourth place tie with Hillsdale. Alma finished first.

Track in 1941 seemed to have lost its appeal. Hope entered the MIAA indoor meet at Jennison Field House in Lansing but none of the competitors placed. Hope men were admonished for the poor turnout in a sarcastic **Anchor** article which appeared in the March 26 issue. Hope's last place finish was inevitable but there would be better days. The baseball team, on the other hand, fared rather well, especially in a non-league sport. Dave Morrison pitched a strong game against Grand Rapids Junior College on April 24, but six Dutch errors resulted in a 2-1 J.C. victory. Morrison got better support against Grand Rapids University on May 2 and Hope came away the victor by a 6-2 count. Wendell Anderson had three hits and Kenny Vanden Berg added a triple. Morrison and Ernie Ensing divided the mound duty against Muskegon Junior College with Ray Spencer behind the plate. The final was Hope 9, Muskegon 6. Vanden Berg and Ray Otteman each had doubles. Jack Baas was the star in Hope's second victory over Grand Rapids Junior College as he connected for a single, double, and triple. First baseman Harold Colenbrander and catcher Ray spencer had triples. Western State's Frosh team beat the Schouten men, 14-2, but a second win over Grand Rapids University, this time 6 to 3, gave Hope a very respectable 4-2 record. Alma won the All-Sports Trophy, followed by Albion, Kalamazoo and Hope.

The fall of 1941 on Hope's campus was probably about like most that had gone before. Its events, however, remain more vivid, as I witnessed them firsthand. Enrolled as a freshman, in due course I was issued a green tie and small cap or "pot." The person in charge of the issuing was senior Bill Tappan, president of the student council, captain of the football team, student representative to the MIAA, member of the Blue Key National Honor Fraternity, pre-med student, and soon to be valedictorian of his class. I was duly impressed. In his case it seemed appropriate to do the sweeping bow, hat in hand, when he commanded, "Pot frosh!" When the freshmen won the annual Pull (tug of war) across Black River we were required to do obeisance only to juniors and seniors. The sophs called foul, claiming that the frosh sneaked in four to six additional men when things were going badly. Also, that anchor man Clarence Stryker was replaced when he injured his hand. They may have been right. It was a long time ago. But I digress ....

The growing stream of those enlisting in the armed forces in '41 prompted MIAA officials to rescind the freshman rule, which had been in force since 1926. The move proved a boon to Hope grid fortunes. By season's end several first-year men had, at one time or another, earned starting assignments. Among them was Dick Higgs from Cedar Springs, a triple threat tailback who fit nicely into Coach Hinga's single wing attack. Other freshmen of note included Gerald "Bud" Karel, a running back with considerable ability from Grand Rapids Central, guards Len Dick and Wayne Purchase from Holland, tackle Len Pape from Grand Rapids South, and end Don Schriemer from Kelloggsville. Hope opened against Grand Rapids Junior College at Houseman Field on September 19. Higgs joined veterans Art Timmer, Don De Fouw, and Roy Davis to make up the starting backfield. Several 1940 squad members were missing. Co-Captain Ray Meyers had enlisted in the Naval Air Corps, as had lineman Chuck Holcomb. Halfback Whitey Riemersma was in the Marine Corps, also in flight training, while Ward Toner was the second lineman to sign up. As the season opened with Grand Rapids J.C., however, Hinga found line stability in veteran tackles Marty Bekken and George Vander Hill. The center position was solid with Captain Bill Tappan. 2,500 watched the teams battle through a scoreless first half. In the second half Higgs lived up to his reputation by breaking loose on a 41-yard run to the J.C. 22. A few plays later Art Timmer scored over right tackle and Roy Davis kicked the point. The 7-0 score stood until Timmer reeled off a 35-yard punt return to set up a 27-yard field goal by Davis. Hope's defense was equal to the task, and the Dutchmen went home with a 10-0 victory.

Hope's second contest was played under the lights at Riverview and was a real standoff. In the first half Hope penetrated to the Michigan Normal 22, was stymied, then saw a Davis field goal attempt from the 29 fall short. The heavier Normal team made its presence felt in the second half and moved to the Hope 11, where a field goal attempt by Osbourne was wide. The Hope defenders survived an 83-yard Normal drive late in the game that moved to the Dutch two-yard line. On the ensuing play, Slabaugh fumbled on the five and Bud Morgan recovered for Hope to preserve the 0-0 tie. Morgan, the scrappy 150 pound end from Herkimer, New York, was the game's star along with tackle Marty Bekken.

In the MIAA opener at Alma, the Dutchmen got off to a good start when Art Timmer passed to Dick Higgs for the score and Davis converted. The Scots retaliated in the second period when Jack Tait connected on a touchdown pass to

Alma's All-everything, Bob Kirby. Both teams threatened in the fourth quarter. Hope moved inside the 10 twice, then missed a field goal from the 18. Alma's final drive was halted on the Hope nine as the game ended. The 7-7 tie was considered a moral victory against the eventual MIAA champions.

A rash of mid-season injuries took its toll as Coach Potsy Clark brought his Grand Grand Rapids University team to Holland on October 17. Clark's assistant coach was none other than Gerald Ford, who would one day become President of the United States. The loss of Tappan, Timmer, Koop, Morgan, Bekken, and Higgs was simply too much to sustain, as evidenced by the 16-0 score. The Lancers scored touchdowns in the second and third quarters and wrapped up the game with a field goal in the fourth. With several players still sidelined, the Dutchmen prepared to host Hillsdale on the 24th. Six of Hope's starters were freshmen. Halfbacks Higgs and Bud Karel were joined by linemen Len Pape, Len Dick, Wayne Purchase, and Leroy "Bud" Korunda. Midway in the first quarter George Vander Hill recovered a blocked punt on the Hope 41. Six plays later Higgs lofted a pass to the speedy Karel who raced into the end zone for the score. The remainder of the contest was decidedly a holding action for Hope. Bill Tappan had a key interception on the Hope 10 and the Dales were stopped at halftime on the Hope seven. At one point in the second half Hillsdale reached Hope's one yard line only to be frustrated by the Dutchmen's stubborn stand. In the fourth quarter a long Hillsdale pass placed the ball on the Hope six, but Marty Bekken broke through to throw Paul Wright for a 10-yard loss and shut down the final threat. In Hope's 6-0 victory several freshmen came of age.

On a rainy November 1 the Hinga men journeyed to Albion for the latter's Homecoming. Despite a stellar performance by Don De Fouw and the Hope defense the Britons managed a second quarter score on a Wauthier to Bob Lynn pass. Paul Schneider's conversion made it 7-0. Hope threatened in the final stanza when the Dutch reached the Albion 7, but De Fouw's pass intended for George Slager was intercepted by Schneider and Hope went home a 7-0 loser. Longtime rival Kalamazoo was Hope's homecoming opponent on November 8, another rainy, dismal day. The Hornets drew first blood when fullback Jack Bockelman rambled 30 yards for the score. Hope's tying touchdown in the fourth quarter was hard-earned. As the third period ended De Fouw passed to George Slager who lateraled to Higgs who reached the five, but the play was nullified by a penalty. A successful De Fouw to Slager pass then placed the ball on the four and on the first play of the fourth quarter De Fouw finally punched into the end zone to tie the score, 6-6. Neither team could score in the remaining time and Hope had to settle for its third tie of the season.

The final game of the '41 campaign was a night contest at Riverview Park against Adrian. There was no rain for a change, but by game time a dense fog rolled in from Black River virtually eliminating the passing game. In the third period Timmer, De Fouw, Karel, and Higgs advanced the ball 80 yards and De Fouw scored from the eight to give Hope the 6-0 victory. Many outside factors had shaped the Dutchmen's destiny and the **Milestone** summarized it well:

> When the smoke of battle had cleared away, Hope had lost only two games, won three, and tied three. Moral victories and bad breaks seemed to be the keynote of the season, but scorebooks do not record weather conditions, injuries, and the other little things that Uncle Sam had not already tinkered with. The frosh stood out as the highlight of the season by their amazing adjustment to collegiate football.[1]

Hope's 2-1-2 MIAA record produced a third place finish behind Alma and Albion. Bill Tappan, Marty Bekken, and Don De Fouw were named to the All-MIAA team as they closed their collegiate careers. Harvey Koop was elected to captain the 1942 squad.

The Hope community now turned its attention to basketball and prospects were bright, to say the least. Coach Hinga had five solid returnees in Co-Captains Ken Vanden Berg and Gil Van Wieren, John Visser, Ets Kleinjans, and Jackie Baas. Sophomore George Dalman had been a second team All-State selectee at Holland High, and was the star of the 1940-41 Hope frosh team. The new rule making freshmen eligible gave Hinga additional guns. Nine of the frosh candidates had captained their high school teams and four were polished enough to join the varsity at once. Dick Higgs, late of the football squad, made the transition without problem. Hinga was especially pleased with the performance of three roommates from the Fraternal House. From Muskegon's Big Reds came Russell Bernard De Vette. Known as "Rusty" by close friends, his game was anything but that. Hinga was quick to spot his athletic talent and later his potential as a coach. In the long history of Hope sports, few would leave as significant an imprint as Russ De Vette. Robert Wayne Van Dis was a product of Kalamazoo Central High School and had played against De Vette on several occasions. His trademark was a continual chatter of encouragement to his teammates that had earned him the affectionate nickname of "Gabby." Natural ability and great enthusiasm combined to make him the sparkplug that every coach seeks.

A recent trip to Ohio took this writer down Route 23 from Ann Arbor to Toledo. Not far from the state line a small green sign proclaimed, "Exit 5 - Blissfield." I was reminded again of Hope's great good fortune when a favorite son of that town came to Hope College in the fall of 1941. Donald Gerrit Mulder was the son of Superintendent Gerrit Mulder of the Blissfield Schools. He was also a basketball player of considerable reputation. Smooth in movement and possessing great quickness, he completed the trio that roomed together on the corner of 10th Street and Columbia Avenue.

Military bases across the country were beginning to field teams and Hope opened the season with the team from Fort Custer . The Dutchmen played well for a first game, leading 22-21 at halftime, but the Army team included seasoned players from Yale and De Paul, and their presence was felt as the soldiers pulled away to a 39-34 victory. John Visser with nine and Ets Kleinjans with eight led the Hope team in the Friday night encounter.

Two days later on a quiet Sunday morning, radio programs were interrupted to announce that Pearl Harbor had been bombed by the Japanese. The following morning President Roosevelt delivered his "Day of Infamy" speech and the Congress responded with a ringing declaration of war. Hope athletes realized at this point that their chances of completing college had lessened considerably. Neutrality and preparedness gave way to direct involvement as the country was suddenly plunged into world conflict. Enlistments ballooned and there was acceleration of the selective service process, but at best government is plagued by bureaucracy. College students would experience a reprieve of several months while official Washington weighed its manpower needs. It was not quite business as usual, but after the initial shock Hope gradually settled into its normal routines.

Hope's second contest was an early indication of the team's potential. In the 50 to 27 victory over Grand Rapids University balanced scoring was in evidence. Co-Captain Kenny Vanden Berg led with 10 and was followed closely by Van Wieren, Kleinjans, and Visser with eight each. Freshmen De Vette, Mulder, and Higgs also broke into the scoring column. Michigan Normal next invaded the Armory in what was described as a dogfight all the way. Only a few points separated the teams throughout, and with 28 seconds remaining the score stood at 28-all. At this point Normal's Ed Gilday stepped to the free throw line and calmly dropped in the

Prep Captains

In 1941 MIAA officials declared freshmen eligible for the first time since 1926. Hope's '41 freshmen crop was unique in that it included nine candidates who had captained their high school teams. **Top Row L to R:** Merle Vanden Berg, Holland; Dick Higgs, Cedar Springs; Russ De Vette, Muskegon; Glenn Bruggers, Coopersville; Gordon Brewer, Martin. **Front Row:** Don Mulder, Blissfield; Bob Van Dis, Kalamazoo Central; Herbert Van Klompenberg, Hudsonville; Ken Leighton, Whitehall.

winning tally. Disappointment in the 29-28 loss was softened by knowledge that the team had performed well on both offense and defense against a highly rated opponent. John Visser led Hope with 10.

A return meeting with Grand Rapids University was almost a carbon copy of the earlier game. Hope again won by a margin of 23, this time 54-31. Vanden Berg was again high with 12, followed by Ets with 10. The Dutchmen were progressing well and Coach Hinga felt they were really ready for Buck Read's Western State five when the teams met in early January. A 20-18 Hope lead at halftime seemed to support Hinga's optimism, but the team was not quite prepared for the exploits of sophomore Harold Gensichen who, with great speed and accuracy, scored 32 of his team's 47 points. George Dalman led Hope with 11 in the respectable 47-43 loss. Near-blizzard conditions kept the team in Kalamazoo overnight.

The tough Western loss was followed by three lopsided wins over MIAA opponents. George Dalman's 16 points led the attack against Hillsdale, while Visser followed with 11. Don Mulder scored eight and De Vette had seven. Final score: Hope 61, Hillsdale 38. Olivet fell, 64-47, and Albion lost to the Dutchmen by 20 as the scoreboard showed a final score of 56-36. The trip to Alma began on a good note as the Hope "B" team defeated Alma in the preliminary, 54-31, with Robert "Hoots" Rowan pouring in 19 and Kenny Leighton getting 16. In the varsity contest, however, Alma's superstars were not to be denied. Jack Howe led the Scots with 17 and Bob Kirby added 10 to sew up a 54-42 victory. Kleinjans with 12 and Visser with 11 were the leaders for Hope. Between halves the MIAA Most Valuable Football Award was presented to Bob Kirby by Holland industrialist Randall Bosch.

Hope's return game at Michigan Normal was a pure case of **deja vu**. Again the contest was close and hard-fought all the way; again the score was tied (43-43) with but seconds remaining; and once again Normal's Ed Gilday stepped to the free throw line and sank the winning point. Smarting from the 44-43 setback, the Dutchmen moved on to Adrian, where sophomore George Dalman took charge with 20 counters and sealed a convincing 72-48 win. Other scorers included Visser with 14, Mulder with eight, De Vette with seven, and "Gabby" with five. The freshmen were beginning to feel at home with Hinga's fast break. Once again in the friendly confines of the Armory, Hope took the measure of Kalamazoo, 44-26. Ets and Dalman led the scoring with 11 and 10. Co-Captain Gil Van Wieren was back in form for the Hillsdale game as he racked up 15. Dalman collected 12 and Vanden Berg, returning to action after an ankle sprain, scored 10 in the 55-37 victory.

Hope's entire squad was seeing plenty of playing time and all seemed to have the scoring touch. Olivet had the misfortune to invade the Armory at this particular juncture. The Comets were soon staring at a 12-0 deficit and their circumstances did not noticeably improve. In a wild second half Coach Hinga used reserves liberally, but any and all combinations worked the run and gun to perfection enroute to a 94-41 victory. Co-Captains Van Wieren and Vanden Berg led the onslaught with 20 and 18 points. Kleinjans followed with 13 while Gabby Van Dis and Jackie Baas each had 11. The 94 points established a new record for the Holland Armory but surprisingly, not for Hope College. It must be recalled that in 1904-05 Hope defeated the Grand Rapids Medical College 101 to 8 and in 1908-09 the Dutchmen took the Grand Rapids Y.M.C.A. 106 to 26.

The Albion game proved considerably tougher, but Hope pulled away in the last period to win, 55 to 37. This time it was Dalman with 15 and Vanden Berg with 14. This set the stage for the home contest with league leading Alma. For the third year in a row the teams had battled for the MIAA title and spectators found standing room only at the Armory. Visser, Vanden Berg, and Van Wieren had been part of all three seasons and the same could be said of Kirby, Howe, and Carey. The game proved to be a classic contest between two fine schools. With four minutes remaining Alma led, 44-42. Bob Kirby then scored two pressure field goals to pad the lead.

But Hope was not finished. By all accounts John Visser played the game of his career. Outscoring his counterpart Keith Carey 16 to 10, John made good on his final shot and Kenny Vanden Berg added another deuce. With the score agonizingly close at 48-46 and the gym reduced to bedlam, the Dutchmen saw the clock run out and the MIAA championship slip away. Jack Howe led the deserving Scots with 15 and Dalman followed Visser's 16 with 14.

The remaining games were anticlimactic to say the least, but Hope played well knowing that second place is better than third. In their last home game the Hinga men bested Adrian, 54-41. Vanden Berg was high with 13 and Visser had 11. Ken Newendorp broke into the scoring column with five. In the season finale at Kalamazoo, the Hornets established a 10-3 lead before the Dutch rebounded to a 39-39 score at the half. The last 20 minutes of the season belonged to Hope and produced a 53-43 victory. The overall record of 12 and six and the MIAA count of eight and two gave evidence of another fine team. The All-MIAA selections also reflected this. John Visser, Ets Kleinjans, and George Dalman made the honor squad, along with Keith Carey, Bob Kirby, and Jack Howe of Alma. Kenny Vanden Berg received honorable mention. Dalman was second only to Howe in league scoring, while Kleinjans was a popular choice to captain the 1942-43 team. On March 24 the teams from Hope, Holland High, and Holland Christian High were feted at a banquet in the Warm Friend Tavern with Western Michigan's fabled Buck Read as speaker.

Spring sports got underway on March 18 with the MIAA indoor track meet at Michigan State's Jenison Field House. Albion edged Kalamazoo 38 5/6 to 37 to win the meet while Hope finished fifth. Hope freshman Hugh Kinneson tied with Alma's Gayle Saxton for first in the pole vault with a new indoor record of 11' 1/2." Hope's freshmen standouts in basketball would go separate ways in spring sports. Russ De Vette, recently chosen as Hope's new student representative to the MIAA, chose baseball. Gabby Van Dis would play most of the season at number one singles in tennis, while Don Mulder opted for golf.

On April 9 with spring practices well underway, word came that American forces on Bataan Peninsula had surrendered to the Japanese. News of the infamous death march would come later. U.S. reverses in this infinitely greater contest, with stakes so high, had a sobering effect on even the most carefree athlete.

Of the four spring sports in 1942, tennis enjoyed the greater success. The team under Coach Bernard Arendshorst opened against a tough team from Grand Rapids Junior College and was edged, 4-3. Bob Van Dis defeated Carl Frans, 6-3, 6-0, and Jackie Baas downed Don Howick, 6-3, 6-0, in singles. In doubles, Hope's team of Bill Tappan and Howard Hoekje defeated Fred Stack and Don Howick, 6-1, 6-2. On April 23 Hope had better luck against a Grand Rapids team as they downed Calvin, 5-2. Van Dis defeated Vandellen, 6-1, 6-1; Howard Hoekje defeated Heinie Scholten, 3-6, 6-2, 6-2; Jackie Baas took Bernard Pekelder, 6-0, 6-4; Bill Tappan defeated Klaus Kuiper, 6-1, 6-2, and the team of Hoekje and Tappan bested Scholten and Vandellen, 6-3, 2-6, 6-4. It was, however, no contest when Kalamazoo came to Holland on April 29 and the Hornets went home with a 7-0 victory.

In a return match with Grand Rapids Junior College, the Grand Rapids crew still held the whammy over Hope, this time 5-2. Bill Tappan at number three singles defeated Tom Blackburn, 6-2, 6-2, and Tappan-Hoekje took Bill Beel and Blackburn, 6-2, 3-6, 6-4. On May 13 Hope shut out Calvin, 7-0, and came close to doing the same to Grand Rapids University the next day. Hope's only loss in the 6-1 contest came when Howard Phillips downed Gabby Van Dis in a three-set match, 6-2, 3-6, 6-4. May 18 found the Dutch struggling again against Kalamazoo on the new courts at Stowe Stadium. Kalamazoo's 6-1 victory was marred only by Bill Moerdyk's 11-9, 6-4 victory over Harris Franklin. The next day Coach Arendshorst's team showed well against Western Michigan despite a 5-2 loss. Howard Hoekje defeated Marsh Campbell, 8-6, 4-6, 8-6, and the team of Gabby Van Dis and Jackie Baas took Walt Warren and Bob Hale, 6-2, 6-4. As expected, in the MIAA meet Hope finished a strong second behind Kalamazoo.

Hope's golf team included Les Nienhuis, Ken Leighton, Don Mulder, Morris Tardiff, and Bob Geldart. Coach Hinga's charges were not successful in dual matches but managed a fourth place finish in the MIAA meet. Jack Schouten's 15-man track squad was unable to produce point getters and finished last in the conference meet. There was some consolation in the fact that Hugh Kinneson took first place in the pole vault with a mark of 11' 2." Rod Funston captured fourth in the discus and the Hope mile relay team of Kinneson, Con Vander Woude, Dick Higgs, and Bill Slocombe also took fourth. Alma and Kalamazoo battled on even terms for the championship with the mile relay the deciding event. The Scots prevailed due largely to their anchor man, who else but Keith Carey. Alma's victory margin was 45 1/2 - 44 1/2 and with it went the MIAA All-Sports Trophy for the second year in a row.

Baseball in 1942 was still non-league and still unfunded, but Jack Schouten's determination to keep it alive was as strong as ever. The venerable coach managed to provide pants and stirrup sox for most of the players, but the upper part of the uniform depended upon individual resourcefulness. The team picture shows a hodge-podge of football jerseys, white sweatshirts, and T-shirts. There was also a variety in the color and quality of caps. Despite its rag-tag appearance, the team took on Grand Rapids Junior College on May 5. With freshman Dick Higgs behind the plate, freshman Russ De Vette took the mound and proceeded to set J.C. down with a two-hit shutout. De Vette issued no walks and only one man reached second base. Ray Otteman drove in two runs and De Vette himself the other in the 3-0 victory. The teams met again three days later at Lamar Park in Grand Rapids. Wildness on the part of pitcher Bud Karel, another freshman, allowed J.C. to build a six-run lead. A Hope rally in the ninth fell short and the game ended at 6-3 J.C. Some Hope athletes managed to participate in two spring sports. Don Mulder and Ken Leighton played both baseball and golf, while Dick Higgs and Ray Otteman took part in track and baseball.

As students made their way back to Hope's campus in the fall of 1942, they became aware of "unknown" places around the globe - - Midway, Dieppe, El Alamein, and Guadalcanal, where U.S. Marines battled for their lives. Rommel, Montgomery, and Eisenhower moved to center stage, and most male students sensed that their days as civilians were numbered. Coach Hinga had nine returning lettermen in football plus a promising crop of freshmen. In addition, he had convinced Bob Van Dis to give the grid game a try. Gabby had never played football, but due to great athletic talent, soon caught up to other squad members. Hinga and Captain Harvey Koop had good reason to expect a successful season, but it was not to be. Early season injuries to senior Don De Fouw and sophomore Bud Karel limited their activity and breaks in general seemed to go the other way.

Hope opened on September 25 in a home night contest against Grand Rapids University. The Lancers had compiled a 6-2 record in '41 but veteran coach "Potsy" Clark had been called to active duty as a Lieutenant Commander in the U.S. Navy. His replacement was Lyle Mc Nitt, who left North Muskegon High School to fill the post. In the opening quarter Hope's only threat went down the drain when a Dick Higgs pass was dropped in the end zone. The game then settled into a defensive battle and ended in a 0-0 tie. Hopes were still high one week later when the team made the long trip to Ypsilanti to meet Michigan Normal. The easterners scored in the second quarter on a pass to end Ben Sladen. The extra point was good on a pass from Chuck Nemeth to Clare Krawczak. Normal made it 13-0 when fullback Jack Brown scored on a 25-yard run. The point attempt failed. Hope came alive in the second half when Carl Schram was smothered in his end zone for a safety. This was followed by Dick Higgs' off tackle touchdown run and Roy Davis' successful conversion making it 13-9. A subsequent Dutch drive ended on the two-yard line as time ran out.

Hope's MIAA season opened on October 10 in Kalamazoo with some bright spots but another loss. The previous night Coach Hinga had suffered an accident while officiating the Zeeland-Hastings game and he walked the sidelines on crutches. The Hornets scored in each quarter and held a 24-0 lead before Gabby Van Dis took over for Don De Fouw who suffered a knee injury. Higgs passed to Van Dis, who took the ball on the 20, eluded several tacklers, and scored. Hope threatened once more moving to the 15, but the comeback was too little too late and the Dutch lost another in the hometown of Hinga and Van Dis.

Hope's best performance of the season came at Hillsdale on October 17. Injuries had forced some major shuffling of personnel by Coach Hinga. Hoots Rowan was shifted from center to left half to replace the injured Bud Karel. Freshman Dale Van Lente took over at center while Captain Harvey Koop was moved from tackle to guard. Freshman Bill Draper assumed the tackle position and Gabby Van Dis moved into the fullback spot for Don De Fouw, whose knee injury was not responding. The juggling act paid off in the third quarter when Van Dis hit Bob Rowan with a touchdown pass and Roy Davis converted. The aerial game continued as Dick Higgs threw a scoring pass to freshman back Joe Northoek making it 13-0. The Dutchmen's defensive effort was outstanding and deserving of a shutout, but in the fourth period the Dales' Tom Ward faded to pass, elected to run, and streaked 72 yards to make the final score 13 to 6. Captain Koop, at a new position, played the finest game of his career to spoil the Hillsdale homecoming.

October 24 marked Hope's own Homecoming with the tough Albion Britons in town. The program for the day included "Hope Hi-Lites" by Rog Koeppe and a page listing 51 of Hope's former athletes now in military service. In the second quarter Hope engineered a dramatic drive to the Albion two, only to be penalized to the seven. A Roy Davis field goal attempt was wide of the mark and the game

The 1942 Hope Baseball Team

Standing L to R: Ken Leighton, Russ De Vette, Ken Vanden Berg, Coach Jack Schouten, Gerald "Bud" Karel, Arnold Whipple, Don De Fouw, John Visser, Gordon Brewer, Bob Glantz, Dick Brown, Ray Otteman, Herk Van Tongeren, Claudius Finger. **Kneeling:** Dick Higgs, Gene Baker, Len Pape. Four years would pass before Hope fielded another baseball team. Leighton, Baker, and Pape would make the supreme sacrifice in World War II.

remained scoreless until the final period. Hope' lack of reserve strength told in the fourth quarter. Bruce Stevens' interception of a Hope pass set up a drive to the Hope two and the Britons plunged over for the 6-0 victory.

In a night game at Riverview on October 30, Hope met Grand Rapids Junior College. On a muddy field the Dutchmen drew first blood when Dick Higgs scored on an end-run and Davis kicked the point. In the third quarter J.C.'s Tom Blackburn intercepted a Hope pass to set up Frederick's eventual touchdown from the one-yard line. Blackburn then ran in the extra point to produce a 7-7 tie.

On November 7 the Dutchmen closed out the season against Coach Gordon Mac Donald's talented Alma 11. The Scots were reigning MIAA champions and seemed well on their way to retaining the title. In the first half it was all Alma. With little more than four minutes gone Dale Wares skirted right end and ran 74 yards for the touchdown. Bill Pink converted. A short time later Alma blocked a Hope punt and recovered on the six. From this point Wares notched his second touchdown, this time on a reverse play. Pink's kick was wide. A Jack Tait to Hanna pass made it 20-0 at halftime and a rout seemed imminent. But somehow in the second half Hinga's patched up collection of underclassmen became a different team. No one, least of all the coach, could know that this would be Bud Hinga's last appearance as Hope's football coach, but there may have been a premonition that this was the last football game for a while. Whatever the incentive, the Dutchmen were inspired and Alma's vaunted attack was stymied. On offense Hope took to the air with some effectiveness. A pass from Dick Higgs to Don Schriemer reached the Alma 27. A second pass from Higgs to Bud Karel was bobbled but retrieved in mid air by Schriemer on the 10. Gabby Van Dis circled right end to the six and on the next play Alma was offside. With the ball on the one yard line Roy Davis plunged in to make it 20-6. The roll continued when Bud Karel intercepted an Alma pass on his own 25 and, in a return to his old form, raced 60 yards to the Alma 15. The Scots, however, held at this point and were able to retain their two-touchdown lead.

As time ran out on football, this last contest for the duration left different impressions. Coach Mac Donald and his team had the satisfaction that comes with a well deserved victory and the resulting championship. But the Dutchmen had something too. In stations around the globe they would recall with pride the great effort in their last 30 minutes of football. Many would play again, and for Hope. Upon reassembling in 1946 they would remember Leonard Pape, that promising tackle from Grand Rapids South, who would be forever 21.

A few post-season details remained. Harvey Koop and Dick Higgs were named to the All-MIAA team. The triple threat Higgs who called signals in the absence of injured Don De Fouw, was chosen Hope's most valuable player. Roy Davis was elected captain of the 1943 team, which of course, would never assemble.

College officials, including Defense Coordinator Bruce Raymond, encouraged Hope men to join the Army's Enlisted Reserve Corps Unassigned or the Navy's counterpart V-12 program. Such action seemed to afford the best chance for deferment until graduation despite the lack of any guarantees. Accordingly, in November a sizable number of us made our way to the Muskegon Armory to sign up for the ERCU. At the same time Don Mulder elected to join the ranks of the Army Air Corps. Enlistments were not for a specified period

Bud Hinga's Last Hope College Football Team - 1942

Back Row L to R: Coach Milton "Bud" Hinga, Manager Seymour Padnos, Harold "Mouse" Van Wieren, Art Slager, Roy Petersen, Dan Yntema, Earl Holkeboer, Glenn Bruggers, Vern Kraai, Ted Wisner, Leroy Koranda, Gordon Brewer, Raymond W. Heemstra, Don Bocks, Assistant Coach and Trainer Jack Schouten. Middle Row: Joe Northoek, Dale Van Lente, Harold "Bud" Groendyk, Dick Loomis, Tony Kempker, Harvey Buter, Harold Van Tongeren, Arnold Schaap, Bill Draper, Harvey Staal, Richard Wierenga, Don Miller, Robert "Gabby" Van Dis. **Front Row:** Len Dick, Don Schriemer, Don De Fouw, Eddie Nieusma, Jack Yeomans, Len Pape, Captain Harvey Koop, Robert "Hoots" Rowan, Roy Davis, Gerald "Bud" Karel, Dick Higgs, George Slager, Merle Vanden Berg.

of time, but for "the duration plus six months." It had an ominous ring.

The starting five for Hope's 1942-43 basketball team was decided early. Russ De Vette, a 6'2" sophomore, was chosen by Coach Hinga to replace 6' 6" John Visser, while George Dalman and Gabby Van Dis took over the forward spots vacated by Gil Van Wieren and Ken Vanden Berg. Don Mulder was at one guard and senior Captain Everett "Ets" Kleinjans directed play from the other. A strong supporting cast included Dick Higgs, Vern Boersma, Bob Rowan, Art Slager, Harv Buter, Paul Van Dort, and Merle Vanden Berg. Dale Van Lente, regular center from the football team, was the efficient manager.

From the start it was obvious to Hope followers that the chemistry was good. The respect of players for coach, and vice versa, was strong enough to allow some flexibility. Good-natured ribbing and practical jokes were rampant in lighter moments, but the players knew their place and on the floor it was all business. Hinga realized that he must offset the team's lack of size in some manner. His brand of fast break basketball was no stranger to Hope fans but it took on new meaning in the hands of this quintet, especially the speedy sophomores, Mulder, De Vette, and Van Dis. At this time the University of Illinois was dominating the Big Ten Conference with Andy Phillip leading the famous "Whiz Kids." Borrowing perhaps from this group and adding wartime terminology, the term "Blitz Kids" was coined to describe the Hope squad. The name stuck and became increasingly appropriate as the season progressed.

The December 3 opener at the Armory found Russ De Vette pitted against some former high school teammates. Muskegon Junior College fell before the Dutch as Don Mulder led with 15 and De Vette collected 13. On December 10 Hope took on a stronger team when they met the Grand Haven Coast Guard in that city, but the Dutchmen's speed and depth were deciding factors in the eventual 52-39 victory. Van Dis and De Vette divided scoring honors with 12 each. Two days later it was more of the same as Grand Rapids Junior College visited the Armory. Hope again dominated play with a winning margin of 18. The 61-43 Dutch win featured De Vette with 18, Van Dis with 16, and Dalman with 14. A return game at Muskegon Junior College became a rout as Hope increased its 21-point halftime lead to 71-37 as the contest ended. This time George "Porky" Dalman scored a season high 21 points while De Vette and Mulder each had 14.

The warm-up games were now over. As the squad prepared to meet Western Michigan the war came a step closer. Word was received that Hope had lost the first of its athletes in service. Marine Lieutenant Wallace "Whitey" Riemersma died when his plane plunged into the Pacific off San Diego. Whitey had been a halfback on Hope's 1940 team. A memorial service was held on December 27 in the Spring Lake Presbyterian Church.

Misfortune struck the Hope team at the start of the new year when Van Dis came down with the flu and could not make the trip to Kalamazoo. His roommates, Mulder and De Vette, were also infected but made the trip and started the game. Five minutes later both were on the bench, completely exhausted. Neither had scored a point. Western built a 27-7 lead, at which point the generous Buck Read used all 14 of his squad members. In the second half Hope's talented reserves made a game of it before falling, 57-42. Kleinjans led Hope with 10, Dick Higgs and Art Slager had eight and Vern Boersma five. Harold Gensichen saw limited duty, but led the Broncos with 13.

The October 9 issue of the **Grand Rapids Herald** had carried a student letter from Calvin College challenging Hope to renew their basketball relationship. The series had lapsed in 1936 in the midst of general ill feeling. Hope now objected to the indirect approach via the **Herald** and considerable haggling ensued. Old bones of contention were revived and used to justify the six seasons of great competition that had been lost. Fortunately for all, perceptive Dutchmen at both schools recognized a good thing when they saw it and seized the opportunity to get back on track. Games were scheduled for January 8 at Hope and February 23 at Calvin. Both games would be filled with drama and somehow set the tone for what would become the nation's top small college series.

Calvin Coach Al Muyskens brought his team to the Armory without the services of star center Jake Hekman, who had entered the Army, but the remaining Knights probably constituted the best team Hope would play, with the possible exception of Western Michigan. Marv Bylsma, who would referee many Hope games in the future, opened the scoring for Calvin. Gabby Van Dis evened the count for Hope and the show was on. The players on both sides set a high standard of sportsmanship, but as always, it was difficult for spectators to do likewise. Feelings ran high. Hope moved to an early 12-5 lead, which proved to be the widest margin of the game. Calvin took a 25-24 halftime lead on Lou Zylstra's patented overhead free throw. In the second half the game was tied at 27 before Hope took the lead for the remainder of the period. Calvin rallied in the closing minutes and Russ De Vette has a vivid recollection of scrambling on the floor for a loose ball as Hope hung on to post a narrow 42-40 victory. Don Mulder, still in a weakened condition from the flu, led Hope's attack with 15. Ets followed with 12. For the Knights it was Marv Bylsma with 14 and Elmer Van Wieren with nine. The Hope **Milestone** later described it as the most exciting game of the year.

On Monday, January 11, Hope got a break in Albion's Kresge Gym when Elkin Isaac, the Britons' scoring leader, fouled out in the first half. George Dalman with 17 points, led the Dutchmen to a convincing 50-29 win. Freshman Joe Canna had seven for the losers.

Champion Alma, led by Jack and Bob Howe, came to the Armory on Friday, January 15. Coach Hinga's charges put it all together on this night in what sports scribe Roger Koeppe termed "the greatest game of a great team." The teams played on even terms for 15 minutes before the Dutchmen pulled away to a 27-18 halftime lead. Fans looked for a second half comeback by the Scots but it was not to be. The Dutchmen reached their season's peak as all five starters scored in double figures and execution seemed flawless. De Vette had 16, Dalman 13, Kleinjans 12, Van Dis 11, and Mulder 10. The 64-39 victory ended a 23-game Alma win streak that went back to Hope's dramatic victory of February 24, 1940.

The Hillsdale team that came to the Armory on January 23 was riddled with illness. Any chance for a Dale victory was gone when three of the five starters were unable to make the trip, and the 40-13 halftime score was evidence of the depleted Hillsdale ranks. Hope reserves played much of the game and scored 40 points in the 85-32 win. De Vette's 14 point performance was high for the Dutch followed by Gabby with 11, and Dick Higgs with nine. Burt Hendrickson led the hampered Hillsdale squad with 13.

In a non-league encounter on January 29 the Dutchmen were surprised in Grand Rapids by a greatly improved Junior College team. Hope managed a four-point halftime lead (33-29) but the count was knotted at 58 with only three minutes remaining. In the stretch it was Hope's splendid sophomores who carried the day. Mulder and Van Dis scored 20 points each and De Vette had 15 in the hard fought 64-60 victory. Vander Mey led J.C. with 21.

Hope's game at Kalamazoo on February 2 included some strange turns. In the first 12 minutes of play the lead changed hands eight times. Then, for the final six minutes of the first half and the first nine minutes of the second half the Hornets were held scoreless. Hope's great defensive effort in this 15 minute period allowed the Dutchmen to widen the gap and notch a 51-33 victory. Russ De Vette was the offensive star of the game with 21 markers. Dalman added 11 while Wayne Thompson and Bob App had 11 and 10 for "K."

At Hillsdale on February 5 the Hope "Blitz" was again in high gear. With an impressive display of speed and shooting accuracy, Hinga's squad established a new MIAA scoring record as they took home a 95-55 win. It was Mulder's night with 21, followed closely by De Vette with 20. Charles Patrick put on a stellar performance with 20 points in the Dales losing cause. At halftime the MIAA Most Valuable Football Player Award was presented to Hillsdale's outstanding fullback, Burr Manby. Randall Bosch of Holland made the presentation, a diamond-studded gold football.

Back in the friendly confines of the Armory, Hope met Albion on February 11. Elkin Isaac, now the MIAA's leading scorer, did not foul out this time. "Ike" led his team with 13 but the Britons lacked additional guns and the Dutch again prevailed, this time 54 to 35. Both De Vette and Mulder matched Isaac's 13 points while Van Dis and Dalman had 11 to complete another night of even scoring.

On February 15 the Dutchmen carried an unblemished MIAA record to Alma knowing that a victory would clinch the league crown. The Howe brothers and Alma's narrow floor were factors to be reckoned with and Coach Hinga had reason to be concerned. Radio broadcasts were not yet part of the Hope sports scene but students hovered near telephones awaiting the outcome. The halftime report did little to relieve tension as the teams were tied at 24. In the second half Hope' guards spelled the difference in bringing home the championship. Mulder and Captain Ets each scored 14 in the hard earned 51-43 win. Jack Howe also had 14 and brother Bob 10. A few days later Hope students and the Holland community had a chance to cheer the new champs in the Armory as the team again downed the Grand Haven Coast Guard in a more relaxed contest. The final was Hope 61, Coast Guard 27.

In only his second year of college Don Mulder had become a household word in the Holland community. On campus his popularity could be attributed to more than basketball. Choosing the challenging pre-med course of study was consistent with his nature and talents, but it was a cheerful disposition and genuine modesty that registered with the rank and file. Fewer than 500 students graced the campus in 1942-43 but all were aware of the "Duke" and his obvious interest in people. Even the most obscure could testify to the warmth of his cordial and upbeat greeting.

It was then, with some dismay that the campus was advised of Don's orders to report for active duty with the Army Air Corps. His departure date was set for February 24, which happened to be the day after the Calvin game. Little remained but to give the Duke a grand send-off. Students and townspeople with cars willingly offered their gasoline ration of four gallons per week, and a sizeable caravan made its way to the Burton Gym in Grand Rapids. Hope entered the game at 14-1 while Calvin stood at 11-5. As expected, the game was closely contested. As the half ended Hope clung to a 25-23 lead. The Dutch led 30-27 on a Van Dis basket early in the second half, but at this point the momentum shifted to Calvin. Despite his aggressive play and proficiency at steals, Don Mulder had committed fewer than two fouls per game in the season thus far. The Hope following therefore, found itself in a state of shock when, with a full 13 minutes remaining, Don made his way to the bench with his fourth and final foul. An otherwise routine occurrence assumed near tragic proportions under the circumstances. Hope fans, some tearful, were aware of the attrition rate among pilots, both in training and combat. Many felt they were seeing Don for the last time. The team, in its disappointment, did not collapse, but according to the **Holland Sentinel**, "Calvin displayed its best form of the season, and showed a vast assortment of shots that had the 1,900 fans on their feet a great deal of the time."[2] At the final buzzer it was Calvin 49, Hope 42. Once again the Knights had defeated the MIAA champion. Marv Bylsma was high for Calvin with 12, followed by Lou Zylstra with 9. Lost in the melee was Russ De Vette's game-high 13 point performance. Dalman and Van Dis had eight apiece and Mulder seven. It is probable that Mulder's recovery was quicker than that of his

(L to R) Roommates Don Mulder, Russ De Vette, and Bob "Gabby" Van Dis were crowd favorites and gave validity to the team nickname, "Blitz Kids."

many fans. The next day he accepted a new challenge as an Air Corps Cadet and subsequently piloted a P-51 Mustang in photo reconnaissance missions over Europe. Without the theatrics of a contemporary general, he would return.

The Blitz Kids made their final appearance at the Armory on Friday, February 26. Old rival Kalamazoo provided the opposition in what appeared to be an anticlimactic end to the season. The Dutchmen, however, had plenty of incentive to do well. No Hope champion had gone undefeated in league play, though the last one (1939-40) had dropped but a single contest to Albion. The team therefore took the floor determined to keep the slate clean. Also, each squad member knew that somewhere a cadet would be giving them strong support. Vern Boersma and Hoots Rowan were given the unenviable job of filling in for the departed Duke. Both performed ably against the Hornets. Boersma, also a pre-med student, would one day return to the Holland community to render outstanding service as a pediatrician.

As usual, Kalamazoo proved a worthy opponent and Hope was hard-pressed. As the half ended, George Dalman's long one hander gave the Dutch a 22-20 lead. An 8-0 run after the half put Hinga's team in the driver's seat and it was never headed. Dalman with 15 led Hope to a 47-35 victory, its 15th against but two defeats. Always a clever passer, Dalman left the fans a classic memento. Midway in the second half the Hornets moved quickly to their end of the floor with four Hope men defending. With quick hands Dalman stole the ball while facing Kalamazoo's basket. Without turning, he snapped a backhand pass to a bewildered Hoots Rowan who had been a bit tardy on defence. The ball traveled two thirds of the floor length at a height of three feet. It was the play of the game and brought a standing ovation. A sheepish Rowan turned and made the uncontested layup.

The All-MIAA team included Russ De Vette, Don Mulder, the Howe brothers from Alma, and Albion's Elkin Isaac. Also in 1943, the **Detroit Free Press** saw fit to select an All-State collegiate team. Its members were:

Harold Gensichen - Western Michigan
Don Mulder - Hope College
Bob Wardrop - Central Michigan
Jack Howe - Alma College
Lee Knorek - University of Detroit

Ets Kleinjans and Russ De Vette received honorable mention. When Mulder was named honorary captain of the team it was evident that his basketball reputation was something more than hometown sentiment.

Some weeks earlier it had been announced that due to growing wartime restrictions, Hope would not participate in spring sports. In the general letdown rumors persisted that members of the Enlisted Reserve Corps would soon be called to active duty. In this state of limbo, those affected found it difficult to concentrate on studies. News from the various fronts frequently added to the unrest. Word came that the troop ship **S.S. Dorchester** had been torpedoed in the icy waters of the North Atlantic. Survivors recounted the heroism of four chaplains who went down with the ship after giving their life preservers to those with none. One of the four was Clark V. Poling, who had played on Hope's 1929 freshman football team.

In mid-March rumor became reality when all members of the E.R.C. were ordered to report to Fort Custer. All members were not as demonstrative as Charles Martindale, who received the news near Graves Hall and expressed his relief by casting an armload of books 15 feet in the air. Our departure date of Monday, March 29, was memorable for this writer. President Wichers presided at the morning chapel service recognizing the 23- man contingent. The group included Art Slager, Hoots Rowan, Harv Buter, and Paul Van Dort from the basketball team. A very serious gentleman from the Gideon Society presented New Testaments to each man, and later a lady in black uniform from the Salvation Army offered a box of cookies. This somewhat somber atmosphere was broken by Coach Jack Schouten, who invited Glenn Bruggers, Preston Stegenga (Stogie's son), and me to have lunch with him at the Owl Restaurant on North River Avenue. The restaurant has long since disappeared, but Jack's caring gesture on an important day for three 19-year-olds, left them with a warm glow and gratitude that remains to this day. In the afternoon a large crowd of well-wishers gathered in front of the Chapel on College Avenue. As the group boarded a bus labeled **People's Rapid Transit**, Jack Schouten in a grey felt hat, stood nearby. Hoots Rowan had spent some time in the National Guard and clued us in on the ways of army life, but at Fort Custer, arrayed in wrinkled

The 1942-43 Hope College "Blitz Kids" - MIAA Champions (15-2)
Hope's first team to go undefeated in MIAA play.

Standing L to R: Coach Milton "Bud" Hinga, Dick Higgs, Harvey Buter, Art Slager, Paul Van Dort, Merle Vanden Berg, Manager Dale Van Lente. **Seated:** Vern Boersma, Don Mulder, Russ De Vette, Captain Everett "Ets" Kleinjans, George "Porky" Dalman, Bob "Gabby" Van Dis, Robert "Hoots" Rowan.

March 29, 1943 - A campus farewell to 23 members of the Army's Enlisted Reserve Corps. The college's male population was depleted by this and subsequent departures to the Navy and Marine Corps.

uniforms all were rookies, including Hoots.

It is beyond the province of this book to trace the wartime experiences of former athletes. Suffice to say that such departure scenes were common across the country in the spring of 1943. Lines from the **Milestone**'s dedication page offered a poignant expression of sentiment on every campus:

> The hoary colleges look down
> On careless boys at play
> But when the bugles sounded war
> They put their games away ...[3]

Hope's next athletic event would occur at Homecoming, 1944. Wearing the men's faded jerseys, co-eds would play a touch football game on the field by Carnegie Gym.

REFERENCES - CHAPTER 7

1. The **Milestone**, 1942.
2. The **Holland (Evening) Sentinel**, Wednesday, February 24, 1943.
3. The **Milestone**, 1943. (Lines taken from The **Spires of Oxford**, by Winifried M. Letts).

CHAPTER 8

POST-WAR SPORTS - CLOSING OUT THE '40S

The unconditional surrender of the Japanese Empire on August 14, 1945, marked the long-awaited end of World War II. Nineteen days later,aboard the **USS Missouri** in Tokyo Bay, official documents were signed and General Douglas Mac Arthur declared, "These proceedings are closed." In a matter of weeks separation centers across the country were flooded with service men and women eager to resume their lives as civilians. By October or November, beribboned men from all branches of service made that all-time sentimental journey home. For this writer the trek began at East Wretham in England, then on to Southampton and the **Queen Mary**, New York harbor, Camp Kilmer, Fort Sheridan, and home for the first time in three years. My return to Hope was delayed until February, but several former classmates were discharged in time to enroll for the fall semester.

Hope College had known and celebrated homecomings for several years, but in the fall of '45 the term took on a deeper meaning. As veterans filtered back to the campus many experienced an eerie feeling that somehow time had stopped at their departure and would now resume with their return. Not born of arrogance or egotism, the emotion stemmed perhaps from the heartfelt welcome home of familiar mentors, and in part from the long-dormant sports program that now would be revived. There was of course, irrefutable evidence that time waits for no one. My original classmates had graduated the previous spring, and a sister three years behind me in high school, had caught up to me in college. In this period of adjustment, Hope's reputation for warmth and friendliness was ever apparent. But in the midst of general euphoria, there lingered the grim reminder that there would be no homecoming for the 36 Hope men who had made the supreme sacrifice.

In May of 1945, the Board of Trustees had selected Irwin J. Lubbers to become the seventh president of Hope College. The critical post war years called for strong leadership, and Lubbers proved more than equal to the challenge. His effectiveness in assembling faculty and staff was soon apparent, as was his confidence in delegating authority. A football program was still not possible in the fall of '45, but MIAA officials laid plans to resume basketball in December. President Lubbers appointed Bud Hinga to the new post of dean of men, and Hinga decided that due to time constraints, he should not continue as football coach. A likely candidate for the grid post was Lt. Alvin Vanderbush, Hope '29, who had enjoyed successful tenures at Grandville and most recently at Grand Rapids South High, a school rich in football tradition. Vanderbush was discharged from the U. S. Navy in October after 32 months of service and was contacted by Hinga. At the President's invitation, Vanderbush joined the Hope faculty as a member of the History Department and as head football coach. He began planning almost immediately for the influx of new and returning football players in the fall of 1946.

In mid-November Coach Hinga, for the first time since 1942, issued the call for basketball candidates. On hand for the first practice were Don Mulder and Art Slager of the '43 "Blitz Kids." There was general rejoicing as the Holland community recalled Mulder's emotional departure nearly three years earlier. The remaining squad members were mostly unfamiliar and it was obvious that Hinga faced a major challenge before the opening game on December 4. At season's end the squad would have a different look, but for the time being it included the following: Lloyd Heneveld, Ken Zuverink, Clare Van Liere, Phil Meengs, Jack Tirrell, Dale Van Lente, Don Oosterbaan, Don Rinkus, Clarence Hopkins, Ernie Post, Jim Yuk, Jack Stegeman, Don Ingham, and

Howard Jalving. Some would become members of the J.V. team and others would opt for the fraternity league as more experienced players returned from the service.

On Tuesday, December 4, 1945, the program of intercollegiate athletics was officially resumed by Hope College. An understandably ragged Hope team made its way to Battle Creek to meet a strong team of servicemen representing the Percy Jones Army Hospital. The host team had earlier defeated Western Michigan, 66-50, and Coach Hinga was philosophical about his team's chances. After posting a 28-17 halftime lead, the soldiers cruised to a 54-45 victory. Lefty Rynstrand led the winners with 21 points, 15 coming in the first half. Lloyd Heneveld, a 1943 Holland High grad, led the Dutchmen with 17. A fine athlete, Heneveld would become better known as a football guard for the University of Michigan and would see action in the Wolverines' 49-0 Rose Bowl victory over USC in 1948. Art Slager added 13 to the Dutch cause, while Mulder and Zuverink each scored seven.

Eight days later a return game was played at the Holland Armory with much the same result. Holland fans had waited a long time for the return of collegiate basketball and were disappointed when Don Mulder was unable to play due to a foot infection. The 58-34 Percy Jones victory proved little but gave Hinga a chance to look at several of his squad members. Heneveld again led with 10 followed by Ken Zuverink with nine. Hope was still without the services of Mulder on December 19 when Hillsdale visited the Armory. In this first post-war MIAA contest freshman Ken Zuverink put on a spectacular performance, scoring 30 points enroute to the 76-47 Hope win. Lloyd Heneveld followed with 15. Mulder returned for the January 2 meeting with Muskegon Junior College and his flashy floor play was much in evidence. Art Slager was high with 10 as the Dutchmen evened their record with a 55-36 victory. Reserves played much of the second half and it appeared that Hope was back in form. But on January 7 the Hinga men found themselves in a real battle at Albion's Kresge Gym. The Britons led at halftime, 26-23, but Hope managed a 46-43 lead late in the game. At this point Albion's veteran Lew Moon sealed the victory with two quick field goals. The final score showed Albion 55 to 47 over Hope. Moon took game honors with 22 points, while his pre-war teammate Elkin Isaac scored 13. "Ike" had rejoined the team only four days prior to the contest. Don Mulder led Hope with 15 and Slager followed with 11.

In a home game with Alma, the Dutchmen built a 36-33 halftime lead, but Alma's aces were also returning from the service and took the lead in the final 10 minutes when, despite the new, more generous five-foul rule, Slager and Heneveld made their way to the bench. The final showed Alma with 73 to 60 for Hope. Alma's three-man scoring punch featured Bud Howe with 21 and the duo of Pete Greenhoe and Al Mc Quaig with 17 each. Ken Zuverink was again hot for Hope with 24 and Heneveld had 13 before fouling out. In spite of the two MIAA setbacks, Hinga was encouraged the next week by the return of two more regulars from the '43 Blitz Kids. Gabby Van Dis and George Dalman were discharged from the Army and Navy respectively, and though not yet in shape, appeared in the January 18 game at Kalamazoo. The Hornets led most of the way but Don "Duke" Mulder was at his best on defense and also led his team with 19 points. Lloyd Heneveld, playing guard for the first time, dropped in 10 counters. The combination enabled Hope to squeeze out a 44-41 victory. Harold Hinkley was high for "K" with 12. The following night the squad met Michigan Normal at Ypsilanti. Art Slager was now switched from center to guard to team with Mulder and give added strength under the defensive board. The game was tied at 47 midway in the second half, but with five minutes remaining the Dutchmen had built a 10 point 62-52 lead and held on to win, 67-62. Howard Messenger was effective in the pivot with 24 for Normal, and Ed Gilday, Hope's pre-war nemesis, added 20. The story for Hope was the aggressive play of Gabby Van Dis, 21 points by Lloyd Heneveld and 17 by Ken Zuverink.

It was a non-league game in Grand Rapids on January 22, but the Calvin contest produced the usual excitement. Townspeople remembered, and a student body that had never witnessed a Hope-Calvin game was soon apprised of the emotional history of the series. The new Calvin coach was Charles "Chuck" Bult, a gentleman of the first order and a genuine credit to the coaching profession. This time the large Hope following did not have to contend with gasoline rationing as it journeyed eastward to the Burton Gym. Van Dis, Mulder, Dalman, and Slager recalled their last game at Burton in February, 1943, and were grateful for the opportunity to once again compete in the charged atmosphere. Missing from the scene were Ets Kleinjans and Russ De Vette. Kleinjans, captain of the '43 squad, had graduated, while De Vette was playing basketball in some rather fast company. Still on active duty, he was touring the Pacific with a U.S. Marine team that boasted six All-Americans. Joe Fulks (Milsaps), Andy Phillip (Illinois), and Bill Closs (Rice) would later perform for the Philadelphia Warriors of the NBA.

The game proved to be another classic with Hope gaining a four-point, 31-27 halftime advantage. Gabby Van Dis, with 24 points, led the way for a Hope team that was not to be denied on this night. Don Mulder followed with 13 and Ken Zuverink contributed 12 in the 60-52 victory. For Calvin, Gene Broene matched Van Dis with 24 and John Vander Molen played a strong game with 18.

As Coach Hinga's team continued to improve, it was strengthened even further by the addition of Harv Buter of the '43 squad and his younger brother Herk, and also tall, blond Don Scholton. Herk and Don now shared the center position while the latter recovered from the ordeal of a Nazi prison camp. As the second semester got underway the Dutchmen again took the measure of Michigan Normal, this time by a score of 65 to 52. Balanced scoring showed Mulder with 14,

Scholton 13, Van Dis 11, and Zuverink 10. Ed Gilday and Bob Messenger again led Normal with 19 and 17. Hope resumed MIAA action by hosting the troublesome Hornets of Kalamazoo College now coached by Bob Nulf. In the course of the game the lead changed hands 15 times but with four minutes remaining the Hornets were ahead, 46-41. Two Hope baskets made it 46-45 as the final minute ticked away. At this point the quick hands of Don Mulder produced an interception. He dribbled the length of the floor to lay in the winning basket and end the nail-biter, 47-46. It was somehow appropriate that the "Duke" also led his team with 16 points. Bob App had 15 for Kalamazoo. It was Mulder again when Albion came to the Armory on February 14. Don was high with 17 but he had good support from Van Dis who scored 16 and Zuverink with 15. The strong Albion team was surprised by the improved Dutchmen and went down to a 17 point defeat, 67-50. Lew Moon had 14 for the Britons. Alma had beaten Hope handily on January 7 and felt confident on their home court, but the final tally favored Hope, 77 to 53. This time Herk Buter led the attack with 14 followed by Mulder's 12. The veteran Bud Howe had 16 for the Scots in the losing cause. Hope's final MIAA contest was played at Hillsdale on February 21 and the lopsided Dutch win was not really a surprise. The undermanned Dales fought gamely against Hope subs but still lost by a score of 79-32. Herk Buter had 10 for Hope as most squad members got into the scoring column. The victory, coupled with a Kalamazoo win over Albion, gave Hope a co-championship with the Britons.

The Dutchmen's stellar performance was gratifying to Coach Hinga, but one item of business remained. The night following the Hillsdale game Hope hosted Calvin in the Armory. On two previous occasions the Knights had put a damper on Hope's championship celebrations, but it was not to be this time. It was Hope all the way as the team closed out the season with a 58-37 victory, their ninth straight win. A victory celebration was held after the game in Carnegie Gym with co-ed Bobby Bilkert in charge of entertainment. She would one day be Mrs. Donald Mulder. The following morning the grand tradition known as Glory Day was revived.

The league's coaches allowed themselves some latitude

Hope College Basketball Team - 1945-46
MIAA Co-Champions With Albion

Seated L to R: Clarie Van Liere, Ken Zuverink, Don Mulder - Captain, Bob "Gabby" Van Dis, George Dalman, Art Timmer. **Standing:** Coach Bud Hinga, Harv Buter, Harold "Herk" Buter, Don Scholton, Art Slager, Phil Meengs, Jimmy Muddle - Manager. Missing from picture: Lloyd Heneveld.

in choosing the All-MIAA team in this first year following the war. Nine men were selected with Hope dominating. Those named were: Don Mulder, Gabby Van Dis, and Art Slager from Hope, Lew Moon and Elkin Isaac from Albion, Harold Hinckley and Bob Rooney from Kalamazoo, Jack Howe from Alma, and Dick De Fay from Hillsdale. As the basketball season came to an end the town of Holland shifted its attention to Holland High School as Coach Malcolm Mackay successfully guided his team through the state tournament and into the Class A finals at Jenison Field House in East Lansing. In a close game on March 23 the Dutch defeated Saginaw Arthur Hill 43-40 to notch the city's first state championship since Coach Cubby Drew's team won it all in 1919.

When the snows finally melted and spring arrived in 1946, the campus became a beehive of sports activity. In marked contrast to the three previous years, eager athletes made their bids for places on five different teams. Using a cadre from his "Theory of Coaching" class, coach Al Vanderbush began spring football drills. After a few weeks work with about 40 candidates, Vanderbush moved on to coach the track team. Track fortunes at Hope had been at a low ebb in the immediate pre-war years and a period of rebuilding would be necessary. The team was off to a good start on April 27 when they traveled to Adrian and took the measure of the Bulldogs 70 1/4 to 60 3/4, but in a triangular at Albion on May 4 the Dutchman began to see the real picture. The final score showed Alma 77, Albion 51, Hope 32. A 108 1/3 to 22 2/3 loss to Kalamazoo was especially discouraging but some individual stars did begin to emerge. The MIAA Field Day meet was held at Albion on May 18 with Albion the winner, followed by Alma and Kalamazoo. Hope managed a fourth place finish on the strength of gold medals by Vern Kraai, Don Lee, and Dell Koop. Kraai took the 100 and 220 in 10.7 and 24.1 while Lee's winning 880 time was 2:10. Koop's winning discus toss was 110'.

Fifteen candidates responded to Coach Albert Timmer's call for golfers. Those remaining after a period of tryouts were Howard Jalving, Baxter Elhart, Don Ladewig, Art Timmer, Paul Mulder, and Clarence Hopkins. The highlights in Hope's two and eight season were a 10 1/2-1 1/2 victory over Albion, a triangular win over both Albion and Kalamazoo, and a fourth place finish in the MIAA Meet at Albion on May 17 and 18. Coach Timmer could maintain that it was a building year, and 1947 would bear him out.

The ever-versatile Bud Hinga took over the tennis squad in '46 and produced an effective team composed of Gabby Van Dis, Don Scholton, Gene Barendse, Jack Tirrell, Bob Holleman, and John Ligtvoet. 4-3 victories were recorded over Grand Rapids J.C. and Muskegon Junior College before taking the measure of Albion by a 6-1 count on May 3. But on May 8 and May 12 the Dutchmen discovered that the Kalamazoo tennis dynasty was still in place. Coach Allen B. "Doc" Stowe had his team more than ready and Hope was beaten, 7-0, on both dates. Somewhat shaken, the team dropped a 4-3 decision to Albion just two days later. Hinga, however, had his unit back in form for the MIAA meet at Albion, where a strong performance netted a second place finish behind the Hornets.

Perhaps the most successful spring sport was baseball, despite its non-league status. With the addition of Al Vanderbush to the coaching staff Jack Schouten was able, for the first time, to concentrate on a single sport in the spring. The squad included Bill Hillegonds and Ralph Cornell behind the plate, Claire Van Liere, Dick Brown, and Don Mulder on the mound, Ray Heemstra, Gordon Brewer, and Bob Danhof dividing duty at the initial sack, Dick Van Doren at second, Ernie Meeusen at third, Don Mulder at short, Bob Dorsch in left field, Chuck Martindale in center, and Jack French and Bob Bennett in right. In the opener at Calvin on April 18, Claire Van Liere, with relief from Mulder, bested the Knights, 7-3. Bob Dorsch contributed a home run to the Dutch cause. On April 23 Muskegon Junior College downed the Dutchmen, 1-0, as pitcher Claire Van Liere walked four in an otherwise superb performance. On May 2 Calvin, in a return game, met the Hope battery of Don Mulder and Bill Hillegonds. Mulder scattered four hits while his team enjoyed a six-run fourth inning and went on to beat the Knights, 12 to 1. Hope's first athletic encounter with Aquinas College took place on May 7 at Riverview Park and proved to be a classic pitcher's battle. In a stellar performance Dick Brown limited the Aquinas team to three hits while Don Doran allowed Hope five hits but no runs in the 2-0 shutout. Dick Van Dorn had two hits including a double for the Dutch and Ralph Cornell replaced the injured Hillegonds behind the plate. Hope's 5-3 victory over Grand Rapids Junior College was significant as it ended a long J.C. win streak. Five days later the Dutchmen again met J.C., this time at Valley Field in Grand Rapids. With the score tied at 2-2, the game was called at 6 as the Grand Rapids City League had reserved the field. Hope tasted defeat at the hands of Western Michigan Frosh in Kalamazoo, but closed out the season on June 3 with a decisive win over Aquinas in Grand Rapids. The final count was 11-3 as the Dutchmen collected 15 hits while Van Liere held Aquinas to three. The 4-3-1 season record was promising, as practically the entire squad would return for 1947.

The long-awaited return of college football occurred on September 3, 1946. New coach Al Vanderbush greeted the largest turnout in the school's history, as 70 candidates began the two-a-day practices leading up to the opening game with Ferris Institute on September 20. Assisting Vanderbush were Russ Waters of Grand Rapids Central High School, and Roy Davis, the former Hope quarterback. The squad's diversity presented a major challenge for the coaches. Included were a hard corps of veterans who had played on former Hope teams, another group that had entered the service directly out of high school towards the end of the war, and the expected number of freshmen coming directly from the high schools. Vanderbush was impressed with the deception afforded by the "T" formation as employed by Clark Shaughnessy, Paul Brown, and others, and had decided to install it instead of the single wing used previously at Hope.

The key figure in such an attack would be the quarterback, and leading contenders for the position were a duo from Muskegon: Nick Yonker, who had been a standout for the Big Reds, and Russ De Vette, who had not played football in high school. De Vette had returned to Hope from the Marine Corps despite Coach Hinga's concern that he might choose to complete his education at a larger institution. De Vette's interest in a coaching career now prompted him to add football to his other three sports. In the early going halfback returnees Dick Higgs and Art Timmer had the edge while Ernie Post and Roseville freshman Bob Emery showed promise at fullback. Interior linemen Bill Draper, Len Dick, and Jack Yeomans were back, and the Grand Rapids trio of Robert "Rip" Collins, Gordon Timmerman, and Abe Moerland were much in evidence as was guard Charlie Davidson, a transfer from Grand Rapids J.C. Veteran Don Schriemer led the contingent of ends along with Harv Buter and Clare De Mull.

Practices were conducted on the field adjacent to Carnegie Gym and from the start there was little doubt that Coach Vanderbush was in charge. Players soon found him to be knowledgeable, sensitive, firm, and fair. These hallmarks of good coaching produced high morale and a cooperative spirit. Coach Waters was also popular with the squad. Like Vanderbush he had been a naval officer and worked well with men in their early twenties. He referred to squad members as "mates" and when helmets were needed for live contact he called upon them to "get the hats." Roy Davis, Hope '44, rounded out the staff and Jack Schouten became a full-time trainer.

A Blue versus Orange scrimmage was conducted at Riverview Park on September 13 to help the coaches decide on a starting 11 for the opener with Ferris on the 20th. There were no films or scouting reports for either team, leaving the coaches little choice but to concentrate on basic football. Hope's Friday night game at Riverview Park attracted a crowd of nearly five thousand, and they were not to be disappointed. The Vanderbush inaugural was off to a good start when Don Ladewig recovered a Ferris fumble on the Hope 43. The Dutch began a 57-yard drive on the ground with ball carriers Dick Higgs, Art Timmer, and Ernie Post alternating. Higgs went off tackle for the final six yards and kicked the extra point. With eight minutes gone in the first quarter Hope led, 7-0. The jittery Bulldogs lost another fumble soon after and this time Timmer went 20 yards for the score. Higgs' kick was not good and the score stood 13-0. Hope continued to capitalize on Ferris mistakes including a blocked punt. Hope fans now had their first look at big Bob Emery, the freshman fullback from Roseville, Michigan. Weighing 215 pounds, Emery took a handoff from Nick Yonker and, shedding would-be tacklers, rambled 30 yards for the score.

Alvin W. Vanderbush
Hope Football Coach 1946-1954

Al brought Hope College its first undisputed MIAA Football Championship in 1953. His '51 team tied with Alma for the title. He also served as director of athletics and later as chairman of Hope's department of political science.

For the extra point try, Vanderbush called a play that would prove effective throughout the year. Left halfback Higgs took a handoff from quarterback Yonker and simulated a right end sweep. With the flow to the right, Yonker circled deep to the left and, completely alone in the end zone, received a picture-perfect transcontinental pass from Higgs. The quarter ended with Hope leading, 20-0. In the second quarter it was Emery again, this time for 48 yards and the game's longest touchdown run. Higgs' kick was blocked, making it 26-0 at the half. In the second half Art Timmer scored his second touchdown on a 30-yard end sweep to make it 32-0. It was Ferris' turn after an interception by Hendrickson and a series of successful passes. Hethering scored on an end run from the eight. With Hope subs in the game Ferris fumbled once more. Hope advanced the ball to the 28, and a Russ De Vette pass to Tony Kempker placed the ball on the eight-yard line. Bob Koop plunged to the one foot line and De Vette scored on a quarterback sneak, making the final score Hope 38, Ferris 6. Vanderbush had obviously accomplished a lot in less than three weeks of practice.

On September 27 the Dutchmen hosted the Albion Britons in a night game at Riverview Park. It marked the first MIAA contest of the season and the Hope coaches had an additional incentive. Hope had not recorded a win over Albion since Bud Hinga's 6-0 victory in 1936. Art Timmer in particular recalled tough losses in 1941 and '42. His satisfaction came early in the game when he plunged over from the one-yard line to give Hope a 6-0 lead. The second Hope score came on a 12-yard end sweep by Timmer. The Dutch continued to be in charge as they scored a third time on the deceptive Higgs-to-Yonker transcontinental pass. Hope's defense proved superb as they shut out the Britons despite some fine runs by fullback Elkin Isaac. Hope's final score came on a brilliant 43-yard run by Gabby Van Dis, whose basketball faking ability was a key factor. The 26-0 victory was decisive and rewarding for players and coaches alike.

Michigan Normal came for another night contest on October 4. Hope's vaunted rushing attack was stymied early on by a strong Normal defense and the Dutch were forced to an aerial game. Hope's first score was set up by a 20-yard Yonker-to-Clare De Mull pass. From the Normal 20 it was once again the Higgs-to-Yonker transcontinental for the touchdown. Later in the half, a Higgs-to-Timmer pass covered 35 yards for the score and Higgs' conversion made it 13-0. The second half was scoreless and Hope had its second shutout of the season. Coach Vanderbush took his team to Houseman Field in Grand Rapids on the night of October 10 to meet Grand Rapids Junior College. In perhaps the roughest game of the season three Hope players were sidelined with injuries. In the era before face masks, Art Timmer suffered a broken nose, Russ De Vette had his two front teeth broken, and Russ Norden had several teeth loosened by a blow. Before his departure Timmer advanced the ball to the J.C. 12. Yonker then passed to Don Schriemer in the end zone for Hope's first score. The kick was not good and the score remained 6-0 until the fourth quarter when Bob Emery and Bob Van Dis engineered a drive to the J.C. 20. At this point Yonker passed to dashman Vern Kraai, who took the ball over his shoulder and streaked into the end zone. Higg's kick made it 13-0. Later in the quarter Hope intercepted a J.C. pass and Roy Zwemer picked up 25 yards in two plays. Quarterback Russ De Vette then threw a touchdown pass to Harv Buter. The conversion by Higgs gave Hope the 20-0 win and their third shutout in a row.

An understandably confident Hope squad made its way to Kalamazoo on October 19, but it was Kalamazoo's Homecoming and also dedication day for the Hornets' splendid new Angell Field Stadium. Coach Bob Nulf had his team more than ready and Hope was in early trouble when Nick Yonker was injured. After a scoreless first quarter Kalamazoo marched from their own 15 to the Hope 35, where a pass from Gene Flowers to Walker reached the five and Reed took it in for the score. Late in the third quarter the Hornets drove from their 40 to the Hope 15. Tom Shopoff then scored on a well-executed Statue of Liberty play and the Dutch were down 13-0. Hope's only threat in the fourth quarter ended with a lost fumble on the Kalamazoo 35. The inspired Kalamazoo team had earned their 13-0 victory and established themselves as a genuine title contender.

October 26 was a golden Indian summer day with ideal conditions for the Dutch Homecoming against Alma. The Holland community responded with a standing room crowd of nearly six thousand. Still smarting from the Kalamazoo defeat, the Dutchmen received the ball on their 28 and marched on the ground via Emery and Van Dis to the Alma two. Van Dis went the final two but Higgs' kick was blocked. It seemed to be Gabby's afternoon as he returned an Alma punt 13 yards, then reeled off a crowd pleasing 42-yard touchdown scamper which included his usual fakes. The kick attempt was wide and Hope had an early 12-0 lead. Coach Steve Sebo's team then made its only threat before the half reaching the one foot line. Hope's next score came when Ernie Post ran back an interception 10 yards before lateraling to Dick Higgs, who advanced to the Alma 25. Bob Koop made it to the 13 on a Statue of Liberty and Emery eventually bucked over from the three. A missed kick left the score at 18-0 as the half ended. In the second half Hope continued its aggressive defense with Abe Moerland blocking an Alma kick. An interception by Van Dis set the stage for the game's longest run. Bob Emery broke loose and raced 48 yards for the touchdown. Higgs' pass for the point was broken up and the Dutch settled for the 24-0 victory.

Adrian had not fielded a football team in 1942 but was back for the '46 season and hosted Hope on November 2, a gray and rainy afternoon. The muddy field severely limited the Hope ground game and Coach Vanderbush was thankful for his team's passing potential. In the first quarter Russ De Vette passed to Art Timmer who got away for 65 yards and the touchdown, giving Hope a 6-0 halftime edge. In the third period Hope worked its way to the Adrian five where Yonker's pass to Dick Higgs was good for the score. Also in the third quarter, Yonker connected with Vern Kraai on the Adrian 30 and the speedster went the distance for the score. This time Higgs broke the jinx and the kick was good. The 19-0 victory was especially meaningful, as it vaulted the Dutchmen into a first place tie with Kalamazoo and Hillsdale with but one game remaining.

Most of Hope's football games at Hillsdale have been memorable, and the November 9 encounter in 1946 was no exception. The new Hillsdale coach was Davy Nelson, a 1942 graduate of the University of Michigan, where he had teamed with Tom Harmon and Forest Evashevski under Fritz Crisler.

Later, at the University of Delaware, he would be recognized as one of the finest minds in college football. Nelson's '46 team boasted two excellent backs in Bill Young and Tom Ward. The Hope coaches expected the game to go down to the wire and knew that it would take every trick in the book to come away with a victory. Hope's first trick occurred early and paid dividends. The Dutch chose to receive and returned the opening kickoff to the 32. On first down Higgs got off a booming quick kick. A surprised Hillsdale defender chased the bouncing ball, touched it, and Hope recovered on the Dale's 30 yard line. Emery gained 14 to the 16 before the going got tough. Higgs got three more and in two plays Emery bulled to the one. On fourth down Yonker went in on a sneak. Higgs kick was true and Hope enjoyed an early 7-0 lead. Near the end of the first quarter Hope punted to safety Bill Young who took the ball on his own 10 and returned it 38 yards to near midfield. A subsequent drive put Hillsdale on the Hope five. Young drove in for the score and Harry Spiteri came off the bench to kick the point. He would be heard from again. With the score 7-7 at halftime, the game was living up to all expectations.

Early in the second half the Dutchmen fumbled on their own 42 and the Dales recovered. In three plays Tom Albright made it to the 13. Three more plays took it to the three and Tom Ward went in for the score. Spiteri again converted and Hope trailed 14-7. The Dutch were down but certainly not out as they received the kickoff and scored in three plays. After Emery had gotten the ball into Dale territory at the 45, Yonker dropped back for a 25-yard aerial to Clare De Mull, who took the ball away from two Hillsdale defenders and raced into the end zone. Higgs' conversion was good and the evenness of the contest was once more in evidence. As the third quarter ended, Hope made its way to mid-field. Van Dis opened the fourth quarter with a six-yard run to the 44 before Emery broke away to the 29. Yonker got three more on a sneak, then passed to flanker Van Dis who made it to the 13 and a first down. Emery then broke through for 12 but was hauled down on the one. Yonker's quarterback sneak was stopped at the one foot line and it was left for the 215 pound Emery to finally break into the end zone. Higgs was having a good day, but his third conversion attempt hit the goal post and bounced away leaving the score at 20-14. The Dutch still led with three minutes remaining, but the determined Dales had driven to the Hope 35. At this point a crucial penalty was assessed against a Hope lineman for unnecessary roughness. The ball was moved to the 20, and on first down tailback Bill Young passed to John Cuddleback for the tying touchdown. For the third time Harry Spiteri came off the bench and split the

Al Vanderbush's First Hope Team - 1946

Front Row L to R: Vern Kraai, Bob Koop, Alfie Vande Waa, Ernie Post, Abe Moerland, Ed Wroblicky, Dick Higgs. **2nd Row:** Ken Lincoln, Manager, John Lightvoet, Gene Nyenhuis, Clare De Mull, Jerry Formsma, Roy Zwemer, Bill Draper, Captain Don Schriemer. **3rd Row:** Robert "Rip" Collins, Head Coach Al Vanderbush, Bill Appledorn, Gordon Timmerman, Don Rinkus, Art Timmer, Bud Newton, Nick Yonker, Ken Weller, Don Oosterbaan, Max Boersma, John Mac Donald - Manager, Clarence Hopkins - Manager. **Top Row:** Bill "Moose" Holwerda, Warren De Witt, Dell Doop, Russ Norden, Ralph Cornell, Don Miller, Russ De Vette, Len Dick, Don Ladewig, Bob Emery, Glenn Bruggers, Charlie Davidson, Harv Buter, Jack Yeomans, Don Bocks, Bob "Gabby" Van Dis, Gordon Brewer.

uprights to give Hillsdale the 21-20 victory and a co-championship with Kalamazoo.

While Hope's third place finish did not sound impressive, its 6-2 season was outstanding in many ways. The six victories were the most ever by a Hope team and four of the six had been shutouts. In a great ball game Hope had come within three minutes of a co-championship. Coach Vanderbush had installed the new "T" formation successfully in a short period of time, and from a squad of great diversity he had molded a team with unusual loyalty and dedication.

In a wind-up of the fall sports season, quarterback Nick Yonker and end Don Schriemer were named to the 11-man All-MIAA team and Schriemer was elected honorary captain of Hope's team. Cross country, which had been discontinued after the 1932 season, was again under discussion, with a subsequent decision to restore the sport for the 1947 season. Jack Schouten would be Hope's coach.

Elsewhere, at Albion, veteran Coach Dale Sprankle announced that he would step down as head football coach. League officials agreed that a person of such stature would be sorely missed.

As the 1946-47 basketball season approached, Coach Hinga's aggregation became an overwhelming favorite to repeat as MIAA champion. Four of the five starters from the 1945-46 co-championship team returned, as did Russ De Vette of the 1942-43 championship team. As a Marine in the V-12 program, De Vette had spent the 1943-44 season as a regular on the Denison University team in Ohio and was named to the All-Ohio team. He subsequently toured the Pacific with a U.S. Marine team that numbered several future NBA pros (see page __). The Hope squad now included five members of the original "Blitz Kids" as well as football stalwarts Nick Yonker and Bill Holwerda.

The season again opened against the Percy Jones Army Hospital team in Battle Creek, but the situation differed markedly from that of 1945. Hope had little trouble in downing the soldiers, 74 to 41, as the box score brought back memories of 1942-43. De Vette led the scoring with 14, followed by George Dalman with 12, Gabby Van Dis with 10, and Don Mulder with nine. On the fifth anniversary of Pearl Harbor, Hope met Grand Rapids Junior College in the Armory. The game was a homecoming of sorts for the new J.C. coach, who was none other than Russ Waters who had so recently served as Hope's backfield coach in football. Waters' second string quarterback now proved his undoing on the hardwoods. Russ De Vette led the Dutchmen with 27 points, 15 in the first eight minutes of the second half. Van Dis had 10 and Dalman eight in the 62-54 win. Jim Horn led J.C. with 12.

The MIAA season opened with Adrian traveling to Holland on December 12. It was more of the same as Hope led, 23-9, after 10 minutes and 30-15 at halftime. The final score of 68-43 showed De Vette with 25, and Van Dis, Herk Buter, and Ken Zuverink with nine each. Fox, who led Adrian with 10, had been an old high school rival of Don Mulder. In a return game at Grand Rapids J.C. on December 15, Hope had some early trouble with Russ Waters' zone defense and could manage only a 24-17 halftime lead. The final count, however, was Hope 53, J.C. 39, with the Dutch scoring balanced. Duke Mulder led with 14, Herk Buter had 13, and De Vette 10. Jim Horn and Jim Montgomery had 11 each for J.C. In a final game before the holidays, Hope notched a convincing 69-33 victory over a highly regarded Michigan Normal team. De Vette and Mulder led the scoring with 16 and 15, but the outstanding feature of the game was the defensive work of center Herk Buter, who held Normal standout Howard Messinger to three points while scoring nine himself.

With their 14th straight victory safely tucked away, the confident Dutchmen awaited the arrival of Western Michigan in the Armory on January 2. But Buck Read's talent-laden squad were also masters of the fast break and it would be a long evening for Hinga's team. From the outset the Broncos' big Don Boven and Mel Van Dis (Gabby's cousin) dominated the boards, a key ingredient in the offense of both teams. Harold Gensichen, top player in the state, led his team to the 76-60 victory. Boven collected 17 and Mel Van Dis had 14. Russ De Vette, however, topped all scorers with 21. Don Mulder had 15 and Gabby 10. Hope licked its wounds and went back to MIAA play.

At Albion on January 6 the Dutchmen managed a 25-13 halftime lead in spite of the Britons' new fan shaped backboards. Mulder led all scorers with 18 and De Vette added nine. Elkin Isaac again was high for Albion with 10 and Lew Moon followed with eight. Hope was back on the victory track with the 49-36 win. Coach Lloyd Grow brought his Kalamazoo Hornets to the Armory on January 10 and his team led the contest for three quarters of the game, but forward Bob App fouled out with K leading 41-38 and the home team took over. Co-captain De Vette kept his team in the game with 14 first-half points and a game high 23. Mulder's floor play and 10 points helped in the stretch and sixth man Harvey Buter was effective off the bench as the Dutch finally prevailed, 55 to 46.

Considering their loss on January 2, the team had reason to be gun shy in the return game at Western on the 14th. Things went bad from the start as the hustling Gabby collected four quick fouls and spent most of the half on the bench. Western's 38-24 halftime lead ballooned to an 84-60 victory as Coach Read substituted freely. Hope's bright spot was Don Mulder's 21 point performance. Gensichen and Mel Van Dis had 13 for Western, and substitute Ray Postema had 10. The trip to Alma four days later helped Hinga's crew forget the Bronco nightmare. Balanced scoring again contributed to a 66-54 Dutch victory. Herk Buter was impressive with 17, as was Mulder with a like number, and De Vette with 16. Rocky Walker kept the Scots in the game with 21 points.

Hope's home contest with Albion on January 23 was

perhaps the finest team effort of the season. Accounts of the game make note of the superb passing and overall teamwork of Van Dis, Mulder, and De Vette. An outstanding defensive performance by Herk Buter helped seal the 83-46 victory. Buter held the Britons' Lew Moon to a single point in the first half. Gabby and Duke Mulder took scoring honors with 22 and 21 points, while Ike Isaac had 19 for Albion. In a gesture of fine sportsmanship after the game, Lew Moon made his way to the Hope locker room to congratulate the winners. Noting Hope's racehorse style, he offered the wry comment, "I'd rather play Kalamazoo, they at least let you rest awhile."

At Ypsilanti on the 25th, Hope struggled in the early going against Michigan Normal. Normal built a 21-11 lead in the first 10 minutes but the Dutch defense tightened and Hope came back for a 23-22 halftime lead on Russ De Vette's long shot. At the three quarter mark the Dutch owned a 40-30 margin and the final count was 49-42.

On Thursday, January 30, Coach Chuck Bult brought a strong Calvin squad to the Armory. The Knights were led by the veteran Marv Bylsma, who had played for Buck Read at Western Michigan during the war. Western had made an appearance in Madison Square Garden, and Bylsma briefly held the Garden scoring record, only to have it broken by the great George Mikan of De Paul. Hinga did not take the contest lightly and the Dutch were ready. Herk Buter seemed especially inspired and played the best game of his career. Buter led Hope with 25 points, continually hustled back on defense, and held 6' 6" Jake Hekman to two points. After holding a 32-25 halftime lead, Hope won the game, 71 to 38. Van Dis had 13, De Vette 12, and Mulder eight while Bylsma led Calvin with 14 and Lou Zondervan followed with 11.

Hope returned to MIAA competition on February 7 when they made the long trip to Hillsdale to meet the team now coached by Harold Westerman. Westerman and Russ De Vette would later coach together at the University of Maine. The Dales made a game of it for 10 minutes, then fell behind 35-24 at halftime. Herk Buter continued his fine performance with 17 points. He was followed by Mulder with 15, and Van Dis and De Vette with 11 each. Gil Edson was strong for Hillsdale with 19, but the Hope victory was almost a foregone conclusion. The final was Hope 71, Dales 45. The evening's high point for the home crowd was the halftime ceremony, which saw halfback Bill Young receive the MIAA's Most Valuable Football Award from Holland industrialist Randall Bosch.

Hinga's squad traveled on to Adrian where the next night they registered their 12th straight MIAA victory, 89 to 60. Hope built a 40-26 halftime lead, and with 12 minutes remaining in the game Hinga cleared the bench. De Vette scored a game-high 24 points and was followed closely by Herk Buter with 22. George Dalman had seven. Of note was the fact that Adrian's high point man was Gregg Arbaugh with 18. Arbaugh would later return to his alma mater and coach many games against Hope teams coached by Russ De Vette.

A truism of sport is that all win streaks come to an end, and Hope's downfall came at Kalamazoo on Valentine's Day. The Dutchmen gained a hard-fought 29-24 halftime lead, then played the Hornets on even terms for the next quarter when the score showed Hope 39, Kalamazoo 34. But soon after, both De Vette and Van Dis fouled out, and with six minutes remaining Kalamazoo knotted the count at 42. K's eventual 51-45 victory was due in large part to the fine floor play of Wayne Thompson, who led his team with 15. Don Mulder was high for Hope with 13 and Herk Buter managed 11. All in all, it was a downer for the Dutchmen.

Calvin took note of Hope's defeat and vowed to extend the Dutch losing streak. The Knights had a new look in the person of guard Wilbur "Slug" Slager of Chicago Christian High. The teams met in the Burton Gym on February 18, and it soon became evident that this was not the same team that Hope had beaten so handily on January 30. By halftime Calvin held a 31-20 lead thanks largely to the efforts of newcomer Slager, who had 11 points. Early in the second half Nick Yonker was summoned from the bench to put the clamps on Slager. Yonker, a great competitor in his own right, limited "Slug" to five points while scoring seven himself. Hope scored eight straight points to begin the second half but the Knights still led by 10 (46-36) at the three-quarter mark. Fans on both sides sensed a repeat of the 1943 Calvin win but Don Mulder finally scored the go-ahead basket to make it 49-48, and the Dutch eked out a 56-53 victory. Mulder's excellent game netted his team 25 points and De Vette followed with 11. Slager led Calvin with 18, Marv Bylsma had 12, and Dave Tuuk eight. Tuuk would later become Calvin's outstanding cross country and track coach, as well as director of athletics for many years.

On February 21 Hope clinched a share of the MIAA crown by defeating Hillsdale for the 20th straight time. The Armory crowd saw Coach Westerman attempt to slow the game down, but Hope's halftime lead was 33-18 despite these tactics. Don Scholton was the defensive star of the game, as he held high scoring Gil Edson to seven points. Russ De Vette led the Hope scoring with 20, Van Dis had 16, and Herk Buter tallied 13. Mulder was limited by a slight case of the flu but his substitute, Nick Yonker, scored 9 in the 72-36 win.

Hope wrapped up the MIAA championship by defeating Alma, 81 to 44, on the last day of February. The contest marked the final home appearance of co-captains Russ De Vette and Gabby Van Dis. Since their arrival in 1941 the duo had displayed superior talent and spirited play. This night they would provide one more "blitz" for an appreciative audience. Don Mulder's superior floor game aided De Vette in scoring 20 and Van Dis in notching 18. With the game well in hand, Hinga removed all three to a standing ovation.

The season, however, was not quite over. Efforts were underway to effect a union of the Reformed Church in America and the United Presbyterian Church. Church officials seemed to feel that an athletic relationship between colleges of the respective denominations would be appropriate and Coach Hinga was persuaded to append a game with Monmouth College to his schedule, which seemingly had reached its logical conclusion. Hope's players traveled to the Illinois school on Monday, March 3, and found themselves in trouble from the start. The Monmouth gym was equipped with fan backboards, which caused the Dutchmen to shoot poorly in the first half. Of greater concern was the deliberate, set style of offense employed by Monmouth, which made effective use of screens. Hinga's practice sessions had not devoted a great deal of time to the defensive art of beating screens or switching men, and by halftime the Hope crew experienced its largest deficit of the season, with the score at 48-26. Things improved somewhat in the second half but the damage had been done and the Scots' decisive 84-58 victory was an unfortunate ending to an outstanding Hope season. Russ De Vette closed out his career with a 20 point performance, followed by Mulder with 13 and Van Dis with 11. Don Armstrong led the winners with 26.

Hope ended with a 16 and four overall record and was impressive at 9-1 in the MIAA. De Vette's 328 season point total included 166 to lead the MIAA. Albion's Elkin Isaac finished second with 130. Named to the All-MIAA team were De Vette and Don Mulder from Hope, Elkin Isaac and Lew Moom from Albion, and Wayne Thompson from Kalamazoo. A worthy Gabby Van Dis found himself on the second team but had honors enough, having been elected president of Hope's Student Council earlier in the year. For the first time the league decided that the Randall Bosch Most Valuable Player Award should be extended to basketball, and to no one's surprise, the first recipient was Russell De Vette.

At the end of the winter season Hope found itself holding a one point lead over Kalamazoo in the race for the All-Sports Trophy. Hope had last won the coveted award a decade earlier in the era of Poppink and Buys. Improved performances in the spring sports would be necessary to maintain the Hope lead. The biggest boost would come from Coach Al Timmer's golf team: the team returned intact with the exception of Art Timmer, who had graduated in February. The Dutch were aided by a new scoring format which allowed one point for each official league dual meet victory in addition to the usual MIAA Field Day points. On April 29 Hope met Alma on the Indian Trails course in Grand Rapids and emerged with a 6 1/2-5 1/2 victory as Earl Holkeboer shot a brillian 69 and Howie Jalving followed with a 70. 6-6 ties with Albion and Hillsdale, plus victories of 12-0 and 6 1/2-5 1/2 over Adrian and Kalamazoo, gave Hope the lead going into the two-day league meet at Kalamazoo. In the MIAA meet it was Hillsdale edging the Dutch 660 to 661, followed by Alma with 664, Kalamazoo 686, and Adrian 814. Howie Jalving was league medalist with a two-day total of 154 and Hope's dual match accumulation was enough to give the college its first golf title since 1934. The season also included a non-league, 15-3 victory over Calvin.

Bud Hinga's tennis team included Jack Tirrell, Gabby Van Dis, Don Scholten, Bob Becksfort, John Ligtvoet, and Gerry Gnade. After dropping 6-1 and 5-4 matches to Calvin and Grand Rapids J.C., the team settled down and registered wins over Adrian, 5-2, Alma, 7-0, Hillsdale, 7-0, and Albion. The usual shutout was suffered at the hands of Kalamazoo. In the conference meet Hope held on to take second place and attention shifted to the track team, which had not been strong since the late thirties.

The track picture was grim for Coach Al Vanderbush in the early going. The annual MIAA indoor meet held at Michigan State College was dominated by Albion with 72 1/2 points. The Britons were followed by Hillsdale with 40 1/2, Alma with 35, Adrian with 22 1/2, Hope 17 1/2, and Kalamazoo with seven. Hillsdale's brilliant Bill Young was high point man with 12. Hope's only first place was scored by Ernie Ross, who went 10' 9" in the pole vault. Coach Vanderbush had hoped to add interest to the track program by conducting some on-campus home meets but was unable to do so due to the construction of a "T" shaped temporary dormitory on the east end of the athletic field. The building took away the east end of the track, which was already less than the regulation 440 yards. Accordingly, Hope met Calvin in a dual meet at Houseman Field on April 23 and scored a surprising 74-57 victory. The Dutchmen scored five firsts in the 13 event meet but had sufficient depth to secure the win. Vern Kraai was a double winner in the 100 and 220, Gordon Brewer won the 440, Don Lee took the 880, and the mile relay team of Milt Peterson, Howard Bruggers, Dennis Shoemaker, and Gordon Brewer closed the meet with a victory. Ten days later Hope met Grand Rapids J.C. on the same track and, despite improved performances, lost the meet by a score of 70 to 60. This time the team managed seven first place finishes as Bob Emery won the shot with a put of 41' 8 1/2", Fred Veltman took the discus with a throw of 108', Ray Heemstra notched a first in the javelin with 155' 6", and Jim Lamb won the pole vault with a height of 11' 3." In the running events Vern Kraai was first in the 220 with 23.6, Brewer took the 440 in 54.8, and the mile relay team of Walt Boerman, Howie Bruggers, Dennis Shoemaker, and Brewer won the blue ribbon in 3:42.8. Bob Paul and Glenn Bruggers took second and third in the two-mile run.

The finals of the MIAA track and field meet were held under the lights at Kalamazoo's Angell Field on Saturday, May 17. Results of Hope's fine showing in golf and tennis were in and Coach Vanderbush communicated to his track team that they were not to be responsible for Hope losing the All-Sports Trophy. The coach's words were enough to inspire an unexpected third place finish. Vern Kraai won the 100 yard dash in the excellent time of 10.1, Jim Lamb took the Pole Vault with 11', and Bob Emery won the Shot with a put of 42' 4 1/2". In addition, a third place finish was recorded by Russ De Vette in the high jump, and a fourth by Fred Veltman in the discus, Brewer in the 440, and Bob Paul in the

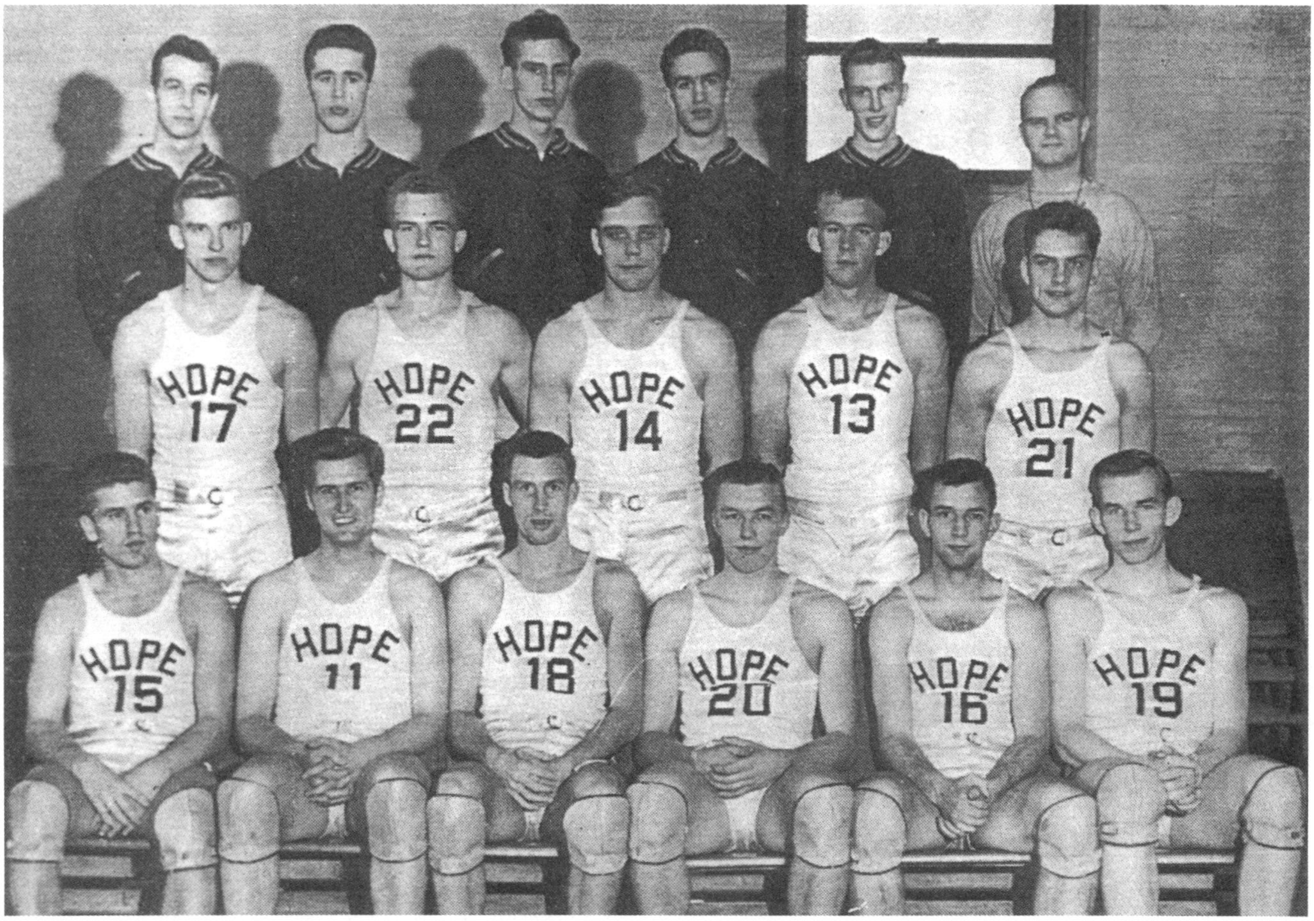

The 1946-47 MIAA Champions
Coach Hinga's Last Championship Team

Seated L to R: Don Mulder, George Dalman, Co-Captain Russ De Vette, Harve Buter, Co-Captain Bob Van Dis, Ken Zuverink. **2nd Row:** Herk Buter, Don Scholton, Chuck Ploegsma, Bill Holwerda, Nick Yonker. **Top Row:** Earl Holkeboer, Fred Brieve, Ron Korver, Paul Hendrickson, Paul Van Dort, Coach Bud Hinga.

Hope College Golf Team - 1947
MIAA Champions

Kneeling L to R: Paul Mulder, Chris Den Herder. **Standing:** Baxter Elhart, Earl Holkeboer, Bob Barkema, Howard Jalving. Howard Jalving was the league medalist.

two-mile. Vern Kraai added a third place in the 220, Jerry Formsma took fifth in the 120 yard high hurdles, Ken Decker had a fifth in the 220 lows, and the mile relay team of Walt Boerman, Jim Lamb, Denny Shoemaker, and Brewer closed out the meet with their best race of the season, good enough for second place. The track team's third place finish was its best since 1937, and gave Hope the MIAA All-Sports Trophy with 40 points. Albion followed with 31, Kalamazoo had 27, Alma 26, Hillsdale 20, and Adrian six. Medals were handed out by the various campus queens. Hope's Myra Brower, later Mrs. Ken Zuverink, presented the All-Sports Trophy to Director of Athletics Milton Hinga.

In baseball's final season as a non-league sport, Jack Schouten's starters were: Bill Hillegonds behind the plate, Dick Higgs at first base, Russ De Vette at second, Ken Rotman at third, Don Mulder at short, Nick Yonker in left field, Harold "Mouse" Van Wieren in center, and Dick Van Dorn in right. Starting pitchers were Claire Van Liere, Bill Ver Hey, and Mike Skaalen. De Vette and Mulder made appearances in relief. The Dutchmen opened with a 10-3 home victory over Grand Rapids J.C., then entertained the Michigan State "B" team at Riverview Park. State eventually won 11 to 4 with Van Liere, Ver Hey, Skaalen, and De Vette all seeing action on the mound. Van Liere, a right handed batter, decided to bat left handed and promptly stroked the ball over the right field fence for a home run. Mulder, with a long poke over the center fielder's head, had an inside-the-park home run, but State's big seven-run fifth inning sealed the victory. A tough 3-2 loss in Kalamazoo to the Western Michigan "B" team was followed by 10-0 shutout of Muskegon Junior College and an 11 to 6 victory over Calvin. On April 3, the Dutch enjoyed revenge in East Lansing when they downed Michigan State's "B" team 6-5 in 10 innings. Ver Hey yielded four runs on eight hits in the first eight innings. Van Liere finished in relief. The winning run in the l0th came on a Rotman single and a long triple by Mouse Van Wieren. Van Liere was the winning pitcher. Western's "B" team continued to be a tough adversary and on May 2 beat the Dutchmen, 11 to 4. Hope was not without offense and matched the Broncos in the early innings. Hope's first score came on first inning singles by Van Dorn and Mulder. In the second it was Dick Higgs with a homer over the right field fence, and in the third back to back doubles by Rotman and Nick Yonker kept Hope in the game. In the fifth Nick Yonker's home run to left field tied the game at four before Western's surge put the game out of reach.

In a May 16 game in Grand Rapids, Harold Van Wieren occupied center stage. Mouse started on the mound against J.C. and gave up three runs before Don Mulder came on in relief. Van Wieren got Hope's first run when he circled the bases on a dropped fly ball and a wild throw to third. In the fourth it was Mouse again with a legitimate home run to make it 3-2 J.C. Hope put the game away with a five-run outburst in the sixth inning that included a steal of home by Mouse Van Wieren, who now had made up for his pitching shortcomings. J.C. rallied for two in the seventh but Don Mulder struck out the last batter to preserve the seven to five victory. Jack Schouten and his charges looked forward to MIAA competition in 1948.

Hope had lost out on the last day of the season in the race for the 1946 football championship and there was reason to believe that the Dutch would be in the thick of the fight in '47. Coach Al Vanderbush welcomed Don Mulder as his assistant and 60 candidates were invited to the opening practice sessions on September 2. Seventeen returning lettermen included quarterback Nick Yonker and fullback Bob Emery plus numerous others who had proven their mettle in the '46 campaign. Dick Higgs was available only for kicking duty, but the presence of linemen Rip Collins, Gordon Timmerman, and Abe Moreland was cause for optimism. Ends Clare De Mull and Bill Holwerda brightened the picture for Yonker.

The season opened at Ferris on September 19. The Bulldogs had been blown out by the Dutch in '46 and they had not forgotten. Harold "Hoppy" Van Zoeren filled in at fullback for the injured Bob Emery and Hope was off to a good start. A short kickoff was taken by Rip Collins on the 45 and advanced to the 49. From that point Yonker and Van Zoeren moved to the Ferris 25. Yonker's pass to Ernie Post was good to the 15. Later from the 11 Yonker broke free on a sneak and went in for the score. Higgs' kick was wide and the score remained 6-0 at halftime. Hope led in first downs eight to two, and it seemed only a matter of time before the Dutch would open up. But the Ferris team was much improved and their passing attack moved them to the Hope five and Hansen went over for the score. The kick was good and the 7-6 score held up for a Ferris victory. Freshmen scatbacks Ted Barrett and Eddie Leverette looked good and "Moose" Holwerda played an outstanding game.

Grand Rapids Junior College came to Riverview for a night game on September 26 and the Dutch were in early trouble. J.C. took the opening kick and drove all the way to the Hope eight-yard line before the Dutch stiffened and got back into the game. Eddie Leverette chalked up runs of 17, seven, and 10 yards, and Bob Emery bulled over from the three. Dick Higgs' kick was good this time, and the 7-0 lead looked good at the half. But in the second half a Higgs punt was blocked and rolled to the Hope 10. Helder later scored from the one and Newara's kick tied the game. Hope opened a drive on their own 36 that netted four first downs. A well-executed reverse to Ernie Post put the ball on the J.C. 20. Leverette then showed some fancy steps around end as he went over for the go-ahead touchdown. Higgs' kick was good and Hope evened its record with a 14-7 victory. The game ended with Hope threatening from the 10 yard line.

The MIAA opener with Hillsdale was considered a key game in the championship race. The season-ending classic of '46 at Hillsdale was recalled and the Riverview stands were full. The first quarter was scoreless. In the second period

Hope worked its way to the Dales' 29 where Bob Emery broke off tackle and went all the way to score. Dick Higgs' kick was good and Hope had the start it wanted. But Bill Young and Tom Ward, Hillsdale's touchdown twins, would be heard from. After a Hope fumble Young connected with end John Cuddleback on a 34-yard pass to the Hope 29. The speedy Young then broke away on a 19-yard scamper to the 10 and Tom Ward took it in for the score. Versatile Bill Young then kicked the point and Hope's impressive start was erased. Coach Nelson's charges mounted a second drive late in the second period but it was cut short by Nick Yonker, who intercepted a Dale pass on the 16 as time ran out. As the second half opened, Ted Barrett returned the Hillsdale kick-off to the 29. The Dutchmen ground out 11 more to the 40, where Yonker found Barrett in the open and the speedster took it all the way to the Hillsdale 17. But a subsequent Yonker pass was intercepted and the drive was dead. Hope threatened again in the third quarter with the ball on its own 26. Yonker threw a five-yard pass to Bill Holwerda, who brought the crowd to its feet as he broke away from tacklers and galloped all the way to the Hillsdale 10. But the Dutch were stymied again as the Dales held and took over on the five. The momentum now shifted and Hillsdale drove 95 yards to score. Young went the final 32 yards and then kicked the point to make it 14-7. In the fourth quarter, against a tiring Hope defense, the Dales again drove to the Hope two and Tom Ward went in for his second touchdown. Young's third kick was perfect and the score stood 21 to 7. As the game slipped away, Hope had enough for one more drive. Bob Emery went the last 14 yards to match Ward with two touchdowns. Dick Higgs' kick made the final score Hillsdale 21, Hope 14. It had been an outstanding game between two excellent small college teams.

After such an effort a letdown might have been expected at Albion a week later, but such was not the case. On the seventh play of the game big Bob Emery broke away off tackle and, with deceptive speed, went 66 yards for the touchdown. With the score at 6-0 Hope fans became aware of an unfamiliar name in the lineup. Halfback Jim Pfingstel intercepted an Albion pass and then, from midfield, threw the halfback transcontinental pass to Nick Yonker for the touchdown. The play covered 50 yards and, with Higgs' conversion, gave the Dutch a 13-0 lead. In the third quarter Pfingstel scored himself on a seven-yard run. Dick Higgs kicked the point and Hope went home with a well-earned 20-0 victory. Hope's game in Ypsilanti on October 18 was played in the rain and there was no score in the first half. Early in the second half a Michigan Normal back intercepted a Hope flat pass and went 60 yards for the touchdown. Normal's 7-0 lead loomed large considering the playing conditions, but late in the quarter Emery scored from the three. The kick, however, was not good and the situation remained grim. But in the fourth quarter fullback Emery scored again on an off tackle play and Hope went home thankful for the 12-7 victory.

Nearly five thousand fans crowded Riverview for Hope's Homecoming game with Kalamazoo College. The Dutchmen needed a victory to get back in the race, and their chances appeared good. Coach Bob Nulf was determined not to be burned by Hope's deceptive transcontinental pass play and alerted the officials to the fact that Nick Yonker, in position as a "T" quarterback, was an ineligible receiver in that he was not at least one yard behind the line of scrimmage. This took away one of Coach Vanderbush's favorite "game-breaker" plays and reduced somewhat the Hope offence. After a first half exchange of punts, Hope drove to midfield from its own 19. At this point Yonker passed to Moose Holwerda who went all the way to the five. On the second play from scrimmage Yonker threw a jump pass to Clair De Mull in the end zone. Higgs' conversion attempt was wide. Kalamazoo then mounted its own drive, which ended on the Hope one yard line as time ran out in the half. In the third quarter Emery kicked to Charlie Stanski on the K 36 and the Hornets began a 64 yard drive to score. Gene Flowers went the last nine yards for the tying touchdown, but Clair De Mull rushed in to block the kick by Reed. Late in the game Hope drove to Kalamazoo's one foot line but a jump pass intended for Moose Holwerda was incomplete and the ball went over to the Hornets. The 6-6 tie would eventually cost Hope a share of the championship.

Hope's game at Alma on November 1 would go down as one of the most exciting in the long history of Hope football. After a scoreless first quarter, big Rex Roseman scored for Alma after a 63-yard drive. Howell's kick was good to make it 7-0. The Dutch were in deeper trouble when they were later called for pass interference, giving Alma an easy touchdown from the one-yard line. Hope managed to get on the scoreboard late in the second quarter when Yonker, on his own 40, connected on a 55-yard pass play to Vern Kraai. With the ball on the five, Kraai circled end to score. Ken Weller's kick was blocked and the score stood 13-6 at halftime. Near the end of the third quarter Yonker scored on a sneak and Weller's kick tied the score at 13. The stage was set for a dramatic fourth quarter. Midway in the period Alma drove to Hope's seven and Hester went in for the score. Howell's kick was wide but Alma led, 19-13. An 80-yard Hope march was impressive but also time consuming. The Dutch were on the Alma four-yard line with just three minutes remaining. Yonker leaped up for a jump pass but finding no one open, came down and rushed into the end zone for the tying touchdown. Ken Weller's kick was wide and it appeared that Hope would have to settle for its second tie. Alma, however, was determined to pull out a victory and launched an effective passing drive. Deep in Hope territory, Nick Yonker, now on defense, continued his heroics with an interception. With slightly more than a minute remaining, a Barrett-to-Holwerda pass placed the ball on the Hope 47. Yonker then hit Vern Kraai with a pass that went all the way to the Scots' 13. Two running plays advanced the ball to the four but used up valuable seconds. In near panic, the Dutchmen called time out, only to find that

Hope fullback Bob Emery had deceptive speed and was hard to bring down.

Hillsdale's Bill Young breaks away for the deciding touchdown in a classic Hope-Hillsdale game - October 4, 1947.

their time-outs were exhausted. This resulted in a five-yard penalty to the nine On the last play of the game Jim Pfingstel passed to Yonker who took the ball on the four, eluded four tacklers, and went into the end zone as the gun sounded. Hope's 25-19 victory could not have been more dramatic, and Nick Yonker's individual performance was, by consensus, one of the greatest in the history of Hope sports.

Hope closed out the season by hosting Adrian on Friday, November 7, in a night game that featured wind, snow, and hail, but especially wind. Before the evening was out the teams had fumbled 14 times. In the first quarter Adrian back Forrest Schultz scored on a fine run, but the play was nullified by an offside penalty. The forces of nature were on Hope's side in the second quarter, when Schultz punted from his own 20. Gale-force winds caught the ball and blew it back over the punter's head, where Hope recovered on the six-yard line. Bob Emery then went off tackle for the game's only score. Dick Higgs' conversion attempt was not good. Adrian mounted a threat in the closing minutes on successive runs by Schultz and Bob Gillis, but the drive ended on the Hope 16 as time ran out.

In his second year as head coach Al Vanderbush had again been denied a share of the championship, this time by the margin of one foot (Kalamazoo game). Hope's 3-1-1 record placed them third behind co-champions Hillsdale and Kalamazoo, but their overall record of 5-2-1 was evidence of another fine season. End Clair De Mull, guard Len Dick, and quarterback Nick Yonker were named to the All-MIAA team. In a post-season team meeting Yonker, to no one's surprise, was voted the team's Most Valuable Player. Center Don Ladewig was elected honorary captain.

For the first time since 1932, cross country was an official MIAA sport. Jack Schouten coached Hope's 1947 team, which included Pete Kraak, Gerald Van Single, Roger Heasty, Hugh Campbell, Collins Ottipoby, and Don Vandenberg. Ottipoby was the son of Hope's beloved athlete of the twenties, James "Chief" Ottipoby. Schouten's fledgling team found the going tough in early dual competition as they were downed by Albion, 15-47, and by Kalamazoo, 18-37. The Dutchmen got their first taste of victory by edging Adrian, 38-40. The MIAA meet was held on November 13 at Albion on a 3.6 mile course. The Britons had things their own way and won handily. Team scores were as follows: Albion 21, Kalamazoo 65, Adrian 81, Hope 88, Alma 132, and Hillsdale 133.

As the 1947-48 basketball season approached, several prominent figures from the 1946-47 championship team were missing. Russ De Vette, Gabby Van Dis, and George Dalman had graduated. De Vette would become a graduate assistant to Coach Ozzie Cowles at the University of Michigan while pursuing a master's degree in physical education. Ken Zuverink married Myra Brower, Hope '47 and took a position with the Brower Furniture Company, and Don Scholten transferred to the University of Michigan. The good news was that Don Mulder was back, and for a second time would serve as the team's captain. Also returning were Herk and Harv Buter, Nick Yonker, Bill Holwerda, Fred Brieve, and Chuck Ploegsma. Hinga also had the good fortune to snare freshman Edwin "Bud" Vande Wege, who had been a member of Holland High's state championship team the previous year. Vande Wege was not long in making his presence known.

In the season opener in the Armory, Hope had little trouble putting away Grand Rapids Junior College. The final read Hope 69, J.C. 32. Vande Wege led the way with 13, followed by Nick Yonker with 12, and Don Boskoel with 10. Jerry Haan had 12 for J.C. Hope's December 13 game with Michigan Normal was closely contested. With 4 1/2 minutes remaining Hope led, 48-47, but a late-game surge led by Herk Buter, made the final, Hope 66, Normal 48. Herk was high for the Dutchman with 20, Vande Wege had 13, Mulder 12, and Yonker 11. Leo Turner had 16 for Normal.

Hope opened the MIAA campaign by hosting Adrian on December 18. It appeared that Coach Hinga had once again found the right combination, and it was more of the same as Hope built a 41-20 halftime lead before coasting to an 83-38 victory. Duke Mulder led his team with 22 counters, amd was followed by Nick Yonker with 14 and Bud Vande Wege with 13. Hoben notched 12 for Adrian.

In a final contest before the Christmas break Hope played host to Monmouth College. The Illinois school's season-ending victory over Hope had put a definite damper on Hope's 1946-47 championship season and the Dutch now had something to prove. The December 20 contest was close throughout the first half. Hope led 33-27 at the intermission, then took charge in the second half. With 10 minutes remaining Hinga's crew had a 20 point lead at 58-38. Captain Don Mulder's 29 points did most of the damage in the eventual 80-54 rout. Yonker also had a fine game with 19 while Vande Wege had 12. Don Armstrong, who had led Monmouth's earlier victory, was again impressive with 22, but it was Hope's night and the Illinois boys could identify with Hope's long trip home the previous March.

The team returned to action on January 8 when Coach Dob Grow brought his Kalamazoo Hornets to town. It proved to be a night when a fine Kalamazoo team could not get untracked. The 33-16 Hope lead at halftime was not characteristic of most Hope-K games. Mulder was again the leader with 18, followed by Herk Buter with 16 and Yonker with 14. Frank "Bucky" Walters and Charlie Stanski had 10 each for Kalmazoo and Bob App added eight. The 66-45 loss would make the Hornets a tough opponent later in Treadway Gym.

In its sixth straight home game Hope met Harold Westerman's improving Hillsdale squad. Westerman's slow-down tactics were effective in the first half, as evidenced by the meager 31-26 Hope lead, but the Dutch eventually pulled away to a 61-46 victory. Freshman Bud Vande Wege led the show with 25 and Yonker had 10. Gil Edson led his team with 17.

A confident Hope squad journeyed to Albion on January

17 to meet an equally confident Briton squad, coached by Walt Sprandle. Hope had first half leads of 22-16 and 31-26, but late in the half Albion went on a 10-0 run and forged ahead 40-34 at the intermission. In the second half, despite a great effort by Moose Holwerda, Albion controlled the boards and thereby the game. Albion's 74-63 victory ended Hope's impressive six-game win streak and served notice that a Dutch championship was not a foregone conclusion. Don Mulder's 21 led Hope followed by 14 from Herk and 10 each from Vande Wege and Harv Buter. Albion's Lou Black matched Mulder with 21 and Lew Moon put in 14. Hope's troubles were not over. The game at Alma on January 24 found the Dutchmen struggling on the narrow floor and behind at halftime, 26-24. Things seemed to go better in the second half and Hope built a 10 point lead with eight minutes remaining. But with a minute left Alma knotted the count at 48. Then, with 20 seconds on the clock, Alma's Mike Budge stepped to the line and dropped in what proved to be the winning point. Vande Wege led Hope with 18 and Mulder was held to 11. Clark was high for the Scots with 17. The narrow 49-48 loss would cost Hinga's crew a share of the championship.

The Dutchmen made their recovery in Battle Creek on January 30 when they easily defeated the team from Percy Jones Hospital. Substitutes played half of the game and Hope's super-sub Harv Buter led all scorers with 18 in the 68-40 win. Herk Buter and Bob Becksfort had nine each while Andacatta had 15 for the soldiers. The Dutch returned to MIAA play on February 5 when they took on the tough Albion Britons in the Armory. Hometown fans were in for a real treat as the lead changed hands 13 times in the first half. Hope held a 42-37 lead as the period ended. The nailbiter continued, and with only five minutes remaining it was Hope 67, Albion 65, but the Dutch were tough in the closing minutes and came away with an 85-71 victory over the eventual champions. Bud Vande Wege had an "on" night with 25 and Mulder contributed another 18. The Buter brothers had 13 apiece. For the Britons it was Larry Edwards with 22 and reliable Lew Moon with 15.

Five days later the Dutch met Chuck Bult's Calvin five in Grand Rapids. The usual tension and excitement prevailed as the Knights jumped out to an 11-1 lead. Hope battled back to take a 24-19 halftime lead, but a late game Calvin surge brought the Knights to within three at 42-39. The closing minutes, however, belonged to the Dutch as they went on a 13 to three run and put the game away, 55 to 42. Mulder again led Hope with 13, while Harv Buter and Vande Wege added nine apiece. Paul Zwier's 16 points took honors for Calvin.

Hope was now on the comeback trail, but trouble awaited in Kalamazoo. On February 13 the Hornets were all business and led 20-10 after 10 minutes. By halftime they enjoyed a commanding 32-15 lead and held on to down the Dutchmen, 53 to 42 Bucky Walters played an outstanding floor game and, along with Bob App, led Kalamazoo with 10 points. Bud Vande Wege had 12 for Hope and Duke Mulder followed with 10. It was Hope's third and final loss of the season but dropped the team out of the championship picture.

Bob "Shorty" Van Dyke had enrolled at Hope in February and was beginning to appear more frequently in the line-up. Van Dyke, at 6' 7," was the tallest man on the squad. He had previously teamed with Bud Vande Wege on Holland High's '47 state championship team. On February 20 he was given the assignment of stopping Hillsdale's high-scoring Gil Edson. Van Dyk's effort held Edson to nine points and was instrumental in Hope's hard-fought 59-51 victory. Mulder and Vande Wege took care of the scoring with 18 and 14 respectively. Harv Buter continued his effective sixth man role by contributing 10 to the cause. Mervin Hobeck was high for Hillsdale and the usually-potent Edson was held to nine.

The following night Hinga's squad moved on to Adrian and were somewhat surprised by Coach Lyman Abbott's team. The Bulldogs led 24-23 at halftime, then slowly fell behind by 10. With five minutes remaining Adrian took charge and were within two points of an upset when time expired. Hope's 53-51 win showed Vande Wege with 19 and Harv Buter with 15. Buter's all round play was excellent and helped save the day for the Dutch. Gregg Arbaugh, Adrian's future coach, dropped in 19 points, most of them from out court. Freddie Fox was also hot from outside with 12.

The days of lopsided wins seemed to be over, and the Dutch found themselves scratching for victories. The team returned to the Armory on February 26 hoping to avenge an earlier loss to Alma. The first half belonged to the Scots and they led 32-24 as the teams left the floor. In the second half Harv Buter sprained an ankle and Nick Yonker fouled out, but the team did not fold. Finally, with eight minutes remaining, Don Mulder scored the go ahead basket and Hope led 42-41 for the first time in the ballgame. With 45 seconds left Hope's lead was 54-50, but Scot Captain Mike Budge intercepted a Hope pass and narrowed the count to 54-52. The Hinga men stalled out the final seconds and spoiled Coach Steve Sebo's bid for a co-championship with Albion. In his final MIAA game Don Mulder led all scorers with 20 points. Vande Wege had 16 and Herk Buter 10. Jack Marema, subbing for Yonker, had three pressure points in the stretch. For the Scots it was Charlie Saxton and Don Carey with 15 apiece. Hope and Alma ended league play in a second place tie with 7-3 records.

A pair of non-league games remained and the Dutch battled against a let-down. The first-half pattern continued at Ypsilanti on February 28, as Michigan Normal led 33-32, but balanced scoring in the second half gave Hope the momentum and an impressive 78-52 victory. Mulder, Yonker, and Vande Wege had 16 each, and big Bob Van Dyke controlled the boards and scored 11 in a substitute's role. Turner had 16 for the losers.

It was fitting indeed that Don Mulder and Harv Buter, the last of the "Blitz Kids," should play their last game against Calvin, but the big news was that Milton "Bud" Hinga would be coaching his last game. After 17 years of coaching at Hope and eight MIAA championships in three different sports,

Hinga announced that he would step down and devote full time to his administrative duties. The desire of the college and community to see these people in action for the last time made for a long waiting line outside the Armory.

In typical Hope-Calvin fashion, the lead changed hands often in the first half, but Hope managed a one point 30-29 lead on Harv Buter's last minute basket. The contest remained agonizingly close throughout the second half until Herk Buter's field goal with three minutes left gave Hope a 61-60 lead. This triggered an 11 point Dutch scoring spree that gave them the game, 72 to 61. Nick Yonker led all Hope scorers with 20 points. Next in line were "Shorty" Van Dyke with 13, Vande Wege with 11, Harv Buter with 10, and Don Mulder with eight. In a gallant effort Elmer Ribbons led the Knights with 25 and Massie Vanderbilt added 13. Hope's season record stood at 14 and three while Hinga's overall tally was a brilliant 178-71.

Freshman Bud Vande Wege led all MIAA scorers with 158 points, followed closely by Mulder with 149. Both were selected to the All-MIAA team. Mulder's final accolade came when he was named the second recipient of the league's Most Valuable Player award. Harv Buter's careful preparation and diligence in practice would serve him well in a subsequent business career in his hometown.

President Lubbers honored Bud Hinga's judgement and proven performance by asking him to name his own successor. There were no search committees or other solicitations. The announcement was made on March 11 that 24-year-old Russell De Vette had been named to fill the big shoes of his mentor. Despite his youth, De Vette had sound credentials and a rich background in the court game, as noted elsewhere in this account. The wisdom of Hinga's choice was borne out by De Vette's long tenure and nine MIAA championships.

Hope now shifted gears for the spring sports campaign. The first activity took place at the annual MIAA indoor track meet, held at Michigan State on March 24. Albion again dominated with 74 1/4 points. Hillsdale was next with 40, followed by Alma with 25, Hope 22, Adrian 18 1/2, and Kalamazoo with 15. Hope opened the outdoor season by traveling to Houseman field to meet the Calvin Knights. Coach Vanderbush had reason to be encouraged by his team's 76-54 victory. Dashman Ted Barrett led the way with 13 points as he took first in the 100 and broad jump as well as second in the 220. Other recorded firsts were Vern Kraai in the 220, Don Vanden Berg in the two-mile run, Ray Heemstra in the javelin, Jim Lamb in the pole vault, and the mile relay team of Bob Koop, Pete Kraak, Howard Bruggers, and Jim Lamb. At Albion on May 24 Hope was not expected to topple the powerful Britons, who took the meet 93 2/3 to 37 1/3. Hope did manage to win three events. Pete Kraak and Con Vander Woude were 1-2 in the 880 (2:11.2), Fred Veltman won the discus with a fine throw of 127' 1/2," and Jim Lamb was first in the pole vault with a mark of 11'.

In Grand Rapids on April 30 it was GRJC 84, Hope 47. As usual in a track meet, there were some bright spots. Ted Barrett had a great day as he won the 100, 220, and broad jump. Fred Veltman again won the discus with a throw of 120' 4," and Jim Lamb's winning vault of 12' 4 1/2" was a new Hope record. In a triangular at Kalamazoo on May 8 it was Kalamazoo 71, Hope 47 1/2, and Calvin 43 1/2. Ted Barrett was again impressive in his specialties with 10.1, 23.3, and 21' 5 3/4."

Bud Hinga Steps Down

After fifteen highly successful seasons as Hope's basketball mentor, Hinga turned over the reins to Russ De Vette, his youthful protege.

In the MIAA Field Day meet at Kalamazoo on May 21, Fred Veltman captured Hope's only gold medal as he won the discus with a throw of 129' 8 1/4." It was otherwise a rather bleak day for the Dutchmen. Albion won as expected, with 75 points, but Adrian was a surprise runner-up with 44 points. An improved Kalamazoo team took third with 38, followed by Hillsdale with 35 1/2, Alma with 17, and Hope with 15 1/2. Disqualification of the Hope mile relay team cost them a fifth place overall. Adrian's splendid Walt Mc Connor led all scorers with 11 1/4 points as he won the 440 and 220, and anchored Adrian's winning mile relay team. His 50.1 in the 440 was a new MIAA record. Hillsdale's Tom Ward, better known for his football prowess, won both hurdle races.

After a 19-year lapse, baseball was once again an MIAA sport. Coach Jack Schouten's association with Hope baseball covered a half century. He had kept the sport alive through some lean years and now was rewarded with an initial turnout of nearly 40 candidates. The '48 team posted an 8-5 record on its way to a second place finish in the league. The season opened on April 13 at Riverview Park against Calvin. The five-inning game featured 11 walks by Calvin pitchers and a

400' grand slam home run by Harold "Mouse" Van Wieren. Mike Skaalen and Lefty Bill Ver Hey saw action on the mound in Hope's 15-2 victory. Three days later the Michigan State J.V. team came to town and it was a different story. Hope was limited to three hits and suffered a 6-0 shutout. On April 22 it was Hillsdale at Riverview and the Dutchmen were forced to overcome a 4-0 lead before posting a 13-9 victory. Lou Vollmer led Hope with three singles and Ver Hey picked up the win. Bill Young and Bob Rowe homered for the Dales.

Hope notched its third win on April 29 when Grand Rapids Junior College visited Riverview. Coach Schouten used Jack Marema, Jim Sector, and Mike Skaalen on the mound. First baseman Lou Vollmer broke a 3-3 deadlock with a single in the eighth inning and the Dutch added one more to register a 5-3 win. A day later Jack's squad traveled to Kalamazoo and was beaten 6-0 by Western Michigan's J.V. team. The state schools were proving to be tough competition, even at the junior varsity level, but on May 1 the Dutch had sweet revenge in East Lansing. Trailing 6-4 in the ninth, Hope rallied for three as Mouse Van Wieren stole home with the winning run. On May 4 it was Western again, this time on home turf. Without question the day belonged to pitcher Jack Marema. Jack scattered seven Western hits, struck out nine, and overcame five Hope errors in the 6-5 victory. He also collected two singles, one of which drove in the winning run in the eighth inning. Warren De Witt was Marema's battery mate.

In a doubleheader with Muskegon Junior College, Mike Skaalen won the opener with a one-hit 9-0 shutout, but the Muskegon team returned the favor in the five-inning nightcap as they got the best of Bill Ver Hey, 1-0. In two final contests before the playoffs Hope shut out Calvin 3-0, then lost to Albion 4 to 1. The MIAA championship was determined by a four-team playoff held in Kalamazoo on May 21-22. Adrian and Kalamazoo did not field teams in this first year of baseball's return. Hope's first opponent was Alma, and Bill Ver Hey and Alma's Charlie Saxton hooked up in a brilliant pitching duel. Ver Hey limited the Scots to three hits over 10 innings and second baseman Chuck Zoet drove in the winning run with a single in the 10th. The final was Hope 2, Alma 1. Against Hillsdale it was a different story as Mike Mc Carthy stopped the Dutch with four hits enroute to a 16-3 victory. Hope's second place finish indicated a sound program that would produce titles in the early '50s.

Hope's new tennis coach was Psychology Professor Harold Haverkamp. His team, certainly one of Hope's best to that time, included John Ligtvoet, Gene Barendse, Jack Tirrell, Bob Becksfort, Ken Etterbeek, Gerry Gnade, Ernie Post, Chuck Votaw, and Wayne Blakeslee. The season opened on April 23 with a tough 4-3 loss to Calvin, as Tirrell and Etterbeek won in singles and the doubles team of Ligtvoet and Becksfort also notched a victory. On April 25 the Dutch blanked Albion 7-0, as all matches were won in straight sets. Adrian was also a 7-0 victim of Haverkamp's team. A second match with Albion found the Britons much improved but the Dutch were still victorious, this time 5-2.

Hope's most impressive performance, however, may well have been its 4-3 dual meet loss to Kalamazoo. It would prove to be one of the stiffest challenges the Hornets would face in their perennial domination of MIAA tennis. In singles Ken Etterbeek defeated K's Marlette, 4-6, 6-2, 7-5, and John Ligtvoet beat W. Des Autels, 6-4, 6-4. In doubles it was Etterbeek and Bob Becksfort getting the best of Des Autels and Marlette 3-6, 7-5, 6-4. In the MIAA Field Day meet, Becksfort, Etterbeek, and Tirrell got through the quarterfinals, and the doubles team of Becksfort-Etterbeek made it to the semi-finals before bowing out. Kalamazoo won the championship with 39 combined points, while Hope was second with 23, and Albion third with 12.

Earl Holkeboer, Bax Elhart, and Chris Den Herder were golf returnees from Hope's '47 championship team, but it wasn't enough and Coach Al Timmer's charges were forced to settle for an overall fifth place finish. In dual matches Hope lost to Kalamazoo 11-8 as Holkeboer led the field with a 74. In other matches it was Hillsdale 15-4 over Hope, and Albion defeated the Dutchmen, 11-8. Hope defeated Adrian 19-0 and in a triangular it was Grand Rapids Junior College 10 1/2, Hope 8, and Calvin 7. In the MIAA meet Hope finished fourth and Earl Holkeboer was runnerup to medalist Blank of Albion.

For the first time in 1947-48, Hope had a female physical education instructor in the person of Louise Jean Van Dommelen. Her many duties included organizing and coaching a women's tennis team to represent Hope in the annual W.M.I.A.A. tournament. The 1948 team included Jeanne Allen, Mary Breid, Irene Demian, Phyllis Dietrich, Edith Gnade, Margaret Moerdyk, Helen Van Alst, and Marcella Westerman. The women bettered the men in posting a 5-4

Louise Van Dommelen

Miss Van Dommelen served in the Hope physical education department from 1947 through 1953. She was Hope's first female staff member.

victory over Calvin, then hosted the W.M.I.A.A. Tournament. Phyl Dietrich won the singles competition and the doubles team of Jeanne Allen and Margaret Moerdyk placed first in doubles.

Hope was forced to surrender the MIAA All-Sports Trophy to Albion, which scored 48 points to 41 for Kalamazoo and 35 for Hope. It had been an "almost" year for Hope, with strong performances in football, basketball, baseball and tennis. Hope's bid for prominence in all sports was taking shape and would be in evidence during the '50s.

Al Vanderbush was guarded in his assessment of Hope's football chances in 1948. There were, however, reasons to be optimistic. Assisting as backfield coach was Russ De Vette, Hope's newly-hired basketball coach. As line coach Vanderbush chose former All-MIAA guard Len Dick. Leading the returnees was two-time, all-conference quarterback Nick Yonker. Halfbacks Jim Pfingstel and Ted Barrett were both explosive and were proven performers. Vanderbush was especially pleased with the veteran line that he had assembled. Six of the seven hailed from Grand Rapids. All-Conference end Clair De Mull had prepped at Wyoming Park, while Bill Holwerda, the other end, was from Grand Rapids South. Tackle Robert "Rip" Collins was also from South and Gordon Van Hoeven, the other tackle, had played at Ottawa Hills. Guards Abe Moerland and Gordon Timmerman were products of Grand Rapids Union. Center Gene Campbell, a friend of Yonker, had played for the Big Reds of Muskegon. All were fine blockers. In the era just before face masks these linemen did not hesitate to stick their heads in the proper segment of opposing anatomy, and scabs on their cheekbones bore testimony to proper technique. Because of the Grand Rapids connection, student writer Gordon Beld dubbed them the "Cabinet Makers." The name stuck and the "Cabinet Maker Line" would become part of Hope folklore. As Vanderbush viewed his prospects, his only real disappointment was the failure of fullback Bob Emery to return to school.

Hope was off to a good start in a night game at Riverview Park on September 24. A strong Michigan Normal team was subdued, 13 to 0. In the last minute of the first half Yonker passed to Moose Holwerda who hauled the ball in on the Normal 25 and went in to make it 6-0 at halftime. The third quarter was scoreless, but in the fourth Yonker lofted a 33-yard pass to Pfingstel who made a great catch and moved to the Normal 21. A few plays later Pfingstel went up the middle for the touchdown and Holwerda's kick closed out the scoring. On October 2 Hope extended its basketball relationship with Monmouth College to the gridiron and made the long trip to the Illinois school. All of Hope's scoring took place in the second quarter. Early in the period, Jim Pfingstel

The 1948 Hope College Women's Tennis Team - WMIAA Champions

Front Row L to R: Mary Breid, Irene Demian, Edith Gnade, Marcella Westerman. **Back Row:** Coach Louise Van Dommelen, Helen Van Alst, Margaret Moerdyk, Jeanne Allen. **Missing from picture:** Phyllis Dietrich.

scored from the one foot line giving the Dutchmen an early 6-0 lead. In the closing minutes Yonker threw a 27-yard scoring pass to Ted Barrett who was open in the end zone. This time the kick was good and Hope led 13-0 at the intermission. Monmouth was not done and midway in the third quarter moved to Hope's one yard line with a first and goal situation. The Dutch line was equal to the task and held for three downs. On fourth down a Scot back was thrown for a loss to the nine and Hope took over, but in the fourth quarter Monmouth was again knocking at the door and surprised the Dutch with a spread formation. Don Armstrong, of basketball fame, scored from the 15. He then ran the extra point and the final score remained Hope 13, Monmouth 7.

On October 8 Coach Lyman Abbott brought his Adrian Bulldogs to Riverview Park for the MIAA opener. On the second play of the second quarter fullback Ted Rycenga scored from the four after a 47-yard Hope drive. Holwerda's kick was wide. Hope seemed to be on the way again but Maynard Clark intercepted a Nick Yonker pass on the Hope 46. Howard Burkhardt then passed to Mike Hoben who lateraled to Maynard Clark,who went all the way. The kick by Buddy Rice was good and Adrian went to the locker room with a 7-6 lead. The inspired Bulldogs continued to dominate play throughout the third period. In the fourth quarter Rice pounced on a Pfingstel fumble and six plays later Bob Gillis scored from the one. Rice was again successful with the conversion and the Adrian lead was extended to 14-6. An aroused Hope team mounted a drive in the closing minutes that featured a 37-yard "Statute of Liberty" scamper by Barrett that placed the ball on the Adrian 17. Yonker then passed to Clair De Mull for the touchdown. Holwerda's kick was good but Hope trailed by one point with less than a minute remaining. Moose Holwerda gave it a good try as he recovered his own on-side kick, but Hope passes fell incomplete and time ran out. Coach Abbott savored the well-earned upset victory and the trip home did not seem long at all.

Hope's game on October 16 was played at Hillsdale in a drizzle. It was Hillsdale's Homecoming but the Dales, now known as the "Bearcats," were without the services of Tom Ward, who was injured. In the second quarter Ted Barrett broke loose on his own 38 and raced 43 yards to the Hillsdale 19. Pfingstel and Rycenga advanced the ball to the two, but a penalty put the Dutch back to the seven. At this point Nick Yonker threw a strike to Moose Holwerda for the score. Holwerda's kick was good and scoring was done for the day. It was Coach Vanderbush's first victory over Hillsdale after two near-misses, and it was Hope's turn to enjoy the trip home.

In a non-league contest Hope met Grand Rapids Junior College on October 21. It was a homecoming of sorts for Rip Collins, Bill Holwerda, and Coach Vanderbush, as the game was played at South Field. In the opening quarter Collins recovered a J.C. fumble on the Hope 18. Hope then marched 82 yards with Ted Barrett going in from the nine. Holwerda's kick was wide. A second Hope drive was stopped on the three. Safety Bill Hinga returned J.C.'s punt to the 14, and Donald "Dutch" Van Ingen went off tackle for Hope's second touchdown and a 12-0 halftime lead. Two quick scores by the Dutchmen early in the third period put the game on ice. Hope took possession on the J.C. 45 and moved methodically to the five, where Jim Pfingstel scored on an end sweep. A Holwerda kick was good for the first time and Hope's lead was 19-0. On the first play after the kick-off, Claus Holtrop intercepted a J.C. pass, then lateraled to Nick Yonker, who went all the way for the score. The kick was blocked making it 25-0 at the end of the third quarter. In the fourth quarter J.C. scored against Hope subs as Owens went in from the one yard line. With the score 25 to 6, Yonker threw to Holwerda who took the ball on the J.C. 45 and went down the sideline for the score. Moose closed out Hope's scoring with a successful conversion. In the closing minutes J.C. recovered a Dutch fumble on the Hope 34 and subsequently scored on a Tietsma to Owens pass making the final 32 to 13.

Hope continued to impress in its Homecoming game with Albion on October 30. Ted Rycenga scored early following a fumble recovery on the Britons' seven. Later a poor Albion punt gave the Dutchmen good field position on their own 39. Barrett broke away to the 13, then scored on a sweep to make it 13-0. Albion came back with a flawless Marvin-to-Martin screen pass from their own 42 that went 52 yards for the score. At halftime it was anyone's game with the score at 13-6. In the second half Hope's Abe Moerland intercepted a Briton pass on his own 38 and, in an unfamiliar role, rambled all the way to the Hope 13. Hope picked up another 10 before Rycenga scored his second touchdown from the three. With the score at 19-6 Moose Holwerda recovered a mishandled Albion punt on the Briton 35. The game was interrupted at this point as Umpire Wendel Emery was carried from the field with a pulled leg muscle. The predicament was resolved when Lee Kleis, Hope's star of the '20s, was called from the stands to complete the game for Emery. Two plays later Ted Barrett attempted a left end sweep but was trapped behind the line. He quickly reversed his field and sped 40 yards down the right sideline to score Hope's fourth touchdown. With the game well in hand, Hope scored a final touchdown. The score was noteworthy in that it came on a pass from ex-coach Hinga's son Bill to basketball star Bud Vande Wege. The 33 to 6 victory seemed in line with the team's potential.

The early-season one-point loss to Adrian had been a blow, but a two-point loss to troublesome Kalamazoo put the Dutchmen out of contention. The November 6 game at Kalamazoo began on a high note. Hope chose to receive. On the second play from scrimmage Yonker passed to Barrett who was hit, but broke away and raced 79 yards for the touchdown. Holwerda's kick was good and the 7-0 lead seemed to be but a continuation of their Albion performance. But the Hornets, with an effective ground game, advanced the kickoff to the Hope 40. Quarterback Charlie Stanski then passed to big Ed Poth, who went the distance to score. A successful conversion made it 7-7 at halftime. The third quarter was a stand-off, but in the fourth period a Kalamazoo punt rolled dead on the Hope two. On the next play a Hope back was nailed behind the goal line for a safety and the game ended 9-7.

Alma came to Riverview on November 12 with a title share already assured. Little remained for Hope but to play the spoiler's role, and for a time it appeared that they would succeed. Claus Holtrop bucked over for the game's first score and shortly thereafter, Moose Holwerda picked up a blocked punt and went in for the touchdown. The 13-0 lead looked good but the talented Scots, led by big Rex Roseman, were not to be denied. Roseman scored in the first quarter, Slotnick in the second, Derby in the third on a flea-flicker, and Roseman again in the fourth to make the final 25 to 13. Coach Steve Sebo's championship team was 5-0 in the MIAA and 8-0 overall. Hope ended at 5-3 overall. The team's 2-3 record in MIAA play resulted in a fourth place tie with Adrian. Nick Yonker, Abe Moerland, and Clair De Mull were named to the All-MIAA team, and the latter two were elected honorary co-captains of Hope's team. Moerland was voted the team's Most Valuable Player award.

As Hope's football squads increased in numbers, Jack Schouten's duty as trainer became a full-time job. Coaching cross country became an impossibility and Psychology Professor Lars Granberg agreed to take the team. In dual meets Hope defeated Adrian 21-34, and Hillsdale, 16-43. A 22-37 loss to Kalamazoo on November 6 was followed by the MIAA championship meet at Albion. Albion again took the crown with 31 points, followed by Alma with 60, Hope with 80, Kalamazoo with 81, Adrian with 97, and Hillsdale with 171. In the combined scoring Hope ended in a third place tie with Kalamazoo. Collins Ottipoby finished 11th for Hope in the MIAA meet, Don Vandenberg was 13th, Pete Kraak 15th, Randy Vande Water 18th, and Hank Parson 23rd. Ottipoby was elected honorary captain for the season.

For the first time since 1931 Hope College had a new basketball coach. Russ De Vette, 25 years old, issued the call for practice in mid-November and eventually settled on a 14-man squad which included Andrew "Jun" Bremer, Fred Brieve, Herk Buter, Bob Dennison, Bill Hinga, who missed playing for his dad by one year, Bill Holwerda, Jack Marema, Paul Muyskens, Duane Peekstock, Ed "Bud" Vande Wege, Jack Van Dorple, Dale Van Dort, Bob "Stretch" Wagner, and Nick Yonker. De Vette decided to have his captain serve throughout the season and Holwerda was elected.

Hope continued its relationship with the Percy Jones Hospital team, but the soldiers lacked the manpower of the immediate post-war years and bowed to the Dutchmen in the December 2 opener at the Armory. Hope's 69-42 victory allowed De Vette to substitute freely. Leading scorer for the evening was Paul Muyskens, a transfer student from Northwestern Junior College in Orange City, Iowa. Muyskens had 14 counters, while Lou Scott scored 19 for the losers.

On December 6 Hope defeated Grand Rapids J.C. by a score of 47 to 32. In a bizarre turn of events the game was shortened by several minutes when it was discovered that J.C.'s inexperienced timekeeper had allowed the clock to run during free throws. Bud Vande Wege still managed to lead both teams with a 20-point performance. He was followed by Muyskens with 10 and Herk Buter with eight. Dave Vander Zee led the J.C. team with 18. On December 9, Hope's young coach was invited to return to his alma mater in Muskegon to put on a clinic for some two thousand high school players. He was accompanied by Holwerda, Yonker, Vande Wege, and Buter, who were used in demonstrations.

In the MIAA opener De Vette locked horns with his good friend Harold Westerman at Hillsdale. In previous years Coach Westerman's team had been outmanned, but on December 11 the teams were evenly matched on the Bearcats' court. Hope managed a 28-27 halftime lead but the score was tied 15 times during the course of the contest. In the closing minutes Hillsdale broke a 55-55 tie and took the game 58-55. It was their first win over Hope since 1935 and was accomplished without the services of star forward Gil Edson, who was out with a leg injury. Bud Vande Wege was high for Hope with 15 and Herk Buter followed with 13. Bob Wagner played well in a reserve role and scored 12. Diminutive guard John Markland led Hillsdale with 13.

Close games would prevail throughout the season, with Hope taking its share of lumps. On December 16 Kalamazoo came to the Armory for the final game before the Christmas break. Guards Charlie Stanski and Bucky Walters were effective in using slow- down tactics and K led 18-17 at the half. The Dutchmen held a 36-28 lead late in the game, but Kalamazoo rallied for a 39-39 tie at the end of regulation play. The Hornets were best in the overtime and rode home the winner by a score of 46-44. Walters played an excellent game and led all scorers with 20 points. Vande Wege with 14 and Holwerda with 10 were best for Hope.

De Vette's charges ushered in 1949 with a 72-32 trouncing of hapless Percy Jones in Battle Creek. In the January 3 game the Dutchmen held a 40-20 halftime lead and substitutes saw a lot of playing time. Scoring was evenly divided with Bud getting 12, Herk 11, Stretch Wagner 10, and Moose eight. Don Collins scored 15 for the losers. In marked contrast, the Dutch were forced to come from behind on January 8 to edge the Michigan Normal team in Ypsilanti. A stellar 24-point performance by Normal's Fred Jackson went for nought as Hope eked out the 51-50 win. It was Vande Wege and Buter again, with 15 and 13.

On January 11 at Adrian, the Bulldogs registered their first victory over Hope since Adrian's MIAA reentry in 1938. The game was played in Adrian's Civic Auditorium and after a see-saw first half Hope held the lead at 27-26. The game was equally close in the second half. Near the end it was Adrian 45, Hope 43. Hope had a chance with the count at 50-49, but the Bulldogs scored one more time and added a free throw to seal the 53-49 victory. Five days later the Dutchmen took on the defending champions in Albion's Kresge Gym. In another close one, Hope led 60-59 with one minute, 25 seconds left. The Britons then made one of two free throws to knot the count at 60. As play proceeded bedlam prevailed and the noise level made it impossible to hear whistles or horns. Hope had possession and Moose Holwerda, thinking that time had expired, stood with the ball, ready to hand it to the official. At this point, Albion's Lou Black snatched the ball from Holwerda and dribbled the length of the floor to score the winning basket in the last few seconds. It was an ugly loss and the Hope squad would remember one month later. Lou Black, with 24, was the consensus hero of the night. Vande Wege's 15 led the Hope squad.

The Dutchmen now stood at an uncharacteristic 0 and 4 in MIAA play. A newspaper article referred to them as "Hope's hapless hoopsters" as they prepared to host Alma on January 18, but De Vette would get a fine performance from his entire team on this night. After a 34-34 halftime deadlock Hope continued to play on near-even terms until the last five minutes, when they pulled away for the 74-65 win. The drought was over. Herk Buter played his best game of the season with 20 points, while Paul Muyskens and Bud Vande Wege each had 16. Nick Yonker added another 11. Lee Boucher was strong for the Scots with 21.

It was Hillsdale in the Armory on January 22. In search of their first title in 19 years, the Bearcats were undefeated in MIAA play. Paul Plodzinski, their fine center, was the league leader in scoring. De Vette worked with Paul Muyskens on defensive techniques to stop Plodzinski, and Muyskens responded by holding his opponent to a total of five points. Nick Yonker's 16 points led Hope to the decisive 63-44 win. Vande Wege was close behind with 15 while Muyskens and Buter each contributed 12. John Markland had 13 for Hillsdale.

Coach Chuck Bult was in town with his Calvin team on February 3. Word had gotten around that slow-down basketball was an effective measure against the Dutch. Fans understood the strategy of deliberate play but they grew impatient when, after 10 minutes, the score stood at 3-3. The tempo picked up somewhat in the second quarter and Hope led 25-18 at the half. Bill Holwerda's second half control of the defensive board made Hope's fast break effective enroute to the eventual 65-43 win. Buter with 17 and Yonker with 15 led the Hope attack. Freshman Duane Rosendahl was high for Calvin with 14. The Holland native would become one of the all-time greats of Calvin basketball.

The Dutchmen carried a three-game win streak to Kalamazoo on February 8 for a typical Kalamazoo-Hope encounter. Considerable bodily contact made for a rough game from the start. Charlie Stanski's floor game in the closing minutes was a deciding factor as the Hornets took the Dutchmen for the second time, this time by a score of 47-44. Bucky Walters and Herk Buter led their respective teams with 13 each.

Things went better when Adrian visited Holland on February 12. Hope's fast break was in full swing but the accurate out-court shooting of Mike Hoben and Gregg Arbaugh kept Adrian in the game. Following a 32-25 halftime lead the Dutch remained consistent and moved to a 71-60 victory. Buter was the Hope leader with 14. Vande Wege, Muyskens, and Yonker each scored 12. For Adrian it was Hoben with 18 and Arbaugh with 17.

Hope's home game with Albion began in similar fashion to the earlier contest. Albion took a one-point halftime lead at 32-31 and the game remained close for the next 10 minutes, but with Muyskens and Holwerda controlling the boards, Hope went on a last quarter scoring spree that netted a 20-point lead at one time. The 75-59 victory was especially sweet for Moose Holwerda who had been victimized in the earlier contest. Hope's balanced scoring included Buter with 17, Vande Wege with 16, Yonker with 15, and Muyskens with 14. Lou Black, hero of the earlier game, again led Albion but was held to 10 points.

Hope's brief two-game comeback was halted at Alma on February 25, when the Dutchmen experienced a cold night on the Scots' narrow floor. Hope held a 23-22 halftime edge and for a time it appeared that victory might be possible in spite of poor shooting, but in the end it was Alma 49, Hope 45. Bud Vande Wege's 13 led the Dutch and Herk Buter had eight. Lee Boucher was again high for Alma with 18. The next night at Ypsilanti the somewhat weary starters found themselves nine points down midway in the second half. De Vette decided to go with his bench and inserted Bill Hinga, Jun Bremer, and Jack Marema. The subs made the most of this opportunity and brought the team back to a three-point lead with 3 1/2 minutes remaining. Stall tactics then netted three more points and the Dutch pulled out the 65-59 win. Scoring was again balanced with Herk getting 13, Muyskens 12, Jun Bremer and Moose 11 each. Hook shot ace Fred Jackson got 25 from the pivot position for Normal, but the brilliant performance wasn't quite enough.

The curtain came down on De Vette's first season at the Burton Gym against Calvin on March 2. Hope had the edge for most of the game and built a 40-29 lead in the second half, only to see it dwindle to 43-42 with 3 1/2 left. The charged-up Knights then stole the ball and scored on two occasions and took over the game. The final was Calvin 49, Hope 45 as Duane Rosendahl and Elmer Ribbons led the way for Calvin with 16 apiece. Slug Slager added eight in the satisfying victory for Coach Chuck Bult. For Hope it was freshman Jun Bremer nearly matching his high school teammate (Rosendahl) with 13. Buter had 11 and Vande Wege nine.

De Vette's initial season was a winning one with an overall 10-7 record. Hillsdale won its first MIAA basketball title since 1935. Hope's 4-5 league record placed the team in an unfamiliar fifth place finish. The defense could not be faulted. In Hope's seven losses throughout the season, the margin of defeat had never been more than four points. Bud Vande Wege and Herk Buter were named to the six-man All-MIAA team. Other selectees were Lou Black of Albion, John Markland and Paul Plodzinski of Hillsdale, and Frank "Bucky" Walters of Kalamazoo. Walters was named the league's Most

Valuable.

Hope's spring sports campaign in 1949 was not a march toward the All-Sports trophy, but as usual, there were some gratifying performances. Coach Harold Haverkamp was able to field a veteran team in Gene Barendse, Jack Tirrell, Bob Becksfort, Ken Etterbeek, Gerry Gnade, and Chuck Votaw. Hope took, Albion 4-3, and Hillsdale, 5-2, but the opposition was generally strong in '49 and the Dutchmen dropped decisions to Calvin, 9-0 and 6-3, to Grand Rapids Junior College, 6-3, and to Kalamazoo, 6-1. In the latter match Hope's doubles team of Gnade and Votaw defeated Kazoo's Gluckenkampe and Hopkins, 4-6, 6-2, and 6-4. A strong performance in the MIAA Field Day meet netted the Dutchmen a second place finish overall behind perennial champion Kalamazoo.

On March 24 Coach Al Vanderbush greeted 40 football hopefuls for the annual spring drills. This responsibility plus a full teaching load made it impossible for him to continue as track coach and the responsibility was turned over to Russ De Vette with assistance from cross country Coach Lars Grandberg. The season's first meet was held at Houseman Field with Calvin winning 75-56. Hope sprinter Ralph Ludwig scored 11 points with firsts in the 100 (10.3), 220 (23.7), and a third in the broad jump. Surprise of the meet was Hope's inexperienced 440 man Bob Ondra, who surged to the front and held on for victory in 53.8. Other firsts were recorded by Ken Dekker in the low hurdles, Fred Yonkman in the high jump, Don Vandenberg in the two-mile, and Clayton Borgman in the javelin.

The season's most exciting meet took place on April 30 at Angell Field in Kalamazoo. Hope's dual meet with Kalamazoo was exceptionally close all the way. Dashman Ralph Ludwig was again the point leader for the Dutch as he took first in the 100 and 220, second in the high jump, and third in the broad jump for 14 points. Fred Yonkman was first in the high jump at 5' 6," Ted Barrett took the broad jump with a mark of 21' 1 3/4," and Fred Veltman captured the discus with a throw of 126' 9 1/2". Hope's cause was further aided by a sweep in the pole vault. Jim Lamb was first with 11', followed by Ernie Ross in second, and Vern Leestma in third. The score stood at 63-all going into the meet's final event, the mile relay. Hope took an early lead, but in the third leg Kalamazoo's Van Horn closed a 24' gap and took a slight lead. Bob Chamberlain, K's anchorman, was able to hold the lead and Hope lost the heartbreaker, 68-63.

On May 4, for the first time in many years, Hope hosted a track meet. The action took place on Holland High's 22nd Street track and the opponent was Calvin. In another close one the Knights again prevailed, this time by a score of 69 1/2 to 61 1/2. First place finishes were evenly divided at seven apiece. In the meet's most exciting race (880) Hope's Pete Kraak edged Calvin's Hooker in a time of 2:09.9. Ludwig had first in the 100, second in the 220, and third in the broad jump. Bob Ondra improved to 53.1 in taking the 440, Veltman won the discus with a fine throw of 132' 9 1/2," Don Vandenberg was first in the two-mile with 11:20, Ted Barrett took the broad jump with 20' 9," and Jim Lamb tied for first in the pole vault with Bekkering of Calvin.

On May 5 the team traveled to Albion for a triangular with the Britons and Kalamazoo. As expected, Albion dominated the meet with 90 points. Kalamazoo followed with 44, and a tired Hope team had to settle for 29. Jim Lamb's 11' 6" first place vault was a highlight for Hope on a discouraging afternoon. Hope's other first place was Barrett's 20' 10 1/2" broad jump. A team victory finally came on May 10 against Grand Rapids Junior College at Houseman Field. Ralph Ludwig, who had spent his first two college years at Junior College, came home this day to win the 100 (10.4) and 220 (24.1) yard dashes. Collins Ottipoby was first in the mile run with a time of 4:59.3, Bob Ondra took the 440 in 54.6, Don Vandenberg bettered his two-mile time with a winning 10:56, Ken Dekker won the 200 yard low hurdles in 27.1, Fred Veltman topped the discus throwers with 121' 11," consistent Jim Lamb won the vault with 11', Fred Yonkman's 5' 8" high jump was good enough to win, Clayt Borgman heaved the javelin 155' 9" for another first, and Hope's mile relay team posted a winning time of 3:41.1 to make the final score 75 2/3 to 55 1/3.

The State Intercollegiate Meet was held at Western's Waldo Stadium on May 14 with Western Michigan edging Wayne State 82 to 81 1/2. Hope placed a respectable fifth on the strength of Fred Veltman's first place discus throw of 130' 4 3/4." Hope also got fifth place finishes from Alex Ebneth in the javelin, Don Vandenberg in the two-mile, and the mile relay team. The team did not fare as well in the MIAA meet at Kalamazoo on May 20. Hope's only points came from a third place throw by Veltman in the discus, a fifth place finish in the mile relay, and Fred Yonkman's tie for fifth in the high jump. Albion won the championship with 76 1/3, Adrian was second with 56, Hillsdale third with 43 1/3, Kalamazoo fourth with 31, Alma fifth with 13, and Hope sixth with 4 1/3.

Coach Al Timmer's golf team posted victories over Davenport-McLaughlin Institute, Calvin, and Kalamazoo but lost to Grand Rapids Junior College, Kalamazoo (non-league), Alma, Albion, Hillsdale, and Adrian. Saving the best to the last, the team did well in the MIAA meet on May 19-20 and pulled out an overall fourth place finish. Bob Kloote was medalist with a 36-hole total of 152 and Howie Jalving was runner-up with 153.

Jack Schouten's baseball team went 7-6 overall on the season but ended in a three-way tie for third place in the MIAA with Adrian and Alma. The season opened at Riverview Park on April 6 against Aquinas. Hope could manage only four hits but Paul Buckhout, Bill Ver Hey, and Mike Skaalen limiited Aquinas to just three. The Dutch pulled out a two-to-one win in the ninth inning as Jack Marema scored on a single by Con Boeve. Jack's crew had an easier time on April 9 when Muskegon Junior College came to town. A six-run second inning helped freshmen pitchers Hardy Ensing and Don Hoffman to an impressive 11-0 shutout. Skaalen finished on the mound. In Kalamazoo on April 12 the Hornets' Gordon Ferris shut down the Dutch machine and then scored the winning run on a single, a balk, and another single to give his team the 1-0 victory. Hope's only consolation was that it was a non-conference game.

The team was back in form on the 14th as they notched a 4-0 shutout of Calvin at Valley Field in Grand Rapids. All four runs came in a big fourth inning. Jack Marema opened with a single and Ernie Meeusen drew a walk. At this point Hope got successive singles from Gordon Van Hoven, Tom Van Wingen, Gordon Brummels, and catcher Jim Harvey. Meanwhile, Mike Skaalen twirled a two-hitter and struck out seven Calvin batters.

The Hope-Alma game on April 22 was halted by a downpour in the second inning with Hope leading 3-2. Four days later seven Hope errors led to a 12-4 beating at Albion with Ver Hey taking the loss. The next day Calvin was at Riverview to avenge their earlier loss. The final was Calvin 3, Hope 1 as the Knights' Mike Van Akker scattered seven hits and struck out 11. In a second meeting with Muskegon Junior College, Hope traveled to Marsh Field to register a 13-2 victory. The 18-hit attack featured four hits by Marema, a home run by Gord Van Hoeven, and two doubles by Tom Van Wingen.

Hope dropped its second MIAA contest at Hillsdale on May 3. The Bearcats' Tim Mc Carthy gave up only two hits, an infield single to Con Boeve and a triple to Mouse Van Wieren, enroute to an 8-0 shutout. Star athlete Bill Young did it to Hope one more time with a three-run homer and five RBI's. On May 7 Hope won an official MIAA contest from Kalamazoo College by a score of 11 to 4. Bill Ver Hey held the Hornets to six hits while the Dutch were collecting 11. Hope's big inning was the sixth when five runners crossed the plate. Gord Van Hoven had three hits and Ver Hey helped his own cause with a double and single. The game was played at Riverview Park as was the one on May 11 with Western Michigan Frosh. In the latter contest Hope spotted Western a 3-2 lead, but in the sixth Mouse Van Wieren tied it with a gigantic home run that went over the left field grandstand and into Black River. A Hope error in the ninth allowed Western to score the winning run and go home with the 4-3 victory.

Hope bounced back the following day at Valley Field in Grand Rapids as Bob Dennison pitched a six-hit 9-5 victory over Grand Rapids Junior College. In a league game at Adrian on May 14, Hope's defense collapsed as the Dutch committed nine errors, two in the 10th inning and the Bulldogs emerged with a 5-4 win. The big blow for Hope was a first inning triple by Ludwig Vollmer with the bases loaded. Paul Buckhout went the route for Hope in downing Alma 4-3 on May 16 in spite of five Hope miscues. Hardy Ensing had a home run to right center in the fourth and Jack's men broke a 3-3 tie in the eighth when Gord Van Hoeven doubled, went to third on a passed ball, and scored on an infield out. Buckhout got the side out in order in the ninth.

The round robin tourney at season's end was rained out and Hope ended in a three-way tie for third place with Adrian and Alma. League officials decided that the tournament was not the best method to determine a champion and henceforth the MIAA championship would be decided on the basis of two league games played with each school.

Coach Al Vanderbush began his fourth season as Hope's football mentor under some pressure. A number of factors labeled Hope as the team to beat in the MIAA campaign of 1949. Russ De Vette returned to assist, and the two were joined by Ken Weller who had just joined the faculty as instructor in Economics and Business Administration. Vanderbush was more than pleased with his assistants and with his returning squad as practice began on September 6. The starting team returned intact from 1948 with the exception of halfback Ted Barrett, who did not enroll. But to compensate for this loss, Eddie Leverette of the '47 team was back after a one-year stint at Central Michigan. Captain Abe Moerland led the veteran "Cabinet Maker" line of Rip Collins, Gordon Van Hoeven, Gordon Timmerman, Gene Campbell, Clair De Mull, and Bill Holwerda. The squad, which eventually numbered 50, included 16 freshmen and numerous other talented underclassmen. At quarterback it was three-time All-Conference Nick Yonker with good backup from Bill Hinga and Ron Schipper. At halfback Jim Pfingstel possessed triple-threat abilities. By any standard the picture was extremely bright and Vanderbush had some difficulty in putting a damper on talk of "great team" and "best in Hope history."

Hope opened at home with a night game on September 23 with Grand Rapids Junior College furnishing the opposition - - but not too much! Even Vanderbush conceded that Hope had the edge, but J.C. was never an easy opponent and the first quarter went scoreless. Early in the second quarter Yonker hit Pfingstel, and the latter raced 10 yards to score. Moose kicked the point to give the Dutchmen a lead they would not relinquish. Late in the quarter it was Yonker to Tom Van Wingen for another touchdown. This time Roy Zwemer converted and Hope's halftime lead was 14-0. It was more of the same in the second half as Yonker's pass was complete to De Mull on the Hope 48. De Mull pleased the crowd by going 52 yards for the score. The kick by Moose made it 21-0. In the fourth quarter Eddie Leverette broke away for a 33-yard touchdown run, but a penalty nullified the score. Roy Zwemer scored a short time later and kicked the point to make it 28-0. Hope's final score came when Don "Dutch" Van Ingen took a handoff from Yonker and ran 37 yards to paydirt. The conversion attempt by Fuzz Bauman was wide. In the closing minutes of the game quarterback Bill Hinga combined with receiver Frank Breen in a drive that neared the J.C. goal once again as time ran out. The 34-0 victory featured Hope's defensive potential as well as ability to cross the goal line.

Hope's second game took place on October 1 against Monmouth, again at Riverview. Near the end of a hard-fought first half Hope capped an 80-yard drive with a 4-yard scoring pass from Yonker to De Mull, and Hope led 7-0 at half time. A defensive struggle followed. Monmouth mounted one serious drive, but James Feehley fumbled into the end zone and Hope recovered. Near the end of the game it was the Dutchmen's turn to fumble on their own 35 yard line. A penalty placed the ball on the 25 and on the first play the Scots' Henry Gildemeister passed into the end zone. Jim Pfingstel was called for interference and Monmouth had the ball, first down on the one yard line. After two running plays the ball was on the one foot line. On third down Monmouth completed a pass in the end zone, but Head Linesman Wendell Emery ruled that time had expired before the snap. Coach Glenn Robinson and his squad disagreed violently with the decision and players and patrons poured onto the field. A general melee featuring Scots and Dutchmen ensued. Order was finally restored by on-duty policemen. The Hope team accepted its slightly tainted victory while the disgruntled Monmouth squad made its way back to Illinois. Meanwhile, proponents of United Presbyterian-Reformed Church union conceded that the cause had taken a few steps backward.

Before embarking for Alma on October 7 Dutchmen baseball aficionados noted with some satisfaction that Detroit Tiger George Kell had edged the great Ted Williams for the American league batting title, 3.429 to 3.427. In the game played at Alma's Bahlke Field Hope stopped an early Scot threat when Bill Bocks intercepted an Alex Kish pass on the Hope five and ran it all the way back to the Alma 33. Running plays moved the ball to the 26. Nick Yonker passed to Bill Holwerda on a short square out pattern and Moose ran it in from the 23. The latter's kick was good and Hope led, 7-0. Alma dominated the remainder of the half but failed to score. Jim Pfingstel took the second half kickoff on the 15 and returned it to the Hope 40. A series of running plays by Pfingstel, Leverette, and Ron Appledorn moved the ball to Alma's one yard line. On the next play Leverette crossed the goal line and Holwerda converted to make it 14-0. Hope's final tally came on a left end pitch-out to Ron Appledorn, who allowed interference to form, then moved 37 yards down the sideline for the touchdown. This time the kick was blocked and the scoring was done for the day. The determined Scots did not give up and drove to the Hope one foot line in the fourth quarter, but the "cabinetmakers" held and the ball went over. Hope's 20-0 victory ended a 12-game Alma win streak.

Hope played another night game on October 15 at Adrian's Island Park Field. An early break got the Dutchmen off to a good start. Bill Bocks recovered an Adrian fumble on the Hope 29. A persistent Hope drive advanced the ball to the Adrian nine. An Appledorn sweep around right end brought the score and Holwerda's kick gave Hope a 7-0 lead and early game momentum. In the second quarter Leverette scored from 10 yards out on a left end sweep. The kick was wide making it 13-0 at the intermission. A second half Hope drive covered 71 yards in eight plays. Included was a 34-yard aerial from Yonker to Holwerda. With the ball on the five, Yonker tried a sneak, broke free, and went in for the score. The kick by Moose was true and Hope's lead was 20-0. Hope's roll continued as another 65-yard drive was climaxed by a Yonker to De Mull scoring pass from the 10. Holwerda's conversion made it 27-0 and Hope was decidedly in charge. At this point Coach Vanderbush rewarded his substitutes with a chance to play. The subs gained a new appreciation of the regulars' effort as Adrian moved quickly to score. The Bulldogs' Jim Jackson went in from the eight and Buddy Rice kicked the point. The ensuing kickoff was fumbled on the Hope 25 and a few plays later Forest Schultz scored from the two. Rice added the point and the game ended, Hope 27, Adrian 14.

Hope's October 22 Homecoming tilt was a showdown between two of the state's three undefeated teams. Hillsdale, under new coach Jack Petoskey, again had an excellent team led by super-star Bill Young. The Dutch left no stone unturned in preparing for what sportswriters felt would be the title-deciding game. At a crowded campus pep rally on Friday night, Captain Abe Moerland crowned Hope's first Homecoming Queen, Delores Freyling of Grand Rapids. She would later become Mrs. Gene Campbell. The contest was billed by the press as Yonker versus Young and a windy day seemed to favor the latter. After an early Hope drive stalled, Hillsdale took charge and moved to the Hope four. The Bearcats' Spud Huston dove in for the score but Young's kick was wide. Still in the first quarter, Young broke away in typical fashion and rambled 37 yards for Hillsdale's second touchdown. This time his kick was good making the score 13-0. In the second quarter Hope fans sensed a momentum swing as the Dutch sustained a drive to the Hillsdale five. Yonker then threw a scoring pass to Moose Holwerda, whose subsequent conversion made it 13-7. The Dutch defense now rose to the occasion and gave the ball back to the offense. The next Hope drive found Jim Pfingstel bucking to the Hillsdale one on third down. Eddie Leverette's fourth down try was stopped at the 6" line. The Dales gained short yardage on two running plays before Clair De Mull, in a brilliant defensive play, broke through to tackle Bill Young in his own end zone. The safety made it 13-9 at the half. The second half featured great defensive play on both sides. A Hillsdale threat was stalled when Pfingstel recovered a fumble on the Hope eight. Hope's last march moved all the way to the Hillsdale four before Leverette was stopped and the ball went over. The game ended with Hillsdale on the Hope 15. The Dutchmen found it hard to believe that six inches had separated them from a probable MIAA championship.

A week later the team found itself making the long trip to Walter O. Briggs Field in Ypsilanti for Michigan Normal's Homecoming. Hope was understandably flat in the first half. A Dutch fumble on their own 30 set up a Normal score as Jim Martin eventually scored from the 3 1/2 yard line. The conversion attempt by Jerry Raymond was wide and the score stood 6-0 at the half. In the third quarter Hope started a drive on its own 24. Ten plays later the ball rested on the Normal 12. A key play in the series was a 25-yard Pfingstel-to-Yonker pass from punt formation. Hope reversed itself for the score when Yonker threw a flat pass to Pfingstel, who made it all the way. Holwerda's kick was blocked leaving the score at 6-6. In the fourth quarter Normal drove all the way to the Hope three, but the Dutch line stiffened and Jerry Raymond attempted a field goal. The kick sailed wide and the threat was over. With nine minutes remaining Hope took its turn at a field goal try. With sure-handed Fuzz Bauman holding, Moose Holwerda split the uprights and Hope was ahead for the first time, 9 to 6. With one minute left in the contest Tom Van Wingen broke free and scored on a left end sweep. Roy Zwemer's kick was good and Hope was back on the winning track with a 16-6 victory.

The game at Albion on November 5 was, by consensus, a Nick Yonker classic. The Hope scoring began early when Yonker intercepted a Briton pass on the 35 and returned it 10 yards to the 25. A few plays later Tom Van Wingen went in from the five and Moose added the point to make it 7-0. Albion came back with an impressive drive to the Hope 12, but at this point defensive end Jack Vander Velde made a great play as he broke through and spilled Frank Joranko for a 12-yard loss to end the threat. Yonker was tough on the Albion aerial game with his second interception, this time on the Briton 25. He then threw a strike to Clair De Mull from the 16 and De Mull was over for the touchdown. Moose made it 14-0. With minutes remaining in the half Yonker threw another touchdown pass, this time to Holwerda, but the play was nullified by a holding penalty. The third quarter was scoreless, but Albion did move as close as Hope's 16 at one point. In the fourth period Hope took possession on the Albion 35 and moved to the five. Yonker's pass to Ron Appledorn was good for the score and Holwerda's third conversion made it 21-0. The Dutch appeared to be heading for a fourth score when Yonker grabbed his third interception of the day, this time hauling in an aerial thrown by the Britons' John Porter. With the ball on the Albion 49, the hard-working Yonker was given a breather by Ron Schipper, but the latter's long pass was intercepted by an Albion back on the 24. Late in the quarter Hope fumbled on their own 17 setting up Albion's only score, a six-yard run by Guilford. The point try was not good. In the closing seconds Fred Yonkman intercepted an Albion desperation pass and ran it to the two-yard line, where he was forced out of bounds as the game ended. The 21-6 victory kept faint hopes alive but there was little prospect that Hillsdale would drop any of its remaining games.

Hope's season finale was played at Riverview Park on November 12 against Kalamazoo. The Dutchmen, despite recent success, had not recorded a win over the Hornets since Bud Hinga's 7-0 victory in 1940, and the desire to prove themselves Hope's best team ever was further incentive. On their own 39 in the first quarter, Hope faced third and nine. Yonker's pass was complete to Ron Appledorn, who eluded tacklers and raced 61 yards for the touchdown. Holwerda kicked his first point of the day for the 7-0 lead. In the second quarter Rip Collins recovered a Bill Glennon fumble. With the help of a penalty Hope moved to the one and Tom Van Wingen dove in for the score. Moose Holerda was gaining consistency and his second kick made it 14-0. The game, however, was far from over. Coach Bob Nulf's crew came back with touchdowns by Jack Davis from the one and Bill Glennon from the 21. A conversion by Conrad Hinz made it 14-13 and it appeared to be anyone's game at the half. In the third quarter Gene Campbell pounced on a Bill Glennon fumble on the Kalamazoo 28. A few plays later, on the 19, Yonker tried a quarterback sneak, broke away, and went all the way to the two. Van Wingen went in for his second touchdown of the afternoon and a Holwerda kick made it 21-13. In the fourth quarter Hope gained possession when Yonker intercepted and moved to the "K" 43. Nick's short pass to Dutch Van Ingen gave Hope fans a special treat as the "Cabinetmakers" did their work. Rip Collins cut down two would-be tacklers, and Abe Moerland a third to spring Dutch into the open. His 40-yard touchdown run plus a fourth conversion by Holwerda made it 28-13. The Hornets' Dick Cain tried vainly to rally his team, but linebacker Bill Bocks intercepted his pass on the Kalamazoo 40 and returned it all the way. Bocks' fine run was called back due to a clipping penalty, and the ball was placed on the 31. Three plays later Eddie Leverette broke free off guard and raced 16 yards to score. Roy Zwemer's kick soared over the goal post and onto Columbia Avenue, making the final score Hope 35, Kalamazoo 13. With seven wins and but a single, four-point loss, it was Hope's best record ever.

Hillsdale closed out an impressive 9-0 season by defeating Indiana State, 48 to 0. The school then accepted a bid to meet the University of Evansville on the latter's field in the "Refrigerator Bowl." In a good game, Evansville downed the MIAA champs, 22-7. Few would dispute the legitimacy of Hillsdale's title, but it is interesting to note that five Hope players were named to the 11-man All-MIAA team while Hillsdale placed but two. Kalamazoo also placed two, while Albion and Adrian each placed one. Hope's honorees included ends Clair De Mull and Bill Holwerda, tackle Rip Collins, guard Abe Moerland, and quarterback Nick Yonker. Gordon Timmerman was named to the second team. Yonker, a fourth-time pick, was also named the league's Most Valuable Player. With one day's rest, Yonker, Holwerda, and Bill Hinga reported to Coach Russ De Vette for basketball practice.

Lars Granberg, in his second season as cross country coach, was encouraged by a 15-man turnout including five lettermen. Collins Ottipoby was elected captain of the team. Coach Granberg was especially pleased at the return of Ivan "Ike" Huyser, who had only been available for the early part of the '48 season. The official course length was now set at four miles as opposed to the previous 3 1/2. Hope opened with a 24-33 victory at Alma on October 7. In 81-degree weather Huyser and Ottipoby finished 1-2. They were followed by Wayne Tripp in fifth place, Jim Rendell in seventh, Hugh

One of Hope's all-time great athletes, Nick Yonker (right) was selected All-MIAA Quarterback four straight years (1946-49). In 1949 he was named the league's Most Valuable Player. Playing in the two-way era of football, he was also an outstanding defensive saftey. A 3-sport man at Hope, he was an all-conference guard in basketball and a regular on the baseball team. Yonker was awarded the Ph. D. degree by Columbia University in 1961 and at this writing, is Professor of Religious Studies at Oregon State University.

Robert "Rip" Collins (left) typified the rugged intensity that made the "Cabinet Maker" line a football legend at Hope in the late 40s. Rip was named to the All-MIAA team in 1949.

Campbell in ninth, Neil Van Heest 10th, and Hank Parson 11th.

At Adrian on October 15 it was Hope 25, University of Toledo 46, and Adrian 59. Scoring in the dual meet showed Hope 19, Adrian 41. Ike Huyser led all runners. In Hope's Homecoming run against Hillsdale on October 22, the Dutchmen took five of the first six places to notch a 16-47 win. Huyser's fourth straight individual victory was the highlight of the meet. The team's winning streak was snapped on November 5 at Albion. The Britons' 17-44 victory featured Ted Hagadone in first place plus numerous other strong runners. Ike Huyser ran a fine race but had to settle for second behind Hagadone. Huyser was back in first place at Kalamazoo on November 12 as the Dutch dropped a heartbreaker to the Hornets, 28 to 30. Three days later Hope College and Coach Granberg hosted the MIAA meet for the first time since Hope's entry into the league. The teams were assembled on 11th Street adjacent to Lincoln School. The starting gun sent them eastward on 11th Street as the four-mile race got under way. At the finish, as expected, it was Albion first with 56 points, Kalamazoo second with 59, Hope third with 72, Alma fourth with 84, Adrian fifth with 98, and Hillsdale sixth with 134. Albion's Ted Hagadone was the individual winner in a time of 22:24. Hope's Ike Huyser was second in 22:42. Jim Rendell finished ninth, Wayne Tripp 14th, Hank Parson 23rd, Neil Van Heest 24th, and Hugh Campbell 27th in the race, which began with 42 participants.

In the summer of 1949 Coach Russ De Vette removed himself from the list of Hope's most eligible bachelors when he married Doris Koskamp, a Wisconsin co-ed who reigned as Hope's May Day Queen. While Doris continued her studies as a senior, Russ greeted nine returning basketball lettermen and prepared for his second season as head mentor. The 20-game schedule for 1949-50 contained a few new wrinkles. Gone were such teams as Percy Jones, Grand Rapids Junior College, and Muskegon Junior College. Added were two games each with Western Michigan and Central Michigan, plus a January MIAA tournament to be held at Albion. The tourney was designed to make money for the league and would not figure in the conference standings.

Led by Co-Captains Moose Holwerda and Paul Muyskens, Hope opened at the Armory against the toughest team it would meet all season. The December 6 game brought Buck Read and his Western Michigan Broncos to Holland. Despite a 27-22 Western lead at halftime, Hope stayed in the game and actually took a 37-35 lead at one point on Jerry Jacobson's field goal. With two minutes to play the score stood 48-all, but a basket by Don Groggell and two free throws by Pat Clysdale gave Western the victory, 52 to 48. Muyskens and Holwerda led Hope with 14 and 13, while Nick Yonker added 12. For the Broncos it was Shaw with 12 and Clysdale with 10.

Hope's MIAA opener was played on December 8 against a good Adrian team that forced the Dutchmen to battle all the way before succumbing 54-48. Hope managed a 23-17 halftime lead but the second half was dead even, thanks in large part to the sharp shooting of the Bulldog's Gregg Arbaugh. Arbaugh was high man for the night with 19, while Yonker and Muyskens had 11 each for Hope and Duane Peekstock put in nine.

The Alma Scots gave the Dutchmen another tussle in the Armory on December 15. The Alma lead at halftime was 32-28 and the Dutch were forced to come from behind in the final two minutes to pull out the 67-62 victory. Yonker led the way with 17, Vande Wege followed with 15, Muyskens had 14 and Peekstock 10. Clark and Mohre led the Scots with 17 and 15.

Four days after Christmas De Vette's squad made its way to Richmond, Indiana, to meet the Quakers of Earlham College. The contest was close all the way, with the home team leading 32-31 at the half. Hope's zone defense proved effective, and at the end the Dutchmen pulled away to a 56-49 victory. Paul Muyskens was high with 15 and Bill Hinga followed with nine. Vance led the Quakers with 12. Hope's 3-1 record was reason for confidence as the team entered the MIAA Tournament at Albion on January 5, but for some reason things did not mesh. The Dutch were trounced 64-47 by Kalamazoo in the opener, then eliminated by Alma, 52 to 45. On January 11 the team traveled to Kalamazoo for a second meeting with a Western Michigan squad that was just hitting its stride. Hope was not able to match its fine performance in the season opener and fell before the Bronco fast break, 73-43. Adams was high for Western with 22, while Muyskens collected 12 for De Vette's crew.

The Dutchmen, somewhat shaken, returned to the Armory on January 14 to tangle with Hillsdale. The 29-25 Bearcat lead at halftime looked like more of the same, but steady play in the second half netted Hope a 52-52 deadlock with two minutes remaining. With home crowd encouragement, the team pulled away and broke its three-game skid with a 57-54 win. Balanced scoring helped as Yonker netted 16, Vande Wege 14, and Jerry Jacobson 12. Hillsdale's Ed Johnson led all scorers with 24. But more losses were in store.

At Albion on January 17 it was Vince Sigren doing the damage with 17 points enroute to a 59-56 Briton victory. Freshman Jerry Jacobson played his best game to date scoring 15, and Muyskens followed with 13 and Holwerda had 11. In the Armory on January 21, Hope dropped a two-point 53-51 decision to Kalamazoo. Bucky Walters' 20- point performance was a key factor, but the game was probably lost at the free throw line, as the Dutch were able to cash in on only nine of 18. Muyskens again led his team with 12. Hope absorbed another defeat at the hands of Calvin on January 24 at the Burton Gym. The first half was close with Calvin leading 25-23, but Chuck Bult's fine team widened the margin in the second half and went on to a 64-51 victory. Duane Rosendahl led his team with a 23-point performance. He had able assistance from Mel De Stigter with 13 and Slug Slager with 11. For Hope it was Jerry Jacobson with 14 and Nick Yonker with 13.

On January 28 the Hope team journeyed to Mount Pleasant determined to reverse the recent trend. Few besides the team felt there was much of a chance against the Chippewas, who owned a 28-game home court win streak, but Bud Vande Wege was back in form this night and put in 21 counters. Jacobson was nearly as effective with 18. Parfitt's 26-point effort was not quite enough for Central, and Hope came away the winner, 63-60. One week later the teams met again at the Holland Armory, and the Dutch made sure their recent victory would not be looked upon as a fluke. Coach De Vette's defensive strategy was much in evidence and shut down the Chips with only 34 points, while the Dutch were scoring 56. Parfitt again led Central, but was reduced from 26 to eight. Vande Wege was high again for Hope with 17, followed closely by Muyskens with 16 and Nick with 11.

It was back to the MIAA on February 11 with Adrian in town. The Bulldogs caught the Dutchmen on a hot streak and could do little to avert the eventual 78-44 defeat. Vande Wege was high for the third game in a row with 13. He was followed by Nick and Bob Wagner with 11 each. Hope and Alma had already divided games when the teams met on the Scots' floor on Valentine's Day. The contest lived up to expectations and was close all the way. It was 39-38 Hope with two minutes left when Alma's Kirk Hamilton put in a field goal to make it 40-39 Alma. An Alma freeze was effective and the clock ticked down to 43 seconds. At this point Nick Yonker, with a history of big plays under pressure, stole the ball, dribbled the length of the floor and scored the winning basket. Bud and Nick led Hope with 11 and 10. Healey had 14 for Alma.

Hope put its four-game win streak on the line at Hillsdale on February 18. The Dutchmen trailed 31-20 after a sluggish first half, but played better after the intermission. A late-game rally almost did it, but the Bearcats hung on for a 53-50 victory as Ed Johnson and Dick Gettings had 10 points each. Vande Wege and Muyskens were high for Hope with 14 and 13. Two days later the Dutchmen bounced back with a 59-48 victory over Albion in the Armory. This time Jun Bremer led all scorers with 18 points. Vande Wege and Yonker gave good support with 13 each. Charlie Frost with 16 and John Porter with 14 stood out for the Britons.

The MIAA finale was played against long-time rival Kalamazoo. A few days earlier the Hornets had cinched the MIAA championship by downing Alma and remained unbeaten on the Treadway floor during the season. Some of the glitter was removed from Kalamazoo's crown when the Dutchmen dominated play on their way to a 65-60 win. Hope established an early 6-4 lead on Paul Muyskens' basket and never trailed. At halftime it was Hope 34, K 22. Muyskens, Holwerda, and Bremer controlled the boards completely and with two minutes remaining, the scoreboard read Hope 64, Kalamazoo 48. De Vette then substituted an entire team. The game was unusually rough and Kalamazoo lost Stanski, Bos, and Walters via the foul route in the closing minutes. Muyskens led his team with 21 and was followed closely by Vande Wege with 19. Bill Bos was high for the losers with 20. The victory was significant for the Dutchmen, as it gave them a solid second place finish with a 7-3 record. Albion, Alma, and Hillsdale tied for third place with 5-5 records. Two non-league encounters remained.

On February 27 Chuck Bult brought his Calvin team to the Armory. The Knights sported a 12-3 record, best of any college team in the state, and it soon became evident that the high rating was no fluke. Calvin led 28-23 at the half and under the generalship of Slug Slager, was especially effective against the Hope zone defense. Elmer Ribbons seemingly could not miss from the corners as he easily led all scorers with 24. Rangy Duane Rosendahl contributed 16 and Elmer Walcott had 11. The Dutchmen experienced a rare evening when no one had a hot hand. Bud Vande Wege managed 14 points, Muyskens 10 and Yonker 9. All in all, it as a Calvin night and Coach Bult could be proud of his team. A **Sentinel** article erroneously reported that it marked the first time Calvin had won both games. Records would show that the Knights had scored double wins in 1928-29, 1932-33, and 1933-34.

Hope closed out the season in the Armory on March 4 against Michigan Normal. The Dutch shooting eye returned as Bud Vande Wege poured in 19 and June Bremer got 17 in the 63-51 Dutch victory. Harry Fosdick had 11 for Normal. Hope's overall record was 11 and nine. Nick Yonker and Bud Vande Wege were named to the six-man All-MIAA team. Paul Muyskens was elected MVP by his team-mates. The squad seemed reluctant to see the season conclude, and on March 6 divided itself into the "Locals" and "Yokels"(outstaters) for a game in Carnegie Gym. Despite the absence of Nick Yonker, the outstaters scored a convincing 66-46 win as Jack Marema led with 25 and Stretch Wagner followed with 20. Fuzz Bauman and Vande Wege had 14 and 11 for the hometown boys. The balls were finally deflated and thoughts were turned to spring.

As usual, the race for the All-Sports Trophy would be decided by performance in four spring sports. Hope held a two-point lead over Kalamazoo in the race, this without benefit of a championship. Creditable showings in all sports had given the Dutchmen a shot, but the spring outlook was bleak. Coach Al Timmer's golf team of Howie Jalving, Bill Kloote, Paul Mulder, Bob Houtman, Dick Kruizenga, and Heinie Visser was given the best chance to bring home a title, and the team lived up to its advance billing by posting an 8-1 overall record in dual competition. The lone loss came at the hands of Alma on April 28 when the Scots won 11 1/2 to 7 1/2. Victories were recorded as follows: Hope 16 1/2 - Muskegon J.C. 1 1/2, Hope 10 1/2 - Hillsdale 8 1/2, Hope 13 1/2 - Calvin 4 1/2, Hope 11 - Kalamazoo 8, Hope 10 1/2 - Albion 8 1/2, Hope 12 1/2 - Muskegon J.C. 2 1/2, Hope 13 1/2 - Calvin 4 1/2, Hope 12 1/2 - G.R.J.C. 2 1/2, and Hope 17 - Adrian 2. The Dutchmen entered the league meet tied with Albion, each team having a 4-1 MIAA mark, but somehow most of the team succumbed to the pressure of the big one and

Kenneth J. Weller

Ken Weller joined the Hope faculty in 1949 after compiling an outstanding graduate school record in economics and business administration at the University of Michigan. His great interest in athletics prompted Al Vanderbush to enlist his aid in football. He served several years as a most capable assistant to Vanderbush and later to Russ De Vette. In 1969 Weller was named president of Central College in Pella, Iowa. During his 21 year tenure he became active in NCAA governance, serving on the NCAA Council and authoring the Division III Statement of Philosophy.

The 1949 Hope College Football Team

The team of unusual talent compiled an overall 7-1 record, best in Hope's history to that time. **Front Row L to R:** Trainer Jack Schouten, Jim Pfingstel, Gordon Van Hoeven, Robert "Rip" Collins, Gordon Timmerman, Captain Ave Moerland, Clair De Mull, Bill "Moose" Holwerda, Nick Yonker (MIAA MVP), Coach Al Vanderbush. **2nd Row:** Manager Alex Ebneth, Bill Aldrich, James Roberts, Ron Appledorn, Roy Zwemer, Don Van Ingen, Eddie Leverette, Tom Van Wingen, Clayt Borgman, Arnie Lankenau, Carl Schultz, Ken Johnson. **3rd Row:** Backfield Coach Russ De Vette, Bill Bocks, Ron Schipper, Jack Vander Velde, Fred Yonkman, Bob Visscher, Harry Visscher, Tom Ritter, John Johnson, Line Coach Ken Weller. **4th Row:** John Newton, Bill Hinga, Jerry Groters, Gene Campbell, Fred Kalsbeek, Gil Bussies, Bob Stone, Richard Hagni, Gene Nyenhuis, Manager Bob Roos. **5th Row:** Ken Van Wieren, Frank Breen, Don Miller, Ken "Fuzz" Bauman, Don Prentice.

Hope finished fourth. Coach Timmer's team did manage to salvage second place overall and Howie Jalving closed out a brilliant career by putting together a two-day 76 and 75 to take MIAA medalist honors with a 151.

Ken Weller became Hope's newest head coach when he took over the tennis team from Harold Haverkamp. Ken's team included Gerry Gnade, Chuck Votaw, Bob Becksfort, Ron Bos, Neil Van Dis, Ken Van Wieren, and Warren Exo. Calvin had one of the better teams in the state and downed the Dutchmen twice by identical scores of 6-3. Kalamazoo defeated Hope 6-1, but Weller's crew avoided the usual shutout when the doubles team of Warren Exo and Ken Van Wieren defeated Bos and Des Autels, 4-6, 7-5, and 8-6. In the victory column Hope won over G.R.J.C., 8-2, over Hillsdale, 5-2, over Albion, 4-3, and over Adrian, 7-0. In the MIAA meet at Kalamazoo, Hope finished a solid second behind the Hornets.

Russ De Vette's rebuilding project with the track team continued. The incentive of performing before the home crowd was a necessary ingredient in building interest and home meets were scheduled on April 28 and May 10. On the 28th Hope lost a close one to GRJC, 69 1/6 to 61 5/6. Hope's top point-getter was Walt Vander Meulen, who took first in the 220 and second in both the 440 and broad jump. He also ran a leg on Hope's winning mile relay team. Other firsts were recorded by Chuck Link in the javelin, Fred Yonkman in the discus, and Ken Dekker in the low hurdles. Gord Van Hoeven and Ron Bos were borrowed from the baseball and tennis teams. They responded by winning the shot put and broad jump. Carl Van Farowe tied for first in the high jump. In a triangular at Kalamazoo on May 2 the Dutch with 29 1/10 points were forced to settle for third place behind Kazoo with 97 1/5 and Grand Rapids J.C. with 35 4/10. Walt Vander Meulen's fine broad jump of 21' 1 1/2" took first, and Van Farowe's high jump of 5' 8" was also a winner. Jim Lamb tied for first in the pole vault with an 11' 2" mark. Hope hosted Albion and Calvin in another triangular on May 10. The powerful Britons ran away with the meet scoring 113 1/2 points, but the Dutchmen got some satisfaction in edging the Knights 24 1/2 to 24. Van Farowe set a new Hope record with a leap of 5' 10 1/2" in the high jump, while Vander Meulen again won the broad jump. Jim Lamb and Ernie Ross were part of a four-way tie for first in the pole vault.

Hope's dual meet at Calvin on May 16 was yet another in the long line of exciting sports contests between the two schools. Going into the final event, the mile relay, the score stood Calvin 64, Hope 62. The Calvin men produced the needed victory and with it went the meet, 69 to 62. Hope's first place winners were Van Farowe in the high jump, Pete Kraak in the 880, Bob Roos in the two-mile, Walt Vander Meulen in the broad jump, Bob Ondra and Jim Lamb, tied for first in the 440, and Lamb, Ross, and Bob Molenaar, tied for first in the pole vault. Alex Ebneth won the javelin throw. Hope ended in fifth place in the MIAA meet at Kalamazoo on May 19. Clayt Borgman took second in the javelin with 163', Jim Lamb was second in the pole vault with 11' 10," and Walt Vander Meulen took third in the broad jump with a fine jump of 21' 5 3/8."

Jack Schouten's baseball team began the season with high hopes and some very solid players. Pitchers included veterans Paul Buckhout and Lefty Bill Ver Hey plus promising Don Hoffman. Behind the plate was Jim Harvey, a proven performer and good man with the bat. Other batters of note were Gord Van Hoeven, Jack Marema, Con Boeve, Ron Appledorn and Tom Van Wingen, but erratic fielding and inconsistent hitting made it a constant struggle for the team to approach its potential.

The season opened in freezing weather at Riverview Park on April 8. Bill Ver Hey went the route to down Calvin 4-3. Hope pulled it out in the ninth when Jack Marema and Gerry Mull crossed the plate. The MIAA opener featured defending champion Hillsdale again at Riverview. Paul Buckhout pitched well for the most part but could not quite overcome five Hope errors and a four-run third inning by Hillsdale that included a Bill Young double. The final was Hillsdale 6, Hope 4.

Bill Ver Hey was in top form on April 18 when the team traveled to Alma. The lefthander limited the Scots to two hits while striking out 11 and issuing but two walks. Hope scored the game's only run in the seventh when Jim Harvey, who had walked, came home on Marema's single. On April 21 it was Hope at Kalamazoo with "Bad Luck" Buckhout on the mound. Paul pitched a five-hitter and struck out nine, but along the way he hit three batters and again had to absorb five Hope errors. Gord Van Hoeven's four hits were wasted as the Hornets scored the winning run in the ninth on an error and a bloop single. The 2-1 setback left the Dutchmen at 1-2 in the league. The following day Hope hosted Grand Rapids Junior College and Jack fielded a team made up largely of reserves. Lefty Hardy Ensing pitched nine strong innings but J.C. led 3-1 as the Dutchmen came to the plate. With Con Boeve on third, Zeke Piersma lifted a long fly to center that bounced off the glove of center fielder Bob Sack. Piersma circled the bases and the score was tied 3-3. Reliefer Don Hoffman retired the side in order in the 10th and in Hope's half, third baseman Don Brink singled home the winning run in the 4-3 victory. Paul "Spike" Van Eck performed well for Hope behind the plate.

For the only time in the season Hope put two victories together when the team shaded Adrian 6-5 on the Bulldogs' home field. Hope had a four-run fifth inning with Gord Van Hoeven's triple the big blow. Bill Ver Hey pitched a four-hitter and struck out 15. In the ninth he struck out the last man with the tying run on third base. The up and down season continued. At Hillsdale on May 2 it was another "almost" game for the Dutchmen. The Bearcats scored all eight of their runs in the first two innings. Meanwhile, Hope pecked away at the lead. Ron Appledorn stroked a left field home run in the sixth, Don Brink had three hits, Zeke Piersma had two, and in the eighth, Gord Van Hoeven's bid for a grand slam went foul by inches. The final was Hillsdale 8, Hope 7.

On a windy May 6 the Alma Scots were at Riverview with Charlie Saxton on the mound. Saxton pitched eight innings of two-hit shutout ball before giving up two runs in the ninth. But it was too little, too late as the Dutchmen suffered a four-to-two defeat. Four days later Don Hoffman got the call in Hope's second encounter with Kalamazoo. Paul Buckhout relieved in the fourth and got credit for the 6-4 win which was punctuated with numerous umpire arguments featuring Hornet coach Henry Lash. Ron Appledorn and Jim Harvey had triples for Hope.

Albion's Britons were the class of the league in 1950, and Coach Del Anderson had them ready when Hope arrived for a double-header on May 13. In the opener Albion's Clark Wurm bested Bill Ver Hey 4-3 in a well-played game. Hardy Ensing led Hope with two singles and a double. In the nightcap, Chappie Marvin pitched a strong game striking out eight Dutchmen and winning over Paul Buckhout, 5-2. The double loss was disheartening, but the low point came two days later when Adrian found Riverview Park to their liking and handed Jack's squad its worst defeat of the season. The Bulldogs crossed the plate 10 times while holding the Dutch to five.

A non-league game was played in Grand Rapids on May 19 against Calvin. Coach Schouten was able to rally his team, and especially pitcher Jack Buchhout. In a brilliant performance Buckhout scattered three hits and struck out 18. Hope's 5-1 victory took some of the sting out of a disappointing league season. In a final contest on May 23 the Dutchmen bowed to Western Michigan's Frosh team, 2-0. The season had its moments, but the overall 6-8 record was hardly a measure of the team's true potential. The 3-7 MIAA mark resulted in a fifth place tie. Albion, with championships in baseball and track, surged ahead of both Kalamazoo and Hope to take the All-Sports Trophy with 50 points. Kalamazoo finished second with 45, and Hope was third with 39. There had been no spring football practice, as league officials decided that such activity interfered with spring sports and gave football an emphasis not consistent with MIAA philosophy. Some coaches would object, but the decision has weathered 40 years.

* * *

The momentous decade of the 40s was over. The nation's return to peacetime pursuits was marked by a seemingly insatiable appetite for sports at all levels. On the college scene athletic programs were bigger than ever, though not always better. The MIAA endeavored not to ape the bigger institutions by following its own course toward sports in proper perspective. A transition had taken place on Hope's campus with the return of Al Vanderbush, Russ De Vette, and Ken Weller to assume important coaching responsibilities, but the influence and example of Hinga and Schouten remained. Hope would shine in the 50s.

CHAPTER 9

HOPE AT MID-CENTURY

As Hope moved into the '50's, Bud Hinga had reason to be pleased with the school's overall program of athletics. In his role as director of athletics he had assembled a fine coaching staff and an array of talented athletes graced the roster of each sport. The MIAA Board of Directors and Judge Advocate De Gay Ernst were providing direction and stability. With the addition of Mary Breid to the Physical Education staff more attention was given to women's sports. It would, however, be another 20 years before women's athletic teams could boast parity with men.

A disturbing incident in this atmosphere of expectancy occurred on Sunday, June 25, 1950, when the North Korean People's Army crossed the 38th Parallel into South Korea. United States forces were soon involved, and though the fighting that followed was termed a "police action," most recognized it for what it was. It seemed unthinkable that a scant five years after the horror of Hiroshima, much of the world would again be engulfed in armed conflict. As in the past, athletic programs were not immediately affected, but uncertainty increased when Adrian Football Coach Lyman Abbott, an Army reservist, was recalled to active duty. There would be more.

Hope's prospects for a winning football season in 1950 were dimmed by the graduation of several outstanding performers. Seven starters were gone, including six of the vaunted "Cabinetmaker" linemen. Only center Gene Campbell returned. His leadership as captain would play a vital role in the team's chances. Bill Hinga and Ron Schipper would attempt to fill the void left by the departure of quarterback Nick Yonker, the league's most valuable player. Coach Al Vanderbush, now in his fifth season, was perhaps resigned to a rebuilding year, but several squad members showed considerable potential. Ends Clair De Mull and Moose Holwerda would not be soon forgotten but Coach Al could turn to Fuzz Bauman, Bob and Harry Visscher, and defensive standout Jack Vander Velde. Jack was the son of former Hope great, Otto Vander Velde, a local physician who donated his time as Hope's team doctor. Gene Nyenhuis at tackle and Lloyd Beekman at guard were proven performers and gave stability to the new line built around Captain Gene Campbell. Despite the departure of Nick Yonker, the backfield included some very able performers, notably Tom Van Wingen, Ron Appledorn, Eddie Leverette, Dutch Van Ingen, and Ted Barrett, who returned after being out of school for a year. Bill Bocks was back in the defensive secondary.

The season opened with a night game on September 22 at Riverview Park against a stronger than usual Michigan Normal team. In the second quarter Ed Skowneski scored the first of his three touchdowns, but the kick was wide and Normal's halftime lead was 6-0. In the third period a jarring tackle by Jack Vander Velde caused a Normal fumble. This led to the tying touchdown by Tom Van Wingen from the two. Bud Prins' kick hit the crossbar and bounced back, leaving the score at 6-6. Quarterback Chuck Paige was effective through the air as he netted 181 yards. Skowneski scored twice in the fourth quarter and Normal went home with a 19-6 victory. Appledorn ran well for Hope throughout the contest, but quarterback Bill Hinga suffered an ankle fracture that ended his football career just as opportunity seemed to be knocking.

Hope's second game was also a night affair, this time played at Waukesha, Wisconsin, in a first-ever meeting with Carroll College. Coaches Vanderbush, Weller, and De Vette were pleased when the Dutchmen exploded for five touchdowns, five Bud Prins conversions, and a safety. Quarterback Ron Schipper earned his spurs by passing for 106 yards and two touchdowns. Ron Appledorn contributed four touchdowns beginning with a 67-yard jaunt on the second play of the game. Carroll came back with two quick scores to take a first quarter lead. Still in the first quarter, it was Appledorn again to make it 14-12 Hope. In the second period Skipper hit Appledorn on a 47-yard pass play that netted Hope's third touchdown. Skipper's second scoring pass went to Fuzz Bauman and covered 17 yards. Hope's fifth touchdown came on a 17-yard run by Appledorn and gave the Dutchmen a very satisfying 37-26 win.

October 7 was a rainy day at Kalamazoo's Angell Field, where the teams met for the MIAA opener. The Hornets drew first blood after a 64-yard drive. Tackle Conrad Hintz converted to make it 7-0. His sure toe would eventually spell the difference in the game. Hope's first score was set up by a 40-yard run by Eddie Leverette. Tom Van Wingen went over from the four but the kick by Prins was not good. Bob Van Horn increased the Kalamazoo lead to 14-6 when he scored on a pitchout from quarterback Phil Dillman. In the third period Ron Appledorn narrowed the gap to 14-13 on a brilliant 87-yard touchdown run, but the Hornets countered with a 40-yard touchdown by Lloyd Johnson, making it 21-13. Appledorn scored once more on a 16-yard run in the fourth quarter, but in the absence of a two-point conversion rule, Hope was the loser, 21-20.

Coach Lloyd Eaton brought his Alma Scots to Holland for a night contest on October 13. After a scoreless first quarter, safety Ted Barrett broke loose for a 67-yard punt return to the Alma nine. Ron Skipper then passed to Fuzz Bauman for the score and Bud Prins kicked the point. The 7-0 lead remained at halftime. Between halves fans were entertained by the bands from both schools, and the Alma aggregation, complete with bagpipes and arrayed in Scottish kilts, stole the show. In the third quarter, quarterback Hess Wever scored for Alma and Alex Kish added the all-important extra point. In the final quarter the Scots moved to the Hope 29, but a fumble recovery by Hope's Neil Droppers ended the threat. The 7-7 tie was the closest any MIAA team would come to beating the Scots, who moved on to the league title with a 4-0-1 record.

Hope played host to an undermanned Grand Rapids Junior College team on October 21 and wrapped up the victory in decisive fashion. Fullback Tom Van Wingen scored twice in the first quarter on short plunges and the Dutchmen were never headed. In the second period Eddie Leverette scored from the four. In the third quarter Ron Appledorn started on a right end sweep, was trapped, reversed his field, and ran 65 yards for the touchdown. Freshman Herb Stouten scored Hope's final two touchdowns on runs of 65 and five yards, making it Hope 39, J.C. 7 when the gun sounded. It should be noted that Bob Wikstrom scored J.C.'s touchdown and kicked the point after. He would be heard from again as an outstanding player and coach for Albion college.

Assistant Coach Johnny Darnton succeeded Lyman Abbott at Adrian and brought the Bulldogs to Riverview for the Dutch Homecoming on October 28. The visitors were in early trouble when Gene Nyenhuis recovered a fumble on the Adrian four-yard line. A Van Wingen plunge was stopped at the 6" line, but Eddie Leverette went in on the next play. Bud Prins' kick was wide but it would be an afternoon when extra points were not crucial. Hope's second score came on a Ron Schipper-to-Fuzz Bauman pass, with the latter making a circus catch in the end zone. This time the Prins kick was true and Hope was out front, 13-0. Misfortune continued to plague the Bulldogs as they fumbled on their own 11 and Lloyd Beekman recovered. Reliable Tom Van Wingen was now generally known as "Terrible Tom" and he scored with little trouble from the seven. A second quarter Herb Stouten touchdown and Bud Prins conversion made it 26-0 at the half. In the third quarter Adrian shanked a punt and Leverette scored shortly thereafter from the 14 to increase the mark to 32-0. Hope's sixth score came when Don Hondorp intercepted a Bill Edinger pass on the Adrian 35 and ran it all the way to the end zone. In the game's waning minutes Quarterback Babe Schultz engineered an Adrian drive to the Hope one-yard line. Bill Edinger then fumbled the ball into the end zone where Guard George Osenko recovered for the only Adrian score. A crowd of 4,500 had witnessed Hope's 39 to 6 Homecoming victory.

A Friday night game at Hillsdale on November 3 was yet another in the long series of hard-fought contests between the two schools. Led by 275 pound tackle George Smallbone, the Dales drew first blood by marching 49 yards in eight plays. Tom Walsh went up the middle for the final 13 yards and the score. Monte Charles' kick was good and the 7-0 lead put pressure on the visitors, but the Dutchmen were able to respond with an 87-yard drive in 11 plays that tied the score. Van Wingen, on his specialty, dove in from the two and Bud Prins' kick made it 7-7 at the end of the quarter. Hillsdale scored their second touchdown in the second quarter when Charles slashed off tackle for 25 yards and kicked the point to make it 14-7. Again the Dutchmen were equal to the challenge. This time Ron Schipper passed to Leverette, who streaked away from the field for 74 yards and the touchdown. The conversion attempt appeared doomed by a bad snap, but Herb Stouten picked up the ball and ran it in to again tie the score. As the clock wound down, Hope was able to capitalize twice on Hillsdale fumbles. Van Wingen went over from the one after a 38-yard drive and Prins made it 21-14. Appledorn went off tackle for the final score and Bud Prins' kick was again accurate to give Hope a well-earned 28 to 14 victory. In total yards it was the Dutchmen with 424 to 164 for the Dales. Ron Schipper was impressive with 194 passing yards.

Hope ended the season at home against Albion. The November 11 contest was played on cold and snowy field with the Britons on the scoreboard first. Harry Hidenfelter circled right end on a 43-yard gallop and Don Carmien converted for the early 7-0 lead. The Dutch offense had trouble finding the right combination and failed to score in the first quarter. In the second period Albion moved to the two-yard line and quarterback Frank Joranko sneaked in to make it 13-0. Following the kickoff the Dutchmen found their intensity and marched to the Albion two and Van Wingen dove in for the score. The conversion attempt by Fuzz Bauman was wide, but the 13-6 score made it a wide open game. Late in the half the Britons were stopped on their own 37, but Mel Larimer, running from punt formation, broke free and ran 67 yards for the touchdown to make it 19-6 at halftime. The third period was scoreless. Hope got a much needed break in the fourth quarter by recovering an Albion bobble, but the Dutch promptly fumbled the ball back and George Gervais broke off tackle for 18 yards and the score to increase the margin to 26-6. With the game out of reach Eddie Leverette got away on the Statue of Liberty play and was finally pulled down on the two. Appledorn scored on the next play. The point was not good and Hope ended on a disappointing note, 26 to 12. With an overall record of 4-3-1 it was still a winning season. Hope's 2-2-1 league mark gave them a fourth place tie with Albion, but along the way they had tied the champions and beaten the second place team. For the first time the league coaches picked an offensive and defensive team for All-MIAA honors. Gene Nyenhuis and Ron Appledorn were named to the offensive team while Jack Vander Velde and Lloyd Beekman were selected on the defensive side. Tom Van Wingen and Bill Bocks were given honorable mention. Team members selected their own Most Valuable Player, and for Hope it was Tom Van Wingen. From the combined ballot the league players then chose the MIAA's Most Valuable. Their choice was Tom Van Wingen. Following in the footsteps of Bob Powers ('39), and Nick Yonker ('49), "Terrible Tom" could enjoy the added satisfaction of having been selected by his peers.

Coach Lars Granberg guided the 1950 cross country team to a third place tie in the MIAA and an overall 4-2 dual meet record. Collins Ottipoby was reelected captain of the squad, which included Bob Roos, Wayne Tripp, Neil Van Heest, John Frandsen, Roger Knopf, Bill Parson, Larry Fabunmi, and Carl Schroeder. The Dutchmen defeated Kalamazoo, 26-29, Alma, 22-36, Central Michigan, 28-30, and Hillsdale, 16-49. Losses were suffered at the hands of Albion, 17-45, and Adrian, 28-29. In the latter meet Adrian's Hewitt edged Bob Roos to give the Bulldogs the narrow victory. Both runners eclipsed the course record. In the MIAA meet at Albion Hope slipped to fourth behind champion Albion, Adrian, and Kalamazoo. Roos finished fourth, Tripp 15th, Ottipoby 22nd, Van Heest 24th, and Knopf 26th. Hope's earlier dual victory over Kalamazoo gave them an overall third place tie with the Hornets.

Basketball Coach Russ De Vette began his third season at the helm with an unusually tough 20 game schedule. Non-league foes included Valparaiso, Western Michigan (two games), Ferris (two games), Detroit Tech, Wooster, and the Dayton Gems, the latter an A.A.U team made up of former college stars. Captain Bud Vande Wege headed the squad, which included Bill Hinga, now nearly recovered from his football injury, Jun Bremer, Ken Van Regenmorter, Zeke Piersma, Jerry Jacobson, Duane Peekstock, Fuzz Bauman, Dick Hagni, Bob Visser, Norm Schuiling, Ron Appledorn, and Ron Bos, a junior out for the first time.

In the opener at Valparaiso Hope stayed with the Crusaders for the first 12 minutes, at which time the score was tied at 21. At this point Ken Van Regenmorter suffered a knee injury and was forced to retire, and Valparaiso then proceeded to build a 50-35 halftime lead. The Dutchmen fought back in the second half and were outscored by only two points, but the damage had been done and the Indiana team won 98-81, largely on the 30 point performance of a forward named Jim Ove. Vande Wege and newcomer Ron Bos led Hope with 17 points apiece.

Tom Van Wingen

The MIAA's Most Valuable Football Player - 1950

Van Wingen's selection marked the second year in succession that a Hope player received the award. Nick Yonker was named in 1949. Hope's only other recipient had been Bob Powers in 1939.

Hope's MIAA opener at the Armory on December 9 fell victim to a power failure. The lights returned briefly but went out for good with 25 seconds remaining in the half. Hope led 40-28 at this juncture and it was agreed to replay the contest only if it would make a difference in the final MIAA standings. The game eventually went into the record books as a 40-28 Hope victory. A few blocks away in Holland Hospital blackness settled in as this writer and wife Lorraine anxiously awaited the arrival of our first child. The hospital's emergency generators plus candles in the hallways were necessary throughout our 36 hour wait. Power was not restored to the city for two days.

Hope's game at Western Michigan on December 12 was pretty much decided by halftime. The Broncos led 38-16, and reserves on both sides played most of the second half. The final was Western 76, Hope 56, but the Dutchmen could take some comfort in the fact that Buck Read's team had earlier defeated the University of Iowa, the season favorite for the Big Ten title. Jun Bremer led Hope with 16, while Ken Van Regenmorter and Ron Appledorn each added 8. For the winners it was Joe Shaw with 18 and Bob Adams with 17.

At Alma on the 14th, the Scots made the best use of their narrow floor, limited Jun Bremer's hook shot, and led at halftime 33-29. The game was close until the final eight minutes, when Alma's surge outscored the Dutchmen 20 to 12 to seal the 72-58 victory. Bill Healy with 20 and Charlie Saxton with 15 led the winners, while Ron Bos took honors for Hope with 17. Vande Wege and Bremer had 10 each. A blizzard kept the team in Ionia for the night.

Hope's next three opponents were Ohio teams, and the Dutchmen did not fare well. The College of Wooster came to the Armory on the 15th with an impressive offensive machine. Hope led 37-34 after 13 minutes, but the Scots moved to a 53-45 halftime advantage and kept it up for the remainder of the game to win, 97-79. An added embarrassment occurred when it was discovered that the Armory scoreboard would only register up to 89. Wooster's Harry Weckesser with 36 points and Pete Williams with 23 did most of the damage. Jun Bremer led Hope's scoring with 18. Ron Bos followed with 16, Bud Vande Wege had 14, and Jerry Jacobson 12.

Hope's December 27 opponent was a team from the National Industrial Basketball League known as the Dayton Air Gems. The game was played in the new University of Dayton Fieldhouse, where the Dutch were out-manned by a stronger, more experienced team. Boasting several ex-university players, the Gems controlled the boards and increased a 44-32 halftime margin to a 90-52 victory. Bob Reed scored 19 for Dayton and Don McIntosh added 16. McIntosh had been a regular for the University of Michigan. Vande Wege was high for Hope with 14 and Bremer had 11. Jerry Jacobson scored 10 before being forced out with a knee injury. The team moved on to Berea the following night. News that Baldwin Wallace had earlier beaten Syracuse University was not exactly a confidence builder. The main problem for the Dutchmen this night was 6' 7" center Dick Retherford, who dropped in 25 points, 10 after missed free throws. A 49-30 Baldwin Wallace lead at halftime became 90-65 at the final whistle. Vande Wege was again high with 17 and Bremer followed with 11.

The Dutchmen hoped to turn the corner at Hillsdale on January 6, but Coach Irv Wisnewskinow had the services of Merv Hobeck, who had returned after a one-year layoff. Hobeck's hot hand produced 22 counters and led the Bearcats to a 65-45 win. Bremer, with 14, was high for Hope. Jerry Jacobson was returning to form with 11, and 6' 5" freshman Bob Visser caught the coach's eye with a fine performance. The Dutchmen, however, were struggling. Aside from the abbreviated Adrian game, the team found itself at 0 and 7. The tide finally turned in the Armory on January 11. The Ferris Bulldogs, somewhat misled by Hope's record, found themselves on the short end of a 36-31 count at halftime. Playing before the home crowd for the first time in nearly a month, De Vette's charges reeled off eight straight points to start the second half and were never headed. The final was Hope 71, Ferris 59. Bremer, Vande Wege, and Bos led the balanced Hope attack with 17, 16, and 14. For Ferris it was Carl Carrington with 15.

Hope's stay in the victors' circle lasted five days. Albion's veteran Coach Walt Sprandel brought his team to the Armory on January 16 and went home with a hard fought 73-67 victory. The improving Hope team held a four-point halftime lead that was gradually erased in the second half due in large part to the fine performance of the Britons' John Porter with 17 points and Chuck Mokl with 15. Porter would later serve as Michigan's superintendent of public instruction and is at this writing, president of Eastern Michigan University. Somewhat obscured in Hope's tough loss was Jun Bremer's game high 23 point performance.

Two days later at Kalamazoo it appeared that Hope finally had it all together. The Dutch lead in the first half reached 17 at one point. At halftime it was Hope 43, Kalamazoo 34. But John Stommen, who led his team with 21, scored 19 in the second half. Steady floor play and 14 points by Roger Winter gave Kalamazoo the five-point victory, 85 to 70. Ron Bos was outstanding for Hope with 18 and Vande Wege had 13.

At Ferris on January 20 the Dutchmen reversed their procedure and came on strong in the second half. It was 39-33 Ferris at the intermission but the final showed Hope 82, Ferris 77 despite a 20 point performance by the Bulldogs' Carl Carrington. It was Bos again for Hope with 17 and Jacobson with 14, but De Vette also got 10 points each from Vande Wege, Zeke Piersma, Bob Visser, and Tim Beerthuis. Hope would taste defeat again, but the Ferris win appears to have been a turning point.

At a special assembly in the Chapel on January 24 the campus community paid tribute to Tom Van Wingen, the league's most valuable football player. Randall Bosch, Holland industrialist, was on hand to present a diamond-studded gold football to the fullback, who had scored 42 points during the 1950 season. Collins Ottipoby, two-time captain of the cross country team, was presented an "H" blanket for being a four-year letter winner in his sport.

Hope visited Detroit Tech on January 26 and for the first time in the season enjoyed back-to-back victories. The Dutchmen led throughout and took the contest, 57 to 42. Bremer was high with 12 while Jacobson and Van Regenmorter each had 11. Back on campus it was semester examination time and the team took a 13-day break from competition.

February 8 found De Vette's squad hosting perennial rival Calvin. The Knights were enjoying one of their best seasons and their 12-1 record made prospects dim for the 3-9 Dutchmen. But strange things happen in Hope-Calvin games and a long waiting line formed on Ninth Street well before the Armory doors were scheduled to open. Hope played with intensity from the opening whistle and, on the strength of a 14 point effort by Ron Bos, built a 43-32 lead at the intermission. In the second half the margin dwindled to three as Jun Bremer made his exit via the foul route, but Ken Van Regenmorter took charge in the waning minutes to help preserve the upset 75-70 victory. Bob Visser's nine points and strong board work were also contributing factors. Balanced scoring aided the Dutch cause as Bos led with 18 and was followed by Bremer with 16, Van Regenmorter with 15, and Jacobson with a like number. Tall Duane Rosendahl was virtually unstoppable for Calvin as he led all scorers with 27. Butts Kool chipped in with 14. The Calvin attack suffered from the loss of Slug Slager, who had graduated at the semester.

Two days later the pumped-up Dutchmen made the long trip to Adrian. This time there was no power outage, but figuratively speaking the lights went out for Hope in the last 20 seconds, as an Adrian basket wiped out Hope's one point lead and gave the Bulldogs a thrilling 58-57 win. Center Bud Bennett led the winners with a splendid 20 point performance while Jun Bremer took honors for Hope with 14. The return game with Alma was played in the Armory on February 13 and, after a halftime deadlock at 23, Hope moved out front and took the contest, 54 to 46. Bremer was once more high man for the Dutchmen with 14, while Charlie Saxton's 16 led Alma. Bud Vande Wege's fine defensive effort held high-scoring Bill Healey to four.

Hopes for a second consecutive MIAA win received a blow when Jun Bremer fell victim to the flu before the Hillsdale game at the Armory on February 17, but De Vette's bench was equal to the task and Hope owned a narrow 39-35 halftime lead. Bob Visser, filling in for Bremer scored 23 and Gene Scrotenboer, also at center, added nine. Jacobson had 14 and Ron Bos 13. Ed Johnson was strong for the Bearcats, but it wasn't enough and Hope avenged its January 6 loss with a 71-59 victory.

With some momentum the Dutchmen made their way to Albion's Kresge Gym on February 20. Another upset appeared in the offing when Jerry Jacobson went on a first half tear with 22 points, but Jake succumbed to a stomach disorder and was unable to play in the second half. Coach Walt Sprandle's charges then proved themselves to be true champions by posting a convincing 101-65 victory. The trio of John Porter, Dick Allen, and Ced Dempsey racked up 26, 19, and 16 points respectively for the Britons.

Jacobson had recovered by February 24, when Dob Grow's Kalamazoo quintet invaded the Armory. The Hornets, who had swamped the Dutch by 15 on January 18, found themselves on the short end of a 54-35 halftime count and never recovered. Hope's team effort included Jacobson with 19, Ken Van Regenmorter with 16, and Bremer and Bos with 10 each. John Stommen and John Sentz had 15 apiece, but the final tally was Hope 83, Kalamazoo 71.

Despite the earlier loss at Albion, De Vette's team seemed to have found itself, and quite appropriately the final contest was against Calvin. Limited seating at the Burton Gym prompted Calvin officials to move the game downtown to the Grand Rapids Civic Auditorium. The rivalry was fast assuming the proportions of a West Michigan classic and fans were again treated to spirited play. A halftime score of 33-33 kept excitement at a high pitch, but the Knights gained the upper hand in the second half on the strength of 20 point performances by both Duane Rosendahl and Butts Kool, plus 17 from Stu Sisco. Van Regenmorter and Bremer were high for Hope with 14 and 13 in the 74-63 loss. Hope's 4-6 MIAA record garnered a fourth place tie with Kalamazoo. Albion was 8-2 for the top spot, followed by Alma at 7-3, and Hillsdale at 6-4. Hope could boast one victory over all league foes except champion Albion, and ended with an overall record of eight and 12 counting the abbreviated game with Adrian. June Bremer and Jerry Jacobson were named to the 10-man All-MIAA team and Jacobson was elected Hope's MVP. It was decided not to select a captain for the 1951-52 season due to uncertainty as to who might be on hand. Only Vande Wege and Hinga would be lost by graduation and the returning nucleus of Bos, Jacobson, Bremer, Visser, and Van Regenmorter boded well for the future - - if only the Korean conflict would somehow not deplete the ranks.

Hope's only championship in the spring of 1951 was provided by the women's tennis team under the direction of Louise Van Domelen and Mary Breid. The MIAA tournament was held at Hillsdale. Hope scored 12 team points, followed by Albion with 5, Kalamazoo 4, Adrian 2, and Hillsdale 0. Hope's Mary Jean Ter Borg captured the singles championship, while Hope's team of Sally Palen and Marilyn Veldman won the doubles title.

Due to the perennial strength of Kalamazoo College, the men's tennis team did not fare quite as well, but Harold Haverkamp's squad finished a strong second. Returnees Ron Bos, Warren Exo, and Chuck Votaw were joined by Dick

Nieusma, Jack Vander Velde, Ron Schipper, Monte Dyer, Johnny Kenwell, and "Tex" Benecke. An opening 9-1 victory over Muskegon Junior College on April 18 was followed by a 6-4 win over Calvin five days later on the home courts. Albion's Britons were in town on April 27 and fell before the Dutch 5-2 as Bos, Exo, and Votaw took the first three singles matches. It was a different story at Kalamazoo on May 3, when the Hornets prevailed, 6-1. Hope's number two doubles team of Chuck Votaw and Dick Nieusma was able to win in straight sets, 7-5, 7-5. The Hillsdale match in Holland on May 8 was close all the way. Bos, Exo, and Nieusma won in singles, but a victory by the number one doubles team of Bos and Exo was necessary to give the Dutchmen the final 4-3 win. The MIAA men's tennis tournament was held at Kalamazoo on May 17 and 18. Any chance of upsetting favored Kalamazoo disappeared when Ron Bos was stricken with illness and could not compete. The Dutch, however, were able to hang on to second place as Chuck Votaw played well and reached the finals.

Only four lettermen returned to Jack Schouten's baseball squad, but 30 candidates turned out and the group included some excellent athletes. When the season opened in early April the infield included Fuzz Bauman at first base, Jim Williard and Jim Van Hoeven at second, Gene Schrotenboer at third, and Zeke Piersma at short. The outfield was equally strong with Tom Van Wingen in left, Dave Kempker in center, and Clarence "Con" Boeve in right. Veteran catcher Jim Harvey had an able backup in Jerry Jacobson, while mound duties were shared by Hardy Ensing, Don Hoffman, and Lefty Bob Dennison. Each of the MIAA meetings were scheduled as double headers, a format that would be abandoned the next year.

In the opener at Calvin on April 10 the Dutchmen combined nine hits, eight walks, and two wild pitches to score 15 runs and down the Knights 15 to 3. Hardy Ensing was the starter and winning pitcher. Calvin's three runs came in the fifth inning off reliever Don Hoffman. In a game played at Riverview a week later the home team suffered a 5-1 setback at the hands of Grand Rapids Junior College. The Dutch were able to score only in the sixth when Piersma singled, Don Howard walked, and Dave Kempker drove Zeke in with a single.

Hope opened league play by taking a double header from Albion by scores of 8-2 and 6-4. In the first game Bob Dennison pitched a two-hitter, Jim Harvey went three for four, and Dave Kempker homered in the sixth. In game two it was pitcher Don Hoffman aiding his own cause with a triple and Dave Kempker getting his second home run of the day in the seventh. The contest was halted by rain in the seventh inning. In the twin bill with Alma Bob Dennison scattered eight hits as Hope took a close one, 4 to 3. The Scots came back to take the nightcap, 8 to 5. Gene Scrotenboer contributed a double and triple in the losing cause. The Dutchmen had another split on April 28 when they entertained Kalamazoo at Riverview Park. In the opener Dennison was touched for 10 hits but the Dutch came from behind to register a 10-5 victory. A five-run seventh inning broke it open for the home team. The game also featured a first inning homer by Jim Williard and two fine running catches by Dave Kempker in center field, one with the bases loaded. In the second game Hornet pitchers Topp and Busman were effective in setting the Dutchmen down, 3 to 1.

Hope's trip to Hillsdale on May 5 resulted in a third straight split. Don Hoffman pitched the opening game for Hope, giving up three runs in the second, but the Dutchmen tied it up and in the eighth Jim Harvey drove Jacobson home from second with what proved to be the winning run in the 4-3 triumph. Hillsdale won the second game as Jake Bloemke's four-hitter bested Bob Dennison. The 6-3 loss was Dennison's first of the season.

A return game was played with Calvin at Riverview on May 8 and it turned out to be a laugher. Jack decided that his reserves deserved a chance to play, and they were used through the sixth inning, at which time the score stood Hope 10, Calvin 8. The regulars were then inserted for a workout and proceeded to score 13 runs in the seventh. The final tally was Hope 25, Calvin 11.

A postponed double header with Adrian was finally squeezed in on May 16. It was a big day for the Dutch as their twin victory boosted them into second place in the final MIAA standings behind champion Alma. Dennison was superb with a four-hit, 9-1 win in game one. A five-run Hope seventh sealed the contest which featured three hits by Tom Van Wingen and a bases loaded triple by Jim Williard in the seventh. Hope could manage only three hits in the abbreviated second game, but the Dutch cause was aided by six walks and four Adrian errors. Van Wingen's double was the big blow in the 7-5 victory.

Hope closed out the season with two non-league encounters with the ever-strong Western Michigan Frosh team. In Kalamazoo on May 18 Western's Jake Emaar held Hope to three safeties in posting a 7-2 win. It was a different story, however, on May 23 at Riverview. The game was tied at 5-all in the eighth and went into extra innings. Western scored in the llth to take a 6-5 lead, but in the top of the 11th Con Boeve singled, then scored on Gene Scrotenboer's double to tie the count. Jim Harvey then singled in the winning run to give Bob Dennison his fifth victory against but a single defeat. Con Boeve had four hits for the day, including a seventh inning home run. Hope ended at 7-3 for second in the MIAA and 10-5 overall, one of its most successful seasons to that time. Shortstop Zeke Piersma, catcher Jim Harvey, and pitcher Bob Dennison were named to the first-ever All-MIAA team.

With each passing month the activation of marine reservist Russ De Vette became more imminent. The prospect of yet another interruption of his chosen vocation did not, however, alter his determination to improve Hope's standing in track and field. Due to inadequate facilities the task was often thankless. Hope's cinder track opposite Carnegie Gym, short of the standard 440 yards, ceased to exist with the erection of the "T" Dorm which took away the east turn. This necessitated use of the Holland High track several blocks away on 22nd Street which did not have space for some of the college field events, notably the discus and javelin. As mentioned earlier, De Vette recognized the necessity of sponsoring home meets to kindle and maintain interest. His only alternative was to construct areas for the field events at the Hope site, conduct those events, and then move on to 22nd Street. The arrangement was less than ideal. In a conventional meet running events and field events are run simultaneously to some extent, and their separation prolonged the meet, not to mention the inconvenience to coaches, athletes, and would-be spectators. De Vette, with the assistance of Lars Granberg, proceeded undaunted.

Hope's first meet was at home on April 21 and the Dutchmen emerged with an 82-41 victory over Grand Rapids Junior College. The home team captured first place in 12 of 15 events. It was an auspicious start, but the situation was reversed on April 25 when the squad traveled to Albion for a triangular with the Britons and Jackson J.C. Accounts show Albion dominating with 100 5/6 points, Hope 49 2/3, and Jackson 10 1/2. Hope's firsts were a 20' 5" broad jump by Walt Vander Meulen, a 159' 3" javelin throw by Clayt Borgman, and a 5' 8" tie for first in the high jump by Carl Van Farowe.

Coaches De Vette and Granberg could only be encouraged by their team's performance against Calvin on April 28. In the meet at Houseman Field Hope won 11 events enroute to a 75-56 victory. The Hope community was becoming aware of the unusual athletic ability of Ron Bos, who was between tennis matches and therefore able to accompany the track team. On the previous afternoon he had been instrumental (victor at number two singles) in Hope's 5-2 win over Albion. This day his 10.0 victory in the 100 yard dash was but a 10th over the Hope record set by Don Martin 16 years before. He also cruised to a first place finish in the 220 in 23.5. Bob Roos continued to impress by taking both the mile and two mile runs. Elsewhere it was a 1-2 Hope finish in the 880 with Fred Yonkman winning in 2:09.2 and Carl Schroeder finishing second. Howie Meyer took the shot with a toss of 40' 2" and Bob Moolenaar was first in the pole vault with 10' 3." Yonkman and Carl Van Farowe were part of a three-way tie for first in the high jump.

Hope's next outing was a three-point, 67-64 loss to Kalamazoo in Holland. The Dutchmen won all of the field events but the Hornets' Mel Reed won both dashes and both hurdle races. The only Dutch victories in the running events were those of Bob Roos in the mile and two mile. Hope field event winners were Clayt Borgman in the javelin, 161' 9;" Bob Moolenaar in the broad jump; Bud Vande Wege in the pole vault, 10' 6;" Howie "Nails" Meyer in the shot put, 40' 10 1/2;" Fred Yonkman in the discus, 109' 3;" Carl Van Farowe and Yonkman in the high jump, 5' 10."

The Dutchmen bounced back from the tough loss with an impressive win over Alma in another home meet on May 5. The 81 2/5 to 48 3/5 victory included nine Hope firsts to five for Alma. Fred Yonkman was a triple winner in the unusual combination of the 880 yard run, discus, and high jump. The latter was a four-way tie including Carl Van Farowe. Vande Wege's 11' vault took that event and was his personal best. Roos again won the distance runs, and football halfback Bill Bocks won the 440. Meyer improved his shot put mark to 40' 11" in chalking up another first, and Jim Dykema won the low hurdles.

Hope's fourth home meet of the season involved an improving Calvin team and was close throughout. A sweep of the shot put by "Nails" Meyer, Neil Droppers, and Jerry Van Duine aided the Dutch cause. Also in the early going it was Vande Wege winning the pole vault and Van Farowe and Yonkman in a tie for first in the high jump. The action then moved to the 22nd Street track where, in the absence of Ron Bos, Calvin won both the 100 and 220. Hope kept pace, with Roos winning the mile and two-mile. Also in the distances, a barefoot Larry Fabunmi added three valuable points by taking second in the mile. Yonkman and Carl Schroeder salvaged second and third in the 880, but Hope could manage only a two-point, 64-62 lead going into the meet's final event, the mile relay. At this point a weary but buoyant Ron Bos arrived at the track. He had just won number one singles and doubles (with Warren Exo) to defeat Hillsdale 4-3 in tennis. As the meet hung in the balance, Bos was pressed into service to run the anchor leg of the mile relay. His longest distance to that point had been 220 yards, but true champions welcome challenges. At the end of a long day Bos responded with a 53-flat 440 to win the relay and give Hope the 69-62 victory.

A 74-57 victory at Alma on May 12 gave the team a 5-2 dual meet record, the best in several years. Hope's point total of 74 was accomplished despite the absence of Yonkman and Vande Wege. Three new Hope records were recorded when Bob Roos ran the mile in 4:37, Jack De Waard did the 220 low hurdles (straightaway) in 26.8, and Carl Van Farowe cleared 5' 11 3/4" in the high jump. Carl's leap bettered the 5' 10 3/4" mark shared by himself and Coach Russ De Vette. Ron Bos was in top form with 10.0 and 22.9 victories in the 100 and 220, and Carl Schdroeder won the 880 in 2:09. Hope's mile relay team of Nevin Webster, Bill Bocks, Jack De Waard, and Jack De Vries, won the event in 3:42. Van Farowe's 16.2 in the high hurdles was also a winner.

The MIAA meet was held at Kalamazoo on May 18. The Hope squad had seemingly peaked at the right time, but misfortune struck as Ron Bos was stricken with the flu and spent most of the week in bed. As the competition got under way Bos made a game effort but had to settle for fourth in the 220 and fifth in the 100. Fred Yonkman recorded Hope's only first with a jump of 6' even. The mark eclipsed Van Farowe's school record of the previous week. Bob Roos set new Hope records in the mile and two- mile with times of 4:35 and 10:26.1, but had to settle for third and second in those races. Van Farowe ended in a five-way tie for second in the high jump and managed a fifth in the high hurdles while Jack De Waard was fourth in the low hurdles. Larry Fabunmi was third behind Roos in the two mile and Carl Schroeder finished fourth the 880. Hope's mile relay team also finished fourth to give the Dutchmen 28 points and a fourth place tie with Adrian. As expected, Albion won the championship with 81 1/2 points, followed by Hillsdale with 37, and Kalamazoo with 36. Alma finished behind Hope and Adrian. Hope's Field Day performance was not spectacular but the program had shown vast improvement and stood poised for a championship run in 1952.

Coach Al Timmer's 1951 golf team also finished fourth. Dich Huff and Dick Kruizenga returned from the '50 squad and were joined by Bob Visser, Arend D. "Don" Lubbers, and Don Prentice. As in track, the team did well in dual matches but stumbled somewhat in the conference meet. Victories were recorded over Muskegon J.C., 15-0, Alma, 9-6, Kalamazoo, 9-6, and Adrian, 11 1/2 -3 1/2. Losses were to Albion, 14 1/2-1/2, Calvin, 8-7, and Hillsdale 14-1. Hope's match with Grand Rapids Junior College ended in a 7 1/2-7 1/2 tie. The MIAA meet was held at the Kalamazoo Country Club on May 17 and 18. Albion freshman Al Nichols was medalist and led his team to the title. Hillsdale finished in the runner-up spot while Kalamazoo was third, Hope fourth, Alma fifth, and Adrian sixth. Dick Huff was low man for Hope with a 2-day total of 165. In the race for the All-Sports Trophy it was Albion winning with 55 points, Kalamazoo second with 40, Alma third with 37, Hope fourth with 36, Hillsdale fifth with 34, and Adrian sixth with 5.

In midsummer, 1951, lst Lt. Russ De Vette was recalled to active duty with the U.S. Marine Corps. He left Holland for the Quantico, Virginia, Marine Base on July 1 accompanied by wife Doris and nine-month old daughter Christie. They would not return until January, 1953. The college was fortunate to find a replacement in Nick Yonker, who had spent the 1950-51 school year at Columbia University pursuing a masters' degree in philosophy. His immediate duties were to serve as backfield coach and instructor in the Department of Physical Education. P.E. instructor Mary Breid was granted a leave of absence to do graduate work at the University of Indiana.

On September 4, Coaches Vanderbush, Weller, and Yonker welcomed a football squad of 35 to pre-season workouts. The 14 lettermen were led by Co-Captains Gene Nyenhuis and Fred Yonkman. Both were tackles. Other linemen included ends Fuzz Bauman and Jack Vander Velde, guards Jim Van Hoeven and Lloyd Beekman, and centers John Newton and Neil Droppers. Quarterback Ron Schipper was the only returning backfield regular, but two talented freshmen runners were soon to be heard from. Halfback Jim Williard had been a standout at Caledonia High School while fullback John Hamilton hailed from Rockford. Donald "Zeke" Piersma nailed down the other starting halfback spot despite the fact that he had never before played college football.

Hope opened against Michigan Normal in a night game at Ypsilanti on September 22. The Hurons scored first in the opening period when Segmen went over from the two, but the conversion attempt by quarterback Paige was blocked. Normal continued to roll when early in the second quarter a bad snap to punter Hamilton gave them the ball on the Hope 21. Paige passed to Pope for the touchdown and this time made good on his conversion. Hope's first-game jitters continued mid-way in the quarter when the Dutchmen mishandled a punt and the Hurons recovered deep in Hope territory. Paige went off tackle for the score, converted, and Normal had a three-touchdown, 20-0 lead. Late in the half Hope got back into the game when Fred Yonkman pounced on a Normal fumble. Ron Schipper threw a touchdown strike to Jack Vander Velde and Bud Prins' kick made it 20-7 at the intermission. Hope was tough on defense in the second half but neither team could cross the goal line, and the Dutchmen went home a 20 to 7 loser.

On September 29 Hope entertained Carroll of Wisconsin in a night contest at Riverview Park. After a scoreless first quarter, Carroll's Emil Pontow scored on a 28- yard end sweep cutback and Dick Irving's kick was good for the 7-0 lead. Hope responded when, from his own 46, Skipper passed to Piersma, who got behind the secondary, took the ball on the 17 and went in for his first college touchdown. Bud Prins made it 7-7. Just before the half freshman Jim Williard electrified the crowd by intercepting a pass and racing 75 yards to score. The play, however, was nullified by a clipping penalty and the teams went to the locker rooms with a 7-7 tie. In the third period quarterback Pete Dellios scored on a bootleg and Irving's kick gave the Pioneers a 13-7 lead. In the game's closing minutes Howie "Nails" Meyer recovered a Carroll fumble on the Hope 45. The Dutchmen moved the ball to the 11, where Hamilton circled right end for the score. Under considerable pressure, Bud Prins made good on the point that would give Hope the narrow 14-13 victory. Williard intercepted a Jim Vetta pass as the gun went off.

Hope traveled to Albion on October 6 to play in a misty rain. For nearly three quarters the game was a stand-off. In games between equals, a lone mistake can often make the difference. Hope was offside on an Albion punt giving the Britons first and 10 on the Hope 49. Frank Joranko methodically moved his team to the 11. Key plays were a Joranko-to-John Walker 12-yard pass and a 16-yard run by Joranko. At this point the Hope defense stiffened and held for three downs. On fourth down guard Ray Loeshner dropped back and kicked a 20-yard field goal for the game's only score. A Hope comeback try began when Williard returned a punt to the Albion 48. On successive running plays it was Piersma to the 35, Hamilton to the 30, and Hamilton to the 10 for a first down. Hamilton and Williard bucked to the two. On fourth down the call was a left end sweep by Piersma. Chuck Stanton, Albion's right end, diagnosed the play and broke through to stop Zeke on the line of scrimmage. Years later, Loeschner, as president of Olivet College, and Joranko, as athletic director at Albion, would recall the sweet 3-0 victory.

In marked contrast to the Albion game, the contest with Kalamazoo was a high-scoring match-up between quarterbacks Ron Schipper and Phil Dillman. The game was played at Riverview on Saturday night, October 6. Kalamazoo drew first blood when diminutive (5' 2") halfback Roger Winter got free off tackle and raced 61 yards to score. The kick was not good and the "K" lead was 6-0. Hope responded when Jim Williard got behind the Kalamazoo secondary and took Schipper's pass for a 42-yard scoring play. Bud Prins' kick gave Hope the early edge, 7-6. In the second quarter Hope moved from its own 35 in nine plays to score on a one-yard plunge by Hamilton. Prins' conversion made it 14-6, but the Hornets came back with five runs and five successful passes to put the ball on the Hope four. Winter went in for his second touchdown, and this time the kick closed the gap to 14-13. Hope lost no time in engineering another drive from the Dutch 36. Three runs and six passes culminated in an eight-yard toss to Piersma for Hope's third touchdown. Prins' consistent toe made it 21-13. Kalamazoo took the kickoff and after five plays, fullback Al Patzer broke through the line, got free, and streaked 75 yards for the score. The missed conversion left Hope with a narrow 21-19 halftime lead. In the third period it was Kalamazoo's turn to move with a long drive from their own 23. Van Horn went the final three yards and this time Monty Nye's kick was good. The Hornets had regained the lead, 26-21, but it was short-lived. With an effective mixture of runs and passes, Schipper moved his team to the Kalamazoo 18, then rifled a touchdown pass to Fuzz Bauman. Prins' fourth point of the day put Hope out front, 28-26. Not satisfied, the Dutchmen added one more score on five Schipper passes and a one-yard touchdown run by Piersma. Sure-handed Fuzz Bauman held the ball for Prins' fifth straight conversion. To the crowd's delight, the game had assumed the proportions of a track meet and the scoring was not finished. A final Kalamazoo drive featured the Dillman to Jim Stefoff combination with Dillman going over. Two missed conversions gave Hope the 35-33 victory. Both quarterbacks were brilliant, as Schipper completed 10 of 18 and Dillman went 12 for 25.

Football gave way to basketball momentarily on October 16, when President Lubbers announced that Hope's new coach would be former All-MIAA center John E. Visser. Visser, an assistant professor of history on the Hope faculty, would be assisted by Nick Yonker. It was agreed that Bud Hinga would act in an advisory capacity until Yonker was free at the end of the football season.

The Hope squad journeyed to Alma on October 20 to meet the favored Scots in their Homecoming game. Coach Lloyd Eaton's team was the pre-season pick to cop the MIAA crown and the Dutch were prepared for a struggle. Miscues marred the opening when Alma fumbled the opening kickoff. Hope moved to the one yard line, then fumbled the ball back to the Scots, but the Hope defense held and Alma's punt into a strong wind went only to the Hope 22. A Schipper-to-Williard pass placed the ball on the four, where three running plays were stymied by the Alma defense. Schipper's fourth down pass found Fuzz Bauman in the end zone and Bud Prins made it 7-0 Hope. A short time later Alma's Bob Mohre intercepted a Schipper pass and the turnover became a score when halfback Dub Martin went in for the touchdown. The kick, however, was not good and Hope still led, 7-6. Three plays after the kickoff John Hamilton broke free for a 41-yard touchdown gallop and Prins added the point to increase Hope's margin to 14-6 at halftime. In the third period Vanderbush turned to the time-honored Statue of Liberty play to cross up the hard-charging Scots. Speedy Jim Williard eluded all defenders as he raced 75 yards to score before the stunned Homecoming crowd. Hope's lead now stood at 21-6. Late in the third quarter Alma narrowed the gap when Dub Martin scored his second touchdown, this time on a left end sweep from the 10. With the score at 21-13 and a quarter to go, the Dutch defenders rose to the challenge. Gene Nyenhuis, Jack Vander Velde, and Bill Bocks were outstanding in preserving the 21-13 victory. It would be Hope's best defensive effort of the season.

Four thousand Homecoming fans turned out on October 27 to witness Hope's first-ever meeting with De Pauw University of Greencastle, Indiana. The Dutchmen chose to receive and in 17 plays, marched the length of the field. Hamilton went the final 10 yards to score and Prins' conversion gave the home team an early 7-0 lead. But on the ensuing kickoff a well-executed reverse brought the ball all the way to the Hope 49. Eight plays later the Tigers were on the board as Steve Nagy took it in from the 10. Bob Stevens' kick was wide, but Hope was offside and his second attempt was good. With the score at 7-7, Dave Kempker recovered a fumble on the Hope 24. Three plays later from the 37, Schipper found Jack Vander Velde behind the defenders on the De Pauw 38. He gathered in the pass and went the rest of the way. Bud Prins' kick was blocked making it Hope 13, De Pauw 7. In the second quarter Neil Droppers was responsible for Hope's second fumble recovery, this one on the De Pauw 26. Hope was stalled on the seven-yard line and Bud Prins was called upon for a field goal attempt. His kick was true and the Dutchmen led, 16-7. Hope capitalized on yet another turnover when Zeke Piersma intercepted a Tiger pass on the Hope 41. Eight plays advanced the ball to the De Pauw 14, where Schipper hit Piersma in the end zone. Prins' kick increased the Hope lead to 23-7. At this point the Tigers, aware of their 5-0 record, tightened up their game with a 10-play scoring drive. The touchdown came on a pass from Bob Stevens to end Penfield Faber. Hope blocked the kick, and the score stood 23-13 at the intermission. The second half belonged to the team from Indiana. A nine-play drive in the third quarter netted their third touchdown as Nagy scored on a sneak. The kick was wide but the once-substantial Hope lead was narrowed to 23-19. De Pauw continued the pressure and late in the fourth quarter Nagy scored again, this time from the two-foot line. The Dutchmen again stormed through to block the kick but the damage had been done and the Tigers increased their season mark to 6-0 with the 25-23 victory.

Conditions were markedly different when Hope traveled to Adrian for a night game on November 3. The Bulldogs of Coach Ted Boyett were without a win and attrition had reduced his squad to 24 men. Virtually no spectators had braved the 20 degree temperature or the snowstorm which swept across Adrian's Island Park Field. The Dutchmen, however, were still smarting from the De Pauw debacle and the weather was not a deterrent. Hope scored in the first quarter when John Hamilton rambled 55 yards on a fullback sweep around right end. Bud Prins' kick hit the crossbar and bounced back to leave the score at 6-0. The next Hope drive began on the Dutch 35 and included nine plays. Hamilton went the final 11 yards and the Prins conversion made it 13-0. Late in the half Piersma intercepted on the Hope 15, and four plays later Hamilton scored his third touchdown, this time 50 yards from the midfield stripe. Co-Captain Gene Nyenhuis was given the honor of attempting the point after and made good on the only kick of his career. With the halftime score at 20-0 and the weather deteriorating, the coaches agreed to shorten the second half quarters from 15 to 12 minutes. In the third period it was Jim Williard's turn to break loose for a 35-yard scoring romp. Howard "Nails" Meyer attempted the extra point, but the kick was not good. Late in the contest Adrian recovered a Hope fumble on the Dutch 19. A Bill Edinger-to-Jim Mohler scoring pass broke the shutout. Gerry Wallace scored the extra point on an end sweep making the final Hope 26, Adrian 7. The Hope bus arrived in Holland at 4:30 a.m. Monday's practice was cancelled.

On a gray November 10, Hope sought to wrap up a co-championship at Riverview Park. As so often in recent years, the force in the way was Hillsdale College. This time, however, the Dale ranks were depleted by injuries and it would be a Hope afternoon. The onslaught began with a first quarter Hope march of 63 yards, with Hamilton going in from the three. The Prins conversion was good and the scoreboard read 7-0. The Dutch lost no time in scoring again. A Schipper-to-Bauman pass covered 50 yards and placed the ball on the Hillsdale four. Hamilton again plunged into the end zone and Prins repeated with the point: 14-0. In the second period Hope ended a 65-yard march with a Schipper-to-Vander Velde pass for the touchdown and Prins made it 21-0 at the half. In the third quarter a screen pass from Schipper to Williard was good for 43 yards. Piersma went over from the one and the Prins kick increased the lead to 28-0. In the fourth period Hope capped an impressive 96-yard march when fullback Don Hondorp scored from the four. Prins' fifth successful conversion made it 35-0. Hope's sixth score was set up by a Bill Bocks interception on the Dale 30 which he returned to the 14. After five plays Williard went over from the two. Bud Prins string was finally broken when he missed the conversion attempt. With the score 41-0, Hope was not finished. Zeke Piersma, who had already scored a touchdown and had two more called back due to penalties, intercepted a Don Tallman pass on the Hillsdale 32 and took it all the way to make it 47-0. Fuzz Bauman attempted the point but lacked Bauman the holder and missed the kick. In the closing minute the Bearcats made it to the Hope one, but Bill Heydorn and Don Vander Toll tackled Jim Nelson to end the game, Hope 47, Hillsdale 0. Al Vanderbush's long- denied championship had been accomplished before the home crowd in no uncertain terms. The record would show that they had also beaten co-champion Alma, 21-13.

A celebration was in order and accordingly, Monday, November 12, was declared "Glory Day", with classes dismissed after chapel. One game remained on the schedule, a non-league contest at Beloit, Wisconsin, on November 17. It was a day when Hope would live and die by the pass. Early in the game a long aerial from Schipper to Bauman put Hope in scoring position and Schipper followed it with a 10-yard strike to Williard for the touchdown. Prins' kick made it 7-0 and the Dutchmen were off and running against a Beloit team boasting a 7-1 record, its best since 1900. In the second quarter it was Schipper passing to Bauman for Hope's second score. The point was missed and Hope's lead was 13-0. The Buccaneers retaliated when quarterback Steve James broke off tackle for 21 yards and the touchdown. The kick by Tony Paris made it 13-7. Again, with but 20 seconds remaining in the half, fullback Paris scored from the one and kicked the point to give Beloit a lead it would not relinquish. Defensive play in the second half was superb by both teams, but midway in the third quarter center Bill Kaulfus intercepted a Schipper pass on the Beloit 37 and turned it into a 63-yard touchdown run. As the season moved to its conclusion, Hope, in a determined drive, reached the Beloit five, but Beloit intercepted Schipper's pass in the end zone and the game was over with Beloit on top, 20 to 13. Coach Al had high praise for the defensive line play of Gene Nyenhuis and Tom Ritter, and also that of Dave Kempker in the secondary. Vanderbush also expressed the opinion that Beloit was the best team Hope had played during the season, and that the Hope aggregation had been well-treated by the host school. Such reflected favorably on the overall class of Beloit College.

Hope ended at 4-1 in the MIAA and 5-4 overall. There were more than enough honors to go around. Eight men were named to the All-MIAA team: Gene Nyenhuis, Lloyd Beekman, Don Piersma, and Jack Vander Velde made the defensive team, while John Hamilton, Ken Bauman, Fred Yonkman, and Jim Van Hoeven were picked offensively.

Quarterback Ron Schipper
Hope's Most Valuable Player - 1951

After leading Hope to a co-championship in 1951, Schipper embarked on a remarkable coaching career. Following eight years in the high school ranks at Northville and Jackson, Michigan, he moved to Central College of Iowa where he would become one of the nation's most successful small college coaches. Competing in the Iowa Intercollegiate Athletic Conference, his teams won the league title an amazing 19 times in a 30 year period. A perennial qualifier for the NCAA Division III playoffs, Central won the national championship in 1974. His son Tim was a member of that team.

The 1951 Hope College Football Squad
MIAA Co-Champions With Alma

Front Row L to R: Trainer Jack Shouten, Howard Meyer, Neil Droppers, Ron Schipper, Co-Captain Fred Yonkman, Co-Captain Gene Nyenhuis, Tom Ritter, Jack Vander Velde, Bill Bocks, Head Coach Al Vanderbush. **Row 2:** Lloyd Beekman, John Hamilton, Donald "Zeke" Piersma, Dave Kempker, Lynn Post, Ken "Fuzz" Bauman, Don Vander Toll, Herb Morgan, Bill Heydorn. **Row 3:** Assistant Coach Ken Weller, Jim Van Hoeven, Tom Keizer, Bob Hoeksema, Paul Bos, Jim Williard, Robert "Bud" Prins, John Newton, Backfield Coach Nick Yonker, Manager John Johnson. **Row 4:** Manager Bill Forth, Don Miller, Don Maxam, Harold Bazan, Paul Klomparens, Bob Schriemer, Don York, Don Howard, Don Prentice, Herman Nienhuis, Manager John Kenwell.

Ron Schipper was edged out in the balloting by Kalamazoo's Phil Dillman, but Schipper was elected Hope's Most Valuable Player by his teammates. The Alumni "H" Club, under President Ekdal Buys, hosted a banquet for the team on November 29. The affair took place in the Juliana Room of Durfee Hall and included guest coaches and players from several high schools. Speaker for the evening was Watson Spoelstra, Hope's first All-MIAA basketball player and now a sportswriter for the **Detroit Times**. He was accompanied by Van Patrick, radio broadcaster for the Detroit Tigers and Lions. Both were well-received, but the evening reached its climax in the simple tribute of Co-Captain Gene Nyenhuis to his coach. Nyenhuis, in presenting "Big Al" with the trophy, commented, "He is the best coach I've ever seen, and one reason is because he's fair. If you play for Big Al's team, you know you've earned the right to play." Vanderbush was named MIAA Coach of the Year by the **Detroit Times**.

The championship season in football obscured, to some extent, a fine performance by the cross country team. Coach Lars Granberg was granted a leave of absence to do graduate work at the University of Chicago. Sociology Professor Bob Vanderham agreed to take over the team. Wayne Tripp was captain of the squad that included Bob Roos, Larry Fabunmi, Jack Corey, Bob Hamilton, Neil Van Heest, Nevin Webster, Walt Vander Meulen, John Schrier, George Van Zoeren, Jim Brower, and John Hume. Hope lost its opening meet at Albion on October 6 but the closeness of the 26-32 score raised some eyebrows. Bob Roos finished first and Wayne Trip was third. Fabunmi tripped and fell but still managed a sixth place finish. Bob Hamilton was 10th and Neil Van Heest 11th.

In a double dual in Kalamazoo on October 13 it was Western Michigan 17, Hope 43, and Albion again 26 to 32 for Hope. The Dutchmen hosted Kalamazoo College on October 27 and were victorious, 17-38. Circumstances necessitated shortening the course to three miles but it is doubtful if this had any bearing on the 1-2-3 finish by Roos, Tripp, and Fabunmi. The only other competition was the season-ending MIAA meet held at Hillsdale. As expected, Albion was again the champion with 24 points, but Hope made a strong showing in second place with 42. Kalamazoo was third with 89 and Alma fourth with 96. Hillsdale was fifth and Adrian sixth, but their scores were not available. It marked Hope's highest finish since the sport was revived by the league in 1947.

Basketball was now underway with new coach John Visser at the helm. Visser announced that he would employ a fast break style of offense similar to that used by Coach Hinga in Visser's playing days. The wealth of talent which greeted him might well have made any offense effective. Bob Visser, younger brother of the coach, Ron Bos, Jun Bremer, Jerry Jacobson, and Ken Van Regenmorter had gained valuable experience while earning their spurs against strong opponents during the 1950-51 season and were ready to go. Zeke Piersma and Dave Kempker were also proven performers. Center Bob Hendrickson from Grand Rapids Ottawa Hills was a blue chip freshman who would be heard from in his four years as a varsity regular.

Coach John E. Visser

In 1951 Visser was chosen to succeed Russ De Vette as basketball coach when De Vette was recalled to active duty with the U.S. Marine Corps. Visser's 1951-52 and '52-'53 teams won MIAA Championships. Following his coaching career he became a college admistrator and served as president of Emporia State University in Kansas.

An early-season scrimmage in Kalamazoo against Western Michigan indicated that Visser's talented individuals were not yet a team. The first test came at Valparaiso on November 24. The Crusaders of Coach Ken Suesens were somewhat surprised when Hope posted a 43-41 halftime lead, but things fell apart in the first five minutes of the second half and Valparaiso went on to an easy 82-68 victory. Willard Doehrman with 23 and Eric Domroese with 20 did most of the damage. Bos and Visser led Hope with 18 and 17.

Captain Jun Bremer, hook shot artist from the pivot, was asked to move to a guard spot to make room for big Bob Hendrickson, and the strategy paid off as Hope opened the MIAA season at Alma on December 8. The Dutchmen started slowly and trailed at halftime, 38-27, but Hendrickson's strong board game kept Hope in the game and his 22 points led all scorers. Hope's chances appeared grim when Bos and Jacobson fouled out late in the second quarter, but Piersma and Kempker quickly took up the slack. With 40 seconds remaining in the game, Bob Visser intercepted an Alma pass and scored drawing Hope within one at 62-61. Hope regained possession and Dave Kempker's outcourt shot with 12 seconds left secured the dramatic 63-62 victory. Visser's 14 points followed Hendrickson in the scoring column, while for

Alma it was Kirk Hamilton with 20 and Bill Healy with 12.

Hope met an undermanned Adrian team in the Armory on December 13. Adrian's slim chances were lessened when leading scorer Bob Ohrman fouled out late in the first half. Hope's 37-22 halftime advantage was too much to overcome, especially when Jack Dace fouled out in the third quarter. Visser substituted freely enroute to the 88-30 victory. Zeke Piersma led Hope with 16, followed by Bos with 13 and Kempker with 12. Hugh Moran had 10 for the Bulldogs. Hope's only negative was a sprained ankle sustained by Hendrickson in the third quarter.

In a rare New Years' Eve appearance, the Dutchmen hosted the Generals of Washington and Lee University. The team from Lexington, Virginia, was coached by Scotty Hamilton and proved to be a tough opponent. Hope's 31-28 halftime margin was due in part to another fine defensive effort by Jun Bremer. The Generals' Dave Hedge fouled out in the fourth quarter with his team down by only three. This seemed to be a turning point and Hope increased the advantage to the final 68-57 win. Jerry Jacobson was hot for Hope with 21 counters and Ron Bos was not far behind with 19. Jay Handlan had 21 for Washington and Lee.

Coach Walt Sprandel brought the defending champion Albion team to the Armory on January 8. In a game that was close all the way, Hope had to contend constantly with the superb talents of Ced Dempsey and John Porter. Late in the game Dempsey scored 7 straight points to give the Britons a brief lead, but a strong finish by the Dutchmen gave them the contest, 79 to 73. Bos and Visser, with 24 and 19, outmatched Dempsey with 23 and Porter with 16. With four straight victories, a confident Hope team looked forward to the season's first meeting with arch-rival Calvin.

Calvin Coach Chuck Bult was well aware of the many facets of Hope-Calvin wars, and his veteran team was well prepared. John Visser, on the other hand, had never really experienced a Calvin game. In his playing days at Hope, Calvin was not on the schedule, and now as a first-year coach it was naturally difficult to anticipate the emotional impact that would place the game in a category by itself. His baptism came on January 11, when 4,400 fans descended on the Grand Rapids Civic Auditorium. From the opening whistle it was a Calvin show, and by halftime the Knights had built an impressive 39-25 lead that ballooned to 30 points midway in the second half. Calvin's team effort included 17 points by Duane Rosendahl, 16 from Roger Postmus, 14 by Stu Sisco, Butts Kool with 12, and Mel De Stigter with 11. Calvin's complete domination of the game was reflected in Hope's 19.5 shooting percentage and by the final 42-point margin of victory. Ron Bos managed to collect 14 points in the 85-43 defeat, but no one else reached double figures.

There was little time to lament the regrettable showing against the Knights. The next day the team journeyed across state to take on Detroit Tech in the motor city. Tech managed a one-point halftime lead at 33-32 but succumbed to strong Dutch defense in the fourth quarter. Bob Visser with 19 points, helped put Hope back in the victory column. He was followed by Hendrickson and Jacobson with 10 each. Westbrook was top man for Tech with 20. The final score was Hope 59, Detroit 54, and the trip home seemed somehow shorter than the previous night's trip from Grand Rapids to Holland.

Hope's troubles were not quite over. In Kalamazoo's Treadway Gym on January 15 the team was unable to match its defensive effort against Detroit Tech. The Hornets of Dob Grow went on a shooting rampage with Manny Glasser's 28 points leading the way. He was joined by John Stommen with 23, John Gideon with 17, Phil Dillman with 11, and Roger Winter, also with 11. Hendrickson was high for Hope with 20, followed by Jacobson with 17, and Bos with 14 in the 91-78 setback.

On January 19, in their fourth straight game away from home, the Dutchmen finally turned the corner against Hillsdale. Coach Visser knew his team was "on" when brother Bob scored 20 first-half points to give Hope a 44-33 lead. The Dutch cause was also aided by 24 of 28 from the free throw line for 86 percent, Hope's best of the season. Visser's 28-point total was backed up by 16 from Bos, 15 from Jacobson, and 13 from Hendrickson. An outstanding 35-point performance by forward Tom Walsh could not prevent the Dales from dropping the contest, 84-72.

In the space of three days Hope notched two victories over hapless Ferris Institute. In Big Rapids on January 23 the "run and gun" Dutchmen hit the century mark with a 100-73 win. Zeke Piersma enjoyed a hot night with 22 points to lead his team. Ron Bos pumped in 21, Visser had 16, and Hendrickson 14. Schubert and Pieropen were high for the Bulldogs with 17 and 16. The game at the Armory on January 26 proved to be somewhat lackluster. Fifty-seven fouls were called and neither team shot well. When Bob Hendrickson fouled out in the third quarter, Jun Bremer was moved to his old spot, where he employed his patented hook shot to lead the team with 17. Hendrickson had 15 before his departure while Bos and Visser each contributed 14. Leno Pieropen showed well for Ferris with 23.

Following the semester break, Hope resumed MIAA action by hosting Alma on February 9. Hope's narrow 41-40 halftime lead was expanded after the intermission, when Visser and Bos took over the game. Their point totals of 31 and 30 led the Dutch attack while Hendrickson added 13. The Scots, who had played Calvin on Tuesday and Lawrence Tech on Thursday, were noticeably tired at the end, but Bob Peuscher, Bill Healy, and Bob Mohre, with 24, 23, and 18 points, performed well in absorbing the 97-78 defeat.

Zeke Piersma did not make the trip to Adrian on February 11 due to a sprained ankle. When the remainder of the team arrived they found things in general disarray. For a variety of reasons Coach Ted Boyett's squad had been reduced to seven players. Coach Visser decided to let each of his squad members play about one half of the game. Under this arrangement the Dutch led 51-25 at halftime and went on to a 93-64 victory. For Hope it was Visser with 20, Bos 18, Jacobson 14, and Al Nelson eight. Adrian's Bob Ohrman, who had fouled out of the game in Holland, remained to the end and collected 25 points.

The game at Albion on February 16 began well for the Dutch, but became a barn burner at the end. Hope built what appeared to be a comfortable halftime lead of 52-38 but saw it gradually reduced to a 73-73 tie in the fourth quarter. There was concern on the Dutch bench when Jun Bremer fouled out with six minutes remaining, but substitute Bob Bolema was equal to the task, as he scored seven points and was strong on defense. Hope's 93-91 victory was finally secured despite 33 points by John Porter and 23 by Ced Dempsey. Hope's team effort showed Visser with 22, Hendrickson and Bos with 21 each, and Bremer with 14.

Hope's chance to wrap up its first title since 1947 came on February 19, when Dob Grow's Kalamazoo quintet invaded the Armory. The only blot on Hope's league record was the 91-78 loss administered by the Hornets on January 15. The Dutch were determined that history should not repeat itself but could manage only a five-point, 43-38 halftime lead. In the second half, however, with the championship on the line and the home crowd behind them, the Hope five pulled away to a 95-76 win and the trophy was theirs. Bob Hendrickson was tough all the way and led his team with 21. He was followed by Bos with 17, Bremer with 15, and Jacobson with 14. Ken Van Regenmorter, playing less than half the game, scored 11. Manny Glasser had 19 and Phil Dillman 18 for Kalamazoo.

The new MIAA champions played their last MIAA game at home on February 23 against Hillsdale. The anticlimactic nature of the contest found the Dutchmen battling a letdown throughout the first half. Hope's narrow 37-35 lead was evidence that a good Hillsdale team was out to take some glitter from the newly-won title. The scare proved incentive enough and the Dutchmen prevailed, 87-72. Hope's rebounding strength was a definite factor, along with 21 points from Visser and 20 each from Hendrickson and Bos. Tom Walsh played a strong game with 21 for the losers and Hinkle added 20.

Incentives were not lacking in the season finale against Calvin on February 26. The Calvin student body descended upon Holland in the late afternoon and lined up along ninth Street waiting for the doors to open. Hope students and townspeople joined the scramble for 1,200 shaky bleacher seats in the Armory. As usual, standing room was at a premium and all hoped there would be no fire. Fire of another sort inspired John Visser's team. On January 11 they had been humbled by the Knights in Hope's worst defeat in the long series. Now, riding the crest of an eight-game winning streak, the team felt the need to prove itself one more time. From the start the ingredients for fast break basketball were in place.

Hours before gametime eager spectators line up outside the Holland Armory for the 1952 Hope-Calvin game. The building's 1,200 seating capacity was decidedly inadequate and standing room crowds posed a treat to fire regulations.

Hendrickson and Bremer dominated the defensive boards and the outlet pass was quickly effected. Numerous three-on-two situations resulted with Bos in the middle, Visser and Jacobson on the sides. Chuck Bult's crew ended up committing more than its share of fouls, and Hope cashed in on 19 of 30 free throws. Calvin, meanwhile, had a cold night from the line, getting only five of 15. Hope left the floor at halftime with a 46-30 lead and did not let up in the second half. Midway in the period the Hope crowd's attention shifted to the individual performance of Ron Bos, who was well on the way to a new Hope scoring record. Sensing this, teammates fed him the ball, but Bos, not a selfish player, often passed it back. This Alphonse-Gaston routine resulted in several missed opportunities to score, but finally, with 36 points and a new Hope record, R. Bos was removed by his coach to a standing ovation. The final talley was Hope 93, Calvin 67. Jacobson followed Bos in scoring with 18, Hendrickson had 13, Bremer 10 and Visser nine. For Calvin it was Rog Postmus with 18, mostly from outcourt, Duane Rosendahl with 16, Stu Sisco with 15, and Preston "Butts" Kool had 10.

Coach Visser's initial year could not have ended on a more positive note. The team stood 14-3 on the season including a nine-game streak to close out the year. Their 9-1 MIAA record was good for an undisputed championship, and yet another exciting chapter had been written in the Hope-Calvin series. Ron Bos and Bob Visser were named to the All-MIAA team and Bremer was elected Hope's Most Valuable Player.

In the All-Sports race Hope found itself in the lead with 27 points to 23 for Albion. The usual projections were made

Hope College Basketball Team - 1951-52
MIAA Champions

Front Row L to R: Bob Bolema, Al Nelson, Captain Andrew "Jun" Bremer, Bob Hendrickson, Bob Visser. **Middle Row:** Assistant Coach Nick Yonker, Willard Rink, Ron Bos, Ken Van Regenmorter, Jerry Jacobson, Head Coach John Visser. **Top Row:** Freshman Team Coach Jack Schouten, Jim Willyard, Don "Zeke" Piersma, Dave Kempker, Director of Athletics Milton "Bud" Hinga. **Missing from picture:** Norm Schuiling.

for spring sports, but this time with considerable anticipation. Track and field had been a question mark for several years, but Russ De Vette's two-year building program was about to pay off despite the fact that he would not be around to witness the results. Coach Al Vanderbush now returned to the post he had relinquished to De Vette in 1949. He was greeted by 14 lettermen plus a group of promising freshmen that included big Bob Hendrickson, late of the basketball team. The team was off to a modest start on March 29 at the Central Michigan relays at Mount Pleasant. Hope's medley relay team of Glenn Straatsma, Carl Schroeder, Bob Roos, and Larry Fabunmi took fifth place and few took notice. But on April 22 at Calvin, Hope captured nine first places enroute to downing the Knights, 85 1/2 - 45 1/2. Fabunmi set a new Hope record in the two-mile with a 10:25.8 performance, Ron Bos won the 100 and 220, Carl Van Farowe won both hurdle races and tied Fred Yonkman for first in the high jump, Clayt Borgman took the javelin, Rod Wissink the pole vault, and the Hope mile relay team closed out the day with a victory.

On April 30 perennial power Albion came to Holland to record its 20th dual meet victory in a row. The Britons, however, were forced to work for the their win as the final score showed Albion with 70 1/2 points to Hope's 60 1/2. The Dutchmen garnered seven firsts to eight for the Britons. Albion's Jack Sharp scored 12 1/4 points as he won both dashes, took third in the broad jump, and anchored the winning relay team. For Hope it was Bob Hendrickson taking both the broad jump and shot put, Van Farowe was again first in both hurdle races, Borgman took the javelin, Fred Yonkman the high jump, and Larry Fabunmi lowered his two-mile record to 10:23.6. In the low hurdle race Jack De Waard was leading Hope to a 1-2 finish when he fell over the final hurdle.

In a meet at Hillsdale on May 3 the Dales won eight firsts to six for Hope, but the final score read Hope 73, Hillsdale 58. Best performance of the day was Walt Vander Meulen's 21' 6" broad jump. Hope's other firsts included Bob Hendrickson in the shot, Bob Roos in the mile, Larry Fabunmi in the two-mile, Nevin Webster in the 440, and Fred Yonkman in the high jump. Ron Appledorn, who had transferred to Hillsdale, won the discus and placed second in the javelin. On the same date several Hope trackmen traveled to Grand Rapids and placed second in the Grand Rapids J.C. relays.

The Dutchmen hosted a triangular on May 7 and emerged victorious with 91 points to 63 for Calvin and eight for Alma. The Alma team consisted of only four men. Yonkman won the discus and high jump, Van Farowe took both hurdle races, Hendrickson was first in the shot, Fabunmi in the two mile, and Dave Hondorp in the 440. Hope's mile relay team of Verne Fuder, Walt Vander Meulen, Al Nelson, and Nevin Webster also placed first.

At Kalamazoo on May 10 Hope took the Hornets handily. In winning 10 of the events, Hope piled up a score of 91 1/2 to 38 1/2. Ron Bos breezed to victory in both dashes, Vander Meulen won the broad jump and 440, Hendrickson was again first in the shot, Yonkman captured the discus, Borgman the javelin, and Roos the mile. Borgman and Moolenaar tied for first in the pole vault, and Larry Fabunmi lowered his two mile record to 10:14. Hope won the mile relay by default.

Hope's final tune-up for the conference meet was held at Houseman Field on May 17 with Grand Rapids J.C. furnishing the opposition. The Dutchmen were again impressive with a 96-35 victory. It was a big day for Bob Hendrickson in his home town. His 20-point performance was the result of firsts in shot, broad jump, 100, and 220. Fabunmi again lowered his record as he finished the two mile in 10:07.8 for the day's best performance. Howie Meyer was first in the discus, the vault belonged to Rod Wissink, Roos took the mile, Borgman the javelin, and Byron Aldrich the 880. The mile relay team of Verne Fuder, Fred Yonkman, Al Nelson, and Dave Hondorp was also victorious, with a time of 3:38.5.

The MIAA Field Day meet was held in Kalamazoo on Saturday, May 24. Ron Bos, who held down Hope's number two singles spot in tennis, found himself scrambling between tennis and track. He managed, however, to qualify in both the 100 and 220 before a deluge of rain forced postponement of the finals until the following Monday evening. Monday, May 26, 1952, would be long remembered in the annals of Hope College track and field as the Dutchmen gained their first ever MIAA championship. In an exciting matchup, Coach Vanderbush got an outstanding team effort from his squad to edge favored Albion by a score of 79 4/20 to 75 17/20. Kalamazoo was third with 31, Hillsdale fourth with 15 19/20, Adrian fifth with 13, and Alma sixth with eight. Hope had five first places to four for Albion. Ron Bos played a key role in the championship effort as he edged the Briton's Jack Sharpe in both the 100 and 220 with excellent times of 10.1 and 22.0. Bob Roos took the mile in 4:35.6, Larry Fabunmi the two mile in 10:13.8, and Walt Vander Meulen the broad jump with 21' 8." Besides the gold medal winners, Hope's "supporting cast" included a third and fourth in the mile by Fabunmi and Glenn Straatsma, a third in the 440 by Dave Hondorp, a second and fifth in the 880 by Fred Yonkman and Carl Schroeder, a third in the 120 high hurdles by Carl Van Farowe, second, fourth, and fifth in the 220 low hurdles by Jack De Waard, Hondorp, and Van Farowe, fourth in both the 100 and 220 by big Bob Hendrickson, third and fifth in the two mile by Roos and Straatsma, third and fifth in the broad jump by Hendrickson and Bob Moolenaar, second and third in the shot put by Hendrickson and Howie Meyer, and fourth in the discus by Fred Yonkman. In the high jump it was Van Farowe tying Albion's Sharpe for second, while Yonkman and Joe Fowler were involved in a four-way tie for fourth. Wes Sikkema took third in the pole vault and Bob Moolenaar and Rod Wissink were part of a five-way tie for fourth. Clayt Borgman was fifth in the javelin and Hope's mile relay team closed out the scoring with a third place finish. When reporters sought comment from Coach Vanderbush on the long awaited championship, his terse reply said it all, "The kids simply came through when it counted."

Hope's tennis fortunes were again guided by Coach Ken Weller. The squad included Ron Bos, Warren Exo, Dick Nieusma, Bill Coventry, Jack Vander Velde, Marv Van Weelden, and Bob Langwig. In an early season non-league match on April 16 the Dutchmen edged Calvin 5-4. Bos, Exo, and Nieusma won their singles matches and the number one doubles team of Bos and Exo posted a win. Hope's number three doubles team of Coventry and Van Weelden was also victorious. Things continued to look good on April 23 when Weller's charges shut out Albion 7-0. A week later it was Hope 4, Alma 3 as Exo and Bos won in singles and the doubles teams of Exo-Box and Nieusma-Vander Velde accounted for Hope's victories.

A trip to the Chicago area ended Hope's winning ways as the Dutchmen were defeated 7-2 by the University of Chicago, and 6-3 by Lake Forest. The downturn continued on May 5 as the perennially strong Kalamazoo Hornets white-washed the Dutchmen 7-0, but two days later the team took a second 5-4 match from Calvin. On May 15 it was Hope 7, G.R. Junior College 3, including several three-set matches. On successive days, May 16 and 17, Hope shut out Hillsdale 6-0 and Adrian 5-0 as both matches were shortened by rain. Several of Hope's reserve players took on the Western Michigan J.V. team on May 19 with the Broncos winning 7-0.

At the MIAA Meet at Kalamazoo on May 23-24 Ron Bos posted a 6-4, 6-0 victory over Alma's John Shields before withdrawing to qualify in the 100 and 220 yards dashes. Bos and Warren Exo subsequently reached the doubles finals before bowing to Kazoo's Tom Wilson and Bob Casler. Hope's overall second place finish was rewarding to coach and team alike.

Only four schools competed in baseball in the spring of '52 although Olivet took part on a non-league basis. Jack Schouten, now in his final season of coaching at Hope, opened the season with a 7-2 victory over Olivet on April 16. A five-run seventh inning provided the margin of victory for pitcher Willie Rink, who took over from Lefty Bob Dennison after the third inning. Zeke Piersma and Jerry Jacobson each had two hits for the Dutchmen. At Riverview Park on April 19, Rink and Dennison combined to pitch a five-hitter against the Michigan State J.V. team. Despite six errors, the Dutchmen prevailed 9-7 on the strength of four hits by Don York and

The 1952 Hope College Track Team
Hope's First MIAA Championship

Front Row L to R: Clayt Borgman, Larry Fabunmi, Fred Cook, Howard Meyer, Rod Wissink, Bob Roos, Byron Aldrich, Coach Al Vanderbush. **Back Row:** Manager Lou Benes, Verne Fuder, Glenn Straatsma, Walt Vander Meulen, Al Nelson, Ken Raak, Bob Hendrickson, Jack De Waard, Joe Fowler. **Missing from the picture:** Ron Bos, Carl Van Farowe, Fred Yonkman, Nevin Webster, Dave Hondorp, Bob Moolenaar, Carl Schroeder, and Wes Sikkema.

three by Morris Witteveen. Three days later Hope hosted Calvin with John Busman giving up four hits and one run over the first four innings. Rink went the rest of the way as the Dutchmen notched an 8-1 victory, their third of the young season.

Coach Schouten's early optimism suffered a blow at Alma on April 26, when his team dropped a double-header to the talented Scots. In the opener the home team combined eight hits with five Hope errors to record a 7-3 win. Mike Bramble limited the Dutch to just five safeties. In the nightcap the Scots collected 19 hits off Hope's Bob Dennison, John Busman, and Jun Bremer enroute to a convincing 16-5 victory.

In Grand Rapids on April 30 Jack's squad launched a 16-hit attack to down the Calvin Knights by a score of 17 to 5. Jun Bremer, of basketball fame, pitched the first six innings for Hope giving up five hits and three runs while striking out five. He was also active at the plate with a home run and two singles. Piersma and York added three hits each.

Hope returned to league play at Riverview Park on May 3 in two superbly-pitched games with the Albion Britons. Bob Dennison and Albion's Bob Betz were about equal in the first encounter as each allowed six hits, but the final score showed Albion 2, Hope 1. Hope's only counter came on a Don York home run. He also had two singles. In the nightcap Willie Rink and Cedric Dempsey hooked up in a pitchers' duel that went 12 innings. Rink fanned 12 and Dempsey nine, but in the top of the 12th the Britons committed two costly errors and the Dutchmen evened the day with a 4-2 victory.

Hope's double-header at Hillsdale on May 10 was similar to the Albion encounter. In the first game Bob Dennison pitched a brilliant three-hitter, only to have the Dale's Le Roy Dorrow counter with a two-hitter. Fuzz Bauman and Morrie Witteveen collected the safeties. Hillsdale scored the game's only run on a controversial play in the l0th inning. On a force play at the plate the umpire ruled that catcher Jim Harvey's foot had been pulled off the base. In the nightcap, Hillsdale led 2-1 in the eighth inning when a Dutch rally netted three runs. Triples by Piersma and Bauman contributed to the 4-2 victory.

In a single game at Grand Rapids J.C. on May 13, J.C.'s John Vander Veen got the best of Bremer and Rink and the Grand Rapids team went on to win, 5-4. Three days later at Olivet Willie Rink pitched a four-hitter to win 5-2 in spite of five Dutch errors. Poor fielding also plagued the Dutchmen at East Lansing on May 28. Hope committed nine miscues but the Michigan State J.V.'s had six of their own. Strong pitching by Rink and a four-run third inning enabled Jack's crew to defeat the State team by two runs for the second time. This time the final was Hope 6, Michigan State J.V.s 4.

Hope's last game of the season was a dreary affair at Riverview Park on May 31. The Western Michigan J.V. team built a 4-0 lead over six rainsoaked innings. The teams had run out of make-up dates and every attempt was made to complete the contest, but to no avail. Play was halted in the seventh and Western went home with a 4-0 shutout. Jack Schouten's final season was a winning one with an overall 8-6 record. In the MIAA, Hope stood fourth with a record of two and four. The Alma Scots took the title with a 4-2 record, while Albion and Hillsdale tied for second at 3-3. Piersma and York were All-MIAA.

Jack Schouten had played on Hope teams before the turn of the century and had coached without pay before being hired in 1919 by President Dimnent. His contribution to Hope men and women had become legendary and extended well beyond courts and playing fields.

Coach Al Timmer's 1952 golf squad included Dick Kruisenga, Bob Kloote, Dick Huff, Bill Kramer, Don Lubbers, and Bob Visser. In dual matches wins were recorded over Grand Rapids J.C., 11 1/2-3 1/2, Calvin, 11-4, Muskegon J.C., 13-2, Alma, 10-5, Hillsdale, 9-6, and Adrian, 15-0. Losses were to Albion, 12-3, Kalamazoo, 9-6, and Muskegon J.C., 9-6. In the second match with Muskegon, Bob Visser recorded a hole in one on the 12th hole. He was also Hope's medalist for the day. Hope's overall record of six and three seemed to indicate a strong finish in the MIAA, but the bottom fell out at the Field Day meet in Kalamazoo on May 22-23 and Hope dropped to fourth place. Albion's first place finish gave the Britons the All-Sports Trophy by the narrowest of margins. The final talley showed Albion with 54 points to Hope's 53.

Hope's women fared somewhat better than the men. Hosting the MIAA on May 22-23 the Dutch ladies captured the title in the first-ever archery tournament. Hope's team of Jean Cloetingh, Gay Tiggelaar, and Arlene De Young scored 3,211 points to 3,102 for Albion, 2,945 for Alma, 2,726 for Hillsdale, 2,520 for Kalamazoo, and 2,507 for Adrian. In tennis it was Hope's Mary Ter Borg winning the singles championship over Albion's Sue Little, 6-1, 6-1. In doubles the semi-finalists were all from Hope and there is no record of the play-off for the title.

The summer months passed quickly, and on September 2 Coach Al Vanderbush greeted 40 football candidates at the Van Raalte practice field on Fairbanks Avenue. It marked the seventh season as head coach for Vanderbush and the fourth for assistant Ken Weller. Guard Lloyd Beekman was captain of the team that traveled to Ypsilanti on September 20 for the opener, a night game at the Hurons' Briggs Stadium (not to be confused with the home of the Detroit Tigers). Vanderbush had lost quarterback Ron Schipper to graduation and anticipated trouble from Eastern's single wing attack. After a scoreless first half the Hurons marched 75 yards, all on the ground, with Warner going in from the 10. The kick by Rod Place was good to put Michigan Normal up 7-0. In the fourth quarter Hope was on the move when the Hurons' Mosely intercepted a Dave Kempker pass and ran it back 75 yards for the score. The kick was wide, making it 13-0. Late in the game Hope moved to the Ypsilanti 10 on the strength of a

Kempker-to-Joe Ypma pass plus runs by John Hamilton and Johnny Adams. Adams then broke through the line on a dive play, veered to his left and went in for Hope's only score of the night. Bud Prins' kick was blocked, making the final score Michigan Normal 13, Hope 6.

The home opener found the Dutchmen hosting a strong Beloit team in a night contest at Riverview on September 27. A stellar Beloit defense prevented Hope from mounting any significant offense and John Hamilton was forced to punt seven times in the first half. Near the end of the second quarter a Hamilton punt was partially blocked, giving the visitors the ball on Hope's 45. A few plays later, with the ball on the 15, halfback Steve Jones threw a transcontinental pass to end Fred Peterson in the end zone. The kick by Tony Paris was good, making it 7-0 Beloit. The Dutchmen were held at bay throughout a frustrating second half. Late in the game Beloit put together an 11-play drive from their own 15 with quarterback Don Spirduso going in from the one yard line. Tony Paris' second placement wrapped up the scoring and gave the Wisconsin team the 14-0 victory.

A third night game found the Dutchmen at Waukesha, Wisconsin, doing battle with Carroll College. Carroll scored twice in the first quarter on runs by halfback Jack Ponta, and early in the second period on a Vetta-to-Foster pass to take a 20-0 lead. The drought finally ended for Hope in the second quarter when Dave Kempker threw a 26-yard touchdown strike to Fuzz Bauman. Bud Prins made it 20-7 with his kick. The comeback continued when John Hamilton went eight yards off tackle to score and Prins added the point. With the score 20-14, Zeke Piersma threw a 22-yard scoring pass to end Paul Bos. Bud Prins made good on his third straight point and Hope had its first lead of the season, 21-20. The third quarter was scoreless but in the fourth period Carroll sustained a drive as reserve back Karris scored with just four minutes remaining. The Dutch were unable to mount a second comeback and Carroll took the contest 27-21, in spite of Hope's domination in all other statistics.

After a week of hard practice the Dutchmen traveled to Hillsdale on October 11, determined to halt the skid. It was Homecoming for Coach Henry Fallon's crew, but this day Hope would be the spoiler. With 10 minutes gone in the opening period John Adams ran 15 yards to score and Bud Prins made it 7-0. Early in the second quarter a 61-yard Hope march featured runs of 16 and 21 yards by Hamilton and Adams. Adams scored from the seven and a second kick by Prins made it 14-0. Ron Appledorn had transferred to Hillsdale and now met his old teammates. His attempted quick kick, still in the second quarter, was partially blocked by big John Hollander and Hope gained possession. A 21-yard Kempker-to-Piersma pass placed the ball on the Hillsdale nine. Hamilton carried on three successive plays, going in on his third try. The kick was not good and Hope went to the locker room leading, 20-0. In the third quarter a 34-yard punt return by safety Zeke Piersma placed the ball on the Dales' 27. Two plays later,fullback John Hamilton broke up the middle for 21 yards and the touchdown. Fuzz Bauman's kick was blocked, but Hope's lead now increased to 26-0. Hillsdale threatened in the fourth quarter but Don Howard intercepted a Leroy Dorrow pass on the Hope seven. The Dutchmen maintained possession in a 93-yard march with Piersma going over from the three, and this time Bauman's kick was good. Hope's 33-0 victory was impressive with 222 yards on the ground and 111 in the air.

It was Homecoming at Riverview on October 18, and a strong Albion team was the opponent. Turnovers would plague the Dutch and lead to eventual defeat. In the course of the afternoon Hope would suffer five interceptions and lose three fumbles. The Britons converted four of the miscues into touchdowns. It was the Dutchmen, however, who drew first blood on a 32-yard end sweep by John Hamilton. Bud Prins' kick was blocked by Ray Loeschner and Hope took its only lead, 6-0. Albion responded with a 13-play drive from their own 30. Halfback Bob Wiksrom dove in from the three and Ray Loeschner added the point to make it 7-6. Four minutes later, after a Hope fumble, Wikstrom scored again, this time from the 15. Loeschner's second point after made it 14-6. The Britons gained possession again when Wikstrom intercepted a Dave Kempker pass. Quarterback Bob Friberg struck quickly with a 53 yard scoring pass to halfback Bob Mac Donald. A Loeschner kick was low and Albion's halftime lead was 20-6. Early in the second half Fritz Shurmur intercepted a Kempker pass on the Albion 25 to set up the next drive. Mac Donald went over guard from the seven to score, but Loeschner's kick was blocked by John Newton to set the score at 26-6. The Hope offense finally came to life on a succession of runs by Hamilton, Piersma, and Adams. A Kempker-to-Paul Bos pass put the ball on the Albion one and Kempker sneaked in for the score. Bud Prins made it 26-13, but the Albion lead was too much to overcome. With three minutes remaining, Bob Kouts recovered a final Dutch fumble on the Hope 27 and a few plays later fullback Mel Larimer went off tackle from the two for Albion's fifth touchdown. Hope's Frank Talarico blocked Loeschner's point try to make it 32-13 and end a frustrating afternoon for the Dutchmen.

Hope's MIAA schedule was interrupted by a non-league game at De Pauw on October 25. The De Pauw trip was perhaps the low point in a thus far disappointing season. Things went badly from the opening kickoff which the Dutchmen allowed to roll into their end zone, where it was recovered for a touchdown by Mc Nairy of De Pauw. The conversion by Stephens gave the Tigers a 7-0 lead before any time had elapsed on the clock. A subsequent score made it 14-0 at the end of the first quarter. De Pauw scored again in the second quarter and twice in the third period to nail down the 34-0 victory. A strong De Pauw pass rush broke down the Hope protection and quarterbacks Dave Kempker and Don York were able to complete only three of 21. The Hope cause was also hindered by leg injuries to John Hamilton and Paul Bos. Coach Vanderbush felt that the Tigers were easily the best team that Hope had encountered to that point.

Despite its 1-5 record, Vanderbush believed that his squad had considerable talent. He was able to convince the team of this fact in a night game at Kalamazoo's Angell Field on November 1. The Dutchmen were off to a shaky start as they fumbled the ball away three times in the first quarter, but the Hope defense held on the 12, the one, and the 20 yard lines to keep the first period scoreless. In the second quarter Kalamazoo drove 62 yards to score. The big play was a perfectly executed split-T option play as quarterback Phil Dillman "turned the corner," then lateraled to halfback Bob Van Horn, who was finally dragged down on the one. Dillman went in from the one and a Bob Vander Veen kick made it 7-0, Kalamazoo. Later in the period Don Howard batted down a Dillman lateral and recovered on the Kalamazoo 27. Kempker passed to Fuzz Bauman, who made it to the two. Two plays later Kempker sneaked in for the score and Bud Prins made it 7-7 at halftime. In the third period a "K" drive stalled and Hope took over. Dave Kempker broke through up the middle, veered to the right and ran 58 yards to the Kalamazoo 15. Frank Talarico then skirted left end on a pitchout and went in for Hope's second touchdown. The point by Prins gave Hope a 14-7 lead, but it was short lived. Once again the Hornets' option play worked to perfection. This time Van Horn took the pitchout and raced 68 yards for the score. Vander Veen's conversion produced the second tie, 14-14. Hope took the kickoff and scored in 12 plays, including runs of 22 and 26 yards by Talarico and Kempker. It was Kempker over left guard for the score. Jack Doyle broke through to block Prins's third kick and the score stood 20-14, with Hope again in the lead. A strong Kalamazoo drive took them to the Hope 29, where the Dutch forced a fumble and Jim Van Hoeven recovered. A Hope punt to the "K" 18 was fumbled by Dillman, and Piersma recovered on the 16. Kempker passed to York for nine yards, then carried to the three. Johnny Adams finally went over from the one, but the play was called back for illegal motion. A delay of game penalty pushed the Dutchmen back even farther and Coach Al elected to attempt a field goal. Bud Prins' kick sailed through the uprights to make it 23-14 with five minutes left in the game. In the waning minutes Dillman attempted a fourth down pass, but Jim Van Hoeven, who seemed to be everywhere, intercepted and ran 35 yards for Hope's final touchdown. Prins' kick made it Hope 30, Kalamazoo 14. The gritty Hornets mounted one more drive, but fullback Sam Grow fumbled on the Hope nine and Van Hoeven closed out a brilliant afternoon with his second recovery of the day. Hope had turned the corner.

The rejuvenated Dutchmen hosted Alma in a Friday night game on November 7. The game's only score came in the first quarter. Dave Kempker threw an incomplete pass but the Scots were called for roughing the passer and the ball was placed on the Alma 15. Quarterback Don York then pitched out to Zeke Piersma, who picked up a key block from Frank Talarico and raced around right end for the touchdown. The conversion attempt was not good and Hope's lead was 6-0. Alma threatened in the third quarter, but the Hope defense rose to the occasion and halted the drive on the six-yard line. A late game Hope drive ended with a Hope fumble on the Alma five, but the Dutchmen had notched their third MIAA victory. Captain Lloyd Beekman was the defensive standout of the game.

Hope closed out the season before a small crowd at Riverview Park on November 15. The Adrian Bulldogs had not enjoyed an impressive season but the spread formation employed by Coach Ted Boyett was cause for concern. Hope got its first break in the second quarter, when Lloyd Beekman recovered a fumble on the Adrian 18. On a fourth down play Dave Kempker passed to Fuzz Bauman for the first score and Bud Prins' conversion put the Dutchmen up, 7-0. Late in the first half Adrian's Clarence Hawkins intercepted John Adams' lateral to Kempker and carried to midfield. A series of plays from the split T formation advanced the ball to the Hope 27, where the drive stalled. At this point Coach Boyett went to the spread formation and quarterback Jim Niebauer passed to end Bob Ohrman for the touchdown. Jim Van Hoeven blocked the extra point try and Hope went to the locker room with a narrow 7-6 halftime lead. After a scoreless third period Hope took the ball on its own 45. A Kempker-to-Talarico pass made it to the Adrian 31, and a Kempker-to-Paul Bos aerial placed the ball on the Adrian 5. A left end sweep by Johnny Adams put the ball in the end zone, but the kick by Prins was wide of the mark. Hope's lead remained at 13-6 until the closing moments, when Joe Ypma intercepted a Niebauer pass and motored 55 yards down the sideline for the touchdown. Captain Lloyd Beekman was given the honor of attempting the season's final tally, and his kick was good. With the 20-6 win Hope stood 4-1 in the MIAA, second behind Albion's perfect 5-0. The strong comeback made the overall 4-5 record seem unimportant. Center John Newton was selected the team's Most Valuable Player, while Jim Van Hoeven and Zeke Piersma were named co-captains for the 1953 season. Bauman, Beekman, Bos, Newton, Van Hoeven and Piersma were named to the All MIAA team. On Tuesday, November 18, the Hope squad was duly feted at a banquet in Durfee Hall under the direction of "H" Club President Bill Poppink.

A significant addition to the Hope Physical Education faculty in the fall of 1952 was Lawrence J. Green. With degrees from Central College of Iowa and Drake University, he would receive his Ph.D from the University of Iowa in 1955 and thereafter be affectionately known as "Doc." The nickname was reinforced when he succeeded Jack Schouten as trainer in all sports.

One of "Doc's" very first assignments was to coach the 1952 cross country team. Included on his first college team were Captain Glen Sraatsma, Jesse King, Carl Schroeder, Bob Hamilton, John Schrier, Roger Knopf, Sam Hofman and Harold Van Zoeren. League placements were determined entirely by the MIAA meet held at Kalamazoo on November 19. All seven league members participated and as expected, Albion won with a near-perfect score of 18 after capturing the first four places. The Britons' Al Nichols was the individual winner, while Hope's top man was Jesse King in sixth place. Straatsma finished 11th, Schroeder 16th, Hamilton 17th, and Knopf 18th. Adrian took second place with 59 points, Hope was third with 68, Alma fourth with 115, Hillsdale fifth with 127, Kalamazoo sixth with 150, and Olivet seventh with 179.

In his second year as Hope's head basketball coach, John Visser tackled an ambitious 21-game schedule. Jun Bremer and Ken Van Regenmorter were lost to graduation, but Ron Bos, Bob Hendrickson, Jerry Jacobson, and Bob Visser were returning starters. The picture was further brightened for the defending champions by the addition of freshman Johnny Adams. The Dutchmen ventured into Hoosier land on November 25 to open the season at Valparaiso. The state of Indiana was noted for the caliber of its basketball, teams and Valparaiso upheld the tradition by trouncing the MIAA champs 104 to 68. The Crusaders' 6' 8" center Bielke led the way with 25 points and generally made life miserable for Bob Hendrickson, who led Hope with 17. Jacobson had 16, Bos 13, and Bob Visser 12. Things went somewhat better at Crawfordsville on November 29, when the Dutchmen trailed a strong Wabash team by the narrow margin of 53-51 at halftime. The Little Giants however, pulled away in the fourth quarter to a 10- point lead. Hope narrowed it to five but finally lost, 92 to 87. Coach Visser got fine performances from Hendrickson, Jacobson, and Bos with 24, 21, and 20 points respectively. Tom Hankinson led Wabash with 23.

Two days later it was more of the same at Greencastle as Hope took on the De Pauw Tigers. The Dutchmen were hampered by the loss of Captain Ron Bos, who was sidelined with the flu, and the team trailed 39-35 at halftime. In the second half a pressing defense plus the fast break brought some success, but in the end it was De Pauw 96, Hope 71. Hendrickson led Hope with 18 and was followed closely by Zeke Piersma, whose excellent performance netted 17. Visser had 13 and Bob Bolema 12. All in all, the Dutchmen were happy to cross the state line into Michigan.

December 6 marked the home opener against the Alma Scots of Coach Fred Lawrence. The flu bug had spread to Bob Visser, and Jerry Jacobson suffered a muscle pull after about 15 minutes of play, but Ron Bos was back and led his team to a 77-54 victory with 27 points. In the second half Coach Visser went to the press capitalizing on the quickness and competitive nature of Piersma and Johnny Adams. The 35-28 halftime margin widened and Hope was never in serious trouble. Bob Hendrickson played his usual steady game and chipped in with 12 points. John Sawyer had 10 for the losers.

At Olivet on December 8, Hope played without the services of Visser and Jacobson but still posted a 54-43 halftime lead. Hendrickson controlled the boards and racked up 23, but the evening belonged to freshman John Adams, who pumped in 20 points as a fill-in for Jacobson. Zeke Piersma sprained an ankle but Holland freshman Alden Klomparens was impressive with 16 and Ron Bos contributed 14 before getting into foul trouble. The final was Hope 100, Olivet 68.

Snow and icy roads forced a postponement of the December 13 contest with Adrian at the Armory, but on the 15th the Dutchmen drove to downtown Grand Rapids to meet Calvin in the Civic Auditorium. Coach John Tuls had the Knights in form and the usual spirited battle took place. Bos scored 15 in the first half but the outcourt shooting of Roger Postmus was the equalizer and the teams were tied at halftime, 38-38. In a hard-fought second half Piersma fouled out but Hendrickson controlled the boards and scored 25 to lead his team to a 70-66 victory. Bos followed with 23, while Roger Postmus was high for the Knights with 24. It was one of the few times that the Dutch emerged victorious in the spacious Civic Auditorium.

On December 27 Hope sought to break the Indiana jinx by hosting Manchester at the Armory. Students were gone for the holidays but 800 fans turned out to see Hope post its fourth straight win. Leading 52-44 at halftime, the Dutchmen were hard pressed to hang on for a final count of 97-92. Bos was high with 24. He was followed by Jacobson with 19 and Hendrickson with 16. Bob Anglin with 22 and Dan Butts with 21 kept the visitors in the game to the very end.

In a similar game at the Armory on January 3, Hope got the best of North Central of Naperville, Illinois. The game was billed as a contest between centers Bill Warden of the Cardinals and Hope's Bob Hendrickson. Warden's credentials included a 40-point performance earlier in the season. The pair waged an even battle, but Hendrickson outscored his opponent, 24 to 23, and the Dutch ended the evening with a 10-point victory, 89 to 79. Bob Visser was back in form with 22 and Bos contributed 17.

MIAA play resumed at Albion on January 7. John Porter and Cedric Dempsey were two of the league's best, but Hendrickson played the best game of his career to that point by pumping in 32 points. He had balanced support from R. Bos with 19, Visser with 14, and Jacobson with 13. Porter tied Dempsey's Albion scoring record with 34 and Dempsey added 21, but the Britons lacked depth and were finally defeated, 92-84. John Visser was prepared for a shoot-out when Coach Dob Grow brought his Kalamazoo quintet to the Armory on January 13. He was not disappointed. The score was tied 15 times enroute to a new Armory record for scoring by two teams. Hope led 61-56 at the half but the Hornets fought to within three at 95-92 with two minutes remaining. Visser's semi stall produced Kalamazoo fouls and the gap widened to a final of Hope 104, Kalamazoo 92. Hendrickson was the scoring leader for Hope with 20. Guard Bob Bolema followed with 18 plus a stellar performance on the boards. Jacobson also garnered 18 while Bos added 14 and Visser 13. The Hornets were well served by Gordon Dudley with 32, Manny Glasser with 25, Phil Dillman with 20, and John Stommen with 15. It was a key victory for Hope in an MIAA race that would tighten as the season moved to its conclusion.

Coach John Visser's squad set an MIAA scoring record on January 17 as they downed Hillsdale 111 to 91 at the Armory. A surprise high-point man for the Dutchmen was freshman John Adams, who pumped in 29. He was followed by the ever-consistent Hendrickson with 23, Ron Bos with 15, and Jacobson with 12. For Hillsdale it was Holland native Ken Schippers leading the way with 21. A week later, again on the home floor, the Dutchmen coasted to a 94-67 win over an outmanned Olivet team. Bos collected 20 points before suffering a knee injury. Visser followed closely with 17. Hendrickson and Jacobson were also in double figures with 13 each. Bud Bryant and Pete Kracala were high for the Comets with 21 and 19.

The snowed-out December 13 game with Adrian was finally squeezed in at the Armory on January 31. Coach Visser, with good reason, was impressed with the depth of talent on his squad. To demonstrate his confidence in the bench he started a team of Zeke Piersma, John Adams, John Brannock, Dwight Riemersma, and Bob Bolema, the latter being the only "regular." Dwight "Whitey" Riemersma of St. Joseph was the son of Ben Riemersma (Hope '25), who had been a mainstay on Jack Schouten's teams of the '20s. Brannock, from neighboring Benton Harbor, was the younger brother of Lee Brannock, co-captain of Hope's 1939-40 MIAA champions. Meanwhile, the Adrian aggregation, which sported a 5-1 MIAA record, was less than enchanted with Visser's decision. After nine minutes of play it was Adrian 13, Hope 12. The regulars now entered, but found the going tough and could only manage a 33-33 tie at halftime. Adrian's set-up style of ball with numerous screens proved effective and, combined with limited service from Ron Bos, kept the Bulldogs in the game. But in the third quarter Adrian's ace forward, Bob Ohrman fouled out along with Captain John Cavas. This turn of events was enough to turn the tide, and the Dutchmen moved on to a 76-64 victory. High scorer for Hope was Bob Visser with 18. Hendrickson had 13, Riemersma 12, and Bolema 10. Smith led Adrian with 14.

In a between-semesters contest at Lake Forest on February 2, the Hope five managed a 40-37 halftime lead and played well into the fourth quarter. At this point ill fortune struck when Captain Ron Bos re-injured his ailing knee, this time seriously. A preliminary examination seemed to indicate that he would be lost for the season. The home team then moved to a 91-84 victory despite a 31 point performance by Bob Hendrickson. Riemersma and Bos had 13 and Visser 10 in the losing cause. Groenberg and Waterfall were high for the Foresters. Back in Holland the team was shocked by news that senior co-ed Claryce Rozeboom had been killed in an auto accident enroute to the home of music Professor Robert Cavanaugh.

Basketball action resumed on February 7 when the Dutchmen, without Ron Bos, met an inspired Alma team on the Scots' narrow floor. The teams battled to a halftime tie at 32 and the Dutch were hard-pressed in the third period. A turning point seemed to come when Brannock, attempting a lob pass to Hendrickson, scored a long basket instead. Hope forged ahead behind 23 points from Brannock and 20 from Hendrickson. Jacobson was also hot with 15 in the eventual 79-67 win. Diminutive George Fox led Alma with 18.

A strong and determined Adrian team was waiting for the Dutchmen when they made the long trip on February 10. A cold first quarter left the Hope team trailing, 20-10. In the uphill battle that ensued Hope narrowed the gap and finally took a slim lead, but in the closing minutes Adrian's Nat Martin sank four straight free throws to give the home team an exciting 81-80 victory. Bob Ohrman's splendid performance netted 27 points for the winners, while Hendrickson and Brannock shared scoring honors for Hope with 19 each. Adams had 11 and Jacobson 10. It was a costly defeat for the Dutchmen in their quest for a second straight championship.

On February 14 the Hope squad displayed its resilience at the Armory by establishing yet another MIAA scoring record against the talented Albion quintet. Halftime showed Hope with 53 to 39 for the Britons and the torrid pace continued to the end of the game. Hot shooting (45.5 percent) and balanced scoring were instrumental in the final 114-86 Hope victory. Leading the way for the Dutchmen were big John Brannock with 29 and Jerry Jacobson with 24. Hendrickson was next with 16, Visser had 14 and Adams 13. Hendrickson, Brannock, and Visser controlled the boards. Lost in the melee were outstanding performances by the Britons' Cedric Dempsey with 27 and Don Roe with 23.

Despite the Adrian loss, Hope had a golden opportunity to sew up the championship at Kalamazoo on February 17. As usual, Hope fans equaled or outnumbered the Kalamazoo following, but the Hornets were at their best in the shadowy confines of the Treadway Gym and held a 39-37 halftime advantage. The third quarter remained close and with six minutes left in the contest Hope was on top 66-64. At this point Kalamazoo's Manny Glasser came through with two picture-perfect hook shots and "K" took a lead it would not relinquish. The Dutchmen went cold in the final quarter and ended the evening on the short end of an 87-76 score. Big guns for the Hornets were John Stommen with 24 and Manny Glasser with 20. Hendrickson, with 20, led the disappointed Dutchmen. Visser had 12 and Adams and Brannock 11 each.

A trip to Hillsdale on February 21 returned Hope to the victory column with a 93-60 win. Coach Visser's brother Bob was high for the Dutch with 17, while Hendrickson netted 16 and Jacobson and Brannock each had 13. Most heartening of all was the return of Ron Bos, who was used sparingly by Coach Visser.

Aside from basketball, February's big sports news was the fact that world heavyweight boxing champion Rocky Marciano would come to Holland to train for his upcoming bout with Jersey Joe Walcott. The Marciano entourage set up camp at the Holland Furnace Recreation Grounds (now known as "Leisure Acres") and Holland was suddenly on the nation's sports map. Scribes of every hue followed for weeks the champion's every move and utterance.

On the last day of February, the Hope team made its way to Naperville, Illinois, for a return game with North Central College. This time their high scoring center Bill Warden took charge early and, after a 51-38 halftime lead, led his team to a 99-86 victory. Warden's 42 points easily took honors for the evening but fell short of an earlier high of 48. Hendrickson had a good night with 27, Visser got 14, and Adams 13. Riemersma and Adams were effective in the late stages with the press as Coach Visser looked ahead to the March 2 encounter with Calvin. With the exception of Hendrickson, no Hope player played more than a half.

The season-ending Calvin game at the Armory was much like all the others. The Knights led by a single point at halftime, 46-45, but pulled away in the third quarter when the Dutch defence faltered. Four of the five Calvin starters proved to be scoring threats and were convincing with a final 91-81 victory. Garris Timmer led the Knight parade with 24, Preston "Butts" Kool scored 19 and was strong on the boards, Roger Hamstra had 18, and Roger Postmus also dropped in 18. Jacobson led Hope with 20 and Hendrickson was close behind with 18.

Adrian lost its bid for the title when upset by Albion, but Kalamazoo and Hope ended with identical 10-2 marks. A playoff to determine the champion was arranged on a neutral floor at Plainwell High School. Plainwell had recently constructed a new gymnasium, and 1,350 of the faithful from each camp crowded in to witness the MIAA's fifth basketball playoff on March 9. Hope received a tremendous psychological boost when it was announced that Ron Bos would be in the starting line-up for the first time since being sidelined on February 2. The game lived up to its billing as the sports spectacle of the season. At halftime Hope held a slender 49-47 lead on the strength of Bos's superb floor play, and in the course of the contest the score was tied nine times. The Dutchmen finally prevailed, 91 to 85. Ron Bos and John Brannock, the latter in a substitute's role, led Hope with 21 each. Bob Hendrickson followed closely with 20, Bob Visser had 15 and Jerry Jacobson 11. For Kalamazoo it was splendid Manny Glasser leading all scorers with 29. Gordon Dudley followed with 20 and Phil Dillman had 17. High scoring John Stommen was held to seven.

Hope's 11-2 MIAA mark brought them a second consecutive league championship while the overall season record stood at 14-8. The Holland Lions Club feted the Champions on March 22 at a banquet in the Warm Friend Tavern. Speaker for the evening was Bill Perigo, head basketball coach at the University of Michigan. A special guest was former heavyweight boxing champion James J. Braddock, who brought a brief message and offered opinions on the upcoming Marciano-Walcott fight. Captain Ron Bos was elected the team's Most Valuable Player, and later was named the MIAA's Co-Most Valuable with Manny Glasser of Kalamazoo. Bob Hendrickson and Bos made the All-MIAA team, along with Glasser, Cedric Dempsey of Albion, and Bob Ohrman of Adrian.

A major coaching transition took place on the Hope campus in the spring of 1953. Russ De Vette had returned from the Marine Corps for the second semester and he now replaced the venerable Jack Schouten as baseball coach. Larry Green took over the track reins from Al Vanderbush, and John Visser was the new golf coach. Visser replaced Professor Albert Timmer while Ken Weller, youngest of the quartet, continued as tennis mentor. Hope had been edged in the All-Sports race by Albion in '52 and there was now a strong belief among the enthusiastic young coaches that the tables could be turned on the Britons in '53.

Coach Green had inherited a number of talented track performers from Al Vanderbush, and he opened the season with an impressive win over Calvin and Alma at Houseman Field on April 22. Hope captured nine firsts to six for Calvin and zero for Alma. Ron Bos, fully recovered from his basketball injury, won both dashes. His 10.0 in the 100 was outstanding for an opening meet. Carl Van Farowe scored 15 points as Hope racked up 82 1/2 points to 65 1/2 for Calvin and 16 for Alma. Van Farowe took the 120 high hurdles, the 220 lows, and the high jump. Carl Schroeder, Byron Aldrich, and Harold Molenaar placed first, second, and fourth in the 880, while Walt Vander Meulen's 21' 5" win in the broad jump was impressive for the first meet of the season. Don Polich and Wes Sikkema tied for first in the pole vault and the mile relay team of Don Brookstra, Byron Aldrich, Carl Schroeder, and Dave Hondorp was also victorious.

Six days later the Calvin team made the trip to Holland for a dual meet at the 22nd Street track with much the same result. The final this time was Hope 76, Calvin 55. The Knights improved their first place production to seven with Hope getting eight. The Dutchmen enjoyed a sweep in the high hurdles with Van Farowe, Don Brookstra, and Jack De Waard. Walt Vander Meulen won the broad jump with a leap of 20'3."

On May 4, Hope met Kalamazoo as part of a double-dual meet under the lights at Allegan High School. Allegan hosted Holland Christian High School in the other half of the meet. Allegan Football Coach Dick Higgs (Hope '48) served as official starter for the evening. From the outset the Dutchmen were in charge, posting a final score of 95-36 on the strength of 13 out of 15 first place finishes. Hope's winning mile relay team consisted of Dave Hondorp, Ron Bos, Carl Schroeder, and Bob Hendrickson.

A May 9 meet in Holland saw Coach Green's squad take

the measure of Grand Rapids Junior College by a score of 83 to 48. Jesse King was the winner in both the mile and two mile runs and Carl Van Farowe again took his specialties, both hurdles and the high jump. Coach Green had urged Ken Bauman to give the discus a try and he emerged the winner with a throw of 108 feet. A Ron Bos victory in the 100 had been expected but he was somewhat surprised when basketball teammate Bob Hendrickson took him to the tape for a dead heat in the 220. Both men were timed in 22.6, no mean accomplishment for shot putter Hendrickson.

Thirteen trackmen and four tennis players journeyed to Beloit College on May 13 to participate in the Great Lakes Invitational. The Hope track contingent finished third with 38 points, behind Wabash with 85 and Beloit with 76. Other participants were Carroll with 18, and Illinois Tech with four. Bos surprised the field by taking the 100 in 10 flat and the 220 in 22.4. Van Farowe had seconds in the high hurdles and high jump while Jesse King was second in the two mile and fourth in the mile. Jack De Waard and Van Farowe finished third and fourth in the low hurdle race, Byron Aldrich was third in the 880, John Brannock fourth in the discus, and Dave Hondorp fifth in the 440. The Hope mile relay team of Hondorp, Aldrich, Schroeder, and Bos finished third.

Ron Bos's delicate juggling act between tennis and track hit a snag on the weekend of May 15-16. Playing number two singles and number one doubles, he was obliged to make the two-day trip to Albion and Wayne State. The track team, meanwhile, traveled to Albion for a triangular with the Britons and Alma on the 16th. Larry Green recruited halfbacks John Adams and Frank Talarico from Russ De Vette's baseball team, but was unable to offset the loss of his speedster. The final showed Albion the victor with 79 1/2 points 66 1/2 for Hope and 17 for Alma. Van Farowe again was first in both hurdles and the high jump, John Brannock took the discus, Don Polich the pole vault, Jesse King the two mile, and Bob Hendrickson bested Fritz Shurmur in the shot put. Frank Talarico managed a second in the broad jump and Johnny Adams' gallant try in the 440 netted a fourth. Needless to say, the latter found the race to be a piece further than his longest touchdown gallop.

Looking to the future, Coach Green sent nine freshmen and sophomores to participate in the Grand Rapids J.C. Invitational on May 20. No team scores were kept, as Western Michigan's Freshman team dominated the field. The big day was finally at hand as Hope's team made its way to Kalamazoo's Angell Field to defend its title on May 22. About 500 spectators viewed the afternoon and evening events. The talented Dutchmen were determined and not to be denied this day. The official scorer's final count showed Hope retaining its MIAA championship with a comfortable 83 3/4 points to 62 for Albion, 33 1/4 for Kalamazoo, 18 1/2 for Adrian, 13 3/4 for Hillsdale, 12 1/2 for Alma, and 2 1/2 for Olivet. The Dutchmen won gold medals in six of the 15 events contested. Ron Bos closed out a brilliant athletic career at Hope with victories in the 100 and 220 yard dashes. His times were outstanding at 10.1 and 22.0. Hendrickson's gold came on a heave of 42' 6" in the shot, John Brannock did likewise in the discus with a throw of 123' 6," and Walt Vander Meulen's 20' 9 1/2" in the broad jump was good enough to win under poor weather conditions. A wet take-off area in the high jump resulted in a six-way tie for first that included Carl Van Farowe and Wes Sikkema. Valuable second place points were added by Jesse King in the mile and two mile, Dave Hondorp in the 440, and Van Farowe in the 220 lows. Don Polich and Wes Sikkema were part of a three-way tie for second in the pole vault and Hope's mile relay team also took a silver medal with the title safely tucked away. Larry Green, in his first year as a college track coach, had helped secure back-to-back championships for Hope. Fourteen years would pass before it happened again.

Ron Bos

By general consensus "R. Bos" was one of the most versatile and talented athletes ever to grace the Hope campus. Leading Hope to two MIAA basketball championships, he was named the league's Co-Most Valuable Player in 1953. He competed concurrently in tennis and track, played number 1 doubles and number 2 singles, and was the MIAA 100 and 200 yard dash champion in both 1952 and 1953.

The 1953 baseball picture at Hope was not necessarily a bright one. Zeke Piersma at shortstop, Jim Van Hoeven at third base, and catcher Don York were returning regulars, along with pitchers Willie Rink and John Busman, but Jerry Jacobson decided to pass up baseball in order to insure his qualification for practice teaching. The remainder of Russ De Vette's squad was essentially untested.

The season opened on a cold and blustery April 18 at Riverview Park with defending champion Alma furnishing the opposition. Scot pitcher Mike Bramble was in mid-season form as he struck out 12 hope batters, but in the bottom of the 13th Hope pitcher Willie Rink tripled to right center. Busman and York then walked to load the bases. At this point Bramble uncorked a wild pitch and the game ended 3-2 in favor of Hope. The nightcap was postponed due to plummeting temperatures.

The Dutchmen hosted Calvin in a non-league encounter on April 22 and edged the Knights, 8-7. The big blow for Hope was a two-run homer into the left field grandstand by Don York in the fifth. Al Dykema, Alden Klomparens, and Don Lubbers had a single an double each. Pitchers John Busman and Vern Hoffman gave up 11 hits but Rink came on in the ninth to preserve the victory. Hope returned to MIAA action with a double-header at Olivet on April 22. Rink was brilliant in the opener as he struck out 14 and allowed a single hit enroute to the 3-1 victory. Duvall struck out 10 Hope batters but passed balls eventually led to his downfall. In the second game, John Busman gave up three runs in the first two innings, then settled down to a five-hit performance. Hope bats boomed and Hope had its second win of the day, 9 to 3.

May 5 saw a return engagement with Calvin in Grand Rapids. The story of the game was a seven-run Hope outburst in the fifth, plus three more in the sixth for the eventual 10-8 Hope victory. Hope pitchers were Rink, Piersma, and Busman. Jim Van Hoeven had a three-run double in the fifth and Don Lubbers stroked a triple in the sixth.

In the first game of a crucial double-header at Albion on May 9 the short (275') left field fence was a factor. Al Dykema cleared the barrier in the first frame to give Hope an early 1-0 lead, but Albion's Jim Murray countered in the second with a three-run blast over the same fence to make it 3-1, Albion. The Dutchmen got one back in the sixth, then sewed up the ball game in the eighth when Al Dykema singled and came home on Don Lubbers' homer, again over the left field fence. The 4-3 victory was sweet for Rink who went the route with nine strikeouts, but a tough loss for Albion's Cedric Dempsey, who whiffed 13 Dutch batters. The Britons came back with a vengeance in the second game, winning 15-2 behind the two-hit pitching of Betz. Hope's only runs came in the second on a two-run homer by Jim Van Hoeven. Hope's other hit was a double by losing pitcher John Busman.

Hope's May 11 twin bill with Hillsdale was moved to Allegan because of Tulip Time activities at Riverview Park. Rink was again in form and twirled a four-hitter to down the Dales, 6-1. The big inning for the Dutch was the second when they pushed across five runs. Hillsdale's lone run was scored by former Hopeite Ron Appledorn after he walked and stole a base. Rink returned to the mound in the sixth inning of the second game with Hillsdale leading 6-3. A seven-run rally in the seventh gave Hope a 10-6 victory as Willie Rink emerged the winner in both contests. The Dutchmen of Coach Russ De Vette now stood at 6-1 in the MIAA and were assured of a title share by news that Alma had taken a double-header from favored Albion.

The all-important makeup game with Alma was played at neutral Valley Field in Grand Rapids on May 20. In a well-played game the Scots prevailed 2-0 on the strength of a five-hitter by Mike Bramble. Rink was also effective with a six-hitter and his teammates played without an error, but several scoring opportunities were missed and the Dutchmen were forced to share their first-ever MIAA championship with a worthy Alma team.

The Dutchmen were back in action the following day in a single game at Riverview Park against the Raiders of Grand Rapids Junior College. John Busman went all the way on the mound to record a 4-2 victory. Busman struck out four and walked one while Piersma led the offense with a double and single. Hope closed out the season by entertaining a strong Western Michigan Freshman team on May 26. Rink went the distance and York delivered a two-run homer but the contest was anticlimactic, to say the least, and Western won, 8 to 3. Hope's overall record in its first championship year was nine and three. Zeke Piersma, Willard Rink, and Don York were honored by being placed on the All-MIAA team.

Ken Weller had little chance of a championship in tennis as Kalamazoo College continued to place year-round emphasis on its program. Hope, however, would field a strong team with the return of Warren Exo, Ron Bos, and Bill Coventry at number one, two, and four singles. Weller could also look forward to strong performances from Grand Rapids J.C. transfer Bill Boeskool. The team was off to a good start as they edged Calvin 5-4 in Holland on April 16. Hope winners in singles were Exo, Bos, Boeskool, and sophomore John Schrier. In doubles it was Exo and Bos taking the measure of Jim Dozema and Al Peelan, 6-2, 1-6, 6-2.

The MIAA season opened for Hope at Adrian on April 23 with the Dutchmen besting the Bulldogs, 5-3. Exo and Bos were again winners in singles and were joined by freshman Glen De Pree in the number five spot. Both doubles teams came out on top as Exo-Bos and Coventry-Boeskool posted victories. A second match with Calvin was played at Franklin Park in Grand Rapids, and this time the Knights reversed the score, winning 5-4. Hope's winners were Exo, Bos, and Boeskool in singles, and Coventry-Boeskool in doubles.

It was another tough day at Alma on May 5. The Dutchmen entered doubles competition trailing 3-2, but Exo and Bos defeated John Fields and Mc Donald, 6-1, 6-1, and Boeskool-Coventry downed Bob Harrison and John Sawyer to give Hope the 4-3 victory. The expected whitewash occurred at Kalamazoo three days later as the Hornets won 7-0. The Dutchmen were unshaken by the setback and performed well when Hillsdale came to Holland on May 11. Hope won four of five singles, losing only at number five. In doubles it was John Schrier and Monte Dyer defeating Bob Morey and Art Burns, 3-6, 6-3, 7-5. Bill Boeskool and Bill Coventry took the measure of Jim Buck and Fred Riggen, 6-1, 6-1, in Hope's overall 6-1 win.

In the Great Lakes Conference Invitational at Beloit on

The 1953 Hope College Baseball Team
MIAA Co-Champions With Alma
Hope's First-Ever Championship In Baseball

Kneeling L to R: John E. Winter, Willard Rink, Don A. Lubbers, Dick Ortquist, Dwight "Whitey" Riemersma, Alan Dykema, Gerald Elenbaas, Vern Hoffman, John Adams, John Busman, Don York. **Standing:** Jerry Jacobson, Dick Schultz, Fred G. Lubbers, Carlton Failor, Don Charpentier, Jim Van Hoeven, Alden Klomparens, Gordon Schipper, Frank Talarico, Tom Harris, Captain Don "Zeke" Piersma. **Missing from the picture:** Coach Russell De Vette.

May 13 it was Kalamazoo the winner with eight points, Beloit second with six, Illinois Tech third with three, Hope and Wabash fourth with two, and Lake Forest failing to score. The Dutchmen continued to do well in MIAA action as they won at Albion five to two on May 15. Bos, Boeskool, Coventry, and Dyer were victorious in singles, and the number one doubles team of Exo and Bos also won. The team continued on to Detroit for a match the next day with Wayne State. The Detroiters prevailed, 7-2, as Hope's only victories came from Exo and Bos at number one and two singles.

Spring sports at Hope surrendered the spotlight briefly on May 19, when senior Guy Vander Jagt won first place in the 11th Annual Hearst Tournament of Orators. The competition took place in Milwaukee, Wisconsin, with a $1,000 check going to the winner. It was Hope's first national championship in oratory since George Steininger accomplished the feat in 1916. Vander Jagt would later represent Western Michigan in the U.S. House of Representatives.

While Vander Jagt was expounding in Milwaukee, Coach Weller's tennis charges were defeating Grand Rapids J.C. in the Furniture City. Exo, Boeskool, Coventry, and John Schrier won in singles, as did the doubles teams of Exo-Boeskool and Schrier-Dyer. The 6-3 win gave the Dutchmen a record of six and three going into the MIAA meet at Kalamazoo on May 21-22. On May 20 the MIAA Board met in Kalamazoo and approved the membership application of Calvin College. There were some reservations due to the fact that Calvin did not sponsor football, but Hope's Bud Hinga urged acceptance of the school, the principles and general philosophy of which were consistent with those of the MIAA. Competition for the Knights would begin with the 1953-54 school year. Calvin's John Tuls hinted that the school might initiate football "in the near future," but 38 years later, no such action had been taken.

In the MIAA Field Day meet, Warren Exo drew Kalamazoo's Bob Casler, the eventual singles champion. Exo gave a good account of himself before bowing out, 3-6, 6-3, 7-5. Bill Boeskool won his first two matches but finally lost to "K"s Dave Moran, the son of Holland High's director of athletics, Joe Moran. Bos, Coventry, and Schrier won first-round matches before being eliminated. Hope's second place finish met pre-season expectations and kept the school in the running for the coveted All-Sports trophy.

Arend Don Lubbers and Bob Visser were returnees on the '53 Hope golf squad, as belatedly was Don Prentiss, but it would not be a banner year. Newcomers Bill Holt, Don Burrows, and John Tamminga showed promise but the team suffered early-season losses to Calvin, 8-7 and, 12-3, to Grand Rapids J.C., 12-3 and 15-0, and to Alma, 9-6. The team finally broke the ice on May 6 as they downed Kalamazoo 10-5 on the strength of a 77 by Bill Holt and a 78 by Don Lubbers. Don Prentiss and John Tamminga had 82s. At Adrian on May 15 the Dutchmen rang up another victory, this time by a score of 13 to 2. Bob Visser was medalist with a 79. In the Conference meet, Albion and Hillsdale tied for first with 22 points, Kalamazoo followed with 12, Hope and Alma each had 10, and Olivet had eight.

While Hope's fourth place tie in golf did not sound impressive, it was considerably better than fifth place, as the All-Sports race went down to the wire. Final tabulations were delayed two days pending the outcome of a rain-delayed tennis match between the doubles teams of John De Vos and Manny Glasser of Kalamazoo, and Bob Siegel and George Clark of Albion. When the Kalamazoo team won, 6-4, 7-5, Albion lost its bid for a fourth straight All-Sports trophy. Hope won the coveted award by the narrowest of margins, with 68 points to 67 for Albion, 46 for Kalamazoo, 37 for Alma, 35 for Hillsdale, 29 for Adrian, and 10 for Olivet. It was Hope's first All-Sports victory since 1947, and the third overall. The hard-earned trophy was impressive, with gold figures representing all MIAA sports. It was placed in a trophy case on the first landing of the stairway in Van Raalte Hall along with others won by Hope teams of the early '50s. When the Dow Center was completed in 1978 its space for trophies was at first inadequate and the '50s awards remained in Van Raalte, only to be consumed when the structure burned in 1980. The excitement of a great year in Hope sports, however, would live on.

Nearly 30 years would pass before womens's sports would count in the All-Sports race, but mention should be made of Hope's fine tennis team of 1953. On May 6 the women under Coach Louise Van Domelyn hosted the team from Western Michigan and shut out the Lady Broncos, 7-0. In singles it was Mary Ter Borg over Georgiana Lewis, 0-6, 6-2, 7-5. Salley Palen defeated Joan Rood, 6-4, 6-2, Suzie Van Slageran took Elly Roegner, 6-3, 6-2, Marjorie Bruins defeated Georgia Myers, 6-2, 6-4, and it was Alyce De Pree over Pat Brabb, 6-4, 6-2. In doubles, Betty Scheppers - Salley Palen defeated Elly Roegner - S. Ames, 6-4, 6-2, and Edith Teune - Mary Schrier defeated B. Spring and Pat Brabb, 6-3, 6-0.

Hope's enrollment in the fall of 1953 was 836 according to the official count of Registrar Paul Hinkamp. Twenty-eight of that number reported for football practice on a hot Wednesday, September 2, and the squad increased to 39 as summer jobs ended and classes began. Coach Al Vanderbush welcomed the return of Russ De Vette as backfield coach and Ken Weller continued as line coach. Graduation losses dictated some changes, and the coaching staff soon switched Bud Prins from tackle to center, Jim Van Hoeven from tackle to end, and Herm Nienhuis from fullback to guard. One week before the opener, quarterback Don York suffered a severe ankle sprain and the job was left in the hands of Muskegon freshman Harry Voss. Fortunately, he had the benefit of veteran running backs in the persons of John Adams, Dave Kempker, and Frank Talarico. Hope's coaches had been favorably impressed by the so-called "Belly" series as employed by Coach Bobby Dodd at Georgia Tech, and added it to the Hope offense. It was a momentous decision. The series afforded unusual deception as the quarterback would place the ball in the fullback's belly, "ride" with him, then either give him the ball or retain it and pitch to a halfback swinging wide. Hope's backfield combination seemed made to order for this innovation.

In a night game on September 19, Hope hosted the Hurons of Michigan Normal under Coach Freddy Trosko. For the Dutchmen, the game was marred by the kind of mistakes that cost ball games. In the first quarter Talarico broke loose on a 41-yard touchdown gallop, only to have it called back for backfield in motion. In the second quarter a bad snap from center on fourth down sailed into the end zone and a scrambling Talarico was only able to get it out to the three. The Hurons' Leroy Manby later went in from the one and quarterback Bob Middlekauff circled left end for the point to make it 7-0. A few minutes later Coach Vanderbush watched in utter disbelief as the punt scenario was repeated. This time Talarico got out to the 10, but four plays later halfback Tom Fagan scored and Badalow kicked the point to make it 14-0 at the half. The teams settled down to a scoreless third period, but in the fourth quarter Harry Voss threw a flat pass that was intercepted by a Huron linebacker who sprinted 22 yards to the Hope three. Manby then scored his second touchdown and Middlekauff kicked the point to make it 21-0. Finally, in the closing minutes, John Adams threw a 20-yard pass to Jim Van Hoeven, then scored on a sweep for Hope's only tally of the night. Bud Prins' kick was wide and the Hurons went home with a 21-6 victory.

Olivet returned to MIAA football competition in 1953 under Coach Warren "Swede" Thomas after an 11-year absence. Using a single wing-unbalanced line formation, the Comets were impressive in an opening 7-6 win over Adrian. Hope hosted Olivet on Friday night, September 25, in a game that saw 186 yards in penalties marched off against the Dutchmen to 65 for the Comets. Near the end of the first quarter Frank Talarico took a pitchout and raced 83 yards to score but the play was nullified by one of the many penalties. With 5 1/2 minutes remaining in the half, fullback Dave Kempker broke free off tackle and with Van Hoeven taking out the last man, went 55 yards for the touchdown. There were no flags and after Prins' kick sailed wide of the mark, the score stood 6-0 at halftime.

The opening play of the second half proved to be the most spectacular of the game. Olivet's Ken Carothers kicked off to Talarico, who took the ball on the 12, dropped it, recovered, and ran up the middle, 88 yards for the score. Fellow halfback John Adams provided a key block at the Hope 48. Kempker's kick was wide, making the score 12-0 with just 23 seconds gone in the second half. Olivet then moved to the Hope 27, where a Charles Twitty jump pass was intercepted by Hermie Nienhuis. Nienhuis was finally pulled down at the Hope 30. A few plays later Harry Voss threw a 20-yard pass to Adams for the score. This time Kempker's kick was good giving Hope a 19-0 lead with 6 1/2 minutes remaining in the third quarter. In the fourth quarter the Dutch put together a 90-yard drive with Talarico going the final 15 for the touchdown. The kick was wide and the game ended, 25-0.

Coach Mickey Mc Cormick brought a fine Carroll College team to Holland for yet another night contest on October 3. The Dutchmen were off to a good start when Jim Van Hoeven blocked Larry Pennewell's punt on the Carroll 40. Five plays later Adams circled left end to score from the Hope 21, and Bud Prins' kick gave Hope an early 7-0 lead. The Pioneers tied the score when end Bob Shutter intercepted a Voss pass on the Carroll 30 and ran it in for the score. George Spellus' kick made it 7-7. Carroll took the lead near the end of the third quarter when halfback Glenn Johnson went over from the three and Spellus again converted. In the fourth quarter a shanked punt by the visitors gave Hope the ball on the Carroll 30. Five plays later Adams scored from the 13 on a well-executed "belly" play. Prins' conversion made it 14-14. Hope's next big break came when Ken Van Wieren recovered a fumble by halfback John Villare on the Carroll 40. Kempker then led a seven-play drive, finally going over from the one. Prins' kick was true, giving the Dutchmen a hard-earned 21-14 victory, their second of the young season.

Hope met Coach Joe Fortunato's Adrian team on October 10 in a night game at the Bulldogs' dusty Island Park Field. In the first quarter Adrian got off what appeared to be an impressive punt, but John Adams gathered it in on the six yard line, broke free, and rambled 94 yards for the first score of the game. Bud Prins made it 7-0. Later in the half Adrian was forced to punt again, this time from their own end zone. Adams' nine yard return placed the ball on the Hope 24. A Voss to Brannock pass was good to the 11, two runs by Kempker took it to the two, and Adams went in for his second touchdown. A Prins kick was again good, making the score 14-0 at halftime despite a tough Adrian defense. In the third quarter, quarterback Joe Davis threw a flat pass while on his own 26. It was intercepted by Harry Voss, who raced into the end zone. A Prins kick was wide and the score remained 20-0 until the fourth quarter, when Walt Mc Callum intercepted a Voss pass and returned it to the Hope 28. On the next play Davis eluded a swarm of Hope tacklers to hit end Ralph Ellison for the touchdown. Davis' kick was good and Adrian avoided a shutout. In the 20-7 Hope victory Coach Vanderbush singled out tackle Warren De Witt for an outstanding defensive performance. A sobering note was the apparent loss of Don York for the season. A blow to the head caused a concussion and doctors advised that he refrain from further football activity.

The fall of 1953 marked the return of Charley Bachman to the coaching ranks. Bachman had guided the fortunes of Michigan State for 16 seasons before his retirement in 1946. After seven years on the sidelines he was persuaded by Hillsdale College to attempt a rejuvenation of their program. Of special significance was his choice of Frank "Muddy" Waters as one of his assistants. Waters and the Michigan State connection would make history at Hillsdale over the next seven years. Bachman brought his squad of young but talented recruits to Riverview on October 17. The game was played before a crowd of 3,500 who saw the Dutchmen capitalize on two early breaks. Quarterback Bill Allinder's pass to end Andy Kincannon was deflected and intercepted by Frank Talarico who returned it to the Dale 23. Five plays later Talarico went over for the touchdown. Bud Prins kicked the point and Hope led 7-0 with less than three minutes gone in the first quarter. Freshman Kincannon fumbled the ensuing kickoff on the 35 and Talarico was there to recover. A nine-play Hope drive ended when Talarico went in from the one and Prins again converted. With the score 14-0 the Hillsdale defense stiffened, but a fourth down penalty against the Dales gave the Dutchmen new life and in four plays they were on the Dale 19. At this point Talarico took a pitchout and behind a key block from Van Hoeven, skirted left end for his third touchdown of the first quarter. The 21-0 score held up through most of the second quarter, but Hillsdale regrouped and with 40 seconds remaining in the half Bill Allinder sneaked in from the three and John Moffat's kick made it 21-7 at the half. Defense was the order of the second half, but with 3 1/2 minutes remaining in the game an Allinder punt went awry and rolled out of bounds on the Hillsdale 30. Coach Vanderbush now inserted his second freshman quarterback, strong-armed John Holmlund from Brooklyn, New York. On his first play Holmlund arched a long pass to end John Brannock, who took the ball over his shoulder and went all the way for the touchdown. The play covered 70 yards. Bud Prins' fourth conversion gave Hope the 28-7 victory. Hillsdale's 46-man squad included 37 talented freshmen who would begin the "Dale dynasty" the following fall.

Hope's preparation for the Beloit contest was handicapped by unseasonably hot weather and the opening day of hunting season. The squad included numerous outdoorsmen, and the coaches finally relented and called off the Tuesday practice. The non-league game at Beloit could not be taken lightly, however. Coach Carl Nelson had enjoyed an undefeated season in 1952, the Buccaneers first in 63 years, and as the game got underway it looked like more of the same. Joe Cibula broke loose for a 54-yard run to the Hope 10, and three plays later quarterback Jack Roberts passed to Cibula for the touchdown and Beloit led 6-0. Johnny Adams responded with a 55-yard run to the Beloit five, but a Harry Voss pass was intercepted in the end zone. A short time later Talarico took a punt on his own 48 and returned it 52 yards for Hope's first score. Bud Prins kicked the point and the Dutchmen led, 7-6. Late in the second quarter Holmlund was trapped, started to run but found Talarico with a pass that covered 54 yards and resulted in the halfback's second touchdown. The kick was not good but Hope went to the locker room leading, 13-6. The Hope coaches made good use of the intermission. It was determined that the inside trap play was not working, as Hope's tackle was not able to get across the hole to the linebacker due to the nose-up defensive tackle in Beloit's five-man front. It was agreed that the tackle and end should switch assignments as the end was "uncovered." The strategy was employed early in the second half and Talarico breezed through virtually untouched, going 68 yards for his third touchdown. The point was blocked, but the complexion of the game had changed and the Dutchmen were in charge, 19 to 6. Also in the third quarter Adams went 39 yards around left end for Hope's fourth touchdown making it 25-6. In the 4th quarter a Holmlund pass set up the final Dutch score and Talarico went in from the six. The point was good and Hope found itself leading a very good team 32 to 6. Substitutes played much of the fourth quarter and Beloit was able to score with eight minutes remaining. The touchdown came on a 23- yard pass from Jack Roberts to Newtson and made the final score 32 to 13. It was Beloit's first loss of the season.

Hope's game at Albion on October 31 was a key contest in the Dutch quest for a championship. The Britons were hampered by limited service from ace quarterback Bob Friberg, but things evened out when Dave Kempker went down with a knee injury in the first quarter. Early in the first quarter John Brannock intercepted a pass on the Albion 23. A few plays later Adams scored on an eight-yard left end sweep. Prins' conversion attempt was wide, and Hope's lead was 6-0. Still in the first quarter, Adams took a handoff on his own 47, picked up a block from Don Vander Toll, and raced 53 yards for his second touchdown. The toe of Bud Prins made it 13-0. The third period was all defense. Hope again threatened, but the Britons forced a fumble on the four yard line. Albion was held on the six and 11 by strong Dutch defense. Two Albion touchdowns were nullified by offside penalties. In the fourth quarter it was Adams again, this time on a 34-yard sweep. Bud Prins made it 20-0 and the game seemed to be out of reach, but in the closing minutes quarterback Tom Schwaderer threw a 12-yard touchdown pass to halfback Norm Weis and guard Joe Dean kicked the point. With the score at 20-7, the Britons successfully executed the on-side kick but time ran out and the Hope victory was preserved.

Hope's chance to clinch the MIAA championship came on the night of November 7 at Riverview Park. It would not be easy. Kalamazoo College had a new coach in the person of Rolla Anderson and his team played inspired ball throughout the contest. Hope was stopped at the four and the 19, and in turn halted the Hornets on the Hope seven. An attempted Prins field goal from the 23 was blocked by tackle Don Hay, and with the score 0-0 at halftime the Dutchmen knew it would be a long night. In the third quarter Kalamazoo punted to Adams, who took the ball on his own 20, crossed the field from south to north, broke into the clear and went 80 yards for the score. Prins' kick was wide but the Dutchmen were finally on the board, 6-0. On the first play of the fourth quarter Adams took a pitchout on the Dutch 44 and got away to the Kalamazoo 20. Jim Van Hoeven made it to the nine on the end-around play. Coach Vanderbush then called for the halfback option pass, with Adams throwing to John Brannock. Brannock made a sensational shoestring catch at the goal line for the touchdown and Hope led 12-0 as Kalamazoo blocked the point try. In the fourth quarter, end John Sweet blocked a Talarico punt on the Hope 10 and Chuck Brown recovered on the six. Quarterback Pete Lenox sneaked in from the one and Bill Howlett kicked the point to make it 12-7. John Hollander recovered the on-side kick and backs Bob De Young and Dave Kuyers moved the ball to the Kalamazoo 20 before the ball went over on a fumble. In the remaining two minutes, the Hornets moved the ball but could not score. The 12-7 victory, coupled with a 0-0 Albion-Hillsdale tie, made Hope's first outright MIAA championship a reality.

The euphoric Dutchmen made an anti climactic trip to Alma to close out the season on November 14. The Scots of Coach Lloyd Eaton were primed to upset the champions and were in charge from the opening kickoff. Halfback Marv Raab scored four touchdowns and passed for a fifth in the 33-19 rout. Hope touchdowns were scored by Talarico, Adams, and Kempker. Hope's title was thus slightly blemished, but the fact of the championship remained, plus 12 points toward the All-Sports Trophy.

The team was feted at a banquet in the Juliana Room of Durfee Hall on November 19. Speaker for the evening was WKZO Sportscaster Len Colby. In the course of the evening, Dr. Otto Vander Velde was presented a set of golf woods by Athletic Director Russ De Vette for his 30 years of service as team physician. James "Grin" Van Hoeven was elected the team's Most Valuable Player, and a short time later was named to the All-MIAA team for the third consecutive year. Bill Heydorn, John Adams, and Frank Talarico also made the all-conference team.

The success of the football team overshadowed somewhat the best cross country performance in the school's history. In his second year at the helm, Coach Larry Green had only two lettermen, Jesse King and Glenn Straatsmaa, but a promising group of newcomers would be equal to the task.

Ron Den Uyl had captained the team at Holland High and Dan Meeuwsen had done the same at Grand Rapids Ottawa Hills. Also on hand were Byron Aldrich, Ron Reinink, Art Schmidt, Harvey Van Farowe, and Henry Young.

Hope played host to Olivet on October 3 in the first dual of the season. In Hope's 21-34 victory it was Den Uyl first, King second, Reinink fifth, Aldrich sixth, and Straatsma 7th. A week later, at Adrian, the Dutchmen won 21-37 with Ron Den Uyl setting a new course record of 21:21 for the four-mile run. King was again second, Aldrich fifth, and Straatsma sixth. A third straight Dutch victory came at the expense of Hillsdale, when the Dales came to Holland on October 17. Hope remained consistent with a 22-36 win that included a first by Den Uyl, a third by King, fifth by Ron Reinink, sixth by Aldrich, seventh by Henry Young, and 8th by Straatsma.

The bubble was broken at Mount Pleasant on October 20, when Central Michigan shut out the Dutchmen 15-49. Jesse King, in eighth place, was the first man to finish for Hope. Den Uyl fell twice on the course and was thus deprived of his usual fine performance. Coach Green and his charges chalked this one up to experience and prepared for the big one at Albion on the last day of October. The powerful Britons had won 39 straight dual meets and captured six straight MIAA titles. The race finished on the 50 yard line of the football field at halftime. Finishing before a cheering crowd was a unique experience for members of college's "loneliest sport." Hope's 1-2 finish with Ron Den Uyl and Jesse King gave the Dutchmen a dramatic 27-28 victory. Ron Reinink finished seventh, Glenn Straatsma eighth, and Byron Aldrich ninth.

Hope won handily in its final two dual meets. On November 7 it was 19-42 over Kalamazoo with Den Uyl and

Hope College Football Team - 1953
MIAA Champions
Hope's first undisputed Championship

Front Row L to R: Warren De Witt, Don Vander Toll, John Brannock, Dave Kempker, Co-Captain Jim Van Hoevan, Herm Nienhuis, Robert "Bud" Prins, Bob Hoeksema, Co-Captain Bill Heydorn, Trainer Jack Schouten. **Row 2:** Assistant Coach Don "Zeke" Piersma, Backfield Coach Russ De Vette, John Walters, Bobby Fales, Dick Schultz, Earl De Witt, Ron De Graw, Harry Voss, John Adams, Frank Talarico. **Row 3:** Don York, Ed Bredeweg, Ian Smith, Maurice Marcus, Tom Harris, Ed Stapert, Bob De Young, Darle Nieneker, Head Coach Al Vanderbush. **Row 4:** Line Coach Ken Weller, Dave St. Aubin, Manager Norm Lager, Ron Boeve, Bob Karsten, Bruce Springsteen, Donald "Doc" Van Hoeven, John Hollander, George Van Antwerp, John Homlund, Dick De Freese, Dave Kuyers, Manager Tom Keizer.

The coaches had reason to smile in 1953.

L to R: Head Coach Al Vanderbush, Line Coach Ken Weller, Backfield Coach Russ De Vette.

1953 Starting 11

Linemen L to R: John Brannock, Co-Captain Bill Heydorn, Hermie Nienhuis, Bud Prins, Don Vandertoll, John Hollander, Co-Captain Jim Van Hoeven (MVP). **Backs:** 37 - John Adams, 35 - Harry Voss, 44 - Dave Kempker, 36 - Frank Talarico.

King finishing together in first place, Henry Young fourth, Art Schmidt fifth, Glenn Straatsma seventh, Harvey Van Farowe eighth, and Ron Reinink ninth. At Alma on November 14 it was Hope 18, Alma 43. Den Uyl finished first, King second, Schmidt fourth, Reinink fifth, Young sixth, Straatsma eighth, and Van Farowe ninth. Hope's 7-0 mark in MIAA dual meets was a source of considerable pride. It counted one half toward the championship and would be on the line at the conference meet.

The MIAA meet was held at Olivet on November 18 with all teams gunning for Hope. Two factors deprived the Dutchmen of an undisputed title. First, Don Wiegant of Hillsdale was an upset winner over Ron Den Uyl who finished second. Secondly, Art Schmidt fell during the race and was unable to deliver his usual points. Morrie Tubergen of Calvin finished third and Jesse King was fourth. Albion's four-point victory forced the Dutchmen to share the title. The Britons' score was 38 to 42 for Hope, 78 for Hillsdale, 101 for Calvin in its first MIAA season, 142 for Adrian, 155 for Alma, 174 for Kalamazoo and 195 for Olivet. Hope's co-championship netted 11 points toward the All-Sports trophy and gave the school a lead in the race at the end of fall sports.

Hopes for a third straight basketball title were dimmed somewhat by the departure by graduation of Ron Bos, the league's Co-Most Valuable Player. Also gone were Jerry Jacobson, Bob Bolema, and Zeke Piersma. The picture, however, was far from dismal with the return of 6'5' Bob Hendrickson, 6'6" Bob Visser, and 6'4" John Brannock. An unexpected plus was the return of 6'7" Bob Wagner after a three-year absence. After a stint in the U.S. Army and in the work force, "Stretch" was back to complete his degree and add rebounding power to Coach Visser's squad. Willie Rink, Whitey Riemersma, Hal Molenaar, John Adams, and Alden Klomparens were also experienced.

Hope's height advantage was not enough to take the day in the home opener on November 28 against Wabash. After building a 46-37 halftime lead, the well-named Little Giants played steady ball to post the 81-68 win. Jay Crittenden was especially effective with 35 points. For Hope it was Bob Hendrickson with 18 and Whitey Riemersma with 13.

The MIAA season opened with the Kalamazoo Hornets invading the Armory on December 4. Hope's fast break was functioning well early in the contest and by halftime the Dutchmen held a commanding 59-38 lead. The home team continued to score at will throughout the third quarter of the game, and when substitutes were inserted defense was thrown to the winds. The result was a 29-point performance by both Manny Glasser and John Gideon of the Hornets. Hope, however, simply had too many guns and racked up a 114 to 95 victory in the track meet-type game. Johnny Adams led all Hope scorers with 23, John Brannock had 18, Hendrickson and Riemersma 16 each, and Norm Kramer and Willie Rink also finished in double figures with 10 apiece.

At Ypsilanti on December 9, the Dutch were bothered by a Michigan Normal pressing defense and fan shaped backboards, but managed a 36-30 lead at the half. The Hurons forged ahead 51-49 in the third period but the Dutchmen enjoyed a hot fourth quarter, outscoring their opponents 25-14, and were victorious 74-65 at the final horn. Bob Hendrickson had one of his better games as did John Adams. Both men scored 25 points, while Preketes had 16 for the losers.

On December 12 the Dutchmen met a disciplined Adrian team on the Bulldogs' home court. Hope took a 32-26 halftime lead but was bothered by the home team's slow down style of play. Henry Hughes, Adrian's freshman center, came alive in the second half to put the Bulldogs ahead. Hope tied it up, Adrian missed a final shot, and the game went into overtime. In the overtime period it was baskets by Adams, Rink, Hendrickson, and a tip-in by Bob Wagner that sealed the 67-61 victory for Hope. Hendrickson led the Dutchmen with 19, Adams had 15, and Riemersma 13, while Henry Hughes scored 18 for the losers. Hope suffered a blow when John Brannock sustained a badly sprained ankle.

Hope's decided height advantage was a factor in the team's 91-53 victory at Hillsdale on December 15. Hendrickson, Wagner, Visser, and Riemersma controlled the boards at all times. In the scoring department it was Adams with 18, Alden Klomparens and Riemersma with 14, and Visser with 11. Hillsdale's 6'6" freshman Floyd Sewell scored 12 in the final quarter and led his team with 18. Confident now with a four-game winning streak, the Dutchmen went home for the holidays.

On January 2 Coach Bob Harvey brought his De Pauw Tigers to the Armory and the Indiana jinx continued. De Pauw's 44-42 halftime lead increased to 15 points in the fourth quarter. A Dutch press narrowed the margin and a final surge made it a three-point game, but the Tigers held on for the 83-80 victory. Freshman Bob Schrier was the big gun for De Pauw with 23. Somewhat obscured by the defeat was a superb performance by Bob Visser, who was everywhere on the floor and led his team with 19. Riemersma followed with 17 and Hendrickson had 15. Failure at the free throw line was costly for Hope, and absence of the injured Brannock was a factor.

Brannock played briefly at Olivet on January 5 but his services were not really needed. Hope enjoyed a 44-24 lead at the half and the Comets were never able to challenge. Adams and Hendrickson led Hope with 14 each in the 81-54 win, which saw substitutes playing early and often. Bob Mason played well and scored 18 for the losers.

Albion's new coach was Elkin "Ike" Isaac, a former basketball and football standout for the Britons. Isaac and his new charges were off to a sensational start, sporting a 9-0 record overall. Both teams were 4-0 in the MIAA as they met in the Armory on January 9. Coach Visser's worst fears were realized when the well-coached Britons took complete command with a 15-0 lead. Visser installed a press and the

Coach Larry Green

Hope Cross Country - 1953
MIAA Co-Champions With Albion

L to R: Harvey Van Farowe, Henry Young, Glenn Straatsma, Ron Den Uyl, Dan Meeuwsen, Jesse King, Manager John De Vries, Ron Reinink, Art Schmidt. **Missing from the picture:** Byron Aldrich.

Dutchmen were able to reduce the deficit to 25-20, but at halftime the visitors were still on top, 38-34. But fouls plagued Albion throughout the contest. Guard Bob Friberg was on the bench with four well before halftime. John Hannett and ace Cedric Dempsey departed in the fourth quarter, leaving Don Roe as the only starter in the game. With Hendrickson at his best, the Dutchmen took advantage of Albion's misfortune, took over the game, and won, 73-67. Hendrickson's 26 points led all scorers. Adams had 11, while Brannock and Wagner each had eight. Despite his foul trouble, splendid Cedric Dempsey led Albion with 21.

Hope and Calvin met amidst the usual hype on January 12, but now the stakes were even higher. For the first time Calvin was a member of the MIAA, and under new coach Barney Steen had lost only to Albion. The game was played before a packed house at the Grand Rapids Civic Auditorium, and as usual the fans got their money's worth. Hope's usual height advantage was negated by tall Paul Newhof and Jim Kok. At halftime the Knights clung to a 36-35 lead and the contest continued in that vein. With 1:09 remaining, Hendrickson dropped in a free throw to give Hope a 65-64 lead, but with 32 seconds left Jim Kok put Calvin up, 66-65. At this point the Knights were in a position to ice the game as Hope fouled four times. But the pressure began to tell and all four tries were missed. Johnny Adams had possession with four seconds left and arched a long one. The ball took an agonizing roll around the rim and dropped off. Calvin's 66-65 victory was perhaps its most significant of the season and was typical of what would become the nation's top small college rivalry. Tony Diekema, who would one day be president of Calvin College, led his team with 18 points. Jim Kok followed with 13. For Hope it was Hendrickson with 19, Adams with 14 and Visser with 11.

The Dutchmen hoped to rebound from the tough loss as they traveled to Beloit on January 16, but it would be a difficult assignment. The Buccaneers boasted a 19-game home winning streak and had already posted victories over the University of Arizona and the College of the Pacific. Hope started well but played poorly in the second quarter, when they were outscored 25-16. The halftime score showed Beloit out front, 48-38. The remainder of the game was played on even terms with a final score of 85-75 and Beloit's victory chain intact. Guard Bob Donahue helped assure the win with 27 points. Bob Hendrickson again led Hope with 22. Visser had 18 and Adams 12.

A return game with Michigan Normal was played at the Armory on January 19. It was generally a bad night for the Dutchmen as a well-executed Normal press seemed to completely rattle the home team. Normal built a 42-33 halftime lead and went on to avenge their earlier defeat. Ray Pogliano, with 27, led his team to an impressive 93-68 win as Cleon Gillman chipped in with 19 and Coleman Jewett got 17. Whitey Riemersma put in 14 for Hope and Adams and Visser each had 12. An impressive floor game by Willie Rink was one of the few bright spots for John Visser's squad.

Hope resumed MIAA action at Alma on January 23. Coach Visser now decided to take advantage of the considerable depth on his squad by employing a platoon system. Hope starters in the contest were Brannock, Klomparens, Kramer, Riemersma, and Rink who employed the press and held a nine-point lead when the so-called regulars entered the game. Hope had a 45-42 halftime edge and led until the final three minutes, when the Scots gained the advantage on free throws. Hope's 83-81 defeat was their fourth in a row and a costly one in the MIAA race. Diminutive George Fox poured in 29 points to lead the inspired Scots, while Bob Visser was high man for Hope with 19. Hendrickson scored 14 while Molenaar and Riemersma each had 10.

The Hope victory drought came to an end at Kalamazoo on February 6. Visser continued with his platoon concept and Hope's wealth of talent wore the Hornets down. Starters included newcomer Ken Armstrong, Rink, Kramer, Brannock, and Riemersma. They were relieved by "regulars" Hendrickson, Visser, Adams, Wagner, and Molenaar. The Dutchmen enjoyed a 44-30 halftime bulge and increased it to 94-65 at the final horn. Hope scoring leaders were Hendrickson with 24 and Adams with 14. Rink and Brannock each had 12 and Kramer put in nine. Manny Glasser was the Hornet leader with 22.

Hard-luck John Brannock was lost a second time when he re-injured his ankle in a minor automobile accident just prior to the Adrian game. Coach Joe Fortunato brought his Bulldogs to the Armory on February 9 hoping to avenge the earlier overtime loss. Hope took a 52-41 halftime lead but Adrian stormed back in the third quarter to go ahead 60-58. The Dutchmen regained the lead in the final stanza and moved on to a 99-89 victory. Visser and Hendrickson led the way with 26 and 25 and were aided by 15 from Rink and 11 from Riemersma. Joe Davis had 23 for Adrian, Henry Hughes 20, and Jim Swoich 19.

Hope scored at will against an outmanned Hillsdale team that came to the Armory on February 13. The Dutchmen breezed to a 58-39 lead at the intermission and Coach Visser used several freshmen in the second half. Ken Armstrong put in the final two field goals to make it Hope 110, Hillsdale 77. The score book showed Adams with 27, Hendrickson and Riemersma with 17 each, Rink with 13, Molenaar with 13, Visser with 10, and Wagner with 10. Freshman Andy Kincannon led the Dales with 18.

Again at the Armory, on February 16, Olivet Coach Swede Thomas tried a press against the Dutch, but by halftime his team was down 52-23 and three of his starters had four fouls. Hope used 14 players in coasting to a 104-54 win. Adams was again the scoring leader, this time with 23. He was followed by Hendrickson with 18 and Visser with 13. Fourteen Hope players saw action in the contest. Don Goudy had 14 to lead Olivet.

Hope's game at Albion on February 20 was the most

crucial of the season. All were aware that a third conference loss would put the Dutchmen out of contention. Hope took an early lead, but a second quarter surge put the Britons ahead at halftime by a score of 40 to 36. Albion controlled the boards in the third period, but a determined Hope team came back in the final quarter and the scoreboard read Albion 80, Hope 79 when Bob Friberg was fouled with four seconds remaining. Friberg swished the first shot to make it 81-79. The second free throw was missed and Hendrickson tapped the ball to Molenaar, who took a few dribbles and fired the game's final shot. The shot missed but Molenaar was fouled in the attempt. With no time remaining, "Mo" stepped to the line. Kresge Gym became as quiet as a tomb as the partisan crowd showed respect for Molenaar's pressure situation. His first shot missed and a roar shook the gym. He made the second to make the final score Albion 81, Hope 80. Molenaar played the finest game of his career in leading his team with 22 points. Adams followed with 15 and Hendrickson had 12. Bob Friberg was outstanding for the Britons with 23 points as were Don Roe and Ced Dempsey with 22 each.

Coach John Visser and his squad took the disappointment in stride and finished the season with a flourish. The Alma Scots were at the Armory on February 23 hoping to repeat their earlier two-point victory, but Hope's height advantage and platoon system wore the visitors down. Hope's halftime advantage was 50-37 and was doubled by game's end. Bob Hendrickson led Hope to the 97-71 victory with 22 points, Rink was stellar with 17, Visser had 12 and Adams 10. George Fox with 23 and Bud Miller with 20 were the Alma leaders.

It was perhaps fitting that champion Calvin and second place Hope should meet in the season finale. An overflow crowd at the Armory was treated to the usual spirited play. John Brannock's long swisher at the horn gave Hope a 53-46 halftime lead, but it was a see-saw contest throughout most of the second half. Near the end the Dutchmen cashed in on eight straight free throws to build a 98-90 margin. In the closing seconds, Whitey Riemersma fired a corner shot that was tipped in by Hendrickson to make the final Hope 100, Calvin 90. Hendrickson was high for Hope with 18, Adams and Rink each had 17 and Molenaar 15. Rink's strong game under pressure drew high praise from Coach Visser. Guard Don Vroon's 26 led the Calvin attack with Tony Diekema and Jim Kok adding 17 each and Paul Newhof 14. Hope won the game, but the Calvin team, in its first year of MIAA competition, notched the championship, a signal accomplishment for first-year coach Barney Steen.

The 1953-1954 Dutchmen were 12-7 overall and 11-3 in the MIAA, good enough for a second place tie with Albion. Hope had knocked at the door, but one-point losses to Calvin and Albion plus a two-point defeat at the hands of Alma kept Coach Visser's squad from a third straight title. Albion's Cedric Dempsey was selected as the league's Most Valuable Player and was a popular choice. Hope's Bob Hendrickson made the All-MIAA team for the second successive year and John Adams was named to the second team. On March 22 the Holland Lions Club honored the Hope team with a banquet at the Warm Friend Tavern.

The month of March was generally devoid of college sports activity but there was news of two former Hope football teammates. On March 4 the **Holland Evening Sentinel** announced that Dick Higgs would move from Allegan High School to St. Joseph as head football coach. Clair De Mull, his assistant for two years, would assume the reigns at Allegan. Abe Moerland, a former Hope grid captain, was released from his coaching contract at Hudsonville to return to Grand Rapids Union, his alma mater. A March 12 release from the college announced the proposed renovation of Carnegie Gymnasium. The refurbished structure would be renamed Carnegie-Schouten Gymnasium in honor of the now-retired Jack Schouten, longtime coach and trainer.

Despite the loss of its basketball title, Hope was still the leader in the MIAA All Sports with 38 points. Albion was in hot pursuit with 36, and once again the issue would be decided by performance in the four spring sports. Coach Russ De Vette welcomed several lettermen from his '53 championship baseball team and hopes were high for another title. After the pre-season shakedown, Hope's starting lineup included Ron Boeve catching, Willie Rink and Jack Kempker on the mound, Don A. Lubbers at first, Dick Ortquist at second, Jim Van Hoeven at third, Carl De Vree or Dick De Freese at short, and Don York, Al Dykema, and John Busman in the outfield. Busman was also available as a relief pitcher.

The Dutchmen were off to a good start in the April 14 opener at Riverview Park. Willie Rink gave Grand Rapids J.C. just three hits over six innings while striking out eight. Don York finished the game in a De Vette pitching experiment. Hope collected 11 hits in the 6-3 victory, including three for four by Don Lubbers. Lubbers and Al Dykema each had triples. Three days later the Dutchmen opened the MIAA season by hosting the Olivet Comets in a doubleheader. The first game was a 22-0 blowout, with Hope collecting 18 hits, three by catcher Ron Boeve. A 10-run seventh inning included a three-run homer by pitcher Willie Rink. Generally-ragged play by the Comets was a contributing factor. In the second game freshman Jack Kempker notched his first collegiate victory by a score of nine to three. Hope scored seven in the first inning to provide the necessary cushion, and Don York contributed three hits.

In a return game at Grand Rapids J.C., Hope made it four straight. Kempker and Rink each pitched three innings and Busman one in the seven inning, 12-0 Hope shutout. The Dutchmen scored five in the final frame and played errorless ball. The second league double-header took place at Hillsdale on April 24 and the De Vette men were again successful. Rink gave six hits and struck out 13 in the opening 3-1 victory. His shutout bid was lost on a ninth inning passed ball. Rink contributed two hits to his own cause, as did Al Dykema. In the nightcap Hope scored four in the second while Jack Kempker scattered seven hits enroute to a 7-1 win. Kempker had two singles of his own and Ron Boeve's double was a key blow.

The six-game win streak came to an end at Riverview on May 1, when Cedric Dempsey and the Albion Britons came to town. Dempsey bested Rink in giving up six hits and striking out nine for the 5-3 victory. Hope left 12 men on base but managed to score three in the fourth on a bases-loaded triple by Ron Boeve. It was a different story in the second game as Kempker set the Britons down with a five-hitter that produced a 4-1 Hope victory. Rink took over an outfield position and contributed four singles, while Don Lubbers had two doubles and two singles.

On May 8 Hope hosted Calvin's first MIAA team at Riverview Park. In the first game it was Hope 8, Calvin 2 behind an eight-hit performance by Rink who also struck out 16. Don Lubbers had three of Hope's nine singles. Hope bats boomed out 12 hits in the nightcap, as Kempker posted a seven-hit, 13-3 victory. Don York had three singles and a triple, while Kempker and Van Hoeven each blasted three-run homers into the left field grandstand.

It was showdown time at Alma on May 15 in the season's final doubleheader. The games were played at nearby St. Louis High School with each team sporting a 7-1 MIAA record. Rink rose to the occasion in the first game with a 5-0 shutout after the Dutchmen scored four in the first inning. A nervous Alma pitcher walked the first three batters. Van Hoeven then singled and John Busman doubled. Hope's other run came in the sixth on a walk and singles by Busman and Ortquist. The Dutchmen, now on the brink of an undisputed championship, fell apart in the season's final game. Six Hope errors, six unearned runs, and eight walks by a struggling Jack Kempker were all that the Scots needed to notch the 7-1 victory that gave them a co-championship with Hope. The lone Dutch run came in the third on singles by Boeve, Ortquist, and York.

There was, however, due cause for celebration. Hope's overall record of 10 and 2 was one of the best in the school's history and had produced a second consecutive co-championship. Rink and York were named to the All-MIAA team, and in a post-season team meeting Willie Rink was elected Hope's Most Valuable Player. Jim Van Hoeven and Don Lubbers were named honorary co-captains for the season just completed. A sobering note came with the announcement that Coach Russ De Vette had accepted an offer to become

Hope Baseball Team - 1954
MIAA Co-Champions With Alma

Front Row L to R: Dick Ortquist, Lowell Huenink, Richard Gould, Robert Smith, Richard Huls. **2nd Row:** Coach Russ De Vette, Carl De Vree, Dick Defreese, Don York, Jan Wagner, Tom Harris, Jack Kempker, John Busman. **3rd Row:** Ron Boeve, Jim Van Hoeven, Bob Verduin, Willard Rink, Bob Wagner, Don A. Lubbers, David Huff, Al Dykema, Doug Elenbaas, Manager Warren Kane.

head basketball coach at the University of Maine at Orono. The offer came via former Hillsdale football coach Harold Westerman, who now served as Maine's head coach. Their friendship dated from graduate school days at the University of Michigan. De Vette would also serve as backfield coach in football.

Coach Larry Green's '54 track squad would miss '53 dash champion Ron Bos, but there was hope that Colorado State transfer Tom Carey would help fill the void. The season opened at home with Hillsdale on April 26. The day was unseasonably hot and wet but Carey made his presence known with firsts in the broad jump and 220 plus a second in the 100. Carey's leap of 22' 4" was outstanding as was Ken Armstrong's second place mark of 22' 3." Other impressive firsts were scored by Hendrickson in the shot with 43' 10 1/4," and John Brannock in he discus with 123' 3." John De Vries won the pole vault, while Joe Fowler, Ken Armstrong, and Dave Hondorp were part of a five-way tie for first in the high jump. Hope's mile relay team won but was disqualified. The lost points were not needed in Hope's 74 2/5 to 56 3/5 final victory.

On April 28 the Dutchmen met Calvin and Olivet at South Field in Grand Rapids. This time the final tally showed Hope with 86 1/2 to 68 1/2 for Calvin and eight for Olivet. Tom Carey, Ron Den Uyl, and John De Vries were all double winners. Carey captured the dashes, Den Uyl won the two distance events, and De Vries was first in the pole vault and broad jump. John Brannock won the discus and Joe Fowler took the high jump to round out a successful afternoon.

The John Bos Relays were held at Houseman Field in Grand Rapids on April 30. No team scores were kept but teams from seven colleges and 18 high schools were represented. Hope was impressive in the 220 low hurdles as Dave Hondorp placed first, Bob De Young second, Ted Bechtel fourth and John Adams fifth. The Dutchmen also had firsts in the pole vault with John De Vries, the mile run with Ron Den Uyl, the high hurdles with Don Brookstra, and the shot put with Bob Hendrickson.

The Hope team continued to roll at the expense of Grand Rapids Junior College on May 8. The 83-48 victory was accomplished at the now-familiar Houseman Field with the Dutchmen winning 10 of the 15 events. Don Brookstra and Bob De Young were 1-2 in the high hurdles, and John Adams and De Young went 1-2 in the 220 lows. Other firsts were recorded by Tom Carey in both dashes, John De Vries in the pole vault and broad jump, Joe Fowler in the high jump, Dave Kuyers in the javelin, and Bob Hendrickson in the shot put. The mile relay team of Bernard Van Ark, Bob Hamilton, Karl Essenberg, and Brian Aldrich was also victorious.

Coach Green's squad experienced a rude awakening on May 11, when the team met a greatly strengthened Albion team at the Allegan High School track. The double-dual, which included Allegan High versus Otsego, found Hope on the short end of a 90 1/2 to 40 1/2 score. The Britons won all of the running events and took 10 of 15 firsts. Joe Fowler and Dave Hondorp tied for first in the high jump, Hendrickson took the shot, Brannock the discus, and De Vries the pole vault, but it was an Albion day and the Dutchmen retreated to Holland to re-group. A week later the team played host to Calvin and reversed the score with a final of Hope 90, Calvin 41. This time Hope took first place in 12 of the 15 events. Tom Carey was a triple winner with victories in the 100, 220, and broad jump. The afternoon's best performance was recorded by John Brannock who set a new Hope discus record with a throw of 133'. Joe Fowler's high jump of 5' 10" also took first place.

The 1954 MIAA track and field meet was held at Kalamazoo's Angell Field on Friday, May 21. In the afternoon field event session Hope built a lead of 30 6/10 to 15 6/10 over favored Albion, but Coach Green knew it would be an uphill battle in the evening finals. One move was to borrow outfielder Don York from Russ De Vette's baseball team. York responded by taking the league championship in the javelin with a throw of 158' 9." Other firsts were recorded by Bob Hendrickson in the shot with a fine put of 45' 2," and by John De Vries in the broad jump with a leap of 21' 3 1/2." De Vries also tied for first in the pole vault at 11' 4." Albion's strength in the running events asserted itself in the evening session and the Britons won the meet in convincing fashion. Final scores were: Albion 90 6/10, Hope 49 6/10, Hillsdale 24 1/10, Adrian 24 1/10, Calvin 20, Kalamazoo 15 6/10, Alma 6, Olivet 0. Hope's second place finishes were recorded by Don Brookstra in the high hurdles, John Brannock in the discus, and Joe Fowler who tied for second in the high jump.

Coach Ken Weller's '54 tennis squad began the season without the services of Warren Exo and Ron Bos, the number one and two singles players who had led the team to a second place finish in '53. Graduation had taken its toll, but Weller could still field a strong contingent with Bill Boeskool at number one, Bill Coventry at two, John Schrier at three, Monte Dyer at four, and GRJC transfer Art Bieri at five. Glenn De Pree and John Warren were also squad members.

The team was off to an impressive start with a two-day sally into neighboring Indiana and Illinois. On April 9 the Dutchmen took the measure of Indiana State, 7-2, as Boeskool, Coventry, Bieri and De Pree were winners in singles. The doubles teams of Boeskool-Coventry, Schrier-Dyer, and Bieri-Warren also recorded victories. The following day the team made a good showing against Eastern Illinois University before bowing 6-3. Boeskool and Bieri were winners in singles while the doubles team of Boeskool and Coventry claimed Hopes other victory.

Hope's first home match was an 8-0 shutout of Grand Rapids J.C. on April 20. Boeskool, Coventry, Schrier, Dyer, Bieri, and De Pree all recorded victories in singles. In doubles it was Boeskool-Coventry and DyerWarren posting wins. Hope's bid for a perfect day was thwarted somewhat when the number two doubles team of Schrier and Bieri was rained out.

With the so-called "warm-ups" out of the way, the Dutchmen moved into MIAA play with an impressive 6-1 win over Albion on April 22. Bill Boeskool defeated Bill Vincent, 6-3, 7-5; Bill Coventry took Joe Roberts, 6-1, 6-2; John Schrier defeated Brad Ungrodt, 6-2, 1-6, 6-2; and Art Bieri won over Don Malton, 6-0, 7-5. In doubles, Boeskool-Coventry defeated Vincent-Roberts, 6-3, 6-2, and Schrier-Bieri were winners over Ungrodt-Jones, 6-4, 6-3.

A week later, in another home match, the Dutchmen repeated the 6-1 score, this time over arch-rival Calvin. Hope winners were Boeskool, Coventry, Schrier, Bieri, and in doubles Boeskool-Coventry, and Schrier-Bieri. Hope's third 6-1 victory came on May 5 against Alma, again on the home courts. Boeskool won over Gordon Mc Donald, 7-5, 6-4; Coventry defeated Harry Anderson, 6-1, 8-6; Schrier took John Sawyer, 7-5, 4-6, 6-4; Dyer defeated Dick Wallace, 6-1, 6-1; and Bieri won over Moe Arnold, 6-2, 6-0. Hope's other win was a 6-3, 6-1 doubles victory by Boeskool and Coventry over Mc Donald and Anderson.

Hope traveled to Olivet on May 6 to shut out the Comets, 7-0, then hosted the powerful Kalamazoo Hornets on May 11. As expected, the Hornets prevailed but did not shut out the Dutchmen. The "1" in Hope's 6-1 defeat was of special significance to Bill Coventry. In perhaps his finest hour in college tennis, Coventry upset Bob Casler, the defending MIAA singles champion in straight sets, 6-3 and 6-4. Both doubles matches went three sets before Kalamazoo claimed victory.

Hope's third shutout of the season came at Adrian on May 14. The 7-0 victory over the Bulldogs seemed to position the Dutchmen well for the contest the following day at Hillsdale, but the Dales proved to be the surprise team of the league. At the end of the afternoon it was Hillsdale 5, Hope 2 with all matches but two going three sets. Art Bieri defeated Art Burns, 7-5, 3-6, 6-3, in singles, and in doubles it was Bieri and Schrier getting the best of Jim Lescrionski and Lou Adams, 6-3, 10-8. The Dales' hard fought victory was legitimate and they proved it again on May 21 in the MIAA meet at Kalamazoo. Final point totals showed Kalamazoo with 50, Hillsdale with 30, and Hope with 25. Albion aided Hope's cause by finishing sixth.

Coach John Visser's '53 golf team had finished in fifth place. The only returnees were Bill Holt and Bob Visser and the outlook was grim in terms of a contribution to the All-Sports race. Junior Jim Hutton and three freshmen rounded out the squad. The first-year men were Joe Martin, Gordon Hondorp, and Dave St. Aubin. On April 24 Hope lost 9-6 to Alma, and on the 26th it was Olivet 7 1/2, Hope 7 1/2, but Olivet's Erso was medalist with a 73 to give the Comets the victory. Dave St. Aubin was Hope's low man in both matches and took medalist honors on April 30 as Hope won at Kalamazoo, 9 1/2 to 5 1/2. It was Bill Holt's turn on May 5 as he carded a 76 to aid in the defeat of Hillsdale, 9 1/2 to 6 1/2. In an away match on May 8, it was Albion 11 1/2, Hope 4 1/2, with Bob Visser playing best for the Dutchmen with a 78.

The up and down season continued. On May 11 Hope hosted Adrian and registered a 15-0 shutout with Bill Holt taking honors with a 79. In Grand Rapids on May 13 it was Calvin 8 1/2, Hope 6 1/2. Hope's 3-4 record going into the conference meet was not impressive, but on May 21 at Kalamazoo, freshman Dave St. Aubin carded a 75 for the first 18 and it was enough to lift the Dutchmen to a third place finish, a major improvement over the fifth place of '53. The golf finish offset the slight drop in tennis and track and allowed Hope to repeat as the MIAA's All-Sports champion. The Dutch teams accumulated 83 points overall to 78 for the Albion Britons. Following the Friday night track finals Russ De Vette, Hope's director of athletics, received the trophy from Ralph Young, retiring director of athletics at Michigan State. Young had been an outstanding coach for Kalamazoo College teams from 1916 to 1923.

*   *   *

As Russ De Vette departed for Maine, the Hope administration elected to cover his former duties by reshuffling various responsibilities. The belt-tightening measure made Al Vanderbush director of athletics while Larry "Doc" Green took De Vette's post as chairman of physical education. John Visser was moved from the History Department to Physical Education, where he would assume the reigns in baseball, continue to coach basketball, and teach classes in P.E. Larry Green moved from cross country to football, where he would work with linemen, and Ken Weller, well acquainted with the Vanderbush offense, would direct backfield play. For the second time in a four-year period, sociologist Bob Vanderham was called upon to take over the cross country team.

With back-to-back All-Sports trophies, Hope College enjoyed new status in MIAA circles. President Lubbers, however, often reminded that being on a pedestal was tantamount to being on the spot. Such was surely the case in the fall of 1954. Athletes will attest that the struggle to stay on top often exceeds the effort to get there. Unforeseen circumstances conspire to bring down a champion.

When Al Vanderbush's football squad assembled on September 1 to defend its title some key figures were missing. Gone via graduation were ends John Brannock and MVP Jim Van Hoeven, also guard Herm Nienhuis, center Bud Prins, and fullback Dave Kempker. Halfback Frank Talarico had joined the Marine Corps, and quarterback Harry Voss was concentrating on studies. As Vanderbush surveyed the scene in this, his ninth season, no one could envision that it would be his final campaign as head coach. Despite the above-mentioned losses, the picture was far from dismal. Co-captains Bill Heydorn and Don Vander Toll were proven leaders and solid performers at guard. Tackles Don Van Hoeven and John Hollander were the biggest men at that position in recent memory and both had considerable playing time in '53, as had back-up Warren De Witt. Center Ron De Graw, a St. Joseph junior, had not played in high school, but was a hard-nosed football player by any standards and had come a long way in the '53 campaign. He was ably supported by Earl De Witt, younger brother of Warren. Lynn Post, a veteran of the '51 co-championship team, returned from military service to take over one end position, and halfback Bob Hoekesema made a smooth transition to the other one. High-scoring John Adams was back at one halfback and Western Colorado transfer Tom Carey was expected to take the spot vacated by Talarico. Fullback Dave Kuyers, with both size and speed, had been impressive in his freshman year. Quarterback candidates included senior Don York, sophomore John Holmlund, and freshmen Mert Vander Lind and Del Grissen.

The '54 season opened at Riverview Park against Fred Trosko's Michigan Normal Hurons. The first half was evenly played, but with 17 seconds remaining quarterback Bob Middlekauff moved his team to the Hope 15 and then passed into the end zone. The ball bounced off two Hope defenders and was deflected into the hands of Doug Wilkens for the touchdown. Middlekauff's point try was not good but the visitors enjoyed a great halftime boost and a 6-0 lead. The Hurons mounted a 69-yard drive in the third quarter with Wilkens going the final distance for the score. This time Middlekauff's kick was good and the score stood 13-0. Hope's comeback attempt was foiled when John Holmlund was intercepted. The Hurons' third score came with 5:30 remaining, when halfback Jerry Miller went in on a right end sweep. The point try was not good, making the final Michigan Normal 19, Hope 0. Coach Al had a good look at his squad as 30 players saw action, including 12 freshmen, but senior Don York suffered a concussion that ended his season almost before it began.

Hope's night game at Olivet on September 25 started well. Speedy Tom Carey took a pitchout from Holmlund and raced 65 yards down the sideline for the touchdown. Van Hoeven's kick was wide, but Hope led 6-0 with only three minutes gone. The lead held up through the first quarter, but in the second the Comets began a 60-yard drive that reached the end zone on a keeper play by quarterback Rolland Wahl. The point try failed and the score remained tied at six until the final 30 seconds of the first half, when Hope scored only to have the touchdown wiped out by a clipping penalty. In the third period a Wahl-to-Compton pass from the Hope 36 went all the way, and Ed Bryant's kick gave Olivet a 13-6 lead. Later, the ball was jarred from Holmlund's grasp as he searched for a receiver. The Comets recovered and moved to the Hope 30, where Wahl passed to Ed Bryant for Olivet's third touchdown. Bryant converted to make it 20-6. Hope's only threat in the fourth quarter came on a Holmlund-to-Paul Wiegerink pass that reached the five yard line. The passing game proved a significant factor in the disappointing Hope defeat. Olivet completed 10 of 18 for 140 yards, while the Dutchmen could muster only three of 10 for 70 yards.

On the rainy weekend of October 2, Hope journeyed to Waukesha, Wisconsin, to take on the Pioneers of Carroll College. The field had been used for a high school contest on the previous evening and the 11-hour downpour which followed reduced the playing area to a sea of mud. Tom Carey was unable to make the trip due to a shoulder separation suffered during practice. Six hundred Mom and Dads' Day fans watched the Pioneers roll up 148 yards, all by rushing. The decision to stay on the ground, combined with five pass interceptions, resulted in a 25-0 Carroll victory. In the first quarter, halfback Glenn Johnson went over from the three and Carroll led 6-0. With 1:54 left in the half, Sid Dodge intercepted a Mert Vander Lind pass on the Hope 20 and halfback Henry Paris later scored on an eight-yard end sweep to make it 13-0 at halftime. In the fourth quarter the Dutchmen fumbled a handoff and Carroll recovered on the Hope five. A delay of game penalty put the ball on the 2 1/2, and quarterback Jack Fendt sneaked in to increase the lead to 19-0. Late in the game Sid Dodge intercepted a John Adams pass and returned it to the Hope seven, and Joe Sydow went in to make the final 25-0. Hope's high point may have been a blocked extra point by Ron De Graw.

The 0 and 3 Dutchmen returned to Holland to prepare for a home game with Alma on October 9. The Scots were sporting an eight-game winning streak over two seasons. They were led by quarterback Denny Stolz and halfbacks Bob Hill and Marv Raab. Raab had been responsible for five touchdowns against Hope in the '53 season finale. Coach Vanderbush began the week by giving his weary charges the day off on Monday. Drills were resumed with new vigor on Tuesday and a productive week of preparation ensued.

When Alma arrived at Riverview the Dutchmen were ready. In the first quarter, five Hope running plays plus a 15-yard penalty against the Scots put the ball on the Alma one, and Adams went over for the game's first score. A successful conversion by Doc Van Hoeven made it 7-0. Freshman Del Grissen had been pressed into service after two minutes of play when quarterback John Holmlund left the game with an injury. In the third quarter freshman Dick Gantos recovered a fumble on the Alma 20. Freshman Ron Wetherbee, filling in for the injured Carey, moved Hope to the 15, where Grissen hit end Bob Hoeksema in the end zone for the score. Senior Warren De Witt added the point to make it 14-0. The Dutchmen were not finished. A fourth quarter drive was led by fullback Dave Kuyers who had 116 yards on the day. Kuyers moved Hope to the Alma 7 where Del Grissen passed to end Bruce Springsteen, who took the ball on the one and dove in for the score. The point after was not good but Hope's 20-0 lead was now insurmountable. Alma scored in the closing minutes against the Dutch subs. Halfback Damon Colburt notched the touchdown on an off-tackle run and quarterback Dick Ayling ran the extra point. It marked one of but two times in the game that the Scots were able to penetrate Dutch territory. The Hope line performed brilliantly on both offense and defense. Marv Raab was held to four yards net in rushing and Bob Hill was limited to eight. Del Grissen went eight for 16 in the passing department, while his twin brother, Duane, subbing for Kuyers, picked up 43 yards in seven carries. The 20-7 victory was a classic example of Coach Vanderbush's ability to inspire an underdog team to perform beyond their own expectations.

Coach Joe Fortunato brought his Adrian team to Riverview for a Friday night game on October 15 and ran into the newly-acquired Dutch momentum. With less than three minutes remaining in the half, quarterback Mert Vander Lind, from his own 23, passed to end Paul Wiegerink, who broke away for a 41 yard gallop to the Bulldog 36. A Vander Lind-to-Tom Carey pass was good to the eight, and Kuyers bulled into the end zone. Doc Van Hoeven's kick was true and the Dutchmen went to the locker room with a 7-0 lead. Defense reigned throughout the third period, but in the fourth quarter Vander Lind intercepted a Joe Davis pass on the Hope 20 and returned it to the 40. Two plays later, after an effective fake to Kuyers, Vander Lind handed off to Johnny Adams who got outside and raced 52 yards down the sideline for Hope's second touchdown. Van Hoeven's kick was wide of the mark, making it 13-0. Adrian scored its touchdown with three minutes left following an 83-yard march. Russ Shindorf finally went in from a half yard out and Joe Davis kicked the point. The hard-earned victory left Hope at two and three with a chance to even the record a week hence at Homecoming.

The Homecoming opponent on October 23 was a solid Beloit team that made few errors. Hope continued to play good ball, but key interceptions took their toll and the Buccaneers emerged on the long end of a 14-6 score. The game proved to be much like Hope's Adrian game, except in reverse. Following a Joe Muscari interception in the second quarter, Beloit scored on a 17-yard pass from quarterback Dan Schroeder to Captain Clyde Butello. Schroeder's kick made it 7-0 at halftime. In the fourth quarter Beloit's fullback scored over center from the three and Schroeder's second placement increased the lead to 14-0. Hope had just four pass completions on the day, with three coming in the final minute of play. The last one was a 31-yarder from John Holmlund to Paul Wiegerink for the only Dutch score. Van Hoeven's kick was wide and Hope's short-lived winning streak was over.

Hillsdale's new head coach was Frank "Muddy" Waters, who assumed the post as Charley Bachman went into retirement for a second time. Waters' teams would win or share the MIAA championship for the next seven years. As mentioned earlier, the former Michigan State fullback enjoyed a close relationship with the Spartans' Biggie Munn and Duffy Daugherty. The MIAA's one-semester transfer rule made it possible for numerous players on the fringe of the State squad to transfer to Hillsdale in January and become eligible for play the following fall. Hope journeyed to Hillsdale on October 30 to continue the long and exciting series between the two schools. Early in the first period Hope's quarterback, Mert Vander Lind, was rushed as he attempted to pass from deep in his own territory. The pass was intercepted by Jack Rosetti, who scored from the Hope 15. John Moffatt's kick was wide and the score stood 6-0. In the second quarter the Dales scored again, this time on a defensive oversight by the Dutchmen. Using Biggie Munn's multiple offense the Dales shifted from the balanced T formation to the single wing with an unbalanced line. The Hope defense failed to shift its linemen one man over allowing Dale halfback Ancel Rogers to break through for a 50-yard touchdown run. The kick was not good, but Hillsdale enjoyed a 12-0 lead at the half. In the third quarter Jack Rossetti recovered a costly Hope fumble on their 12. An offside penalty moved the Dales back to the 17, but on the next play flashy halfback Nate Clark went all the way for the score. This time the kick by Bud Temple was good and the Hillsdale lead was 19-0. Still in the third period, with Del Grissen at the helm, Hope mounted an impressive 75-yard drive through the air. Grissen, master of the short pass, completed five aerials to Tom Carey, and one each to Ron Wetherbee and Lynn Post. Grissen's final throw was from the 10 to Carey and netted a touchdown. The kick was not good, but with the score at 19-6 the Dutchmen were still in the ball game. The Hillsdale defense stiffened in the fourth quarter and Hope was forced to punt. At this critical juncture the center's snap sailed over kicker Carey's head and Dale tackle Ed St. Clair recovered in the end zone for Hillsdale's fourth touchdown. The extra point failed, making it 25-6. The Dutchmen were not finished. Two Holmlund passes to Adams and one to Carey put the ball on the visitors' 20. A 15-yard penalty against the Dales put the ball on the five, but on the next play Holmlund was sacked on the 15. His next pass to Adams was good to the six. A subsequent off side penalty put the ball on the one and Adams went in for the score. The kick was not good and the game ended, Hillsdale 25, Hope 12.

Once again Coach Al rallied his discouraged forces. A confident Albion team came to Riverview on November 6 sporting a six-game winning streak. Dave Kuyers got the Dutchmen off to a great start by intercepting a Briton pass on the Hope 35 and returning it 46 yards to the Albion 19. On the next play Ron Wetherbee broke off tackle and went all the way for the touchdown. Doc Van Hoeven's kick was good, and Hope led 7-0 with only 53 seconds gone in the contest. There was no further scoring until the final minute of the half. With 14 seconds remaining a Holmlund-to-Adams pass was complete and the latter, faking out two defenders, went 28 yards for Hope's second touchdown. A high pass from center negated the point try, and the Dutch halftime lead was 13-0. With three minutes gone in the third quarter, Holmlund again connected with Adams. This time the play covered 64 yards with Adams going over for his second touchdown. Van Hoeven's kick was wide, leaving the score at 19-0. The Britons finally got on the board after a 67-yard drive that culminated with Murray's six-yard left end sweep. The conversion attempt failed, and the Hope lead was now 19-6. Holmlund's hot hand continued with a completion to Wetherbee, who romped 50 yards to the Albion 18. Two plays later Holmlund hit Mert Vander Lind with a scoring pass, but the touchdown was wiped out by a holding penalty. The quarterback's next pass was intercepted by Albion's Virgil Hall on the two. Hall advanced to the 22, where he fumbled. Hope Co-Captain Bill Heydorn was on hand to recover and give the Dutchmen another chance. Sub fullback Dick De Freese then scored after three successive carries. The conversion attempt by co-captain Don Vander Toll was not good, but nobody cared. The Britons were held at bay for the remaining six minutes and the jubilant Dutchmen had their second upset of the season, this time by an impressive 25 to 6 score.

Twenty-five hundred spectators turned out at Kalamazoo's Angell Field on November 13 to watch the Hornets and Dutchmen battle it out for a second place tie in the MIAA. Kalamazoo drew first blood when big Bob Steward bulled in from the five yard line. Rudy Walchena's point try was blocked by Warren De Witt to make it 6-0. Early in the second quarter the Hornets added to their lead when Herb Lipshitz went 15 yards off tackle and into the end zone. The kick by Walchena was good and the Dutchmen were down 13-0. The Hope defense now stiffened but its offense was stymied until the final quarter. With 4:30 remaining in the game a Holmlund-to-Carey pass was good, with the latter going in for the score. Warren De Witt's kick was good and the margin was narrowed to 13-7. The De Witt brothers became a real factor in the game when, with three minutes remaining, Earl recovered a fumble by Kalamazoo's Jim Smith. Warren's earlier block of a Kalamazoo point try, coupled with his own successful conversion, now loomed large. Holmlund now began a drive with completions to Kuyers and Adams. A third aerial to Bruce Springsteen placed the ball on the six. On a third down play Kuyers was stopped at the five. On fourth down with 45 seconds remaining, Holmlund threw a final pass into the end zone only to see it batted down by Hornet co-captain Paul Coash. A gallant comeback try had failed by the narrowest of margins. Kalamazoo ended in a second place tie with Albion with a 4-2 record, and second year coach Rolla Anderson's overall 6-2 mark was the best at Kalamazoo since 1946. The fates of football are not kind to losers. Instead of a second place tie, the Dutchmen now dropped to fourth place at 3-3. As the silent Greyhound made its way back to Holland, the coaches were left to mull over the "might-have-beens" without the anticipation of a better performance seven days later.

At a banquet on November 18 Bill Heydorn was named Hope's Most Valuable Player while John Adams and Lynn Post were co-captains-elect for the 1955 season. The MIAA coaches showed their respect for Hope's fourth place team by naming Adams, Heydorn, Kuyers, and Van Hoeven to the All-MIAA team. Al Vanderbush pondered the prospects for 1955, while Russ De Vette began his first season as head basketball coach at the University of Maine.

Sam Hofman was captain of Coach Bob Vander Ham's 1954 cross country team, which ended in an overall fourth place tie with Hillsdale. Squad members included Ron Den Uyl, John Docherty, Allen Durham, Jim Cooper, John Fikse, Lowell Huenink, John Schrier, and George Schipper. Hope opened the season with a 23-36 victory at Olivet. Ron Den Uyl finished first, John Fikse fourth, Jim Cooper fifth, Schrier and Schipper tied for sixth, Durham was eighth, and Hofman ninth. The Dutch harriers tasted defeat at Calvin on October 6 as Calvin ace Morrie Tubergen led all runners with a time of 22:32 for the four mile course. The final score was 19-42 in favor of the Knights. Den Uyl finished third and Hofman sixth.

In a close meet at the American Legion course on October 9, the Dutchmen came back to edge Alma, 24-33, with Den Uyl again the winner. Lowell Huenink was fourth, John Fikse fifth, Sam Hofman sixth, and Jim Cooper eighth. Hope's third and final victory was a 21-38 win over Adrian, again on the home course. Den Uyl's first place finish was followed by Fikse in third, Huenink fourth, Durham sixth, Cooper seventh, Docherty ninth, and Hofman tenth. The meet took place on October 15 and was followed by a loss to Grand Rapids JC on the 23rd.

The October 30 meet at Hillsdale was timed to finish at halftime of the football game and hometown fans were pleased when the Dales' Ron Wiegandt crossed the 50 yard line first for his 16th victory in a row. Den Uyl was second, Fikse ninth, Huenink 10th, Hofman 12th, Docherty 13th, and Cooper 15th. The final score showed Hillsdale 29, Hope 36. As expected, Albion dominated the November 6 meeting at the Legion course by a score of 19-39. Den Uyl was second behind Albion's ace Jim Chapman, Hofman finished seventh, Huenink ninth, Fikse l0th, and Cooper 11th. On November 13 the Dutchmen were unable to alleviate Hope's football disappointment, as the Hornets took a convincing 18-46 victory. Kalamazoo's Frank Grimm and Dick Erhle crossed the finish line together. Den Uyl's third place was followed by three more men from "K."

The MIAA meet was held at Adrian on Wednesday, November 17. Albion finished first with 26 points after staving off a Kalamazoo threat. The Hornets had 34, Calvin 96, Hope 127, Hillsdale 133, Alma 169, Adrian 173, and Olivet 178. Hope's overall finish was good enough for a fourth place tie. As late November snows blanketed the Hope campus, attention shifted to basketball. John Adams moved from regular halfback to regular forward for John Visser, now in his fourth year as head coach. Dwight Riemersma, Willard Rink, Harold Molenaar, and two-time All-MIAA Bob Hendrickson filled out the starting five. All were proven veterans. Coach Visser's problem in the 1954-55 campaign would be depth and by the Christmas break this weakness would hamper the Dutch effort. Norm Kramer's second semester transfer to Kalamazoo College would force Visser to look to untried freshmen.

Big news in the fall of '54 was the completion of the new Holland Civic Center at the corner of Eighth Street and Pine Avenue. City fathers engaged the famous Harlem Globetrotters to play, or perhaps "perform" the first game in the new auditorium on October 26. With the accent on fun, the large crowd was regaled by the antics of "Goose" Tatum, dribbler Marcus Haynes, and other members of the cast. The new structure had a seating capacity of 2,500 for basketball. Nine hundred and ninety-four theater-type seats graced the balcony and afforded maximum comfort. A formal dedication took place on November 16 and 17. Hope continued to practice in the refurbished Carnegie-Schouten Gym and at the Armory, with an occasional session at the Civic.

The first intercollegiate contest in the spacious new structure pitted Hope against Central of Iowa on November 27 before about 1,500 spectators. Hope led 30-26 at the intermission, but early in the second half the Dutchmen from Iowa tied it at 32, and with 12 minutes remaining Hope led by a single point, 38-37. The home team finally found its rhythm and pulled away to a 65-56 victory. To no one's surprise Bob Hendrickson led Hope with 19. He was followed by Whitey Riemersma 15 and Hal Molenaar with 13. Arnie Ver Hoef was high for Central with 15.

Hope's MIAA opener with Adrian on December 4 was a nail-biter all the way with the Civic crowd much involved. Jim Swoish's shot at the halftime buzzer gave the Bulldogs a 42-40 lead, but two minutes into the second half play-maker Willie Rink was on the bench with five fouls. The Dutchmen did not fold and managed to hold a 76-74 lead with one minute remaining, but the Bulldogs' final shot forced the game into overtime. In the extra period Jim Swoish and freshman Henry Hughes combined for 13 of Adrians's 15 points to give the visitors the 91-84 victory. Molenaar led Hope with 23 and was followed closely by Hendrickson with 21. Adams and Riemersma each contributed 13. Swoish and Hughes were the Adrian leaders with 24 and 22.

The December 7 game at Hillsdale was played before 200 noisy fans and proved to be a rough contest. The Dutchmen built a 41-28 halftime lead but lost momentum in the second half and trailed 64-56 with seven minutes left. At this point Visser's fast break began to function and his charges tied it at 66 with four minutes remaining. Hope sub John Jeltes forced several turnovers and Hillsdale's Rog Davis fouled out with five minutes left. Hope's 23-6 run in the final seven minutes gave the team its first league victory by a score of 79 to 70. Riemersma was high with 21, Rink had 15, Hendrickson 14, and Molenaar 13. Rog Davis tallied 19 for the losers.

Coach Visser used 16 players against an outmanned Olivet team in the Civic Center on December 11. In spite of the numerous substitutions, Hope's 44-31 halftime margin ballooned into an 83-59 victory. Riemersma led the way with 16, followed by Hendrickson's 12, 11 from Rink, and 10 from Norm Kramer. Olivet's James Mason had 21 in the losing the cause and Maynard Stafford had 14.

It was a different story at Michigan Normal two days later. The game was played in the Ypsilanti Central High School Gym and Jim Skala's Hurons appeared to be in mid-season form as they shot 42 percent from the floor to 27 percent for the Dutch. After an early 12-12 tie, the Normal team took a 44-34 lead at the intermission and coasted to an 86-59 win. A crowd of 750 watched Web Kirksey lead his team with 26 points, most from outcourt. Dave Parks added 15. Whitey Riemersma led Hope for the third straight game, but he was limited to 14 points.

Hope made the long trip to Pella, Iowa, for a return game on December 16 with Central College. Hope's sister institution now stood at 5-1, with its only loss in the season opener at Hope. Coach Visser's five held a four-point, 35-31 halftime lead, but the Iowans played steady ball, cashed in on 35 of 46 free throws, and avenged their earlier loss. The final was Central 77, Hope 71. Hendrickson led Hope with 22, Adams had 20, and Riemersma 16. Gus Youngberg was high man for the winners with 25.

In an attempt to make full use of the new Civic Center, Hope had scheduled a "Holiday Classic" on December 29 and 30. Participants were Lake Forest, Beloit, Albion, and Hope. An "opponent exchange" format was agreed upon to insure that Hope and Albion would not meet for a third time. It became apparent in the first evening's play that the MIAA teams would not fare well. In the first game, Albion was beaten 84-62 by Beloit and Hope absorbed a 103-73 thrashing at the hands of Lake Forest. The Foresters were led by Ev Cocallas with 25 and 6' 9" George Wolz with 20. Adams was the leader for Hope with 19. Coach Ray Ragelis had substituted freely after his team established an early 41-11 lead. But the worst was yet to come. The second night's activity began with Lake Forest downing Albion, 71 to 55. The Dutchmen, determined to make a better showing, actually led Beloit 46-45 with 4:26 remaining in the half, but the roof fell in when the Buccaneers went on a 21-4 tear and led at halftime, 66-50. The visitors were unchallenged in the second half and ended with the most decisive victory of the classic, 126 to 81.

The shell-shocked Dutchmen had little time to lick their wounds. On the following Monday, January 3, the Hurons of Michigan Normal came to the Civic intent on repeating their triumph of December 13. Hope's 878 students had not yet returned from the holiday break and disenchanted townspeople stayed away in droves. Three hundred and fifty of the faithful had their pick of seats and though their voices echoed in the 2,500 seat auditorium, they witnessed Hope's best game to that point. The Dutchmen, beaten by 27 in the earlier contest, fought to a 39-36 halftime lead and kept the score close throughout. With the score tied at 84 and 27 seconds remaining, Hal Molenaar launched a 15-footer that parted the net and gave Hope the dramatic 86-84 victory. Hendrickson led all scorers with 20 while balanced scoring came from the other starters. Adams had 17, Molenaar 16, Riemersma 14, and Rink 13.

It was a case of two teams that knew each other very well when Hope and Albion squared off in the Kresge Gym on January 8. The Britons led 32-27 at halftime, but the game remained close and was tied at 66 with one minute remaining. Bob Meeth and George Vivlamore then added free throws to make it 68-66. The Dutchmen had two more shots at the basket, but neither connected and Albion had the win in a well-played game.

Hope hosted Calvin for the first time in the Civic Center on January 13, 1955. Coach Barney Steen's MIAA champions were enjoying another good year but expected the usual tussle from Hope. The Knights' 38-33 halftime advantage was challenged several times in the second half, but Tony Diekema was the difference as the game wound down. The future Calvin president scored five field goals in the last eight minutes to seal the 93-82 victory. In overall scoring it was tall Tom Newhof leading a balanced attack with 19. Don Vroon followed closely with 18, Diekema had 17, and Gord De Kruyter 16. Hendrickson's 24 was tops for Hope. Adams added 17, Molenaar and Riemersma 14 each and Rink had 12. A serious snowball fight ensued in the parking lot, but there is no record of the outcome.

The Dutchmen returned to the win column on January 15 when the Alma Scots visited the Civic. In a ragged game the home team could manage only 26 percent from the floor, but built on a 37-29 lead at the half and went on to a comfortable 90-76 victory. Several freshmen saw service and Mert Vander Lind was among the scoring leaders. Molenaar led with 17, Adams was next with 15, Rink had 14, and Vander Lind 13. For Alma it was Jim Ford with 20 and Dick Ayling with 12.

In 1955 Kalamazoo grid coach Rolla Anderson was also coaching basketball. On January 29 the Hornets hosted Hope at the Tredway Gym in what Anderson termed their "best game of the season." The home team was not bothered by the Hope press, shot nearly 46 percent from the floor, posted a 44-36 halftime lead, and went on to win, 98 to 70. Gary Morrison pumped in 25 points, John Frueh had 19, and big Doug Steward was tough on the boards. For the losers it was Hendrickson with 18, Molenaar 17, Riemersma 14, and Rink 13. As the first semester ended Coach Visser lost a strong reserve when Norm Kramer transferred to Kalamazoo College in his home town.

The second round of MIAA play found the Dutchmen hosting Hillsdale on February 5. Coach Doug Wicken's team trailed 44-27 at halftime but stayed in the game by making good on 31 of 34 free throws. The teams played on even terms throughout the second half, with Hope finishing 18 points on the plus side. The eventual 87-69 victory was due in large part to strong performances by Riemersma and Hendrickson, who scored 21 and 20 points respectively. Guards Rink and Molenaar added 14 and 11. Coach Wickens was pleased with work of 6' 6" transfer Ken Blizzard, who led his team with 17. Ron Ford was next for the Dales with 15.

At Olivet on February 8 Coach Swede Thomas had his Comets ready and Coach Visser was concerned at halftime to find his team trailing 37-36. However, the Dutchmen reeled off 10 straight points to start the second half as the fast break functioned smoothly. The Comets regained control with slow-down tactics, but the damage had been done and Hope emerged with a 79-63 victory. The scorebook showed Riemersma leading with 24, Hendrickson with 18, and Adams 16. Coach Thomas got 18 points from Maynard Stafford and 15 from Buck Schultz.

Ike Isaac brought his Albion Britons to the Civic on February 12 for another in a long line of exciting match-ups. Hope fought to a 33-32 halftime lead, then used a tight zone to hold down center Bill Collison. In the end the Dutchmen pulled ahead 72-66, thanks to the 23-point effort of Willie Rink, who led his team for the first time. Hendrickson and Molenaar each had 12 and Adams 11. George Vivlamore was top man for the Britons with 19. Collison managed 14 in spite of the zone, and Bob Meeth had 13.

Hope's three-game spurt was halted in a heart-breaker at Alma on February 16. The Dutchmen played well throughout the first half and led 40-34 at the intermission, but with 10 minutes left Rink got into foul trouble and a comfortable lead disappeared. With the score tied at 72, Ron Lude, a 6' 5" Central Michigan transfer, put in the deciding free throw and Hope's late season comeback was stymied. Lude and Jim Ford led the Scots with 15 each while Molenaar with 23 and Hendrickson with 22 were high for the disappointed Dutch.

Two days later the team made its way to Grand Rapids to meet the high-flying Calvin Knights. Despite Hope's so-so record, 4,200 fans crowded into the Grand Rapids Civic Auditorium to cheer and jeer in what some now termed, "the battle of the denominations." In the first half John Visser's five seemingly could do no wrong. At halftime, fans from both sides viewed the scoreboard in disbelief as Hope led by 16, 45-29. Calvin concern increased when Hope built its lead to 20 at 53-33 with four minutes gone in the second half. The talented Knights were far from finished and an abrupt change of momentum saw the home team gradually close the gap. It appeared, however, that the Dutchmen would hold on to win with a 78-76 lead, but Don Vroon's patented two-hander with three seconds left sent the game into overtime. The drama continued in the extra period as the din from the crowd reduced the coaches to hand signals. The Dutchmen were not done and once again appeared on the verge of victory as they led 89-87, with only nine seconds remaining. This time it was Ed Start who prolonged the agony. As Start put in the game-tying basket he was fouled and Dutch hopes faded. The scenario reached its climax as the free throw attempt bounced back to Willie Rink who passed quickly to Molenaar. Molenaar in turn went cross court to John Adams who, for the second year in a row, took the final shot. Adams' attempt in '54 had rimmed the hoop and dropped off, leaving Hope with a heartbreaking 66-65 loss. This night the fates were kinder and the Saginaw junior's shot parted the net to make the final Hope 91, Calvin 89. In terms of sheer excitement, Adams' shot probably matched his longest touchdown run. Molenaar and Rink led Hope with 26 and 25 and Riemersma had 17 while Hendrickson and freshman Jim Hilmert were outstanding on the boards. Paul Newhof connected for 26 Calvin points and Jim Kok, out all week with the flu, came through with 22. Don Vroon had 17 and almost made the difference with his long-Tom at the end of regulation play. Another Hope-Calvin classic had gone into the books and Hope's trip home was over almost before it began.

Fifteen hundred turned out on February 22 to witness the last home appearance of Bob Hendrickson and Willard Rink. Furnishing the opposition were the troublesome Hornets of Kalamazoo College. Building on the Calvin success, the Dutchmen used the fast break effectively and moved to a 46-36 halftime advantage. The second half going was tough, but Hope's season-high 42 field goals netted the eventual 98-92 victory. Coach Visser employed a zone defense which worked to the advantage of his sometimes-tired regulars. Forwards Riemersma and Adams stole the scoring show with 28 and 26, while the hard-working Hendrickson had 17. For Kalamazoo it was Gary Morrison with 25 and Wayne Shell with 23.

Hope closed out the 1954-55 season by making the long trip to Adrian on Saturday, February 26. The Bulldogs were a team on the march. A victory over Hope would give them a co-championship with Calvin and they were not to be denied. A 46 percent shooting average helped produce a 49-38 lead at halftime and the Dutchmen, meanwhile, had difficulty finding the intensity that had generated the Calvin and Kalamazoo victories. When guards Rink and Molenaar both fouled out early there remained little doubt as to the outcome. Hope reserves played nearly half of the game that found a deserving Adrian team finally winning by 20 points, 98-78. The duo of Leon Harper and Henry Hughes poured in 27 and 22 respectively, and Jim Swoish had 13. In his final game Bob Hendrickson led his team with 21. John Adams had 15. Adrian and Calvin, each with 12 and two records, were declared MIAA co-champions. A playoff was arranged to determine who would advance in the NAIA tournament. The Bulldogs prevailed, 76-67, and after disposing of Detroit Tech, reached the tourney in Kansas City. They were finally eliminated by Texas Southern, 102 to 83, but the 1954-55 season remains one of the finest in Adrian basketball history.

Hope's 8-6 record spelled fourth place in the MIAA, while the overall mark of 10-10 included its share of excitement. Especially pleasing to Coach John Visser was the strong second round of MIAA play. Bob Hendrickson was named to the All-MIAA team for the third straight year, and Harold Molenaar made the second team.

Coach Visser was given little time to brood about the "might-have-beens" of basketball. As Hope's new baseball mentor, Visser greeted eight lettermen from Russ De Vette's '54 co-championship team. After a year's absence, John Adams returned to become one of the college's very few three-sport men. In short order he took over at first base, as talent will out. Other infielders were Dick Ortquist at second, Dick De Freese at third, and Carl De Vree at short. Starting outfielders were Don York, Al Dykema, and freshman Ron

Bob Hendrickson was a four-year starting center for Coach John Visser and 3 times All-MIAA. One of the all-time greats of Hope basketball, he also competed in track and was the MIAA shot put champion in 1953, '54, and '55. Following graduation he enjoyed a successful career as basketball coach at Grand Rapids Ottawa Hills High School, twice winning the Michigan State Class "A" Championship.

Wetherbee. The usual Michigan spring weather forced workouts in "spacious Carnegie-Schouten Gym" in preparation for the April 15 opener with Ferris. The pitching chores would be handled by All-MIAA Willard Rink and John Holmlund, the erstwhile quarterback. York and Mert VanderLind also had limited mound duty.

The series of fourth place finishes in the fall and winter of 1954-55 eliminated any talk of the All-Sports trophy. Instead, each spring sports coach simply endeavored to compile the best record possible. Visser's April 15 debut was successful, as his Dutchmen beat Ferris 8-6 at Riverview Park. Carl De Vree stroked a bases loaded triple in Hope's four-run fourth and Don York came through with a two-run homer in the fifth. Adams had two for three and Wetherbee went two for five. Fink, who struck out 10, was the winner.

The MIAA abandoned its double-header format for the spring of '55 and Hope opened the league season at Olivet on April 19. The Comets scored one in the first and two more in the fifth. With the score 3-1 in the ninth, singles by Adams and Rink produced one more Hope run, but the rally fell short and Rink's 14 strikeout performance was wasted in the 3-2 loss. Two days later Hope hosted Grand Rapids J.C. and scored nine runs in the first six innings. J.C. tied the count with a seven-run seventh, but lost the game 11-10 on two shortstop errors in the ninth. Ron Boeve led the Hope hitters with two doubles. Holmlund and York pitched most of the way, but it was Rink in relief who got the win. The loser was Bob Andree who, two years later, would be a first-line hurler for Hope.

Hope lost a pitchers' battle to Adrian at Riverview on April 26. There were no hits in the ball game until the eighth inning. Rink struck out 10 and walked none, but the Bulldogs pushed across three runs in the top of the ninth and went home with a 3-0 shutout. Singles by Carl De Vree and Al Dykema were the only hits allowed by winning pitcher Doug Kane.

The Dutchmen faced pitching of a different sort at Hillsdale on April 29. Seven Dale pitchers managed to walk 17 Hope batters. The free passes, combined with eight Hope hits, produced a 15-2 victory. Rink struck out 14, three in the ninth to end the game. The Dutch bats continued to boom on May 3 at Riverview, as Hope hosted Kalamazoo in temperatures of 85 degrees. A 10-run second inning for Hope sealed a 13-6 Dutch victory. The big second included a single and home run by Al Dykema, a triple by Carl De Vree, three walks, and three Kalamazoo errors. Dick Ortquist also had a banner day at the plate with three hits, including a home run. Winning pitcher Willie Rink struck out 13 while giving up seven hits. Gary Morrison had two doubles for Kalamazoo and drove in two runs.

Hope met Calvin in Grand Rapids at Valley Field on May 7. The teams played evenly and the score was tied at six in the last of the ninth. With two out and two strikes on first baseman Keith Dykstra, Rink uncharacteristically let go a wild pitch that allowed Tony Diekema to score the winning run from third base. Ortquist again went three for four, but the Knights' 7-6 victory redeemed in part, their recent basketball loss to the Dutchmen.

The May 11 game with Albion was played at the Zeeland High School diamond due to Tulip Time activities at Riverview Park. Willard Rink was in top form as he twirled a three-hitter, striking out 12 and walking but a single batter. The result was a 7-0 shutout that featured four for four by Carl De Vree and an eighth inning triple by Don York. Winning streaks, however, seemed hard to establish and the Dutchmen dropped a tough 3-2 decision at Alma on May 14. All runs were scored in the first three innings. A first inning triple by the Scots' Jack Westerhof scored two runs and pitcher Gord Rutherford drove in what proved to be the winning run in the third. Dick De Freese had two hits and scored both Hope runs. The teams also played a seven-inning non-league game and the Scots again squeezed out a one-run victory, this time 5-4. Ron Boeve led Hope with a homer and single. Pitcher John Holmlund struck out nine and walked three but gave up two home runs, one the game winner in the last of the seventh.

Hope College played its first-ever night baseball game at Riverview on May 18. Quite appropriately the opponent was Calvin College. The 18-11 Hope win was also gratifying, the only problem being that it was a non-league contest. Williard Rink gave up one hit and struck out nine over five innings before giving way to John Holmlund, who pitched the final four. Hope's 13-hit attack included four for four by Ron Wetherbee.

Hope closed out the season by traveling to Detroit for a double-header with Wayne University. In the opener the Dutchmen outhit their big city opponents 10-6, but eight costly errors contributed to the eventual 6-3 Wayne victory. Rink went the distance striking out six and walking one. Adams and Dykema each went three for four. In the seven-inning nightcap the Hope nine could muster only three hits and Wayne went on to register a 10-0 shutout. As the team made its way back to Holland thoughts turned to graduation and summer jobs. In his first and only year as Hope's coach, John Visser's team compiled an overall record of six and seven. The team finished fourth in the MIAA at three and four. Hope was represented on the 15-man All-MIAA team by its battery of Willie Rink and Ron Boeve.

Coach Al Timmer's '55 golf team also finished fourth in MIAA play. The team was strengthened by the addition of freshman Ray DeDoes who took medalist honors with a 73 in his very first match, an 8-7 victory over Grand Rapids J.C. Other team members were Bill Holt, Bill Kramer, Jim Hutton, Dave Hondorp, and John Van Dyke. After the April 21 opener, the team met Adrian and Hillsdale in a triangular at Hillsdale. The Dutchmen were victorious over Adrian 10-6 but were beaten by the Dales 15 to 1.

De Does was again medalist (71) on April 26 as Hope downed Kalamazoo 13-3 at Saugatuck. On May 5 the team repeated the 13-3 score, this time at Olivet. C. Burton of the

Comets was medalist with a 73, while De Does was tops for Hope with a 78. Hope defeated Calvin, 10-6, on May 10, with De Does leading both teams with a 74. In the other part of the Saugatuck triangular, it was Albion 9 1/2, Hope 6 1/2. In the MIAA Field Day meet at Kalamazoo on May 20, Bill Kramer placed third with a two-day total of 157. Team scores were: Albion 821, Hillsdale 839, Alma 880, Hope 881, Calvin 894, Kalamazoo 902, Adrian 979, and Olivet 989.

Coach Ken Weller continued to do an outstanding job with the men's tennis team. The 1955 squad posted an impressive 9-2 dual meet record and finished second only to powerful Kalamazoo. Five of the dual wins were shutouts. Bill Coventry, John Schrier, Art Bieri, Glenn De Pree and John Warren returned from the '54 squad and were joined by freshmen John Jeltes, Ken Van Wieren, and Dwayne "Tiger" Teusink. In two days of early season competition the team ventured into Indiana and Ohio. The April 11 match with Earlham was forced inside because of rain. The unfamiliar indoor facilities did not bother the Dutchmen, who were off to a good start with an 8-0 victory. Coventry, Van Wieren, Jeltes, and Schrier won at singles, while four Hope doubles teams also came out on top. The teams were: Coventry-Jeltes, Schrier-Van Wieren, Bieri-Teusink, and De Pree-Warren. The next day it was Hope 10, Wittenberg 1. Coventry's singles match, a tough three-setter, was Hope's only loss.

When Hope hosted Adrian on April 19, Coach Weller had completed his shakedown and the team shut out the Bulldogs, 7-0. Winning in singles were Jeltes, Van Wieren, Coventry, Schrier, and Bieri. In doubles this day it was John Warren-Art Bieri, and Glenn De Pree-Dwayne Teusink. In Grand Rapids on April 21 it was Hope 9, Grand Rapids J.C. 0. This time the singles victories went to Jeltes, Van Wieren, Coventry, Schrier, Bieri, and Teusink. The winners in doubles were Jeltes-Van Wieren, Schrier-Bieri, and De Pree-Warren.

Five days later, the team was back in Grand Rapids to meet the Calvin Knights at Franklin Park. In the 6-1 Hope win Jeltes defeated Dave Scheur, 6-3, 6-2, Coventry defeated Jim Kok, 6-0, 6-1, Schrier defeated Rich Sharda, 9-7, 6-4, and Bieri defeated Warren Boer, 6-1, 6-1, 6-3. Hope's only loss of the day came when Rod Boersma defeated Van Wieren in a three-setter, 6-2, 2-6, 6-3. The doubles team of Jeltes Van Wieren defeated Scheur-Sharda, 9-7, 6-4 and Coventry-Bieri defeated Boersma-Bouwkamp, 5-7, 7-5, 6-4.

At Alma on April 29 Hope's top performers were at their best and the result was another 7-0 shutout. At home against Olivet on May 3 Coach Weller took advantage of an opportunity to get more of his squad into the act. After Jeltes, Coventry, Van Wieren, Bieri, and Schrier had secured the match with singles victories, the doubles team of Jeltes and Teusink proved effective, as did De Pree and Warren in the overall 7-0 win.

Hope was not the only MIAA team to administer shut outs. At Kalamazoo on May 5, after seven straight victories, the Dutchmen found out what it was like to be on the receiving end. Kalamazoo's 7-0 shutout was accomplished in straight sets down the line. The Hornets, with one of their strongest teams, had earlier taken the measure of both Illinois and Indiana of the Big Ten.

Hillsdale found Weller's team still smarting from the Kalamazoo encounter when they came to Holland on May 10. With something to prove, the Dutchmen got back on the winning track with a convincing 6-1 victory over one of the MIAA's better teams. The Dales won only the number one doubles match. Two days later in Detroit, Hope ran into a strong Wayne University team. Jeltes and Coventry were the only Hope winners in the 5-2 setback. Not overly troubled by the non-league loss, the team was at Albion the next day to post another 6-1 victory. Jeltes, Van Wieren, Coventry, Bieri, and Schrier came through in singles while Jeltes and Van Wieren got the sixth win in doubles.

Hope entered the MIAA meet at Kalamazoo with 18 points and picked up an additional 12 to finish with 30 for second place overall. Hillsdale was third with 26. Other teams in order of finish were Albion, Calvin, Alma, Adrian, and Olivet. Hopeites were pleased to have one of its teams finally break the fourth place jinx which seemed to have dogged the Dutchmen throughout the 1954-55 school year.

Coach Lawrence "Doc" Green began his third track season with a few veteran performers and a very promising crop of freshmen. Particularly impressive were the hurdlers. Leading the way was Paul Wiegerink from Grand Rapids Ottawa Hills High School, State Class A champion in both the high and low hurdles. He was joined by 6' 7" Jim Hilmert of Kalamazoo Central, who had placed fifth in the highs in the state meet. Also on hand was Everett Nienhouse of Oak Park, Illinois, who was the Illinois state champion in the high hurdles. Not to be forgotten was junior Don Brookstra, who had finished second in the highs in the '54 MIAA meet. Athletic Director Al Vanderbush conceded that it was "almost embarrassing" to have so much talent in a single event.

The opening meet at Ferris on April 22 was canceled due to rain, but Hope took second place in a triangular in Grand Rapids on the 25th. Kalamazoo won the meet with 85 points to 55 for Hope and 24 for Grand Rapids J.C. Jim Hilmert scored 13 points for Hope with firsts in the high hurdles and discus, plus a second in the high jump. Paul Wiegerink set a new Hope record by winning the 220 low hurdles in a time of 26.2, and Dave Spaan won the 440 in 52.9. Bob Hendrickson took the shot put and John De Vries was first in the broad jump.

Coach Green took eight freshmen and two sophomores to the John Bos Relays in Grand Rapids on April 30, and the underclassmen came home with two firsts and four seconds. Wiegerink lowered his record to 25.7 in taking the low hurdles, while Hilmert won the highs in 15.8. Ev Nienhouse was second in both hurdle races, and Dave Spaan took second in the 440. Wiegerink also claimed a second in the 100 yard dash.

Hope and Kalamazoo met in a classic dual meet at Allegan on May 3. The Hornets claimed eight first places to seven for the Dutchmen, but Hope led 62 2/3 to 59 1/3 going into the meet's final event. The men from "K" were able to win the mile relay and with it the meet by a score of 64 1/3 to 62 2/3. Hope's double winners were Hilmert in the highs and the discus, and De Vries in the broad jump and pole vault. Dave Spaan won the 440 in 51.0 to break George Douma's Hope record of 51.4, set in 1935. Wiegerink again won the low hurdles and Hendrickson the shot.

Hope was back at Houseman Field on May 7 for a quadrangular with Calvin, Olivet, and Alma. Paul Wiegerink, in his home town, was in top form as he contributed 19 points to his team's winning total of 99 1/2. Calvin came in second with 59, and Olivet edged Alma 28 1/2 to 28. Wiegerink's big day consisted of firsts in the high hurdles, low hurdles, and 100 yard dash plus a second in the broad jump. Ron Den Uyl was a double winner in the mile and two mile, and De Vries was again first in the broad jump and pole vault. Hendrickson took the shot, Spaan the 440, and Hope's mile relay team of Jim Cooper, Curt Menning, Dave De Jong, and Dave Spaan made it 10 of 15 firsts in the meet overall.

Albion outscored Hope 81 to 50 in a night meet at Allegan on May 10. The Britons swept the discus, 880, and two mile, and the Dutchmen never quite recovered. John De Vries won his specialties, the broad jump and pole vault, and Don York was excused from baseball practice to throw the javelin. York won the event with a heave of 159' 2 1/2." Ev Nienhouse was first in the high hurdles and Wiegerink took the lows. Hope's other first was by Hendrickson in the shot put.

At the Elmhurst Relays on May 14 the Dutchmen met even stronger competition. In a field of 21, Hope finished eighth with 12 1/2 points. A talented University of Chicago team took first with 35 1/2 points. De Vries managed a second in the broad jump and third in the pole vault, Wiegerink was third in both hurdle races, and Nienhouse, back in his home state, was fifth in the highs.

The MIAA meet at Kalamazoo on May 20 found Albion successfully defending its championship with 75 3/4 points. Hope beat out Kalamazoo for second place with 46 3/4 to 44 3/4 for the Hornets. Hillsdale followed with 22 3/4, Adrian with 19, Calvin 11, Olivet 5, and Alma 0. Hope's two-point margin over Kalamazoo was accomplished when the Dutch mile relay team reversed the earlier dual meet result and edged the Hornet team for third place in the meet's final event. John De Vries was at his best as he won the broad jump with a leap of 22' 5" and the pole vault with a mark of 12' 1 5/8." The broad jump was a new Hope record. Paul Wiegerink was Hope's leading scorer with firsts in the high and low hurdles plus a third in the 100 yard dash. His time of 24.7 in the lows lowered his own Hope record. Bob Hendrickson won the shot put for the third straight year with a throw of 41' 10 1/2." Dave Spaan finished fourth in a fast field of 440 men, but was able to lower his own Hope record to 50.7. Hope's one, two, three finish in the high hurdles was yet another highlight of the meet.

As the 1954-55 school year came to an end Hope's only championship came in women's tennis, as Coach Mary Breid's team won the WMIAA title on May 14. Hope's Betty Schepers won the singles championship by defeating Sue Buckle of Albion, 6-4, 6-1. Miss Schepers was also the first recipient of the Sue Little Sportsmanship Award. In doubles Hope's team of Alice Warren and Suzie Van Slageren defeated the Kalamazoo entry, 6-4, 5-7, 6-1. Hope's archery team of Joan Pyle, Mary Wolters, and Marcia Tasma finished second.

* * *

In the spring of 1955 Al Vanderbush reached a decision. With mixed emotions he had reviewed his taxing responsibilities as professor of history and political science, director of athletics, and head football coach. Still in the prime years of a coaching career, he loved the game and its associations, but he had viewed with some dismay the departure of Russ De Vette when a major coaching position was not available at Hope. Now with the blessing of President Lubbers, he composed a lengthy letter to De Vette in Orono, Maine. It contained an offer of the head football post if his former assistant would return. De Vette's short tenure at the University of Maine had been rewarding, especially the association with good friend Harold Westerman, but with roots at Hope and the football challenge he accepted with little hesitation. An era in Hope sports had come to an end, a new one was about to begin.

Many in the Hope community were caught off guard by the announcement in the **Sentinel** of April 21. In a terse statement Vanderbush explained his decision: "I would not retire this year if I had not been able to persuade De Vette to take over this spot. He is a splendid coach and I have no hesitancy in turning the position over to him. He returns reluctantly because he has so recently taken a new job at Maine, but the ties of his alma mater are strong." [2]

Coaches of course, come and go in the ever-changing world of sports, but Vanderbush left a mark that would not soon be erased. Team candidates learned quickly that their best effort was demanded at all times. He had little patience with those who feigned injuries or "coasted" in practice. At the same time he had a warm spot for the industrious "underdog" who might be plagued with limited ability. Those who played knew they had earned the right and it became an unusual badge of honor. Vanderbush was capable of harsh words in moments of high emotion, but equally capable of remorse if the words were unjust. This quality of contrition endeared him to players and increased his stature among them. Always knowledgeable in his sport, he sought out the best clinics and stayed abreast of the latest trends. A hallmark of successful coaching is the ability to bring a team back from a discouraging loss, and Vanderbush was especially adept in this area. Behind a stern exterior he was known as a deeply caring person whose concern extended well beyond the playing field.

REFERENCES - CHAPTER 9

1. The **Holland (Evening) Sentinel**, Friday, November 30, 1951.
2. The **Holland Evening Sentinel**, Thursday, April 21, 1955.

EPILOGUE

REFLECTIONS - PROJECTIONS

From the Civil War autumn of 1862 to the peaceful spring of 1955: 93 years of Hope College athletic endeavor! Throughout it all, Hope students and coaches have tailored their sports activity to fit their avowed purpose for being at Hope, namely to secure an education and give something back to society. An objective of this work has been that the reader might experience vicariously the evolution of this process. Through these pages it is my hope that scores of former athletes may step forward for one final bow before fading into the oblivion of games past. Many, of course, have passed to their reward, some even as I recorded their accomplishments. Others walk our streets or sit in the stands to cheer their latter-day counterparts. A select few achieved stardom while the vast majority just did their part . . . ."but how they played the game!" Grantland Rice would be proud.

A subsequent volume will recount the glory years of the late '50s, success in the "troubled waters" of the '60s, new faces and facilities in the '70s, domination in the '80s, and finally, the promising '90s. Hope's athletic odyssey continues.

Gordon M. Brewer
October, 1992

BIBLIOGRAPHY

Books

Harburn, Todd E. and Gerald E. Harburn. **MIAA Football**. Chelsea, Michigan: Booi Crafters, Inc., 1986.
Hackensmith, C.W. **History of Physical Education**. New York: Harper and Row Publishers, 1966.
MIAA Handbook. 1939.
Renner, Thomas, ed. **Celebrating a Century of the Student Athlete**.
Holland: The Michigan Intercollegiate Athletic Association, 1988.
Stegenga, Preston J. **Anchor of Hope**. Grand Rapids: William B. Eerdmans, 1954.
Wichers, Wynand. **A Century of Hope**. Grand Rapids: William B. Eerdmans, 1968.

Newspapers

The Detroit Free Press
The Grand Rapids Herald
The Grand Rapids Press
Holland City News
The Holland (Evening) Sentinel
The Hope College Anchor
The Kalamazoo Gazette

Other Sources

Hope College Alumni Magazine
Hope College Annual. One issue only, 1905.
Hope College Catalogs. Some titled, **Hope College Bulletin**. **Hope Preparatory School.**
Minutes, 1913.
Hope College Council Minutes, 1914.
Hope College Milestone, annual since 1916.

INDEX